SHEPHERDS FOR SALE

ALSO BY MEGAN BASHAM

Beside Every Successful Man: A Woman's Guide to Having It All

SHEPHERDS FOR SALE

HOW EVANGELICAL LEADERS TRADED
THE TRUTH FOR A LEFTIST AGENDA

MEGAN BASHAM

BROADSIDE BOOKS
An Imprint of HarperCollinsPublishers

FIRST EDITION

Library of Congress Cataloging-in-Publication Data

Names: Basham, Megan, author.
Title: Shepherds for sale : how evangelical leaders traded the truth for a
   leftist agenda / Megan Basham.
Description: First edition. | New York, NY : HarperCollins Publishers,
   [2024] | Includes index. |
Identifiers: LCCN 2024008756 (print) | LCCN 2024008757 (ebook) | ISBN
   9780063413443 (hardcover) | ISBN 9780063413450 (ebook)
Subjects: LCSH: Evangelicalism—United States—History—21st century. |
   Progressivism (United States politics)—History—21st century. |
   Christianity and politics—History—21st century
Classification: LCC BR1642.U5 B38 2024 (print) | LCC BR1642.U5 (ebook) |
   DDC 277.308/3—dc23/eng/20240430
LC record available at https://lccn.loc.gov/2024008756
LC ebook record available at https://lccn.loc.gov/2024008757
24 25 26 27 28 LBC 5 4 3 2 1

For my father, who taught me to stand alone when it means standing on the Truth. And for Brighton and Shelby, who I hope to teach the same.

In vain do they worship me, teaching as doctrines the commandments of men.

—Matthew 15:9 ESV

Presenting an issue sharply is indeed by no means a popular business at the present time; there are many who prefer to fight their intellectual battles in what [has been] aptly called a "condition of low visibility." Clear-cut definition of terms in religious matters, bold facing [*sic*] of the logical implications of religious views, is by many persons regarded as an impious proceeding. . . . But with such persons we cannot possibly bring ourselves to agree. Light may seem at times to be an impertinent intruder, but it is always beneficial in the end. The type of religion which rejoices in the pious sound of traditional phrases, regardless of their meanings, or shrinks from "controversial" matters, will never stand amid the shocks of life. In the sphere of religion, as in other spheres, the things about which men are agreed are apt to be the things that are least worth holding; the really important things are the things about which men will fight.

—J. Gresham Machen, *Christianity and Liberalism* (1923)

Contents

Introduction: How Do You Solve a Problem Like the Christians? xi

CHAPTER 1 Climate Change: Sneaking Past the Watchful Dragons 1

CHAPTER 2 Illegal Immigration: Strangers, Neighbors, and Aliens...........31

CHAPTER 3 Hijacking the Pro-life Movement....................................51

CHAPTER 4 Christian Media and the Money Men 72

CHAPTER 5 Gracious Dialogue: How the Government Used Pastors to
Spread Covid-19 Propaganda 90

CHAPTER 6 Critical Race Prophets....................................121

CHAPTER 7 #MeToo, #ChurchToo, and an Apocalypse 152

CHAPTER 8 None Dare Call It Sin: LGBTQ in the Church 194

CONCLUSION.. 232

Acknowledgments...245

Notes..247

Index..301

INTRODUCTION

How Do You Solve a Problem Like the Christians?

Even in church, we worry about world problems we cannot understand
or master, and we waste our time and substance on committees whose
announced purpose is to save the world and whose real purpose turns out
to be getting some politician elected. Even in church, we are so shaky in our
faith in the next world that we often talk as if the teachings and promises
of our Lord were a mere convenience for putting this world to rights ...

Well, but mustn't the churches adapt Christianity to suit the ideas of
our time? No, they must not. Our ideas are killing us spiritually. When
your child swallows poison, you don't sit around thinking of ways to
adapt his constitution to a poisonous diet. You give him an emetic.

—Joy Davidman (aka Mrs. C. S. Lewis)

When a group of friends from church invited Bailey Anderson to put on
a pink knitted hat and join them at the 2017 Women's March, she assumed her confusion was a matter of geography.

She and her husband, James, didn't just live in California; they lived in
deep-blue Los Angeles, where James worked as a software engineer for a major film studio. They'd relocated to America's second-largest city five years
before, from a rural town an hour outside of Atlanta where they hadn't been
able to walk to the grocery store but also hadn't encountered heroin addicts
shooting up on the sidewalk on Sunday afternoons. Finding a good church
quickly became one of their first priorities. "We were this young, evangelical
couple with a fourteen-month-old toddler and a baby on the way. We knew

we needed community if we were going to survive," Bailey told me with a chuckle, only half-joking.

In Georgia, they'd attended a contemporary nondenominational church, so they looked for similar options in L.A. And they took the quest seriously, averaging two services in two different congregations every Sunday morning. "On Saturday nights, we did this whole complicated thing of looking at different churches on a map and plotting out service times and distance, trying to figure out, if we went to a nine a.m. service at one location, if we could make it to a ten thirty a.m. service at another," James recalled.

They also did their homework, researching pastoral blogs and online statements of faith, eliminating options that didn't seem doctrinally sound. Once they were sitting in a pew (or, more often, a row of padded chairs), they paid close attention to the sermons, asked questions during the pastor meet-and-greets, and spent several weeks attending likely candidates. They didn't view themselves as especially partisan, but they also didn't view issues like abortion and the definition of marriage as political. These were matters of spiritual conviction, and they knew that whatever church they settled in, it had to have biblical positions on sexuality and the sanctity of life, even if those subjects were rarely addressed from the pulpit.

"It wasn't as easy you might think," said James. "You kind of had to listen for the buzzwords and know how to interpret them. Like if the pastor talked about how Jesus came to 'fix' our 'brokenness,' you knew that probably meant 'sin.' And that was especially true if he applied 'brokenness' to sexuality. You knew what he meant but wasn't willing to outright say."

It took a few months, some trial and error, and a couple of extended false starts, but eventually, they settled into a church that, if a little lacking in theological depth, still felt like a place where they could grow among likeminded believers.

Now, as she sat before the LED glare of her laptop screen, scrolling through the search returns for "Women's March" and "pussycat hat," Bailey felt disoriented. *Climate change. LGBTQ rights. Workers' rights. Immigration reform. Racial justice. Abortion. Abortion. Abortion.* She had some sympathy for one or two of the grab bag of issues this march was supposed to represent, but she couldn't understand why Christians would want to take part in an event almost entirely opposed to a holistic understanding of biblical ethics. "I was so naïve at the time," she told me in a soft southern drawl, "I didn't even know what the hat meant, that it was supposed to represent female genitalia."

More than disoriented, she was discouraged. Even in L.A., church was supposed to be the one place her family could find fellowship with other committed Christians.

The couple wrote the experience off as a locational hazard. "We just assumed it was California," James said. "What are you going to do?"

When they moved back home to Georgia a year later, they thought things would be different. Safely ensconced back in the Bible Belt, they figured they'd plug right back into the megachurch they'd left. But it, too, had changed. The pastor had always embraced a "seeker-sensitive" model, meaning the worship style (pop and rock) and sermon focus (practical life improvement) were designed to be as inoffensive and culturally familiar to non-Christian visitors as possible. But in the intervening years, sensitivity had tipped over into the doctrinally dubious. One weekend, the pastor preached a sermon in which he suggested that some of the Bible's moral standards were no longer applicable to modern society. He was cagey about what he meant, but he would later imply it's unloving for believers to define homosexuality and transgenderism as sins.

By then it was 2019, and some church staffers invited James to join a racial reconciliation study group titled "Be the Bridge."[1] Once there, he was told that new white members weren't allowed to speak for the first six months. They were only to "do the work" of listening and completing a "Whiteness 101" reading list. James abided by those rules for a few weeks, keeping notes on his now-glaring concerns. Even more than the division this particular curriculum seemed sure to stoke, he was alarmed at how the instructors were applying it to broader areas of life. "I started noticing that a lot of the discussions centered not just on racial justice, but on quite a lot of leftist causes. The women who led the group would frequently talk about oppressed-oppressor dynamics. At one point they told us we needed to read more books from 'queer authors' because they were an oppressed group, too. And that's when it really started to click for me that this was a slippery slope to all sorts of dynamics."

James never made it through the probationary period. When another white member who had managed to stay mute for six months got sent back to a three-month talking time-out for politely challenging the moderators' claims regarding police shooting data, James left the group.

The straw that broke the camel's back came one Sunday when the worship pastor told the congregation that God went looking for Adam and Eve after they ate the apple because He wanted to tell them, "There's nothing you could do to ever separate you from my love."

"I just turned to Bailey and said, 'I can't do this anymore,'" James remembered. "It was straight heresy. If sin doesn't separate you from God, then what are we doing? We were just so hungry for real teaching at that point."

Their next stop was a Presbyterian Church of America (PCA) church. Though they are Reformed Baptists by conviction, they were happy to agree to disagree on secondary doctrines so long as the preaching was sound. A few weeks in, the pastor began a series on justice, by which he meant solely racial justice. The final sermon—the last Sunday the Andersons attended—was on generational sins. At the end, the pastor asked all the white people in the service to stand up and applaud for the black people, to let them know they were personally repenting of America's history of racism and systemic injustice.

"It was a really awkward moment," James said. "Just a few minutes before, you were smiling and chatting with the African American next to you. And then, suddenly, you're being put through this kind of struggle session. And even though you're not good with what's happening, you don't want to stay seated and have people go, 'Oh, there's a racist, right there!' So, we stood."

It especially grated on Bailey to hear these pastors make the broad-brush claim that white families had accumulated wealth and advantages at the expense of black suffering. She had grown up in an abusive home to an alcoholic mother who eventually abandoned her and her three younger brothers. Her father was semi-present, but his failure at a string of blue-collar businesses like lawncare and carpentry had left the family living paycheck to paycheck, and there was a parade of women in and out of the house. At sixteen, Bailey found herself stepping into the role of parent to her siblings—making their meals, driving them to school. Through it all, the church had been her sanctuary. She'd first heard the Gospel as a young child, at Awana. She came to saving faith at seventeen, in her high school's youth group. Yet now, as an adult, she could not find that same haven away from the turmoil and conflict of the world, where the unchanging wisdom of the Word, rather than trendy social issues, would be preached.

"I think that was when it really hit us: 'this is a bigger problem,'" she says. "'This is not just California craziness. It's not a red state or a blue state thing. This is something in the Church.'"

I have talked with dozens of Jameses and Baileys over the last few years, people who have reached out to me due to my reporting on the evangelical world. They are ordinary Christians who feel confused and dismayed to see well-known pastors and ministry leaders letting the culture rather than Scripture dictate the content of their teaching. They see leaders insisting that Jesus requires them to get Covid-19 vaccinations and lobby for immigration bills, but doesn't require them to speak clearly about sexual morality. They feel, frankly, like sheep without shepherds. What they all want to know: What is going on? Why is this happening *everywhere*?

Infiltrating the Last Fortress

A couple of years ago, my husband and I took an anniversary trip to Boston and visited the King's Chapel. As our guide explained, the "King's" part of that moniker is noteworthy. The Lord Bishop of London established America's first Church of England congregation in 1686, in part to shore up the Crown's authority over belligerent Puritan colonists who had a penchant for defying English law.

Today, the media and publishing industries insist that the political right is playing the role of King James, leveraging churches to fulfill political aims. The last few years have seen a barrage of high-profile authors and filmmakers proclaiming that something sinister has driven the evangelical preference for conservative candidates for decades. Every major news outlet from CBS to the BBC fêted *Jesus and John Wayne*, a book that claims even Billy Graham was motivated more by politics than faith, "wedding patriarchal gender roles to a rising Christian nationalism."[2] Tim Alberta's similarly celebrated *The Kingdom, the Power, and the Glory* argues that American church leaders of the late twentieth century opposed "pornography, homosexuality, drug use, rising divorce rates, secularism in public schools, and, above all, abortion" not because the Bible speaks to these topics, but because these leaders "needed an issue set that would satisfy the lowest common denominator of their socially conservative constituency."[3] (You have to wonder what nefarious political powers Alberta thinks were at work in the first-century Church that caused it to likewise prioritize sobriety, marriage, sexual purity, and protecting the innocent.)

The narrative that the GOP has dangerously co-opted the American Church is built almost entirely on speculation, subjective stories, and the fact that evangelicals voted for Donald Trump at about the same rate as they voted for previous Republican presidential candidates.[4] But it serves a dual purpose. If churchgoers can be convinced there's something shameful and unchristian in bringing their values to the democratic process, first, it will blunt their influence on the culture. Second, they will be distracted from noticing the secular left's long and well-documented history of infiltrating churches and buying influence among church leaders—a history that still marches on today.

In his book *The Devil and Karl Marx*, political science professor Paul Kengor describes the process the Communist Party USA used between 1920 and 1950 to deliberately infiltrate mainline Protestant churches and woo pastors to their socialist program:

> I found repeatedly, dating back a century, beginning with the launch of the Soviet Comintern and Communist Party USA in 1919, atheistic communists clearly tapping social-justice language not because they believed in Jesus (quite the contrary) but to dupe believers in Jesus . . .
>
> Documents in the Soviet Comintern Archives on Communist Party USA show how communist officials in Moscow and New York[5] deliberately targeted [prominent Methodist seminary professor Reverend Harry] Ward to help push their propaganda. In one letter from December 1920, Ward is listed by Comintern officials as a source to get their materials on the shelves at the seminary library.[6]

Kengor especially draws on the recollections of ex-communist Herbert Romerstein. Archived at Stanford's Hoover Institution, Romerstein's papers represent one of the United States' most comprehensive collections on the subversive activities of communist front organizations. Before he went to work for the Reagan administration, Romerstein testified before Congress on the long lists he and his comrades had compiled of people and organizations they planned to target for exploitation. They called them suckers lists. One group, Romerstein told Kengor, represented "the biggest suckers of them all"—pastors, because communist operatives had more success infiltrating their ranks than those of any other group.

Members of the Soviet Comintern, the international socialist organization that included the Communist Party USA, were atheists—after all, the founder of their belief system called religion "the opium of the people"[7]— but they knew how to ape biblical terms for political ends. Their pseudo-religious jargon worked especially well on the National Council of Churches, a Protestant umbrella group that had a keen interest in social justice causes like wealth inequality. Other government records showed that the Episcopal Church, which today ranks as one of the farthest-left Protestant denominations, was deeply compromised, with an estimated 20.5 percent of its rectors associated with communist activities.[8]

According to now-declassified records, American communists acting under Soviet orders founded the front group American Peace Mobilization with a particular goal: to convince religious leaders to promote the Kremlin's aims. In 1941, it successfully enlisted pastors to lobby FDR to keep America out of World War II because Stalin and Hitler were, at that time, allies. Presumptuously calling itself "we of the church," the group published an open letter in the *New York Times*. It said their "belief in God and the worth and dignity of the human personality expressed in His image" compelled them to call on President Roosevelt to "put an end to what we deem is an aggressive, militant foreign policy, which will inevitably lead to . . . the destruction of democracy." As soon as Stalin changed positions and wanted America to join the Allies, however, these religious leaders immediately became pro-war, and changed their name to the American *People's* Mobilization.

Congress would later call the American Peace Mobilization "one of the most seditious organizations which ever operated in the United States."[9] And pastors, claiming to speak for the "the church," were a part of it.

Illustrating just how little is new under the sun, the Gray Lady did its (hopefully unwitting) part to provide cover for this Soviet-engineered group, referring to it with the innocuous descriptor "a group of clergymen."

As you read through this book, it's important to remember such history. You will see eerily similar parallels to events happening today. Secular, leftist organizations that have no interest in furthering God's kingdom or seeing biblical morality enacted in the public square are funneling money into front groups with names like the "Evangelical Environmental Network" and the "Evangelical Immigration Table." Well-known evangelical leaders, posing as representatives of average Christians in the pews, are once again publishing open letters in national newspapers on behalf of leftist causes.

While these leaders' motives for such activities may be complex and sometimes unclear, the motives of their secular backers are simple. Around 32 percent of the U.S. electorate describe themselves as evangelical, and the vast majority of that group leans right.[10] Among Americans who describe themselves as conservatives, Protestant evangelicals are the single largest religious group by 23 points.[11] As The Atlantic put it in 2021, evangelicals are simply "America's most powerful voting bloc."[12] They don't always win at the ballot box, but in most regions of the country, they always present a massive hurdle to leftist power grabs. If the Democratic Party could manage to shave off even 10 percent of their support for Republicans, it would face little opposition to its agenda. So far, it has failed in that objective.

Look at nearly any issue that represents a key priority for progressives, and you will find that even when all other major demographics have signed on, Christians, and evangelicals in particular, represent the most formidable roadblock. Whether it's the LGBTQ movement, climate change, or illegal immigration, again and again, polling research shows that evangelicals still stand as a fortress in the way of the political left.[13] Indeed, they often stand in the way of the political right as well, earning the ire of many GOP leaders and their large donors who would just as soon see social conservatism die.[14] Keeping alive the spirit of American resistance to the agendas of the powerful that so vexed King James, evangelicals just won't get with the program.

Correction: the rank and file won't get with the program. Certain high-profile leaders are a different story.

"Faith Voices"

In the early 2000s, foundations funded by secular billionaires began to speak earnestly, if not very openly, about how to take down this fortress.

By the time it concluded spending down its endowment in 2020, the Bermuda-based grant maker Atlantic Philanthropies was one of the largest funders of left-wing causes in a number of countries, including the United States.[15] In 2010, for instance, it spent $27 million to safeguard the passage of the Affordable Care Act.[16]

That same year, it issued a report on its failing efforts to break down opposition to gay marriage in Ireland.[17] Titled "A Meeting of Queer Minds" the report highlighted the resistance of Ireland's devout Catholics and Protestants. "Organized religion is at the heart of LGBTI oppression and needs to be deconstructed," the authors wrote. But they quickly identified the roadblock they would face in achieving that aim: "How can one deconstruct an institution that provides hope and comfort to millions of desperate people?" Rather than go on opposing churches, the gay lobby would need to co-opt them. "An engagement needs to come from groups within the churches," the report advised. "LGBTI organizations *need to appropriate Christian values for a progressive rights agenda*" (emphasis mine).

The president and CEO of Atlantic Philanthropies at that time was Gara LaMarche, a man who has spent his entire career hopping from one elite leftist donor group to another. He had previously served as the director of U.S. Programs for George Soros's Open Society Foundations (OSF). His former employer was still a close associate, though, through their mutual membership in the Democracy Alliance, an exclusive group of ultra-rich left-wing patrons whom Politico once described as "the country's most powerful liberal donor club."[18] (LaMarche would eventually take the helm of that group as well.)

This likely explains why the same question—how to solve a problem like the Christians—also began to preoccupy Soros's organization.

On February 3, 2012, another director at OSF, Bill Vandenberg, sent an internal memo to the U.S. Programs board regarding discussions they had been having on "the role of religion in public life" and how the organization, founded by an atheist, could leverage "strategies that engage faith-based communities in debate, advocacy, and mobilization."[19]

Vandenberg reviewed the fact that "faith communities" had become a particular funding priority for OSF because of their "significance in a nation as religiously identified as the US" and because of church leaders' ability to bring "faith-based perspectives into the public square and into policy making processes." Most especially, he noted, faith communities could help OSF "reach beyond the choir of [O]pen [S]ociety's usual suspects,'" which presumably didn't include a lot of churchgoing folk.

After bemoaning presidential candidates' tendency to "pander to the 're-ligious right,'" as with the "anti-abortion movement," he acknowledged that religion's influence is "powerful and here to stay." Then he laid out a strategy for harnessing some of that power for OSF. It included "invest[ing] in faith-based advocacy and the engagement of the faith community in Open Society campaigns," "fund[ing] strategic communications work," and "award[ing] fellowships to faith-based thinkers." In other words, OSF would start spreading a lot of money around those Christian types to create astroturf campaigns.

At the top of OSF's list for how it hoped to use "faith voices" was immigration reform and, using a term that could have come from the communists of a century ago, "economic equity."

The foundation also planned to do plenty of oppo research on the "'religious right's' organizational infrastructure, funding, and reach," in the hope of identifying "generational divides" it could exploit: "Awareness of these generational divides, the differences of opinion and nuance on public policies that exist between younger and older evangelicals will help our grantees build greater public support for issues such as economic equity, climate change, immigrants' rights, LGBT equality, and reproductive health," Vandenberg wrote.

So, if your daughter or granddaughter suddenly starts quoting a pastor who claims the Bible has nothing to say about abortion, you may have George Soros to thank for it. But he is hardly alone.

A few years later, in 2018, another billionaire, eBay founder and long-time Democratic donor Pierre Omidyar, a Buddhist, dipped a toe into the evangelical influence game.[20] His foundation made the first of several fifty-thousand-dollar grants to the Ethics and Religious Liberty Commission, the legislative lobbying arm of the nation's largest Protestant denomination, the

Southern Baptist Convention.[21] This contribution's stated purpose was to help combat America's alleged white supremacy problem. Omidyar would go on to make many, many more donations to mainstream evangelical institutions, his money joining rivers of funding that had started to flow into the church from other left-wing foundations.

Then, in 2020, the largest foundation in the world, the U.S. federal government, leveraged the influence of well-known ministry leaders to promote its Covid-19 lies and guilt average churchgoers into submitting to authoritarian lockdowns and vaccine mandates. The Billy Graham Center at Wheaton College went so far as to partner formally with the Centers for Disease Control and Prevention and the National Institutes of Health, setting up the website Coronavirus and the Church, which center director Ed Stetzer urged pastors to share with their congregations.

Two years later, perhaps seeing how successful other federal agencies had been at co-opting evangelical pulpits and platforms, the head of the National Oceanic and Atmospheric Administration announced his intention to use "faith-based organizations to potentially host climate and equity roundtables."[22] Dr. Rick Spinrad shared that NOAA had already had "multiple discussions with the faith community" about how it could help "the Biden-Harris Administration . . . address the threats of climate change." Though he admitted that turning to churches had not been "part of [NOAA's] organizational construct" in the past, he pledged that, going forward, the "agency [would] build these partnerships and channels of communication into [its] DNA."

Wolves, Cowards, Mercenaries, and Fools

The question is: Why have so many well-known evangelical institutions and leaders in recent years started promoting causes that no plain reading of Scripture would demand, like lobbying for fossil fuel regulations or dismantling white privilege, while issues that unequivocally call for Christian clarity find them silent and stymied? When the guy who created the Christian children's program VeggieTales starts arguing that evangelicals should take a more "nuanced" position on abortion,[23] and when two successive presidents of the Southern Baptist Convention say the Bible only "whispers" about sexual sins,[24] something is badly off in mainstream evangelicalism.

Are they dupes or deceivers? Is it organic or orchestrated? Certainly, money is playing a role in some of these evolutions, and there is no doubt, as we'll see, that once-trusted evangelical leaders and institutions have yoked themselves to left-wing billionaires and their pet projects. But it need not always be explicitly transactional. Institutional prestige, seeing oneself lauded on CNN and in the *Washington Post* as more intellectually and morally advanced than the rest of the evangelical rabble, can also be a potent elixir. So can gilded invitations to the most exclusive parties in the world.

Pastor Rick Warren boasts of his role as a "global influencer" to the United Nations and the World Economic Forum.[25] *Christianity Today*'s editor in chief, Russell Moore, opens his latest book[26] with an off-topic recollection of being a guest at President Obama's White House Christmas party. Is it a coincidence that both these men now habitually push progressive views that directly conflict with the feelings of the men and women the media claims they represent?

Perhaps some are simply weary of being the bad guys and are eager to sign on to something, *anything*, that will draw the culture's approval. They may not reject clear biblical morality, but they instead emphasize those things our society doesn't find offensive and, in fact, rewards.

When the National Association of Evangelicals took money from a pro-abortion foundation that also funds Planned Parenthood as part of a program to promote contraception to teens, a former board member put the compromise down to a desire for worldly status.[27] She felt the NAE leaders were just foolish, naïve people whose craving for wider respectability made them susceptible to political influence. It's true the savvy, cynical world is always eager to seize on Christians who fail to follow Christ's command to be wise as serpents, but I have my doubts that NAE leaders were quite the innocent doves the woman believed, for reasons we'll explore.

Others in positions of influence and authority see the cultural accommodation and are unhappy about it (or so they tell me privately), but not enough to confront old friends, not enough to lose their place among the speakers at the next big discipleship conference. Why join Elijah and get a reputation as a "troubler of Israel" when you can stay quiet and be esteemed by all? And so, they speak some truth, even a lot of truth, but they fail to do as Paul does in Acts 20—present the *whole* counsel of God. *So, you have to overlook the unbiblical excesses of the MeToo movement to hold on to your lofty administrative position—what does it matter if it leaves a few women with burdened consciences?*

A prominent former editor of an evangelical magazine told me he was moderating his approach with regard to issues like abortion and critical race theory (never mind that he didn't moderate it at all on issues championed by the political right) because he hoped to model for evangelicals how to "hold the center." His idea was that if theologically conservative Christians exemplified charitable compromise, progressives would look for areas of agreement as well. I don't think he was a coward or a wolf, but I do think he wanted the applause of the magazine's young, woke reporters. And I believe in thinking himself wise, he became a fool. The Bible instructs us to proclaim truth, not to hold centers—and anyway, the center is far too liberal a place for biblical orthodoxy. So is most of the right these days, for that matter. All that editor was going to do was cede more and more ground to progressives, who, by definition, are always looking to gain it.

These days, he retweets *New York Times* columnists who defend Christian support for gay marriage and recommends podcasts by Democratic strategists who argue that abortion should be allowed up to fifteen weeks. The center certainly has shifted.

This is not to say that Christians can't have disagreements on whether science proves climate change is a serious problem or what gun regulations might be prudent. Even where Christians agree on principle, reason and conviction can lead to different views regarding solutions. But these issues aren't being argued in good faith. They're being smuggled in through shallow religious manipulation and a demand for consensus that Scripture does not require.

Knowing they don't have the backing of their claimed constituencies, these evangelical leaders turn their pulpits and platforms into vehicles for shaming the rank and file because they will not agree that supporting, say, the Black Lives Matter movement is a "Gospel issue," necessary to show the world what it means to be faithful followers of Christ.[28] Often, those arguing for these progressive priorities don't even bother bringing much biblical application to the table. No matter the issue, all are thrown into the basket of "Love your neighbor."

Why should the United States reward tens of millions of illegal immigrants with citizenship despite the fact they broke our laws and it drives down wages for blue-collar workers? *Love your neighbor.* Why should I take an experimental Covid-19 vaccine I don't want when I'm statistically extremely unlikely to experience anything more than mild symptoms? *Love your neighbor.* Why should I support cap-and-trade carbon emission limits that will make everything, from gas to groceries, more expensive? *Love your neighbor.* No less a public Christian than former vice president Mike Pence said he supports laws that allow gender-confused adults to mutilate their bodies under the principle of "Love your neighbor."

Using the Bible for cheap sloganeering in this way misses the point that the reverse of every one of these actions can also have a detrimental effect on our neighbors. Which is why a lot of our neighbors disagree with them!

Eventually, thoughtless usage had so cheapened Jesus's profound teaching to meaningless catchphrases that political and media leaders who had no role in the Church also began to use it like a Swiss army knife—a convenient tool to unlock any policy preference. In late May 2023, Alyssa Farah, cohost of *The View*, argued on CNN that conservatives shouldn't boycott Target over Pride merchandise like "tuck-friendly" swimsuits and queer-themed kids clothing because they should "love their neighbors." The year before, California governor Gavin Newsom put up billboards in Texas that advertised his state's up-to-birth abortion laws with the message "California Is Ready to Help. Love Your Neighbor as Yourself."

There is a reason the Book of Jude urges all Christians, not just pastors, to "contend for the faith" and be on the lookout for those who "secretly slip in" among us, dividing us by distorting the clear teaching of the Word for their own ends. Some are, yes, wolves—unfaithful pastors and teachers deliberately leading the sheep astray. I believe that you'll have little trouble pinpointing in these pages who they are. But there are different degrees of error. Passivity, fear of reprisal, and plain old lack of discernment are also reasons pastors may compromise with the culture. For those who are not outright wolves, forthright, brotherly confrontation, such as when Paul opposed Peter over those who wanted to add Jewish custom to God's grace in Galatians 2, may bring about sincere repentance. And we should take heart in knowing ours is hardly the first era to necessitate unpleasant conflict.

In 1983, theologian Francis Schaeffer grew alarmed by evangelical groups concerning themselves with fashionable issues like "unjust structures" and inequitable wealth distribution rather than sinful human hearts. He had no doubt he was seeing capitulation to the spirit of the age. And he had no doubt where such socialist, utopian thinking would lead:

> Here the gospel has been reduced to a program for transforming social structures. This is the Marxist line. It does not mean that those who take this position are Communists. But it does mean they have made a complete confusion of the kingdom of God with the basic socialistic concepts. In back of this stands the Enlightenment idea of the perfectibility of man if only the cultural and economic chains are removed . . .
>
> But think further what this means theologically. What has happened to the fall and sin? [Evangelicals for Social Action] seem to be saying that changing economic structures is the means of salvation for modern man since only this deals with the basic "causes of the disease." Ironically their program is not radical enough! The basic problem is that of the fall and sin and the heart of man. The basic problem is much deeper than social structures, and by not recognizing this[,] ESA ends up with an understanding of salvation which is very different from what the Scriptures teach.[29]

This is not to say God's Word has nothing to say to the political or social issues of our time. There are rich Scriptural arguments to be made about the sacredness of human life, God's design for sex and marriage, and even private property rights. But they *are* rich; they aren't yard signs. And if you argue that Christians should steward their voting rights as citizens to reflect these biblical priorities, the same figures who have taken up the cause of climate change and reforming the police system will accuse you of politicizing the Church and "culture-warring."

Again and again in these pages, you will note the manipulation of Church leaders who claim that to stand where the Bible stands is "political," yet not accepting their view on some issue where biblical application is disputable is somehow—even when they're pressing you to lobby for legislative remedies—paradoxically *not* political. Republicans who speak of how their faith prompts them to vote for a certain candidate are grasping for power. Democrats who do the same are illustrating faithfulness in the public sphere.

The Eleventh Commandment

There's a running joke in evangelical institutions, especially among Southern Baptists, about an unspoken Eleventh Commandment: Thou shalt not criticize church leaders. Like all Pharisaical traditions, it has the appearance of godliness but is not especially biblical. (See not only Jesus's and John the Baptist's choice words for the compromised religious elite, but also Paul's remonstration of Peter in Galatians 2 or the Judaizers in Galatians 5 or Alexander the coppersmith in 2 Timothy 4.)

What the Eleventh Commandment has meant in practice is that even as prominent pastors and theologians have spent the last few years accommodating every sort of secular, progressive influence, critical or even cautioning voices have been slow to respond. When they do respond, leaders like J. D. Greear, then president of the Southern Baptist Convention, have wielded the Eleventh Commandment like a rocket launcher, firing descriptors like "divisive" and "demonic" at any who raise objections to the promotion of critical race theory, feminism, or LGBTQ ideology in SBC ministries.[30] Greear went on to liken those leaving churches over woke teaching to a "synagogue of Satan."[31]

"We should mourn when closet racists and neo-Confederates feel more at home in our churches than do many of our people of color," he thundered from the platform of the SBC's national convention in 2021.[32] Of course, the megachurch pastor did not back up this shocking accusation with evidence or identify these rank and unrepentant sinners.

Greear's hyperbolic rhetoric is hardly unusual for elite evangelicals discussing average people in the pews. In a 2018 Vox essay, Ed Stetzer, who was then executive director of the Billy Graham Center at Wheaton College, claimed that "far too many white evangelicals are motivated by racial anxiety and xenophobia."[33] Again, no examples were provided. Sift through many ministry leaders' recent sermons and conference addresses, and you will find that such unspecific and unsupported indictments, which confirm the worst stereotypes the left lobs at Christians, are rampant. In other words, the Eleventh Commandment runs in only one direction. As they demand that the rank and file address them with gentle and kind words, the shepherds are building their platforms by becoming public accusers of the sheep.

Along with not being especially biblical, the Eleventh Commandment is far from journalistic. Thus, in this book, I will provide accounts of specific people. But my guidelines will be this: I will name names where the events are public or the comments were made on the record. I will not name names where the comments were not public or where they were made in the context of a personal conversation with an expectation of confidentiality.

It is also important to note that none of the pastors, theologians, or Christian influencers included in this book are associated with the political left, though they have been pushing progressive ideologies. I don't bother with open liberals like *Sojourners*'s Jim Wallis or MSNBC's Al Sharpton, as they are known Democratic operatives. They have little to no sway among theological conservatives or with the broad swath of mainstream evangelicalism.

Every name I put forward as evidence of liberal drift and infiltration is commonly trusted and welcomed by orthodox American Protestantism. They are men and women whom I, too, at one time trusted and still sometimes learn from, though with a much more cautious posture than I once had.

Naming them is not a question of punishing or singling out, but of understanding what is taking place in the Church so we can put it right. Josh Abbotoy, executive director of the Protestant politics and culture journal *American Reformer*, describes it as upgrading our antivirus software. "Evangelicals need to learn to be more careful readers of their leaders' actions and rhetoric, and much more thoughtful about who they elevate," he said. "There are discernible patterns that should be studied and addressed so they can be solved . . . We aren't judging the state of [a church leader's] soul, but rather, his fitness for leadership."

You will notice that the Southern Baptist Convention features heavily in some chapters. This is not because I am a member of an SBC church (though I am), but because, as America's largest Protestant denomination, the SBC is not only emblematic of issues happening throughout the Church, but it also represents the greatest number of conservative evangelicals in the country. Indeed, it represents around 5 percent of the total U.S. population.[34] If you are a progressive intent on using churches to move evangelicals to the left, Southern Baptists offer the most bang for your buck (which is why the left spends so many bucks on that very project).[35]

Finally, this book is not a theological treatise or a work of political argument. I am not here to persuade the reader that homosexuality is a sin or that the push for equity (which guarantees outcomes) rather than equality (which guarantees opportunity) is simply a repackaged version of Marx's politics of envy. I presume there are enough readers still orthodox enough in their thinking that I do not have to start at square one by outlining God's intent in designing humanity as male and female and who are sensible enough to know that no nation can long remain a nation that does not police its borders. There are plenty of authors who do theology and political theory very well, and you will find recommendations for some of their works in these pages.

My ultimate purpose is to confirm for average evangelicals in the pews that the uneasy feelings many of you have been having (perhaps for some years now) that your pulpits and your institutions are being co-opted by political forces with explicitly secular progressive aims are justified. That is indeed happening. (Though one development that has cheered me immensely is to see how many of my fellow sheep have not, for the most part, wandered away with their shepherds. You are pushing back against that which you know is not biblical. My prayer is that this book will arm you to do so to an even greater degree.)

It benefits no one to be like the prophets in Ezekiel 13, covering up crumbling walls with whitewash so we don't have to confront how close those walls are to tumbling down. We do not worry for the future of the Church. The gates of Hell will not prevail against it. Its victory, and thus the victory of every true Christian within it, is secure. But it is certainly fair to worry about our nation and what will become of it if the restraining influence of the Church is withdrawn. And we should certainly pray for weary, wounded sinners who are coming to the Church in need of the transcendent power of the eternal and who are, instead, given temporal preoccupations with social issues.

Let us learn from what is happening now so that we can elevate the right leaders, those like King Hezekiah, who will tear down the false idols, eject the false prophets, and restore the temple. Hebrews 10:25 commands Christians not to give up meeting together, and as we learned during Covid-19, there are very good reasons for that. Iron cannot sharpen iron while we watch online sermons from the couch. Nor should we abandon the seminaries and Christian colleges to liberals without a fight—these are the institutions training the majority of our nation's pastors and ministry leaders. I am not here to call for a leaderless church—we need pastors, deacons, and elders who exercise godly authority.

Finally, while this book focuses on false or misguided shepherds, this country is still blessed with many, many good shepherds, many of whom are laboring in obscurity. As the Andersons did, we must put in the effort to find them and become members of their local bodies. (I'm happy to report that the Andersons did eventually find a church home where James is teaching Bible study classes.) And as we expose darkness, let it inspire us all the more to thank God for such good and faithful shepherds bringing His Word to light.

SHEPHERDS FOR SALE

CHAPTER 1

Climate Change

Sneaking Past the Watchful Dragons

> By these waters also the world of that time was deluged and destroyed.
> By the same word the present heavens and earth are reserved for fire,
> being kept for the day of judgment and destruction of the ungodly.
>
> —2 Peter 3:6–7

Everyone has that friend who gets a little too enthusiastic about Christmas—the one who plays carols as soon as Starbucks starts serving pumpkin spice lattes in late August, whose tree is up and fully decorated just after Halloween. Mine is a member of the Christian Reformed Church, a small Calvinist denomination that has roots in her family's Dutch heritage. Every year, she bakes *kerstkransjes* and *kerststol* (wreath-shaped almond cookies and fruitcake) with her daughters, she tells her granddaughters folktales about both Sinterklaas and Saint Nick, and she cheerfully drags her friends into every Christmas boutique she passes, even in the dog days of July.

But just after Thanksgiving in 2022, I got a call from her. She was fuming about a four-week Advent devotional her pastor had sent out with the church newsletter, one that sounded nothing like any traditional meditation on the incarnation of Christ.

"Listen to this," she seethed, reading from the introduction: "'We don't have to look far to see injustice, to see creation groaning under the weight of the climate crisis and environmental destruction, and to see people turning away from seeing and addressing these realities.'

"What does this have to do with Christmas?" she demanded. "I mean this is just depressing. Hang on." I listened to laptop keys clicking furiously as she hunted for another selection. "This is from week three: 'It can often be hard to find joy today, especially when we allow the reality of the role our actions play in our changing climate to truly sink in.' I dunno, I guess I'm old-fashioned. I thought an Advent calendar should talk a little bit more about the birth of Jesus."

Ironically, my friend is in line with her synod on this issue. She believes climate change is primarily driven by human-induced carbon emissions, and she supports policies to limit the use of fossil fuels. But, as she told me, "It feels like they're making everything about this. It's Christmas! Some things should be sacred!"

When she tentatively asked her pastor about the Advent calendar, he defended it by telling her, "If Joseph and Mary were alive today, they would be the ones most impacted by environmental disasters. So, it's important we think as world citizens and consider how our choices affect the poor in other parts of the world."

His rebuke revealed that he had little idea how the choices of environmentalists in wealthy Western nations are impacting the world.

World Citizens

In 2019, formerly impoverished Sri Lanka was a nation on the upswing. After successive years of impressive economic growth and an increasing gross national income, the World Bank upgraded it from a lower-middle-income rating to an upper-middle, bringing it on par with Argentina, China, and Russia.[1]

Three years later, its economy collapsed.

By June 2022, fuel supplies were so short that buses, medical vehicles, and other basic services had stopped running. A foreign exchange crisis meant imported necessities like antibiotics, canned milk, and even toilet paper were suddenly unavailable. Babies were born underweight, and malnourished children started fainting in school as food shortages left around 30 percent of the population hungry.[2] Eventually, protestors stormed government buildings, and the president fled the country.

A range of culprits contributed to the crisis, but the most significant was a 2021 green policy banning imports of chemical fertilizers and pesticides. As a result, rice yields dropped 30 percent, and exports of tea, which had been Sri Lanka's major cash crop, fell to their lowest point in twenty-three years.[3]

Around the same time in another part of the world, the Dutch government announced a plan to forcibly buy out three thousand farms and mandate a 30 percent reduction in livestock as part of its effort to comply with EU carbon regulations. Dairy farmer Erik Luiten spoke for many of his countrymen when he told NBC he had no interest in selling the land that had been in his family for generations.[4] He and thousands of others took to the streets in protest, just as had farmers facing new taxes, pesticide bans, and herd reduction in Germany, Ireland, and other EU nations.[5] For now, the Netherlands remains the second largest food exporter in the world, right behind the United States—an astonishingly productive output for a country that's roughly the size of Maryland. That will end if the newly formed Farmer-Citizen Movement, an anti-climate regulation party that won a historic parliamentary election in 2023, isn't able to stave off the European Union's wholesale land grab and cattle slaughter.

Fossil fuels, fertilizer, and cows have also all been targeted in the tiny West African nation of Ghana. In 2018, the formerly impoverished country boasted one of the fastest-growing economies in the world, with the biggest gains coming from a thriving cocoa bean trade and recently discovered offshore oil deposits.[6] As the *New York Times* put it that year, "Cocoa is Ghana's other natural bounty, and producers are piggybacking on the oil boom." Unfortunately, all that bounty drew the attention of the World Bank, which struck a deal with the Ghanian government to transition away from "polluting and expensive oil-burning electricity" and toward solar and hydropower.[7] In essence, the World Bank was telling a developing African country to give up a huge source of wealth that would transform the lives of future generations and go back to the fields and grow chocolate.

By 2021, Ghana went from a net exporter of electricity to experiencing the prolonged, frequent blackouts of its developing world past. No electricity meant farmers could no longer access the water they needed to irrigate crops that were already dwindling under less-effective organic fertilizers *mandated by Paris Accord climate commitments*. When the war in Ukraine compounded

Ghana's fertilizer troubles, the European Union refused to help because "supporting fertilizer production in developing nations would be inconsistent with the EU energy and environment policies."[8]

In the end, Ghanian police turned tear gas and rubber bullets on citizens protesting the policies that had left many of them hungry and suffering,[9] in the words of the BBC, "the worst economic crisis in a generation."[10]

Meanwhile, in the United States, the National Association of Evangelicals released a 2022 report telling American Christians that supporting the very policies responsible for all this is what it means to love "the least of these."[11]

To successfully introduce some left-wing priority to the Church, progressives must often begin with a buzzword (or buzz phrase, as the case may be). Think of it as an inversion of C. S. Lewis's "watchful dragons" metaphor. Lewis, writing for the *New York Times* in 1956, explained that he began to realize that the fairy stories that bubbled up in his imagination might, when married to some quality of Christ he wished to communicate, have the power to reach a reader inured or even hostile to theological language. He supposed that by casting the truths of the Gospel into a mythical world and "stripping them of their stained-glass and Sunday school associations," he might steal past the "watchful dragons" of a religion-wary reader and penetrate the heart.[12]

Those who want to see the Church take up the preoccupations of the left are following a similar process, but in reverse—they bring the secular into the sacred by disguising it with "Christianese" terminology.

According to the Pew Research Center, religious Americans are the least likely group to fall prey to climate alarmism, and evangelicals are the least likely subgroup to feel great concern over the issue.[13] Only 34 percent of them believe global warming is a serious problem, and they tend to attribute it more to natural fluctuations in weather patterns than to human activity.

Even if the average believer in the pews hasn't made an in-depth study of the impact a net-zero economy would have on GDP, he's skeptical of the apocalyptic claims in the headlines that, if he is over age thirty-five, he has seen for decades now. His Christian worldview tells him how the world will actually end and that a sparrow does not fall from the sky without God's seeing it and that he's to test all things and hold fast to what is sound (1 Thessalonians 5:21). Therefore, he's not given to panic.

The only way to persuade him to take up a cause that goes against his common sense and theological instincts is to convince him that it isn't a political or even a scientific matter, but a matter of Christian witness and biblical obedience.

To turn "environmentalism" into "creation care" would take a branding campaign.

What Would Jesus Drive?

Though there were some attempts to persuade conservative Protestants to join the environmentalist movement in the 1980s, the effort didn't really start to gain momentum until the next decade. That was when the ecumenical National Religious Partnership for the Environment realized that the millions it was receiving from left-wing grant makers like the Hewlett, Rockefeller, and MacArthur Foundations hadn't been enough to put significant legislative points on the board.[14] It needed to expand beyond the borders of its liberal mainline, Catholic, and Jewish coalition and look toward the roughly 45 percent of voters who then identified as evangelical.[15] Thus, in 1993, the Evangelical Environmental Network was born.[16] Its mission: to win average churchgoers to the green cause by leveraging the influence of trusted institutions like *Christianity Today* and the National Association of Evangelicals.

A decade before, it would have been difficult to imagine the NAE pushing legislation as progressive as cap-and-trade carbon emission limits. After all, it had then been so influential among conservatives that Ronald Reagan delivered his famous "Evil Empire" speech to its 1983 national convention.[17] It would have been even more difficult to envision the magazine founded by Billy Graham promoting "climate vigil songs" that turn biblical metaphors about the earth groaning under the curse of sin into environmental parables.[18]

But that was before a group of leaders susceptible to the lure of Beltway media prestige took the helms of these two organizations. In 2015, the George Soros–funded think tank New America, which counts among its executives a number of Obama administration alumni, dissected the tactics the EEN used to try to co-opt evangelical institutions. New America's hope was that they could learn from the EEN's experience to find more success leveraging churches in the future.[19] Drawn largely from interviews with a number of principal actors, the report described the EEN's top-down strategy, both in the type of organizations it chose to target and the sort of people it sidled up to.[20]

There's not much question as to why the NAE, which represents some 45,000 churches and 30 million churchgoers, was its primary target. But *Christianity Today*, known as the flagship magazine of evangelicalism, would have made an equally attractive partner. Pastors of that era tell me nearly every Protestant church office maintained a subscription. That would have fit perfectly with a key element of the EEN's approach, which, as the New America report details, centered on recruiting "elite evangelicals" who would use their influence to give spiritual legitimacy to deeply anti-human climate policies:

> From 2000 to 2004, the EEN slowly laid the groundwork for national evangelical institutions to grasp climate change as a moral issue. EEN's strategy was to integrate "climate care" into the core of the evangelical subculture, by building a bench of national evangelical elites who framed climate change as a moral issue and called for decisive policy action. The expectation was that these ideas would then "trickle down" to rank-and-file evangelicals.[21]

That description was a bit more circumspect than the one New America researchers offered at a 2015 presentation where they called this the "rent an evangelical" model.[22] By this, they meant using a leader in a trusted organization who knows the lingo to persuasively sell a message to what would otherwise have been an unreceptive audience. They explained that the object was to "collect strange bedfellows" and "sort of sneakily break down" the faith coalition from the inside. That is, the EEN had hoped to peel off a percentage of evangelicals because it recognized them as a "core group in the Republican Party and the conservative movement." Ideally, this "evangelical voice" would then "give cover to Republican members of Congress to support climate action."

There was one other group the EEN had especially hoped to draft into its project—the largest Protestant denomination in the country, the Southern Baptist Convention. Its strategy was to start with the Ethics and Religious Liberty Commission, the denomination's legislative lobbying arm:

> The ERLC had historically been a challenging target, because of its core role in the Republican Party and its tight focus on issues related to abortion, gender, and sexuality. Yet EEN leaders hoped to win the ERLC's support for Creation Care, because even just neutralizing the Southern Baptist Convention in the debate on global warming could disrupt the solid Republican opposition to measures like cap and trade.

In other words, while this early incarnation of the creation care movement wore religious clothes, its aims were explicitly political, from start to finish. And as we'll see, evangelical leaders are still being rented to perform the same function in churches today.

The ERLC proved a tough nut to crack, largely because its policy director at that time, Barrett Duke, was skeptical about the sweeping government solutions his organization was being asked to support. He took the time to seek out other expert views before committing. What he heard convinced him that, contrary to the EEN's claims, the science on climate change was still very much open to debate. And he saw no reason to lend the weight of Southern Baptist influence to a project that did not have clear biblical aims. The EEN had no choice but to make do with only two Christian lodestars, *Christianity Today* and the NAE, and get to work.

In 1999, the trio embarked on their first major collaboration, cohosting a "care of creation" conference at Malone College, a small Christian school in Northeast Ohio. A few years later, EEN vice president Rev. Jim Ball took NAE vice president Richard Cizik to the United Kingdom for a climate conference. Ball was in only his mid-thirties at the time, and in photos from that period, he is more gangly youth than polished NGO executive, but inexperienced though he might have been, he already had a flair for marketing. As he was loitering around the gift shop of Westminster Abbey, browsing knickknacks bearing religious slogans, it occurred to him that what would really give the EEN's efforts a boost (at least with the more malleable brand of Christian) was a vehicle for virtue-signaling.[23] This being shortly before the dawn of social media, he went with the old-school version—a bumper sticker crusade. The slogan that would stave off environmental apocalypse: "What Would Jesus Drive?"

To fully capitalize on Ball's idea, the EEN enlisted the help of the public relations firm Fenton, then best known for liberal clients—it handled an ACLU campaign for abortion and another for then–San Francisco mayor Gavin Newsom promoting same-sex marriage.[24] The EEN then bought TV ads in key markets. The goal was for Charlotte, St. Louis, Des Moines, and Indianapolis (cities that tend to play home to upwardly aspirant megachurchgoers with enough social anxiety to be easy marks for shallow spiritualism) to be overrun with fuel-efficient hybrids sporting the anti-SUV message. But as is often the case with such gimmicks, in the end it sparked more of a media trend than a movement.

For a few months, there was hardly a mainstream outlet in the country that failed to give Ball and his WWJD bumper stickers their fifteen minutes of fame, though many, like CBS, seemed to have their tongues planted firmly in their cheeks when they dubbed the EEN the "green Jesus group." Even Jay Leno got in on the act, opining on the *Tonight Show* that Jesus would have driven "a dented-up pickup—he was a carpenter, after all." When the hubbub eventually died down, the only enduring impact of the bumper stickers came from some English rockers who adopted the kitschy slogan as a band name.

Still, two noteworthy developments would arise from the "What Would Jesus Drive" flash in the pan. The first was that Ball might have been one of the earliest progressive activists to apply the "love your neighbor" catchall to a left-wing cause, telling *Good Morning America* about his SUV shaming, "The most basic teaching of Jesus is to love your neighbor like yourself. How can you do that when you are filling your neighbor's lungs with pollution?" (He apparently gave little thought to how much lower his neighbor's survival rate would be if he got into a high-speed collision while driving a compact car, or how his neighbor with multiple children was going to shuttle them and a few friends to soccer practice.) Since then, no incursion of leftism into the Church has failed to apply this all-purpose generalization in ways that have nothing to do with the state of an individual's heart or with showing hands-on kindness to the people in one's actual community.

The other development was that Ball now had recruiting help in Cizik, who was ten years older and far more established in mainstream evangelicalism.[25] The two convened a private meeting of about thirty evangelical leaders, including representation from *Christianity Today*, and in the summer of 2004, the group gathered on the Maryland side of the Chesapeake Bay and made a "'covenant' to engage the evangelical community on climate change and produce a 'consensus statement' within a year."[26]

It took them a couple of years to get to the statement, but *Christianity Today* editors did immediately endorse a bill from Senators John McCain and Joe Lieberman that would place carbon emission restrictions on businesses. The bill failed due to lack of support from conservatives, but the movement was still making progress. By 2006, fourteen member schools of the Council for Christian Colleges and Universities had launched creation care initiatives, largely as a result of the EEN's efforts.

Then, in 2006, the EEN received an influx of cash from left-wing donors that allowed it to found a new, more aggressive front organization. One of the funders was the Clinton Global Initiative—yes, those Clintons—which kicked in five hundred thousand dollars.[27] The Hewlett Foundation, one of the world's largest grant makers, which has long invested vast sums in abortion and family planning programs as part of its interest in controlling population, provided about the same.[28] With full coffers and elite backing, the Evangelical Climate Initiative was launched at a National Press Club breakfast hosted by Senators McCain and Lieberman.

Like the bumper stickers, the ECI was designed to make a media splash, and it did. Cizik was catapulted into the highest echelon of celebrity, landing a *Vanity Fair* spread.[29] It depicted him walking barefoot on water, clad all in black like a prophet of doom, against a ghostly, mist-shrouded wasteland, his only company a giant gray owl perched precariously on a dead tree branch. (Ironically, the caption says the image was photographed in New York City.)[30] The upscale celebrity gossip rag labeled him "the good reverend," and he was listed alongside Arnold Schwarzenegger, Bette Midler, and Bono's wife as an environmental hero. Ball wasn't quite so lucky (or perhaps unlucky), but he still scored plenty of mentions in outlets like the *New York Times*, the *Los Angeles Times*, and Salon.

With the ECI in place, the EEN was on the cusp of success in its decade-long effort to subdue Republican resistance to environmental regulations by convincing the party's most reliable voting bloc that climate change activism was a requirement of faithful Christian practice. As New America noted, "It seemed like climate care was now enshrined as a moral issue for evangelical Christians." To that end, the ECI released a public letter titled, "Climate Change: An Evangelical Call to Action."

The letter was drafted by David Gushee, Christian ethics professor and self-branded public intellectual (who has since gone on to reject the Bible's teaching that homosexual and transgender behaviors are sinful).[31] It ran as a full-page ad in the New York Times and was accompanied by radio and TV ads in fifteen red states that would have been key to any legislative success.

The letter left no room for theological or scientific debate, stating starkly that "evangelicals must engage this issue without any further lingering over the basic reality of the problem." In a Christianity Today report (that included no disclosure about the magazine's "covenant" meeting with the EEN), Ball insisted the statement was not politically motivated.[32] Yet the crux of the ECI's ask—buried within the letter's vague generalizations about loving neighbors and overwrought, unsourced claims like "millions of people could die in this century because of climate change"—was this: "The most important immediate step that can be taken at the federal level is to pass and implement national legislation requiring sufficient economy-wide reductions in carbon dioxide emissions . . . such as a cap-and-trade program."

This made it clear that the EEN/ECI was not simply encouraging Christians to consider the issue from biblical principle, but was lobbying for the U.S. government to increase its control over businesses and individuals, to the economic detriment of both. As Hayden Ludwig at the conservative financial think tank Capital Research put it, "This was cheap eco-fearmongering at its worst, advocacy deceptively masquerading as a message from Scripture."[33] Indeed, the letter closed with this admonition: "In the name of Jesus Christ our Lord, we urge all who read this declaration to join us in this effort."

Apparently, none of the signers considered that it should be a rather fearful thing to urge people to vote for any legislation in the name of Jesus Christ where the impact is debatable and the morality biblically ambiguous. But the glittering list of pastoral and ministerial signatories did not seem daunted in employing the Lord's name so cavalierly.

Along with the expected endorsements from various *Christianity Today* editors and writers, the list included Saddleback Church pastor and *The Purpose Driven Life* author Rick Warren, who has acted as spiritual adviser to both Republican and Democratic presidents; Salvation Army head W. Todd Bassett; president of the Council for Christian Colleges and Universities Robert Andringa; World Vision president Richard Stearns (who in 2014, in the name of "Christian unity," changed the nonprofit's hiring policy to include practicing homosexuals); and emergent church poster pastor Brian McLaren (who would later deny the doctrine of Hell, question the existence of a historical Jesus, and fully embrace LGBTQ affirmation).[34] One name was conspicuously missing. Cizik (who left the NAE in 2008 and endorsed gay marriage in 2015 [35]) ironically did not sign due to blowback from other NAE leaders, who were less enamored with how his new media profile was impacting the organization's formerly staid public image.

Also missing from among the signatories? Any climate scientists. The document's key scientific citation was the Intergovernmental Panel on Climate Change, a UN offshoot the letter described as "the world's most authoritative body of scientists and policy experts on the issue of global warming." Eventually, that authoritative body would find itself rocked by multiple data-skewing scandals. But that was still a few years into the future. As to specific evidence that human activity was the primary driver of climate change, the statement noted only that the previous fifty years had seen a "steady rise in global temperatures." It provided no more persuasive or precise substantiation.

That was not the case for a less-fêted statement written in response.

When a group of evangelicals involved in the climate change debate heard about the EEN/ECI statement, they immediately tried to persuade the NAE to rethink any endorsement. The letter they sent the organization did not demand wholesale rejection of the notion that climate change is primarily caused by human activity, but they did argue that opinion on the "cause, severity, and solution" to climate change should be a matter of Christian liberty. Some of the NAE's own members were among the signers urging their leaders not to "adopt any official position on the issue of global climate change" because "love for the Creator and respect for His creation does [*sic*] not require us to take a position."

Most of all, these dissenters pointed out that, biblically, there is no clear mandate to spread the gospel of global warming. Evangelicals, they said, "are to be first and foremost messengers of the good news of the gospel to a lost and dying world. We are to promote those things that please God and oppose those things in the world that clearly violate His righteous standard of conduct." They were gracious enough not to directly point out that climate change, however popular a cause it might be with the rich and powerful, did not meet this standard.

Then they got to work drafting an open statement of their own.

The Other Creation-Loving Evangelicals

While Professor Cal Beisner's formal academic background centers on theology, economic ethics, and public policy, he has spent two-plus decades in the trenches of the environmental debate.[36] During that time, he estimates that he has read upward of seventy books and many thousands of articles on climate change, plus a nearly equal number on the economics of climate and energy policy. "I have done far more study in the science of climate change than I ever did for my PhD," he told me with a self-deprecating chuckle when we met over Zoom.

Given how large Beisner's reputation looms in the evangelical climate clash, I expected someone aggressively academic, perhaps with that scholarly tendency to forget the person in front of him scrambling to take notes as he expounded on his area of expertise. But he spoke slowly and patiently, frequently pausing to invite follow-ups, quietly assessing my expression to make sure I understood the information he was sharing, offering points of clarification where it was clear I was confused. The only thing that was exactly as I envisioned was his shock of artlessly tousled gray hair, which was straight out of central casting. Toward the end of our discussion, which went on more than thirty minutes past the time I requested, he noticed that I was both a little under the weather and a little overwhelmed and asked if he could say a quick prayer for me before we said goodbye.

So, when Beisner explained that it was his love for people that spurred him to found the Cornwall Alliance for the Stewardship of Creation, it was easy to believe.

"When I was young, my family lived in Calcutta, India," he told me. "My father was a journalist working for the State Department. Part of his job was ensuring U.S. grain shipments actually reached the poor they were intended for. That was no small task because of the widespread corruption in the Indian government in the late 1950s." When Beisner was four or five, his mother was suddenly struck by paralysis. Her illness, which was never diagnosed but may have been Guillain-Barre syndrome, lasted six months. His older sisters were sent to Loreto House, the school that counted Mother Teresa among its former teachers, while he spent his days with an Indian family while his father was at work.

"Early in the morning my *aia* [nurse] would walk me to their house," Beisner recalled. "And in the courtyard of our apartment building we would pass by a beautiful tree with a vine bearing red flowers. Then we would walk out onto the street where I had to step over the bodies of people who had died of starvation and disease overnight." Years later, when he became a Christian, Beisner began to grapple with the Bible's teaching on caring for the needy. "I saw how so many of the environmental movement's favorite policies were really harmful to the poor by slowing, stopping, or reversing economic development." Those early images and memories of Calcutta would fill his mind. "That's what motivated me to get involved in all of this," he said.

Though Beisner leads the Cornwall Alliance, the group also includes experts like award-winning NASA climate scientist Dr. Roy Spencer and the former director of the University of Delaware's Center for Climatic Research, Dr. David Legates. In 2006, with the help of environmental economist Dr. Ross McKitrick and energy policy analyst Paul Driessen, they produced a response to the EEN.[37]

Unlike its counterpart, their letter was deeply sourced. It pointed out that the EEN statement had referenced only the IPCC's executive summary, which had been compiled by government negotiators, not scientists, in a notoriously politicized process. The actual report from which the IPCC summary drew was much more ambivalent about the impact of human activity on the climate. Beisner and company argued that it was irresponsible for the EEN signers, given their shallow understanding of the issue, to use their ministry platforms to call evangelicals to specific action. "[Good intentions] must be linked to sound understanding of relevant principles, theories, and facts . . . That linkage is lacking [in the EEN statement]," they wrote.

For all its careful, gracious wording, what Beisner and his colleagues carried out from there can only be described as a shellacking. As they walked through the detailed, relevant research via nearly fifty scientific citations, the Cornwall group did not deny that global warming was occurring. But they did demonstrate how much uncertainty remained about the degree to which it was human-induced, and they disagreed that it was an extreme problem requiring an extreme solution. "Foreseeable global warming will have moderate and mixed (not only harmful but also helpful), not catastrophic, consequences for humanity—including the poor—and the rest of the world's inhabitants," they wrote. They also provided study results contending that a large part, arguably even the majority, of climate change was naturally occurring and that attempts to regulate it by reducing carbon emissions would be an extremely costly exercise in futility.

The Cornwall Alliance finished by saying that they agreed with Cizik, Ball, *Christianity Today*, Warren, and the rest of the EEN's coalition that Christians are called to love their neighbors and act as faithful stewards over the earth. But given the conflicting expert opinion, they rejected the assertion that Christians should be spiritually guilted into promoting cap-and-trade legislation:

> Government-mandated reductions in carbon dioxide emissions not only would not significantly curtail global warming or reduce its harmful effects but would also cause greater harm than good to humanity— especially the poor—while offering virtually no benefit to the rest of the world's inhabitants. In light of all the above, the most prudent response is not to try to prevent or reduce whatever slight warming might really occur . . . The world's poor are much better served by enhancing their wealth through economic development than by whatever minute reductions might be achieved in future global warming by reducing CO emissions.

The list of signatures for this statement did not include any big-name megachurch pastors—none was featured in *Vanity Fair* or even in its lower-rent cousin *People*—but it did include over a hundred scientists in the fields of climatology, meteorology, physics, biology, and earth sciences, as well as energy engineers.

As New America lamented in its report, the resistance mounted by Beisner and his compatriots was enough to stall the momentum the EEN had built. But efforts to turn evangelicals into environmental activists continued.

In 2008, two years after the ECI released its statement, Jonathan Merritt, son of former Southern Baptist Convention president James Merritt, tried again to co-opt the massive denomination that had been the EEN's white whale.[38] He penned an open letter declaring that the SBC's "denominational engagement" with climate change was too timid and called for Southern Baptists to have a "unified moral voice" on global warming, demonstrated by "actively preach[ing], promot[ing], or practic[ing]" creation care in their churches.[39] Lest there be any confusion about whether this meant simply studying Bible passages related to responsible conservation, he finished by noting that "government is often needed" to address the issue.

While a number of heavy hitters (including Southeastern Baptist Theological Seminary president Danny Akin, then-SBC president Frank Page, and, of course, Merritt's father) signed the statement, it failed to gain traction. It was clear that Merritt had hoped to follow in the ECI's footsteps. He borrowed the ECI's name, calling his group the Southern Baptist Environment and Climate Initiative (SB-ECI), and, just like them, had arranged to launch his program at the National Press Club. But this plan was scuttled when other denominational leaders got wind of it and resisted. Perhaps the evangelical world had simply tired of dueling letters by then.

Still, this didn't mean that leftist secular foundations had tired of funding Christian-branded groups to infiltrate churches so they would begin preaching that the end was nigh because of climate change rather than the return of Christ. During the next fifteen years, the EEN continued to receive vast sums from groups like the Natural Resources Defense Council, Marisla Foundation, Environmental Defense Fund, Rockefeller Brothers Fund, and the Hewlett Foundation. Nor did the EEN remain the only game in town. New green evangelical groups ripe for funding were popping up all the time. There would always be more opportunities.

Selling Indulgences

New America concluded its 2015 postmortem report by recommending that the next generation of environmental activists pursue a tortoise rather than a hare model of drafting churches into their cause. "It is in evangelical universities and in individual congregations that the next battle for Creation Care will be fought," they wrote.

They were right.

As the 2020s dawned, Danny Akin demonstrated that he hadn't lost his willingness to promote climate change activism within the Church. In February 2021 he held a conference dedicated to the subject at Southeastern Baptist Theological Seminary, located in the lush, green Raleigh suburb of Wake Forest.[40] All six speakers took the position that climate change is a problem of catastrophic proportions and that Christians have a duty to take up the issue.

Oxford theology professor Alister McGrath, for instance, argued that believers who do not view climate change as an existential crisis possess less love for God's creation. That was marginally better than comments made by atmospheric scientist and well-known environmental activist Katharine Hayhoe. In an interview for the seminary's podcast, she likened Christians who are skeptical of man-made climate change to Pharisees and antebellum slavery defenders. While analyzing what she called the "relationship between climate change and slavery," she said, "letters to the editor and comments that people would publish in the newspaper back in the pre Civil War era . . . compared to the letters to the editor and the comments that people publish today in support of continuing a fossil fuel based economy . . . you could literally take out slavery and replace it with fossil fuels. The same economic arguments were used for both of them. And of course, everyone wants a healthy economy. Of course, everyone wants people to have good jobs, to be able to feed their families. But do we want it at the price of truth and justice?"

Not only did her interviewer, SEBTS theology professor Ken Keathley, offer no pushback to the suggestion that Christians opposed to fossil fuel regulation are as morally blinkered as those who once opposed abolition, he joined the analogy, and "model[ed] the love of Christ."[41]

In a related podcast interview with SEBTS theology professor Ken

Keathley, she likened Christians who are skeptical of man-made climate change to Pharisees and said they make the same arguments. Even leaving aside her slavery comments, Hayhoe was a particularly provocative invite. A cherubic darling of the World Economic Forum, she once shared a stage with President Obama and Leonardo DiCaprio at the South by South Lawn film festival.[42] The trio were there to premiere the actor's documentary *Before the Flood*, a movie that claims, with utmost sincerity, "the number one public enemy is the cow." But when not hanging out with the Hollywood lothario known as the green movement's biggest hypocrite[43] or allowing a blood-red painted priestess to blow the spirits of the dead in her face as part of a Davos shamanic ritual,[44] Hayhoe serves as scientific adviser to the EEN. And she has made a special cause of spreading climate alarmism to churchgoers. Her entire presentation at the SEBTS conference centered on convincing theology and ministry students that global warming is a cataclysmic, man-made problem that faithful Christians must mobilize to solve.

The conference did not include any evangelical scientists from Cornwall Alliance or any other organizations who might have provided a counterpoint to Hayhoe's talk, though they should have been easy enough to locate. In fact, I could not find that SEBTS has *ever* hosted a speaker who has challenged climate change catastrophizing, though the school regularly welcomes those who promote it.

In the fall semester of 2022, the school's L. Russ Bush Center for Faith and Culture welcomed Jonathan Moo, professor of environmental studies at Whitworth University, to give a guest lecture titled "Loving God and Neighbor in an Age of Climate Crisis."[45]

Known for their theological conservatism, the Southern Baptist Convention's six seminaries educate at least a quarter of all Protestants who go into ministry, another reason groups like the EEN have been so keen to sway them.[46] Before he died in 2008, theologian and apologist L. Russ Bush set up the center to help inure SEBTS from the influence of worldly and unbiblical ideologies. Yet as Moo's lecture would show, even the best-planned temples can fall prey to moneychangers.

Moo began by sharing his love of the terrain of the Pacific Northwest, waxing poetic about local flora like thimbleberries and Rocky Mountain maples. He then lamented the trees and local wildlife lost to the lumber industry, the mountain caribou that no longer populate the forests. This part of the presentation would surely have resonated with any Christian who wants to preserve the glory and variety of God's handiwork by stewarding it with care. (Few things make me grumpier than when a housing developer in my area begins a new project by bulldozing all the trees.)

But as Moo went on, he made it clear that he was not merely encouraging responsible conservation but creating a new class of extrabiblical commands. Creation care, he said, is necessary "in order to be faithful to the Gospel": "It's not an option. It's not just something we might add on to lots of other programs we might do ... And the reason why this is absolutely vital and should be woven into all that we do and proclaim, is first and foremost, because it is part of the Gospel."

It might be good to pause for a moment and remember something as elementary as what the Gospel actually is, given that the climate change activists won't be the last group we encounter who have decided their pet project deserves inclusion. It is the Good News that God has provided a way to salvation through the death and resurrection of Jesus Christ (Romans 1:16). Christ, who Himself is God incarnate, satisfied God's wrath and paid the penalty for our sin on the Cross so that "whosoever believes in him would not perish but have eternal life" (John 3:16). The Gospel is a message of deliverance not from earthly difficulties or circumstances, but from the power of sin in our hearts and the penalty of sin in Hell (Revelation 21:1–8). It's not self-help advice for a more comfortable life or a series of steps to winning God's favor, but rather, it is the uniquely Christian message that salvation is an unearned gift from God (Ephesians 2:1–10). It is all about what God has done to reconcile us to Him, so that we might be able to stand justified before Him despite the sins we commit against Him every day (2 Corinthians 5:17–21).

The proper response to the Gospel is repentance from sin and faith in the sufficient work of Christ (Mark 1:15; Romans 10:9). To live faithfully in light of that Gospel is to endure in belief in Jesus to the end (Matthew 24:13–14), to carry the Good News of salvation to the lost (Matthew 28:19–20), and to contend for the faith once delivered to all the saints by standing against any doctrine that adds to or takes away from that message (Jude 1:3; Galatians 2:11–16).

Moo's explanation for how creation care, as he would later define it, plays a necessary role in the Gospel was "if we love our neighbor, we cannot help but care for the world of which they are a part." It's true that love for our neighbors should prompt us to take care of the part of the world we inhabit, but as Beisner and the Cornwall Alliance have shown, other Christians have different, legitimate ideas about how that love is expressed through the stewardship of creation. They might pursue technological innovations to yield more crops or increase energy availability or create more personal wealth for impoverished people—all loving priorities Moo's lecture didn't acknowledge. Worse, as he went on, he not so subtly downgraded the importance of mankind as the pinnacle of God's creation, the only living thing fashioned for eternal life.

He stressed "proper biblical humility," because "it turns out all other creatures also have that breath of God's life." While he acknowledged that man alone is made in God's image, he added that Jesus "gave up his very life on behalf of all of creation." Not sinful mankind, *creation*. An imprecisely phrased statement? Perhaps. But as Moo moved on to discuss passages like Romans 8:22 (commonly misused by environmentalists who claim it refers to creation "groaning" not just under the weight of sin but of CO2 emissions) he highlighted the population increase since Jesus's time. "Now we're adding a billion [people] within twelve years or so," he said. "That more than exponential rise in human population means, of course, an impact. Every one of these people needs resources to survive."

With this, Moo accepted the environmental movement's narrative that the fruitful multiplication of humanity, which the Bible describes as a blessing, is instead a curse on the earth (Genesis 1:28 and 9:1). He then expanded on this premise, implying that people are a blight on the natural world. "We have affected directly probably eighty-five percent of land on earth and, indirectly, much more than that," he fretted, stressing that "seventy percent of the earth's grasslands we now use to grow food."

This was all before he came to the point of his lecture, which was that climate change is caused "by human activity" and that the United States bears the lion's share of guilt because of how "rich and prosperous" our use of fossil fuels has made us. Americans, he argued, are especially obligated to "sacrifice" by adopting emission-restricting policies.

Moo then outlined ways the seminary students might respond to what he had presented as massive existential problems. Less driving and flying were high on his list for "living lives of personal virtue." If the seminary students must fly, he suggested that they "acknowledge the cost by paying for it with carbon credits." Where might the students buy these credits? "There's a great organization," he said, "Climate Stewards, linked to A Rocha, this Christian organization that is doing fantastic projects in the majority world that qualify for carbon offsets."

Moo, who sits on the board of A Rocha International,[47] was quite literally selling the students indulgences to pay for the "sins" of driving a car or taking a flight.

Anything compared to that medieval-style virtue hawking seems rather dull, but Moo did have a few more suggestions for environmental activism. "Above all," he encouraged those assembled to pressure their churches to engage the issue. This, he said, would provide "a witness to a world that has been waiting for Christians to step up and show what it looks like to be distinctively Christian."

Climate change activism as a *distinctively Christian* witness? One wonders if Moo missed that of all the issues in which Christians might involve themselves, climate change is the one where they're most likely to get lost in the crowd. It's hard to be distinct when nearly every major corporation, the world's largest fund managers, A-list Hollywood, the United Nations, the World Economic Forum, and the vast majority of the Western world's national governments got there before you did and are arguing for the exact same policies. It's a little like the old Eddie Murphy joke about Johnny Carson's wife getting a job at a boutique so she could "do her share" and add her seventy-dollar paycheck to Carson's hundreds of millions: *Now the climate change movement has three hundred million and seventy dollars.*

As for where A Rocha gets its dollars, along with individual donations, government grants, and funding from secular environmentalist groups like the Chino Cienega Foundation, Moo's organization receives operational support from the Annenberg Foundation,[48] a left-of-center grant maker that also funds the National Abortion Rights Action League,[49] Planned Parenthood, and the Center for Reproductive Rights. As with many other secular purse holders, Annenberg's interest in environmental activism is married to a desire to reduce the population through abortion.

It wouldn't be the first time A Rocha's leaders would show little compunction about partnering with a group focused on destroying rather than preserving life. Its executive director, Ben Lowe, ran for Illinois's Sixth Congressional District as a Democrat, assuring voters that his personal pro-life views did not mean he would support overturning *Roe v. Wade*.[50] It's difficult to imagine anything less "distinctively Christian" than turning a blind eye to the clearest moral horror of our age for the sake of glomming onto the same issue that preoccupies the world's wealthiest and most powerful non-Christians. But A Rocha's strange hymns and prayers that sound more like Marxist Gaia worship than anything recognizably biblical give such abortion indifference a run for its money.[51]

Among the sins A Rocha calls humanity to repent from in its recommended prayers are "ecological violence" and "act[ing] like parasites instead of gardeners."[52] It suggests praying for the "courage to speak out against increased nuclear capability" and lamenting our "exploitive economic system [that] has encroached into holy habitats."

Another prayer, titled "Woe to the Unholy Trinity," reads more like a cultish chant than a prayer:

> ...We have acted as cheerleaders and chaplains to this unholy trinity
> Lord have Mercy.
> And so we name the unholy beast.
> We renounce it.
> We repent of it.
> Unrestrained Capitalism,
> Consumerism,
> Individualism ...
> This unholy trinity
> That oppresses the poor,
> Ransacks the Earth.[53]

One has to wonder what average Southern Baptists would have thought had they known their "unholy" capitalist tithes, which help support SEBTS, were going to pay the lecture fees of a representative from A Rocha, who then used the invite to do a bit of capitalist carbon trading himself.

Moo finished his lecture by enjoining the students not to demonstrate their commitment to stopping climate change through protesting. Rather, they should vote for fossil fuel legislation and write to their representatives. He stressed that students should emphasize in these messages that they're demanding these climate change policies "because [they're] Christian[s]."

"Smuggled into a Discipleship Class"

What Moo mapped out was a new approach for pushing a climate change agenda through the Church. Instead of recruiting marquee names to sign on to high-profile public statements in the hope that the masses would want to follow the examples of their evangelical stars, it would quietly pressure churches, seminaries, and everyday people in the pews to become grassroots activists. The GOP would thus become convinced that if it wanted to retain the evangelical support it depends on to win elections, it would need to back carbon emission caps, fracking bans, and other net-zero policies.

This was exactly the strategy that New America recommended at the conclusion of its 2015 autopsy report on the failure of the EEN's top-down strategy. "This lack of grassroots support made it difficult for sympathetic evangelical elites to engage in public conflict with Christian Right leaders who opposed climate action," the authors wrote, specifically citing Beisner. EEN president Mitch Hescox agreed with that assessment, telling New America that if his coalition had done more to recruit churches rather than big, recognizable names, their efforts might have produced better results.

Not that they had no success with average evangelicals. New America's report authors made it clear that the EEN and its allies were able to convince some churches to embrace nonpolitical environmental measures that centered on personal responsibility, like recycling. Their frustration was that they weren't able to mobilize them on behalf of *legislation*. "[EEN leader] Peter Illyn found it difficult to persuade local pastors to engage Creation Care in their congregation, unless it was hyper-local and *disconnected from public policy* [emphasis mine]," they wrote. That is, they weren't willing to agitate for more centralized government restrictions.

But New America did cite one exception to this failure. Episcopal priest Alexis Chase had extensive experience merging progressive political activism with her ministerial role. As a member of a group of clergy known as the Marriage Militia Project, Chase has helped marry as many homosexual couples in the Church as possible in a bid to increase acceptance for same-sex marriage.

She described how her environmental group, Georgia Interfaith Power and Light, successfully convinced a group of Southern Baptist lay leaders in five Georgia churches to lobby to stop plans for three coal-fired power plants. Her strategy in one word: subterfuge.

First, "motivated lay leaders" in evangelical megachurches would invite Chase to teach a general creation care class to their small group or Bible study. (This raises the question of why Southern Baptist churches, whose statement of faith prohibits both women in the pastorate and the affirmation of homosexuality, would provide spiritual leaders like Chase access to their members in the first place.) From there, Chase suggested some presentations on how to lower energy bills that allowed her to disguise her ultimate lobbying aims. At the end of the class, she gave those assembled phone numbers to call to register complaints about the coal plants: "Partly as a result, two proposed coal-fire plant projects were shut down completely. But the policy campaign was smuggled into the class as an extension of personal discipleship."

Read that again: the policy campaign was *smuggled into a discipleship class*.

In 2022, the year before he took the helm of A Rocha, Lowe cited the New America report in a study.[54] His conclusions on the "generational divide over climate change among American evangelicals" largely agreed with New America that trying to mobilize a grassroots effort would be more effective than relying on the trickle-down influence of elite evangelicals, but he added one wrinkle: He particularly wanted to see climate activists focus on the young Christians his research told him were more persuadable. His hypothesis was that given "the influential role of evangelicals in American society and politics," if enough of them were co-opted, "it could change the political calculus around climate policies and also bring bipartisan action within greater reach."

Getting Political and Doing Your Homework

What we see is that from the earliest stages of the creation care movement, it has never been simply an effort to encourage personal righteousness or reflection on how individual Christians might steward the earth responsibly or practice conservation in our own spheres of influence. It isn't even about volunteering or fund-raising for planting nurseries or cleaning up marine ecosystems, though this is often the front-facing focus on creation care websites. That may have been the mechanism the EEN, A Rocha, and other groups sometimes used to gain access to churches, and if their focus stayed on these elements, various individual Christians and churches would take up those initiatives as they felt led, and few would complain.

But their ultimate aim has been to press for political action on a biblically debatable matter—to use the Church to produce a groundswell of evangelical demand for centralized government policy. And not just federal authoritarianism like the Green New Deal. These same organizations urge Christians to pressure our representatives to sign away our national interests to legally binding international authoritarianism—the kind of UN oversight that is playing havoc in Europe and developing nations.

Yet, those Christians who resist being drafted into this project are the ones creation care activists accuse of being political.

California pastor Gavin Ortlund may not have reached the name recognition of Rick Warren or the institutional heights of Richard Cizik, but as New America has illustrated, that model didn't work for the EEN anyway. And Ortlund, whose laid-back Ventura County style and hushed manner of speaking give him something of a preppy guru vibe, would certainly live up to Lowe's ideal of a grassroots campaign catalyst among young evangelicals. Ortlund's not only a popular author, but also a fellow with *The Gospel Coalition*'s recently inaugurated Keller Center for Cultural Apologetics—an entity specifically designed to speak to "the next generation."[55] His YouTube channel, Truth Unites, has developed a wide following of young seminarians and ministers through its accessible exploration of apologetics and theology. In 2022, though, Ortlund released a video that did not delve into either of those areas.

The key theme of the episode titled "Climate Change: Why Christians

Should Engage,"[56] is that evangelicals have been "very skeptical or apathetic" about the issue because they've been politicized by the right. He begins in characteristically soft tones by asking his audience to consider "orienting their postures" to the subject in such a way as not to be "closed off." He then shares that he's "deeply burdened" that too many Christians have dismissed the idea that human-caused climate change poses a significant risk to humanity "without having studied it, not based on the evidence, but based on the socio-political associations."

"I think the main thing is just in the United States in recent decades, though not back in earlier times, issues of environmental stewardship, and particularly climate change, have been associated with political liberalism," he says. "And evangelicals have tended to be politically conservative. And I think that is the biggest single factor for why more Christians aren't more active in leading the charge on something like climate change." From there, Ortlund launches into a layman's recitation of the most common tenets of the climate change movement—namely, that it is settled science because "every other scientific body of national or international standing agrees that human-caused global warming is a serious problem."

His descriptions of the wages of climate change are as hyperbolic as anything coming from United Nations climate star Greta Thunberg, beginning with the claim that it is a very "big deal."

> The consequences are very severe. . . . a lot of the things that you might not think of is just the increase in extreme local weather events. . . . And people living closer together causes greater spread of infectious diseases . . . Let's say you don't have any snowcap, or you don't have enough [water] and all your crops die . . . Because when there's a drought or a famine in a poor country, people die; when there's flooding and wildfires, people die. And the scary thing is, you know, seeing the ripple effects of famine and things like that causes political problems, and that can lead to war.

Ortlund finishes this portion of the video by saying he is not trying to be apocalyptic or a "doomsday person," but it's hard to imagine what he might have said differently if he were.

Ortlund takes it on faith that extreme local weather events are increasing, even though, when you compare actual data with models, you get different answers. The 2022 hurricane season, for example, saw the weakest storm levels in forty-two years, part of an overall downward trend.[57] The number of hurricanes hasn't seen a particular uptick, either, as even the National Oceanic and Atmospheric Administration had to concede in May 2023. "We conclude the historical Atlantic hurricane data at this stage do not provide compelling evidence for a substantial greenhouse warming–induced century-scale increase in: frequency of tropical storms, hurricanes, or major hurricanes, or in the proportion of hurricanes that become major hurricanes," they wrote.[58] Claims regarding prolonged record heat also require reading the fine print to discover that the most severe heat waves in U.S. history occurred in the 1930s.[59]

Ortlund cites only one scientific authority in his video, the same one the ECI cited 16 years earlier: the Intergovernmental Panel on Climate Change, which he describes as a group of leading scientists from all over the world. He goes on to say that every "scientific body of national or international standing agrees that human-caused global warming is a serious problem." To not accept that consensus, he says, is to buy into "conspiracy and hoax;" it is a failure to "take a responsible posture" as a Christian.

As for why Ortlund feels his brothers and sisters must accept the prevailing climate change narrative, he offers nothing more original than those three magic words: *love your neighbor.*

Yet it's worth pointing out that research is beginning to show that this kind of rhetoric has been fairly detrimental to our neighbors, driving an epidemic of fear and despair among young people, giving rise to a new term, *eco-anxiety.* One 2021 study conducted by five UK universities surveyed ten thousand young people between the ages of sixteen and twenty-five in ten different countries, including the United States. It found that nearly 60 percent think that humanity is "doomed" because of climate change.[60] Nearly half said their fears for the environment are negatively impacting their mental health on a daily basis. Perhaps if Moo wants the Church to offer a "distinctively Christian witness," he and Ortlund could consider what words of calm assurance, rooted in a loving God and His stable creation, would mean to generations who are deeply worried about climate change.

Also, Ortlund doesn't seem to have done the full breadth of study on the issue himself, or he would know what is meant by scientific consensus. As Dr. Roy Spencer (the NASA climate scientist who helped Beisner write the Cornwall Alliance's response to the EEN's 2006 letter) pointed out in the *Wall Street Journal*, the oft-cited claim that there is a 97 percent consensus in the scientific community on climate change is a myth,[61] one cobbled together from agreement on a variety of premises. The vast majority of scientists agree that temperature averages have increased slightly in the last 150 years and that man-made greenhouse gas emissions have contributed to some of that rise. What many don't agree on is how much humans are contributing or how serious a threat this poses.

Spencer stressed that he would be included in the consensus even though he's a well-known dissident in the climate science community because he questions the degree to which fossil fuels are driving warming and is adamantly opposed to draconian government regulations to address the issue. He even believes warming has had some positive impact on the planet.

Ortlund's appeal to consensus also fails to consider the severe professional and reputational damage any scientist who questions the conventional wisdom risks. In September 2023, climatologist Dr. Patrick Brown admitted in the Free Press that in order to get his paper published in *Nature* magazine, he deliberately left out other factors that contributed to increased wildfires in California and focused solely on climate change.[62] As consulting meteorologist Anthony Sadar pointed out in 2022, "No [human-caused climate change] challenger wants to get blacklisted or de-platformed or lose an opportunity for good grant money or miss a chance for an advanced degree or end his science career."[63]

Ortlund both began and ended his presentation by stressing (albeit in those same soothing tones) that Christians should discuss the issue respectfully and not attack one another. But however softly his words were uttered, it's hard to square that with his insistence that those who hold views that differ from his can be doing so only because they are motivated by politics or haven't "hit the books."

When I asked Beisner about Ortlund's assertion that Christians resist engaging on climate change because they've been politicized, he minced few words: "The Christians who have become activists regarding that issue are almost invariably doing so because *they've* been politicized. I can almost guarantee you that Gavin Ortlund has never read any significant part of the scientific reports of the IPCC. He may have read press releases from it, he might possibly have read the summary for policymakers for the latest IPCC assessment report. But that would be about it."

Beisner noted that the IPCC's releases are far from sound scientific reports. Government representatives, not scientists, are the final authors of the IPCC summaries that policymakers and the media cite. The government-appointed delegates go over the scientists' initial draft summary line by line and then, Beisner explained, they get to vote on the wording of every sentence. "The task of every delegate there is to make sure that nothing in it undermines the policy of the government he represents," he told me. "The most important people in the IPCC are not the scientists. They are the delegates who represent the desired policies of their own nations."

It's also worth remembering that the IPCC, a bureaucratic division of the United Nations, has a history of scandal specifically related to climate data. In 2009, hacked emails revealed that its climate scientists had concealed data and attempted to silence colleagues who didn't align with that consensus Ortlund mentioned.[64] Though the IPCC denied any fraud, the data that leaked in the affair that became known as "Climategate" demonstrated that the scientists' climate models were not playing out as expected in real-life temperature patterns.

In 2017, "Climategate 2.0" hit. In its next report after the scandal, IPCC scientists had to admit that temperature warming appeared to have stalled. It was terrible timing for those who hoped to create more global oversight at the Paris Accords. In an apparent attempt at damage control that would ensure that nations still agreed to carbon emission regulations, scientists at NOAA then got caught falsifying data.[65]

Is an influential Gospel Coalition pastor like Gavin Ortlund aware of these scandals when he encourages Christians to look to the IPCC as the authority? Is he aware of how IPCC summaries are assembled and disseminated when he dismisses as conspiracy theorists fellow Christians who, he says, have failed to "hit the books"? Most important, does he know about the United Nations' partnership with Planned Parenthood[66] to restrict population growth through an aggressive "reproductive health and rights" program, and does he think his audience deserves to have this information?

This is not to single out Ortlund, who is certainly not the only young pastor promoting climate change activism as a Christian practice, nor the only one citing the IPCC as an authority. But he is well positioned with the Keller Center and *The Gospel Coalition* to be the sort of mainstream, conservative evangelical influence New America was hoping to see. In 2023, *The Gospel Coalition* hosted a "debate" on climate change between two men who had no scientific expertise and who both agreed that climate change is largely human-caused and represents a serious problem.[67] Their only serious disagreement was in how to address it.

This raises a question—why don't these organizations seek out experts, like the climatologists at the Cornwall Alliance, who are certainly more credentialed in climate science than people like Dr. Moo? Or if the issue is a combination of theological and environmental expertise, why not call Dr. Beisner?

When I asked Beisner if seminaries like SEBTS ever invite Cornwall Alliance climate scientists or theologians to present an argument for stewardship rather than creation care, he was blunt. "No, they don't." And when *The Gospel Coalition* was setting up debates about how Christians are to care for the environment, did the Cornwall Alliance's phone ring? Again, "No." This despite the fact that the Cornwall Alliance is well known, well respected, and virtually the only evangelical game in town when it comes to offering a counter view. Thus, Beisner offered this reasonable plea for such institutions: "Let people hear two sides, at least, to an issue. If you want to have a group like A Rocha in, I'd encourage you to have somebody from Cornwall Alliance as well." That doesn't seem too much to expect.

In keeping with the Cornwall Alliance's initial 2006 letter to the NAE,[68] I'm not here to argue for one side of the climate change debate or the other. But I am here to remind evangelical leaders who would use their offices to draft the Church into the battle that there *is* a debate. As we have seen over the course of the Covid-19 pandemic, few things are more detrimental to the discovery of truth than beating the drum of scientific "consensus" when it is clear how much consensus is created through media manipulation and fear of professional and reputational damage.

The climate scientists and experts at the Cornwall Alliance ably explode many of the cheap narratives peddled as arguments for draconian government action. The fact is, 98 percent fewer people now die in climate-related deaths annually than did one hundred years ago.[69] That is actual numbers, not model projections. Is trying to artificially hamper the world economy really a better solution to shifting temperatures and weather patterns than giving the world's poor the same economic tools that wealthy nations used to develop the kind of infrastructure that can withstand floods, hurricanes, and freezes?

The trade-offs on loving our neighbors by agitating for "legislation that helps speed up the transition to renewable energy" are never as simple as they seem.

Remember that 2022 NAE report about "loving the least of these"? That report (which, similarly to Ortlund, warned its readers not to listen to "polarizing voices" who refer to "conspiracy theories") was primarily a patchwork of sad, weather-related stories—floods in Vietnam, droughts in Bangladesh—that provided not an ounce of hard scientific evidence that these events were caused by carbon emissions or man-made climate change. Yet the regulations to address emissions come with a lot of sad stories, too, and their cause is not debatable.

Take the lithium-ion batteries needed to power electric cars and store solar energy. Producing such batteries requires cobalt, cobalt that right now is being dug out of the ground by slaves in the Congo, including many children,[70] some as young as four. They toil in tunnels and pits in the heat for sixteen hours at a stretch, breathing in toxic fumes. There is no other option for work, as their villages were bulldozed to make way for the cobalt mines. Walls and tunnels frequently collapse, amputating the lucky, burying the rest alive. The mines are destroying the local ecosystem, poisoning the water, requiring the clear-cutting of trees.

These are complex topics. It is not wrong for pastors and Christian leaders to weigh them and debate them. But it *is* wrong for them to make agreement on environmental policies a test of biblical faithfulness. It is wrong to make climate change activism a measure of one's commitment to the Gospel. And it is wrong to bind consciences with a blithe and unthinking "Love your neighbor."

CHAPTER 2

Illegal Immigration

Strangers, Neighbors, and Aliens

Peace be within your walls and security within your towers!

—Psalm 122:7

When Maureen Maloney saw the tagline for the Evangelical Immigration Table, "Welcoming the Stranger," she couldn't help but feel a wave of bitterness. The same went when she saw Christian celebrities sending open letters to the *Washington Post* demanding that lawmakers admit more immigrants under programs that grant refugee status to many who are in no danger of persecution, war, or violence in their home countries.[1] The group said they wanted to see more immigration because they "value the opportunity" to "live out the biblical commandments to love our neighbors and to practice hospitality." She wondered why they didn't have much interest in ministering to people like her. She wondered if they considered her their neighbor.

I spoke to Maloney three days after the twelfth anniversary of her son's death.

When I asked her about Matthew, she still, at odd moments, inadvertently slipped into the present tense. "Matthew is one of those people who's loved by everybody," she told me. But in her next sentence, as she recounted what happened to him, her brain evidently clicked back into recognition that he was gone.

"He was voted most dependable in high school and graduated college three months before he was killed," she remembered. "On the day that it happened, he was coming home in the early evening, like after dinnertime, and he was riding his motorcycle in a residential area. An illegal alien who had been drinking all day was driving a truck. He ran through a Stop sign and collided with Matthew's motorcycle."

It wasn't the collision that killed Maloney's son, though; it was the fact that the driver of the truck tried to flee, perhaps with deportation in mind. At first, Matthew landed on the windshield of the truck and rolled off. He was getting up to make his way off the road when the driver stepped on the gas. As he drove off, he ran over Matthew, who got stuck in the truck's wheel well and was dragged to his death.

"It was a beautiful summer evening," Maloney said, "so lots of people were out barbecuing and just sitting outside in the shade. There were a lot of witnesses and people running after the truck, banging on it, trying to stop this person and save Matthew's life." I expected to hear emotion in Maloney's voice as I probed for more details about that day. But her tone was flat, matter-of-fact—perhaps from so many years of telling her story, trying to get people to listen. "At the quarter-mile mark," she went on, "the man ran over a curb, and Matthew became dislodged. At that point—I don't know, maybe the guy was panicking—he backed up over Matthew again. Then he took off."

I asked what she thought about the argument put forth by various evangelical groups who insist that Christ's command to love our neighbors means we must support various amnesty policies. She told me they're cherry-picking Scripture. "I think our basic religious principle should be that God expects us to follow the law," she said. She felt that Christian institutions are aiding and abetting illegal immigration by "incentivizing people to make this dangerous journey up to the U.S. border." When the man who killed her son was arrested, she discovered that because he'd had a child while living in the United States, he was receiving welfare, free state health care, and government-subsidized housing. "Why wouldn't people rush to come here when word of things like that gets out?" she asked me. Because word *has* gotten out, the news cycle in the last few years has been dominated by the record numbers of illegal aliens coming across the border.[2] According to a joint study conducted by Yale and MIT, there are now as many as 22 million living in the United States[3] If that figure is accurate, that would make them nearly 7 percent of our population. But even if that estimate is high, there is no question that we have been welcoming a lot of strangers.

After Matthew's death, Maloney joined Advocates for Victims of Illegal Alien Crime (AVIAC), a group that banded together to give a voice to people in whom evangelical leaders seem to have little interest—those who have lost loved ones due to illegal immigrant homicides, murders, and manslaughters. It is notoriously difficult to get a clear accounting of just how many people that is, as the last report the U.S. Government Accountability Office produced on illegal alien crime was in 2018. That report showed that between 2010 and 2015, illegal migrants who were incarcerated were responsible for the deaths of 33,000 people.[4] Simple back-of-the-envelope math suggests that the total over the last thirteen years could easily top 85,000. As Maureen Maloney said, even though this is far from the full tally, it is not a small number.

When I asked her if AVIAC and its members ever hear from evangelical groups interested in ministering to them in their suffering, she minced no words. "No. We never have. And we represent the loved ones of victims from all over the country; it's not a local organization. But these church groups are not interested in us." Reflecting on groups like the Evangelical Immigration Table protesting family separation policies, Maloney pointed out that she and other AVIAC members have "suffered the ultimate in family separation."

Perhaps these ministries and parachurch organizations don't care because there are no left-wing billionaires or federal programs funding them to care.

Gang of Eight

In January 2020, *Baptist Press*, the house organ of the Southern Baptist Convention, published a lie. The question is whether the outlet knew at the time that it was a lie.

The article was not attributed to any specific author and was labeled an "explainer."[5] It claimed to debunk reporting from the conservative news outlet Breitbart, which revealed that the Evangelical Immigration Table, a group that lobbies for various amnesty policies in the name of Jesus, was funded by left-wing, atheist billionaire George Soros. This was not a small matter because, largely under the direction of, first, Richard Land, and then Russell Moore, the SBC's Ethics and Religious Liberty Commission had become a key leader in the EIT. Nor were Land and Moore alone. Leadership for a host of trusted evangelical organizations, including the Council for Christian Colleges and Universities, the NAE, World Relief, InterVarsity Christian Fellowship, Focus on the Family, Prison Fellowship Ministries, and the Wesleyan Church, had joined hands with the EIT. If it was being bankrolled by Soros, they would all have a lot of explaining to do.

The EIT officially launched in June 2012, after the NAE and Clergy and Laity United for Economic Justice (a progressive interfaith group) began working with the left-wing National Immigration Forum.[6] Its purpose was to act as a front group to promote the NIF's open-border policies, such as granting legal status to most illegal immigrants, among evangelicals.[7]

From the outset, the group focused not on encouraging Christians to meet the material and spiritual needs of immigrants in their own communities, something few would object to, but on pushing them to lobby lawmakers for specific legislation. CNN, for example, reported shortly after the EIT's debut that it was "fundraising and placing people in three states, Colorado, Florida and Texas, to lay the groundwork with local evangelical leaders" in the hope that they would create a "highly reactive group of evangelicals ready to push for immigration reform."[8] The EIT's own documents support this characterization. By late 2013, the group was soliciting proposals for "mobilizers" to "activate" pastors and congregations, explaining that "81 Republicans in the House who may vote for immigration reform represent districts whose population is at least 20% evangelical Christian. Over the last year, the [EIT] has worked to engage pastors and congregants in 16 of the 20 states that are home to these districts."[9] Later, a group of Pepperdine and Chapman sociologists studying immigration policy would note that President Obama appeared to have waited to issue his executive order on Dreamers until just after a 2014 EIT press conference that claimed evangelicals had reached a "tipping point" on amnesty. That support, the researchers wrote, gave Obama "the political cover he needed in order to take this step."[10]

Claiming to speak for evangelicals across the country, the EIT demanded not just general immigration reform but the passage of the Gang of Eight bill. Backed by New York Democratic senator Chuck Schumer and moderate Arizona Republican senator John McCain, the sweeping overhaul of U.S. immigration laws would have granted citizenship to nearly 11 million illegals and paved the way for a further surge in unlawful migration.[11] Alabama Republican senator Jeff Sessions, then the ranking member of the Senate Budget Committee, warned at the time that, if successful, the bill would have caused "economic catastrophe."[12]

The EIT's efforts to see the bill passed began in earnest in January 2013, as the group pushed churches to join a forty-day study of cherry-picked Bible verses, titled "I Was a Stranger," that they insisted applied to U.S. immigration law.[13] Instead of studying the Bible, churches involved with the EIT began recruiting their congregants for political activism. One North Carolina church, for instance, that promoted a six-week workshop[14] on:

- The History of Immigration in the United States;
- Immigration in NC—Understanding Our Newest Immigrant Neighbors;
- Developing Your Moral Voice in Immigration and Diversity;
- Stranger-to-Neighbor Storytelling Workshop;
- Understanding Secure Communities and the DREAM Act; and
- Strategies for Voicing Your Value and Taking Action.

Two months later, Moore, along with seven other church leaders, including NAE board member Samuel Rodriguez, met with President Obama in something of a publicity blitz to convince Republican lawmakers that even evangelicals wanted to see "pathways to citizenship" like the Gang of Eight bill.[15] The proposal would have required an illegal alien to pay only a fine of a thousand dollars to receive provisional legal status and another thousand-dollar fee ten years later to become a permanent resident.[16] It's not hard to guess why so many border crossers are unwilling to wait as much as decades in the normal green card process when immediate entry might be had so cheaply.[17] But the EIT insisted that evangelicals wanted what Schumer and McCain were selling because, as ABC noted at the time, "Religious groups have played a key role in organizing public support for immigration reform, especially from conservative churchgoers who may not otherwise support the effort."[18]

The problem was Moore did not represent the majority of his supposed constituents, and the "support" that ABC and other major media outlets were breathlessly covering was basically astroturf. At the time that Moore and other EIT leaders were claiming to speak for them, a Pew Forum poll found that evangelicals ranked by a ratio of nearly three to one "better border security" as more important than "creating a path to citizenship."[19] When asked how they preferred to reduce the illegal immigrant population—by enforcing current laws or creating a pathway to citizenship—a Pulse Opinion Research poll that same year found that 79 percent picked "enforce the law."[20] Only 13 percent chose conditional legalization. It's hard to see on what basis Moore and his compatriots could make any reasonable claim to be representing the views of anyone but themselves.

Nonetheless, the EIT set about making a media splash with the narrative that evangelicals were demanding more progressive border policies.

Before he was disgraced in a sex scandal in 2018,[21] few American pastors boasted more star power than Bill Hybels, founder of Willow Creek Community Church and pioneer of the seeker-sensitive church growth movement. It was thanks to Hybels that so many evangelical pastors became convinced in the 1990s that the best way to grow their churches was to embrace entertaining multimedia worship services and avoid sermons on culturally unpopular topics like sin. Hybels clearly did not, however, have much concern about turning off conservatives or getting involved in contentious and biblically disputable political debates. The EIT recruited his wife, Lynne, to act as a spokesperson,[22] and it quickly became clear that the group hoped that such Christian celebrities would lead what one progressive gay columnist called a "grasstops" movement.[23] As opposed to a grassroots effort, just like with the Evangelical Environmental Network, these mascots would leverage the power of their name recognition to convince rank-and-file believers to jump on the Gang of Eight bandwagon. Along with Hybels, they collected signatures from notables like bestselling author and political pundit Eric Metaxas under the pretext that they were simply voicing general Christian principles regarding immigration. As the Center for Immigration Studies noted at the time, the EIT's statement represented a "rhetorical Rorshach [sic] test—vague enough to mean whatever you want it to mean. In other words, the EIT 'principles' are intended to deceive."[24] And deceive they would.

When the EIT announced its first $250,000 expenditure of what would eventually be at least $650,000 on radio ads to promote the legislation in Republican-led districts,[25] this naturally brought up the question of who was footing the bill. For that matter, where had the nearly $1 million the group had spent in its first year of existence come from?

Conservative think tanks and political commentators opposed to amnesty were aware from the outset that the EIT began as a project of the National Immigration Forum,[26] a well-known home of progressive immigration activists and business interests who benefit from cheap labor. The NIF's board includes representatives from the landscapers' lobby and the United Food and Commercial Workers International. It also has close ties to the hard-left militant group La Raza. William Hawkins, senior fellow with the U.S. Business and Industry Council, has given a concise summary of the NIF's aims: "[The group] is particularly keen on opening the borders to unskilled, low-income workers and then making them eligible for welfare and social service programs. Under this scheme, the country would be importing a new underclass living in poverty.... Once legalized, this expanded wave of immigrants are to be encouraged to vote."[27]

George Soros has made no secret of the fact that his aim is also to open the borders, saying in 2009 that "sovereignty is an anachronistic concept originating in bygone times."[28] Starting in 1996, he began directing hundreds of millions of dollars to the cause of unrestricted immigration, though it has often been difficult, if not impossible, for watchdog groups to follow his money.[29] In 2016, for instance, the global transparency rating group Transparify named Soros's foundation the "least transparent" in the world.[30] Still, it was widely reported that Open Society was the NIF's largest backer, granting the organization $3 million in 2009/2010 alone.[31]

Shortly after EIT announced the ad campaign, Breitbart discovered that not only was it connected to the NIF, but there was no meaningful distinction between the two groups.[32] The EIT did not legally exist as a separate entity, leading Breitbart to report that the EIT was receiving funding from Soros.[33]

No doubt the NIF and EIT expected Metaxas to follow along with the rest of their statement's prominent signatories and overlook the identity of their backer. After all, Metaxas had graduated from Yale and lived in Manhattan. He hosted witty, intellectual salons titled Socrates in the City, had been invited to speak at the National Prayer Breakfast during the Obama administration, and favored natty pinstripe suits and silk pocket squares. Surely if anyone was a fellow elite EIT traveler, he was. Except, he wasn't.

Showing the nonconformist streak that led him to support Donald Trump and become persona non grata among Christian high society, when Metaxas learned of the EIT's Soros connection and realized his signature on a statement of very general beliefs was being used to lobby for legislation he disagreed with, he immediately withdrew his name. "When you sign on to something that says we agree with these values as Christians, [but then] translate that into specific policy, like this Gang of Eight immigration bill—which I think is bad policy—then you really need to make that clear," he told the *Christian Post*.[34] The EIT had no choice but to soldier on without the bestselling Bonhoeffer biographer.

Likely to head off any more defections, NIF's then-president, Ali Noorani, who is so far left that he even criticized Biden's cap on refugees,[35] moved to clean up the Soros mess. He insisted that none of the money that had gone to the EIT had come from the man who has long worn his ambition to destroy national borders on his sleeve.[36] Rather, Noorani said the U.S. Chamber of Commerce had given the NIF money for a "Bibles, Badges, and Business" project, which he described as a "network of religious, law enforcement and business leaders in support of immigration reform." The "Bible" part of the title was where the EIT came in—Noorani was clear it represented the faith leaders and religious groups embodied in the program's name. And he said the Chamber's funding for the BBB program paid for the EIT's advertising blitz. The NIF, he said, helped the evangelical group only with "logistics functions." He further told the *Christian Post* that "each and every decision" made by the EIT was made by EIT members—while legally they might have been the same organization, he maintained that the EIT's work was separate.

In the meantime, Moore and the rest of his group kept up their best efforts to convince Republican members of the House that their largest and most loyal constituency, evangelicals, wanted them to pass the Gang of Eight bill. Moore and several others met with Obama again in November 2013, then for a third time in April 2014 in order to, according to the *Wall Street Journal*, "keep pressure on Congress to act."[37] None of it was to any avail.

Much like Cal Beisner and the Cornwall Alliance thwarted the efforts of the Evangelical Environmental Network, a second Christian immigration group that had Metaxas joined stymied the EIT's efforts. The open letter the Evangelicals for Biblical Immigration sent to Congress had been co-penned by Kelly Monroe Kullberg.[38] Like Metaxas, the soft-spoken blonde was of Ivy League pedigree. While a chaplain at Harvard, she had founded Veritas Forum, a group that promotes the exploration of Christianity in disciplines like philosophy, literature, and politics on hundreds of college campuses. And a book of essays she edited titled *Finding God at Harvard*, about religious experiences in the Ivy League, had become a bestseller, well reviewed by everyone from Father Richard Neuhaus to civil rights icon John Perkins. She'd also spent years volunteering as a missionary to impoverished nations like Peru, Guatemala, and El Salvador, so was well-equipped to answer the general statements of the EIT with not just biblical counterarguments, but firsthand experiences. Kullberg wrote that while the Church can and always has helped suffering people displaced by war and famine, God himself invented nations and places people in them. She further pointed out that though the United States has always been a generous nation, immigration policy must be a matter of prudence that first considers the safety and security of citizens and that foreigners who "do not mean to come as blessing, [do] not belong in America...":

While the Bible teaches us to be kind to the sojourner or "resident alien," it also teaches that kindness to the sojourner ought not to be injustice to local citizens and their unique culture. To steward and cultivate, whether a garden or a nation, involves wisdom and discernment. We, like our Founders, want to conserve what is true, good and beautiful. We want to nurture a nation that would welcome our children as well as the well-intended sojourner. That would mean making distinctions. Lawlessness with escalating violence and incivility cannot yield peace...

God loves the "sojourner." No question. Amen. God also loves the citizen. He is a God of love and of order, peace, freedom from debt, wise boundaries, and of nations. In some contexts Scripture teaches us to welcome. In other contexts it teaches us to be distinct, set apart, and, at times, to build walls...

Let's leave behind the sloganeering and confront the hard task of discernment. Just as Paul taught the Church (1 Timothy 5) to delineate among widows for whom the Church should provide, we are called to discern among "sojourners" (like Ruth and Rahab who intend to assimilate and bless) and "foreigners" (who do not intend to assimilate and bless) and to welcome the former with hospitality.

Whether it was Kullberg and her fellow signers' efforts or simply that House Republicans knew the minds of their evangelical constituents better than Moore and the rest of the EIT thought they did, the Gang of Eight bill never made it out of Congress. But the EIT would regroup for future fights, continuing to deny any connection to Soros.

Bibles, Badges, and Business

As the Obama administration gave way to the Trump administration, which no one in DC saw coming, the efforts of the EIT and its partner organizations did not let up. Joined by new Christian celebrities like New York City pastor Tim Keller and bestselling authors Ann Voskamp and Max Lucado, they called on President Trump to break his campaign promises regarding immigration—the promises that had played an integral role in propelling him into the Oval Office. In a full-page ad in the *Washington Post*, they said evangelicals were "concerned by the dramatic reduction in arrivals of refugees to the United States . . . Jesus makes it clear that our 'neighbor' includes the stranger and anyone fleeing persecution and violence . . ."[39] Either they did not know or were intentionally overlooking the fact that many of those granted refugee status today are, like most other immigrants, fleeing poor conditions rather than war or religious, racial, or political oppression.[40] And the reduction wasn't all that dramatic. The final fiscal year of the Obama administration had seen 85,000 refugees admitted. Trump's new policy allowed for 50,000.[41]

Though the EIT backed and promoted the open letter, its partner organization, World Relief, the refugee resettlement agency housed within the National Association of Evangelicals, officially spearheaded this campaign. While talking to Christian media outlets, World Relief executives routinely tout the idea that a greater number of refugees admitted into the country gives groups like them greater opportunity to spread the Good News of salvation. "God might move one of his image-bearers halfway around the world so he or she can hear the hope of the gospel," Matthew Soerens, World Relief VP of policy and former EIT field director, wrote in for *The Gospel Coalition* 2015.[42] In fact, while Christians *should* do all they can to tell all new arrivals to the United States about the hope found in Jesus, that's not a part of World Relief's work. The nonprofit is legally barred from proselytizing. It actually has more freedom to spread the Gospel in other nations than it does on its home turf, though that is not the sort of work that will be rewarded with hefty government grants and contracts.

Just like other major religious NGOs that do the administrative part of refugee resettlement, World Relief also has a massive financial incentive for wanting lawmakers to admit a high rate of refugees and asylum seekers into the country. As Capital Research Center put it, "In reality, they are simply government contractors paid handsomely for their services."[43] How handsomely? The financial watchdog group found that in 2018 alone, World Relief received $215.3 million from taxpayers for administering federal refugee grants.

■ ■ ■

There was another tactic in which the EIT followed in the Evangelical Environmental Network's footsteps. It made a particular target of the Southern Baptist Convention, highlighting how many Southern Baptist leaders had become involved with its work, including then-president J. D. Greear, Southeastern Baptist Theological Seminary president Danny Akin, North American Mission Board head Kevin Ezell, and "many others."[44] That's to say nothing of the new leaders it recruited from the denomination, giving them plum jobs. However, questions from ordinary Southern Baptists (the people whose tithes support the denomination's entities) about Soros funding continued to dog the EIT's steps. So much so that *Baptist Press* published its 2020 explainer saying that "a number of blogs have circulated these rumors."[45] It didn't mention that some of those "blogs" included *National Review*, the premier conservative journal founded by William F. Buckley in 1955; the public policy think tank Center for Immigration Studies, founded in 1985; and the Institute on Religion and Democracy, whose board once included such esteemed Christian intellectuals as Carl F. H. Henry and Father Neuhaus.

Baptist Press also provided a new quote from Noorani: "Quite simply, there has never been a single penny from George Soros that has gone toward the work of the Evangelical Immigration Table." Neither Noorani nor *Baptist Press* offered any documentation on who *did* fund the EIT.

■ ■ ■

Two developments—one an international bombshell and the other a quiet, inadvertent revelation about a pastor's job title—would finally put the question of Soros's financial backing to rest.

In 2007, SBC pastor Alan Cross started Community Development Initiatives, a racial-reconciliation government consulting firm, and from there developed an interest in immigration policy. According to Cross's bio, after pastoring for sixteen years in Montgomery, Alabama, he began to "work with churches across the southeastern United States to help them engage their immigrant and refugee neighbors with love, good deeds, and the gospel with the Evangelical Immigration Table."[46] In 2016, he announced that as the southeast regional coordinator for the EIT, he would be helping lead the group's booth at the annual Southern Baptist Convention. He noted that he had been "working with the EIT, which is a consortium of ministries such as the Ethics & Religious Liberty Commission."[47]

Along with that, Cross authored numerous immigration op-eds, including in the *New York Times*, positioning himself as an employee of the EIT.[48] Then, in 2017, an NIF press release revealed a different title, indeed a different place of employment, for Cross.[49] He was not, according to the National Immigration Forum, a coordinator for the EIT but, rather, a southeast regional mobilizer for the Bibles, Badges, and Business program under the NIF. A job description that the NIF had posted for Cross's role made it unequivocally clear that while the applicant was expected to serve the EIT through active participation in the BBB program, the NIF was in charge: "The National Immigration Forum is retaining a Southeast Regional Mobilizer to coordinate specific constituencies"—the "constituency" in this case meaning conservative Christians.[50] The BBB mobilizer answered to and received pay from the NIF. The role reported to the NIF's BBB manager. And what the NIF required from this role was someone who would recruit pastors and churches to the cause of open borders for the purpose of connecting them to legislators. These were just a few of the responsibilities Cross had signed up for:

- Utilize our existing network of connections in the ... faith communities to reach their counterparts in other states and build and nurture those relationships in order to educate them on the benefits of immigration and convince them to support the campaign and enable them and others to take action.
- Over the 7-month period, coordinate at least 1 in-person meeting in each target district between key constituents (pastors/ministry leaders ...) and the Member of Congress (or his/her staff).
- Recruit at least five (5) pastors per month to be included as new signatories to the Evangelical Statement of Principles.
- Work with leaders of fifteen (15) churches to engage congregations on immigration from a biblical perspective during the period.
- Provide coaching and oversight for Evangelical Immigration Table volunteer Church Mobilizers working in their region.
- Focus on educating and organizing conservative faith ... constituencies in key target states and districts within the region. Exact states and districts will be determined with consultant, Director of Field and Constituencies and Bibles, Badges, and Business (BBB) campaign manager. Note that states may be adjusted based on further research into target districts.

Whatever else this job was, it was not ministry to impoverished immigrants.

The employment posting left no question that the BBB initiative was being spearheaded and controlled by the NIF, but there remained a fig leaf of plausibility that funding for the EIT's part of the program was cordoned off from the Soros money. A global news story of epic proportions put an end to any speculation there.

In June 2016, a group of anonymous hackers known as DCLeaks published a trove of private emails and other records from a host of powerful political figures from across Europe and the United States.[51] Among the staggering revelations contained in the documents was the fact that Soros was using his billions to buy access to Democratic politicians for the purpose of manipulating elections. It also showed he was buying access to evangelical leaders for the same reason.

Buried in a 2013 report prepared for Open Society's board about the foundation's annual expenditures and goals was a notation that two hundred thousand dollars had gone to the "NIF Action Fund" for "Businesses, Bibles, and Badges." (Whoever put the report together can probably be forgiven for transposing the title of the program a bit.) The report also included future plans to divide one million dollars between the BBB program and another initiative because "evangelical, business, and law enforcement support [has been] highly influential in engaging conservative lawmakers."[52] Again, this was just as the EIT was ramping up its efforts to see the Gang of Eight bill passed.

Nor were the revelations limited to cold expenditures listed on a spreadsheet. A paragraph in the 2015 board book specifically noted Open Society's efforts to co-opt the Southern Baptists:

> In the course of our work, we were able to generate engagement by a group of mayors through Emma Lazarus II Fund grantee Cities United for Immigration Action . . . and *some conservative voices such as evangelical Christians and Southern Baptists through grantee NIF.* In the face of this pressure, the Obama administration announced Sept. 20 that by 2017, it would raise to 100,000 the total number of refugees the US takes worldwide each year [emphasis mine].[53]

And when it all went bust and the Gang of Eight bill failed? Open Society's 2016 board book provided a postmortem that described how money went from the foundation to the pass-through group Alliance for Citizenship, before finally ending up at the National Immigration Forum:

> When it became evident that there might be an opportunity to pass

[comprehensive immigration reform] in early 2013, a group of organizations and labor unions came together to form a coalition: the Alliance for Citizenship (A4C). *A4C was intended to serve as a coordinating body as well as a conduit for pass-through funding.* A4C's mandate was to develop a coordinated national campaign, strengthen and align the progressive movement around immigration reform as well as *coordinate with nontraditional allies (e.g., faith-based groups, business interests, law enforcement)* [the BBB], recruit additional advocates, lobby key members of the Senate, and influence development of the legislation . . .

A4C [the Soros-backed steering committee] coordinated with different organizations also working for [comprehensive immigration reform] . . . *NIF was also among the groups working with faith based organizations . . . through its Bibles, Badges and Business coalition and since it was a Working Group member, it was well positioned to bridge and align the work* [emphasis mine].[54]

In other words, Soros's foundation was unequivocal that its money went to make sure the EIT's Bibles, Badges, and Business work was "bridged and aligned" with Soros's broader effort to see a pathway to citizenship passed and the refugee cap raised. As if that weren't enough, in a 2013 article on Open Society's own website titled, "Building Momentum for a Roadmap to Citizenship," Noorani wrote enthusiastically of the evangelical leaders in the EIT making "a clear call for a road to earned citizenship. And he explained that the BBB program (the same BBB program he told the *Christian Post* the EIT was a part of and to whom the Open Society board listed payments) had been "urg[ing] quick action" on Congress.

Not only is it possible that the Soros network paid for some EIT efforts, but Soros's own organization claimed responsibility for them in its internal records. Note that this leak was well before *Baptist Press* claimed in 2020 that it had debunked the EIT's Soros ties. So, either the SBC news outlet was outright lying to average Southern Baptist readers or it was willfully choosing to take Noorani's highly implausible claims at face value rather than do a little digging.

As of 2021, Soros was still funding the NIF,[55] the NIF was still controlling the EIT, and a host of evangelical leaders were still involved in their efforts. If they were simply teaching Christians how to apply Scripture to immigration, why would they have to hide and dissemble about what they're doing?

Jon Whitehead, a trustee for the ERLC (the Southern Baptist Convention's lobbying arm, which has been deeply involved with the EIT) texted me after reviewing the Leaks documents: "Evangelicals (especially Southern Baptists) were shamelessly hung out for sale by their leaders. In exchange for subsidized meetings with their EIT friends, leaders looked the other way as their churches and pews were exploited. They even used *Baptist Press* to mislead people, claiming 'not a penny' of Soros money went toward EIT. It looks more like tens of millions of pennies!"

And the push from SBC leaders to convince the rank and file to accept the NIF's agenda continues. Most resolutions that Southern Baptists vote on at their annual convention are proposed by local pastors or church members. At the 2023 convention, however, the resolutions committee itself, which was appointed by President Bart Barber and is guided by an ERLC liaison, authored a proposal on immigration.[56] It resolved that the SBC should "implore" the government to "maintain robust avenues" for asylum seekers. It did *not* suggest that the government also reform its heavily abused asylum policies that allow virtually anyone who makes it across our border to claim asylum. But the wording of the resolution was largely irrelevant, one ERLC source told me. The point is it provides cover for the NIF, in partnership with the ERLC, to continue to set the immigration agenda for the most influential Protestant denomination among conservatives.

Groups like the EIT pepper their speeches with Bible verses about the fatherless and the widow but fail to acknowledge how the positions they've staked out have created plenty of both. And it's not just an issue of victims of illegal immigrants, but also of Americans who lose out on job opportunities and see their wages depressed, their housing prices driven up, and their social services diminished because needed resources are devoted to supporting newly arrived people who are often not equipped to support themselves. As I was writing this chapter, news broke that the July–August 2023 employment report showed that more than 1.2 million native-born Americans had lost jobs. At the same time, nearly 700,000 foreign-born workers gained them. As the *Daily Mail* reported, this increase represented the "highest July-to-August jump in the last 10 years," though the trend of replacing

American workers with non-natives was already gaining speed before the pandemic.[57] It only slowed for a few years during the Trump administration. And that's to say nothing of the flow of fentanyl across our border, which is up 860 percent over the last four years, or the scourge of human trafficking.[58] The Congressional Research Service found that in the first ten months of 2023, border agents apprehended more than 110,000 unaccompanied minors, a record high.[59] An estimated 75 to 80 percent of those are trafficking victims.[60] Did the pastors and evangelical noteworthies opposing Trump's policies consider how it might be kinder to disincentivize this chaos and evil? Being concerned about the costs of immigration does not make someone anti-immigrant any more than being concerned about the costs of flooding makes someone anti-water.

Unequal Standards

The strangest thing about the concern so many church leaders have expressed about refugee policy is how much it fluctuates depending on who's occupying the Oval Office.

In the ad they took out in the *Washington Post*, Keller, Voskamp, Lucado, and company opposed Trump's ninety-day moratorium on refugees from seven Muslim-majority nations that were hotbeds for terrorist activity because "'neighbor' includes . . . anyone fleeing persecution and violence, regardless of their faith or country."[61]

You might assume they showed similar distress when Biden's Department of Homeland Security secretary, Alejandro Mayorkas, said in 2021 that Cubans trying to flee a country *not* known for terrorism to escape undeniable persecution and torture were not welcome in the United States.[62]

You would be wrong. The group issued no letter, let alone published one in a major national newspaper. Beth Moore, whose social media posts and activism criticizing Trump's border policies were widely covered between 2016 and 2020, said nothing about the hunger, sickness, and general deprivation unfolding in the island nation.[63] She made no objection to Biden keeping the doors of this country shut tight to Cubans despite the fact that the government there was reportedly beating, arresting, and detaining Christian pastors.[64] Nor did she offer general support for welcoming Cubans fleeing the threat of torture. She didn't even mention Biden's overall policy of keeping refugee admissions historically low, the point that so distressed her during the Trump years.

The same goes for the man with whom she shares a last name but no relation. Trump's border positions featured prominently in Russell Moore's criticism of evangelicals over their support for the former president.[65]

Claiming to speak for 13 million Southern Baptists, Moore published an open letter and gave national interviews blasting Trump's so-called Muslim ban.[66] At the height of the media storm surrounding Trump's plans for building the wall, Moore tweeted, "Immigrants, & those fleeing from persecution, are not political ideas. They bear the image of [God]."[67] Yet when the totalitarian Cuban regime was cutting off social media from its people and scores of protestors were going missing and women were crying in the streets about their children dying of hunger,[68] how many op-eds did the prolific media commentator write about Biden's lack of response? How many interviews did he give? How many tweets did he post? If you guessed zero, you would be correct. When pro-Palestinian protestors that included a good number of immigrants from Muslim nations took to the streets across Europe and even thronged the U.S. Capitol, defacing monuments and clashing with police, Moore failed to concede that perhaps there's good reason for Western nations to consider whether the ideology of the people they're admitting is compatible with democratic values.[69]

The hypocrisy of the two Moores would be easy to dismiss if they were outliers. But the list of evangelical authors and mega-pastors who lent their names to campaigns explicitly and implicitly condemning Trump's immigration policies is a staggeringly long and elite one.

Quoting Sen. Ben Sasse (R-NE), J. D. Greear called Trump's border policies "wicked" and said "Americans (should be) better than this."[70] He then appeared on PBS's *Firing Line*, arguing that any believers who voted for Trump must speak about the "dignity of immigrants" lest they damage their Christian witness.[71] Again, not just any believers, period, but *those who voted for Trump*. While Greear's ire toward Trump's six-week-long policy of family separation might have been a legitimate point of debate, the megachurch pastor never indicated that it bothered him when the Obama administration sometimes employed the same tactic.[72]

And where was Greear's clarity on Cuba or when the Biden administration maintained Trump's refugee cap? Though he was happy to sign and promote Russell Moore's ERLC statement demanding Congress maintain Obama's deferred action on Dreamers,[73] he uttered not a word about the crisis in Cuba or the Biden administration's ghastly bungling of immigration in general that has led to significant suffering at the border.[74]

Republicans in Congress offered direct resolutions to support the Cuban people as they were protesting brutal communist oppression.[75] No Democrats backed it. Neither did any of the aforementioned religious leaders. The EIT did not rally support for it, even though the overwhelming majority of those persecuted by Prime Minister Manuel Cruz were Catholic. While it might be possible to believe that one or two of these leading Christian lights simply didn't have the time to address the issue, the fact that none of them did, despite their very active social media accounts, suggests that something else was going on.

It's important to reiterate that the comments from these leaders who supported the Gang of Eight bill and condemned the Trump administration were far from ambiguous and went well beyond general biblical principle. The letters, essays, ads, tweets, and interviews took an explicitly activist tone, demanding action on specific policies. Certainly, different Christians will support a range of different policies regarding citizenship and how many immigrants the United States should admit, as well as who should take priority and what the process should look like. Convictions on this issue will differ, and part of a Christian's responsibility in a representative republic is debating those convictions in good faith. But the leaders associated with the EIT did not allow room for disagreement or even acknowledge that someone could be loving while seeing the issue differently than they did.

What did their later disinterest suggest but that all that effort to "welcome the stranger" was less about Christian conviction and more about political posturing to win the affection of the progressive media and other left-leaning demographics? Scripture has much to say about leaders who strive to appear righteous before men and show partiality to those whose favor they would like to have. It has much to say on those who use unequal weights and measures. None of it befits those who claim the title pastor or ministry leader.

Metaxas captured well what was happening with groups like the EIT when I asked him about his brief involvement with them: "It's disturbing that some Christians seem quite happy to twist the scripture that says we are to 'care for the strangers and aliens among us' into a carte blanche invitation to enact dramatically destructive immigration policies, as though painting a smiley face over the monstrous reality of encouraging vicious drug cartels and child-sex traffickers. It's hard to overstate the blasphemy of using God's Word in that way."

Of course, believers are to preach Christ crucified to all, no matter how they arrived here. Of course, we should provide for those in real need, no matter how the needy came to cross our path. But "welcome the stranger" was Christ's command to his followers to personally emulate the Good Samaritan. To insist that it was meant to be used as a blanket immigration policy is spiritual manipulation that cheapens its meaning. And to insist that pastors should use their pulpits to shame congregants into becoming activists for debatable legislation cheapens the mission of the Church.

Scripture does not require us to sacrifice national sovereignty. In fact, Acts 17:26 tells us that God "marked out [our] appointed times in history and the boundaries of [our] lands." The Lord is not opposed to borders; He invented them. Nor does this command require us to abandon good sense and prudence when setting limits for how many immigrants we admit and what qualifications we use for doing so.

A humane society requires well-ordered government that sees to the needs of its citizens, while setting clear expectations that the rule of law will be enforced. Anything else quickly devolves into abuse and anarchy, as we are seeing by the scourge of drug- and sex-trafficking and gang violence that unregulated immigration has created. The United States should and always has welcomed "huddled masses yearning to breathe free" to share in the blessings God has bestowed on us. But if we incentivize illegal immigration by rewarding those who ignore our laws and fail to ensure that those to whom we grant citizenship understand and respect the founding ideals that made this nation great, the United States will soon look little different from the countries these immigrants are fleeing. We will no longer have anything good to share.

CHAPTER 3

Hijacking the Pro-life Movement

Rescue those being led away to death; hold back those staggering toward slaughter. If you say, "But we knew nothing about this," does not he who weighs the heart perceive it? Does not he who guards your life know it?

—Proverbs 24:11–12

"I had heard screaming, and I went to see if I could help. I thought maybe someone was delivering a baby." Ginna Cross was telling me about the time she witnessed an abortion

It was 2007, and as a twenty-two-year-old, newly minted nursing school grad, she had gone to East Africa to spend a year as a medical missionary, caring for the littlest and most vulnerable of patients, orphans ages zero to two. In between treating common issues like malaria, ear infections, and malnutrition at the clinic, she and another nurse occasionally found themselves with downtime.

Given that the health care system in Mozambique ranks among the world's worst, with severely understaffed facilities at every level, they figured their inability to speak Chitwe, the local dialect, wouldn't preclude them from helping out at a nearby hospital. "The hospitals there are such a mess," Cross told me, "There were always things you could do. Even if it was just praying with people."

That language barrier, though, meant Cross had no idea what she was walking into when she entered the open, mostly bare room of exam tables that served as a labor and delivery area.

When she walked over to the sobbing teenager on a cold, metal table at the far side of the room, the girl threw her arms around Cross's waist and buried her head in her abdomen. That was when Cross realized what was happening. "The woman performing the abortion quickly said something to me, then seemed irritated that I didn't understand. She was using long metal tools, what I then realized was a curette, to scrape the uterus." As Cross stood there with the girl's arms locked around her, she watched copious amounts of blood and tissue clots flow into a large plastic container at the end of the table that the abortionist whisked away a few minutes later when the procedure was finished. The woman had the girl stand up and walk to a recovery area, where she sat and cried. Cross sat and cried with her for about half an hour until hospital workers came by and told the girl she could go home.

"It was horrifying," Cross told me. "From that time on, I was just broken about the reality that this was happening everywhere."

She came home with a passion to protect babies in her own country. In between working as a pediatric nurse in the ICU and raising six kids of her own, the energetic blonde supported a local Kenosha, Wisconsin, pro-life pregnancy center. This led to a seat on its board. Eventually, Cross left hospital work altogether to become Alliance Family Service's executive director.

When the U.S. Supreme Court issued the ruling that overturned *Roe v. Wade* on June 24, 2022, Cross felt it was a moment she had been working toward her entire adult life. "I mean, this was something that was strived for and prayed for by Christians for half a century," she told me. "So, when the decision came down, it was surreal. Like, is this actually happening? All of us [working in pregnancy centers] felt like we never really expected it in our lifetimes, but the Lord is so good to us that this has happened kind of against all odds."

It came as something of a shock, then, when many of the big-name evangelical leaders who were supposed to represent pro-life activists like her sounded distinctly less than celebratory. Instead, a number of them used the fall of *Roe* as an opportunity to argue for bigger government and to bolster the pro-abortion narrative that Christians only care about babies before they're born.

While Religion News Service columnist and author Karen Swallow Prior acknowledged in a strangely somber *New York Times* op-ed that *Roe* fundamentally violated a right to life, the thrust of her piece was that women choose abortion because the United States is insufficiently feminist and fails to provide enough entitlements.

Legalized elective abortion was the consolation prize given to women in 1973 for the centuries of inequality and oppression that stemmed from their sin of not being men...[I]t does take a village to become who we are. Thankfully, America's romance with radical autonomy and rugged individualism is cooling. Roe gave our nation some of the most liberal abortion laws in the industrialized world and a high rate of abortion compared with that of many other industrialized countries, in no small part because of our individualist cultural and economic ethos. . . .We can do better than asking women (and men) to choose between their children and themselves.[1]

Prior expanded that idea on Twitter, where she said, "Our work now is just starting: we must help and support moms, dads, and babies."[2]

Prior's framing—that pregnancy forces women to "choose between their children and themselves"—sounded disconcertingly close to the pro-abortion narrative that babies are a fundamental obstacle to female fulfillment. It legitimized the erroneous and self-focused worldview that career achievement and material wealth provide women more satisfaction than starting a family. (Even if not the ideal reason to get married, unplanned pregnancies have historically had a way of sending young people down the aisle. And as sociologists have repeatedly demonstrated, marriage and kids are far more important to women's happiness than professional success).[3] That's to say nothing of the fact that Prior completely failed to take into account the millions of families on waitlists to adopt.[4] No one who believes a baby will impede their opportunities to pursue a good life is obligated to raise one. The death of Roe just meant that, in some states, they would no longer be permitted to kill one.

But the biggest issue with the essay was that it was explicitly secular and progressive in outlook, finding solutions in collectivist social programs rather than in policies that encourage a return to biblical standards of husbands caring for wives and children (2 Thessalonians 3:6–14, 1 Timothy 5:8). When Prior favorably quoted another writer who argued that a "post-Roe world is one that compels a greater claim on public resources to support expectant mothers," she was promoting the very forces that have crushed the American family.

Reams of data have shown how the Johnson administration's 1964 introduction of new welfare programs, many specifically designed to address black poverty, decimated marriage in the black community.[5] While marriage rates have declined among all ethnicities, black families have been by far the hardest hit.[6] Today, nearly half of black men and women have never married by age forty—the highest percentage of any ethnic group by a full 19 points.[7] Because of that, almost 70 percent of black children are born to single mothers, and nearly 40 percent of women who get abortions are black, even though African Americans are only 12 percent of the population.[8] Yet more than half of Americans who receive food assistance (SNAP), income supplements (TANF), and rental subsidies, are black.[9]

As economist Thomas Sowell put it, "The black family, which had survived centuries of slavery and discrimination, began rapidly disintegrating in the liberal welfare state that subsidized unwed pregnancy and changed welfare from an emergency rescue to a way of life."[10] High levels of government support have not been beneficial to black moms and kids. Why would the fall of *Roe* make us believe more of the same is a good idea?

Her response to *Dobbs*, so steeped in worldly reasoning, would hardly be worth mentioning if Prior were simply another left-leaning academic. But the fact that she spent twenty-plus years combined on the faculties of Southeastern Baptist Theological Seminary and Liberty University, two Christian institutions widely advertised as conservative alternatives to liberal secular and religious schools, reveals much about the state of evangelical higher education today.

Bestselling Bible teacher and conference speaker Beth Moore similarly used the occasion of *Dobbs* to chide evangelicals for not doing enough to help women who, but for lack of Christian care, might not choose death. "Yes. Step up, church. Take responsibility for the fact that pro-life is either pro-all-life—which is in step with the truth of the gospel—or pro-some-life which for many is in step with political expediency," she replied to Prior on Twitter. "Unborn/born. Babies/Girls/Women need immense support, compassion, care."[11] After claiming to be pro-life for her entire forty-plus years in ministry, Moore had this and this alone to say about the end of *Roe*. She has never publicly acknowledged it since.

This "step up" response, of which Prior and Moore were only two high-profile examples, especially irked Cross. She knew firsthand not just the vast amounts of effort pro-life Christians were expending to care for moms and babies, but also the significant financial investments they were making. "It was presented as if this was this new idea that we should care about both, but that's exactly what the pro-life movement has been doing since 1973," she told me.

To Cross's point, in recent years, 82,000 volunteers in nearly 3,000 pro-life centers across the country have annually served roughly 2 million clients—more than three times the number of abortions procured.[12] In 2019, before there was any serious inkling that *Roe* might be overturned, pro-life centers provided $270 million worth of services and goods to at-risk women, including medical care, education, and baby items like diapers, car seats, and clothing.[13] Indeed, even before new laws in many red states forced Planned Parenthood and other abortionists to close their doors, *Time* magazine complained that centers doing the work Prior and Moore were calling for already outnumbered abortion clinics three to one.[14] And that was only counting official pregnancy centers; it did not include the churches that have long provided care through their own in-house ministries. To Cross, it bordered on dishonest that the first and, for a number of these voices, *only* thing they would say about *Dobbs* was to imply that pro-lifers hadn't been caring for moms.

Still, Prior's and Moore's ungenerous responses were marginally better than those of some other evangelical leaders whose reactions didn't even imply that *Roe* being overturned was a good thing. Author, pastor, and frequent Gospel Coalition contributor Mika Edmondson sounded downright apologetic, suggesting, like Prior, that outlawing abortion would only be morally legitimate if accompanied by an expanded welfare state. "Now that Roe is overturned, I pray that we will provide the access to healthcare, childcare, living wages, education and job opportunities that will support the lives of people in desperate situations," he said.[15] It was akin to telling abolitionists on the day of the Emancipation Proclamation that the end of slavery would be worthwhile only if Lincoln also announced a mandatory minimum wage and scholarship program for freed slaves. Those might have been worthy goals, but whether they were pursued would not have altered the evil of slavery or the unmitigated good of ending it.

Other comments from Edmondson that day were indistinguishable from the laments of pro-abortion progressives who profess to be Christians. "May the Lord give grace to victims of rape whose pregnancies are daily reminders of the worst violation," he said. "May the Lord give grace to women whose lives are at risk in their pregnancies & to medical providers wondering if they can intervene to save their lives. Lord, have mercy."[16] At no point since the *Dobbs* decision has Edmondson publicly characterized the ruling (which, again, established only that the people's legislative representatives hold the power to ban or limit abortion) as an unadulterated good.

Strangest of all the responses, though, may have been the utter silence of *Christianity Today*'s public theologian, Russell Moore. For years, Moore had been the media's go-to expert on evangelicals' grassroots efforts to fight abortion, regularly quoted in major newspapers and given frequent cable news appearances to discuss the issue. During his eight years leading the ERLC, he dined out on his pro-life bona fides, delivering speeches, publishing essays, and even writing a book on the topic. As the key moral voice at evangelicalism's flagship magazine, Moore's primary job responsibility was writing about such monumental developments.

When much lesser political events struck, that cast those he disliked in a negative light, he would often post his take within a day, sometimes within hours. After Trump was indicted for mishandling classified documents, Moore tweeted immediately. And when the Southern Baptist Convention released a report on abuse that lambasted Moore's denominational enemies, he had a nearly fifteen-hundred-word essay out within the space of an hour.[17] He was more than capable of responding quickly given sufficient provocation. Yet, for weeks after the most important legal decision pro-life Christians would see in their lifetimes, he published no essays, recorded no episode for his podcast, posted nothing on social media.

Christianity Today evidently felt the silence from the man it was two months away from naming its editor in chief was growing awkward. After almost a week went by with no word from Moore, it posted a "bonus episode" of his podcast titled "A Conversation with Stephen Prothero on Culture Wars Now that 'Roe' Is Gone."[18] Except, that was misleading.

The interview was a pre-taped discussion about a *Dobbs* draft opinion that had leaked in early May and might not have represented the final opinion. For three weeks, Moore would neither write nor record anything about the most consequential legal decision of the modern era. When he finally did publish an essay about it, like Prior, Beth Moore (no relation), and Edmondson, he focused on the social programs that churches and lawmakers might offer as a response. His suggestions, like theirs, made zero mention of marriage, fathers, or how the men involved in unwanted pregnancies might be induced to provide the care expecting mothers need.[19]

A month after *Dobbs* dropped, it would it come to light that Moore had, in fact, commented on the decision the week it was released, during an already scheduled panel at the Faith Angle Forum, a high-status think tank convention where secular journalists interact with religious intellectuals (though the evangelical representatives often use the opportunity to express disdain for the rest of their demographic).[20] Moore's remarks there gave some indication as to why he remained otherwise silent so long. When *Time* magazine's Molly Ball asked him during a wide-ranging discussion if *Roe*'s reversal vindicated evangelicals who had voted for Donald Trump because he kept his promise to appoint pro-life justices, Moore refused to give the former president an ounce of credit. "The author of the *Dobbs* case is a George W. Bush appointee," he said, ignoring the fact that the other Bush appointee, Chief Justice John Roberts, did not sign on to the majority opinion and actively lobbied for a much narrower ruling that would have left *Roe* in place. Meanwhile, all three Trump appointees voted to overturn *Roe* completely, making the score Bush 1–2, Trump 3–3.

Nevertheless, Moore summarized his view: "I don't think that you would have had largely any different decision from a Jeb Bush court or Marco Rubio court, a Ted Cruz court." Of course, at the end of the day, the choice evangelicals had was not between Bush, Rubio, or Cruz and Trump. It was between Hillary Clinton and Trump, and there would have been a radically different Court and a radically different America today if they had not ultimately decided to pull the lever for the latter.

He Who Must Not Be Credited

Moore's dismissal of President Trump as a significant factor in energizing the pro-life movement reflected the rhetoric and reasoning of quite a number of elite evangelical figures who had proudly worn the "Never Trump" moniker.

While for decades it had been uncontroversial for Christians to place significant weight on a candidate's stance on abortion when evaluating how to vote, suddenly, after 2016, it wasn't so important anymore. Trump had changed the calculus.

I will never forget the moment I came face-to-face with the pervasiveness of this shift. I was in an editorial meeting with former *World* magazine editor in chief Marvin Olasky, who had always discussed abortion as our nation's greatest moral evil. He'd always been clear that he felt it was among the most important factors (if not *the* most important) when weighing one's choice in political representatives. Of course, we didn't promote candidates in our reporting, but I'd never before heard Olasky suggest that our work should challenge Christian readers to moderate their tendency to rank abortion as the "single issue" that settled their vote.

Yet, there he was, in late 2019, telling his team of reporters that there might be more important ways for voters to promote pro-life policies than simply electing politicians who promised to restrict or end abortion. One might decide that the best way to vote for life would be to select a candidate whose official platform was pro-abortion but who supported subsidizing day care or paid family leave, making children more appealing. Perhaps another might feel that a candidate who supported abortion but who promised to address systemic racism would be more pro-life, given that better education and higher-paying jobs might lead more minorities to keep their babies. This was a man who'd previously championed Sowell and advocated for personal responsibility and free markets. In more ways than one, I could not believe what I was hearing.

Olasky finished this soliloquy with a little snicker about the lack of political sophistication in theologian R. C. Sproul's famous pronouncement that he would "never vote for a candidate for any office, including dogcatcher, who is pro-abortion." Apparently, at some point after the election of Trump, Olasky had decided this sentiment was worthy of light mockery.

I was less surprised to later see Tim Keller (a significant influence on Olasky and, thus, on *World*'s editorial positions) make an almost identical argument on Twitter about how Christians should "relate the Bible to politics":

> Here are two Biblical MORAL norms: 1) It is a sin to worship idols or any God other than the true God & 2) do not murder. If you ask evangelicals if we should be forbidden by law to worship any other God than the God of the Bible—they'd say "no."
>
> We allow that terrible sin to be legal. But if you ask them if Americans should be forbidden by law to abort a baby, they'd say "yes." Now why make the first sin legal and NEVER talk about it and the second sin illegal and a main moral/political talking point? . . .
>
> The Bible tells us that idolatry, abortion, and ignoring the poor are all grievous sins. But it doesn't tell us exactly HOW we are to apply these norms to a pluralistic democracy. . . . I know abortion is a sin, but the Bible doesn't tell me the best political policy to decrease or end abortion in this country, nor which political or legal policies are most effective to that end.[21]

Leaving aside the fact that worshipping an idol does not deprive another human being of his right to life, Keller misunderstood the purpose of government. As established by God, it is to execute just laws and punish lawbreakers (Romans 13:3–8). Governments may do more, but they should not do less. Those blessed to be citizens of representative democracies should, likewise, steward their votes so that which is self-evident from nature and nature's God is enshrined in law, or else we have no basis to argue for any form of moral order. Again, legislators can do more to discourage murder besides outlaw it, but they should not do less.

We already acknowledge in myriad ways that homicide and violence are illegal and therefore punishable. The crux of the abortion debate is simply whether a baby in the womb is a person. Keller acknowledged that, for Christians, Scripture had already settled that issue. Our governing documents tell us, then, that the baby has an inalienable right to life, just as those who were once enslaved had a right to liberty. It is incumbent on us, the governed, to ensure that our representatives are securing those rights as they are required to do according to the highest law of our land, the Constitution, just as the abolitionists did. As a *Christian Post* op-ed put it, replace the word *abortion* with the word *slavery* and imagine if Keller would have still felt comfortable signing his name to that tweet.[22]

Yet, while Keller argued that the Bible does not tell Christians how to oppose abortion, there was one way he clearly felt was wrong—by voting for Donald Trump. Being a Christian Trump supporter, he told *The Atlantic*, meant that you were focused on "power and saying, How are we going to use power to live life the way we want?"[23] Well, yes, to the degree that an election is choosing a political leader to enact policies you prefer and that someone else opposes, voting for any candidate is always a vote for power regarding some question of how life in this nation should be lived. (I'm struggling not to say "duh" here.) And, of course, that includes voting for a candidate who will use his power to restrict abortion.

Evangelicals, as the media pointed out ad nauseam in the run-up to both the 2016 and the 2020 elections, made a political wager that a hotel magnate and reality TV star might do as he promised and appoint justices who would overturn *Roe*. The decision was not a difficult one for many pro-lifers, given that their other options were the aggressively pro-abortion Hillary Clinton and Joe Biden or refusing to vote for either of the two major-party candidates, which also would have helped the pro-abortion side.

Considering that pro-life evangelicals had been electing Republicans for decades with little to show for it, the Trump campaign's pitch to black voters—"What do you have to lose?"—was probably ringing in a lot of their ears as well when they went to the ballot box.

Keller and others who pretended that it was not a binary choice when it came to abortion conveniently ignored the fact that, according to Pew polling, in the Republican primaries of 2016, "evangelicals were among those most skeptical of Trump."[24] As late as April of that year, 66 percent of regular churchgoers did not back him. If Keller, Moore, Prior, and others felt that Trump's personal moral character should have made him less attractive to evangelicals, it did. It wasn't until he won the nomination and headed into the general election that they lined up behind him. Their enthusiasm for him was most demonstrated with the 2020 general election and 2024 Republican primaries, after he'd kept his word on judicial nominees and a number of other campaign promises.

Somehow, Keller found support for Donald Trump uniquely discrediting in a way that voting for Joe Biden—who had plenty of evangelical Democrats in his corner even though Biden had also been accused of sexual assault—was not. And Biden was promising to protect abortion access, expand LGBTQ power, and erase religious liberty protections to boot.

After extensive searching, I could find no public comments from Keller chiding Christians who supported Biden or rebuking groups like "evangelicals for Biden" for politicizing the Church, even though that movement was widely covered by outlets like NPR, ABC, the *New York Times*, the *Washington Post*, *Newsweek*, and the United Kingdom's *Guardian*.

In contrast, Keller had no compunction about participating in a 2018 meeting of church leaders whose stated purpose was to "self-[reflect] on the current condition of Evangelicalism" in light of "the support of 'eighty-one per cent of self-identifying white evangelicals' for Donald Trump."[25] It takes a fair bit of hubris to decide that the defensible political choice of other evangelicals requires a meeting to "self-reflect" on their behalf. But what the gathering didn't appear to note was that white evangelicals also happen to be the religious group most opposed to abortion in all or most cases, at around 74 percent.[26] They're also the religious group most motivated to vote based on their abortion views.[27] As the Associated Press put it, "White evangelical Protestants stand noticeably apart from other religious people on abortion restrictions."[28] So, it should hardly have surprised Keller and the other leaders that this particular cluster of voters aligned with Donald Trump, given his campaign promises and their political priorities.

For their commitment to the pro-life cause that led these Christians to pull the lever for Trump, Keller also slighted them in the pages of *The New Yorker*[29] and the radio station Premier Christian News, saying they'd made it harder to evangelize.[30] "'Evangelical' used to denote people who claimed the high moral ground; now, in popular usage, the word is nearly synonymous with 'hypocrite,'" he wrote. Instead of trying to explain to the urban professionals who made up his primary mission field why evangelicals have such a great commitment to protecting babies (a possible form of evangelism itself), Keller denigrated the motives of his brothers and sisters as being power-driven. What witness did it provide young city dwellers to confirm their already low opinion of those suburban and rural red state voters? (Incidentally, Keller's claim that "the high number of white evangelicals who have identified with Donald Trump and the Republican Party [is] a stronger political identification [than has] ever happened in my lifetime" was also wrong. It was about the same as it was for both George W. Bush and Mitt Romney and within the margin of error.[31])

By contrast, the district Keller was in went 79 percent for Clinton in 2016 and 77 percent for Biden in 2020.[32] How many of those who attended Keller's church or church plants were represented in that heavily tilted majority? Though only a handful of staffers at Keller's church network and preacher-training ministry have donated to political campaigns since 2015, those who did, donated frequently, and according to Federal Election Commission records, they gave exclusively to Democrats. Again, out of hundreds of donations from employees of Redeemer Churches and City to City, not one went to *any* Republican, let alone a Republican presidential candidate. Surely, it's reasonable to ask why, if Keller had so many words for Christian Trump voters about the perils of mixing politics and faith, he couldn't have spared a few for progressive evangelicals, especially given how many fell under his close influence and authority.

In fact, he and the evangelical publication he founded *promoted* Democratic operatives who used faith as a basis to make political appeals.

Power Games

In 2020, when former Obama administration staffer Michael Wear began to lobby evangelicals to turn out the vote for Biden, neither Keller nor *The Gospel Coalition* seemed the least concerned that the veteran campaign strategist might be motivated by political power. Keller took Wear's self-professed commitment to justice at face value and recommended his 2017 book, *Reclaiming Hope: Lessons Learned in the Obama White House About the Future of Faith in America*, as a "road map for navigating the unprecedented social and cultural changes we are facing." This, even though Wear made his living arguing that evangelicals should back Democrats despite their support for abortion.

Wear was a chief strategist for the AND Campaign, a left-leaning social justice group that ranks abortion as less important than alleged systemic racism as a voting priority. And he was the senior adviser to Not Our Faith, a hastily formed super PAC that spent the final weeks of the 2020 election buying up hundreds of thousands of dollars' worth of ad time to convince Christians not to reelect Trump. ("Trump eked out 2016 with unprecedented support from white evangelicals. . . . We're going after all of it. We think Christian support is on the table in this election," Wear told the AP in comments that sound a bit like he might have had a bit of a power preoccupation.)[33]

The Gospel Coalition presented Wear as an authoritative voice on political ethics, posting his video lectures on "how Christians should think about politics" and endorsing him as a model for "faithful and responsible participation in American public life."[34] The outlet justified this promotion with the fig leaf claim that Wear is personally pro-life.[35]

Immediately after *Roe*'s fall, however, when red states moved to enact laws to protect babies in the womb, the ostensibly pro-life Wear rushed out a proposal on his Substack for what he called a "sustainable [federal] compromise."[36] It suggested that states allow abortion for any reason somewhere between nine and fifteen weeks, regardless of the will of the state's voters. Given that 93 percent of abortions are performed within that time frame and that he was allowing exceptions for rape and incest up to birth, Wear's compromise would have outlawed only around 6 percent of abortions.[37] This, he said, would recast abortion in U.S. politics to make it what it is in Europe, "a second or third-tier issue, but never an issue around which their politics revolves." So, he was willing to allow nearly all the killing to continue if it meant Republicans could no longer use abortion as a wedge issue. But to Keller and the publication he founded, Wear had not been discredited by this.

Perhaps more revealing of Wear's supposed convictions, in a *New York Times* piece immediately after Biden's 2020 election, the Democratic strategist offered the new administration some advice.[38] To soothe the feelings of Republicans, he suggested that it "wait to act on overturning the Trump administration's version of the so-called Mexico City Policy" (the order that blocked federal funds from going to nongovernmental organizations that perform or promote abortion) until after the anniversary of *Roe*. This, he said, would act as the White House's "signal that while there will be disagreements about abortion policy, they're uninterested in promoting a new round of culture wars." In other words, instead of suggesting that Biden *actually* compromise to save the lives of some babies, Wear just told him to put on a little PR performance.

Yet it was Wear who was deemed a principled political thinker by a host of leading evangelicals who found Trump supporters grasping and embarrassing. Wear was elevated to the status of senior fellow at the allegedly pro-life Christian think tank Trinity Forum on the basis of his "civility and courage" in politics.[39] And it was Wear who was given Keller's outstretched hand while truly pro-life Trump voters received his disapproval. Certainly, no Trump campaign strategist or any member of the Trump administration has been featured on *The Gospel Coaliton*'s website as "an evangelical Christian whose faith led him to seek justice and mercy," as Wear was. In this, at least, *The Gospel Coalition* has been editorially consistent.

Of the vast number of essays the outlet published about Donald Trump, nearly all were negative, with titles like "Why I Think a Trump Presidency Is Intolerable," "How Donald Trump Ushered in the Apocalypse," and "The Cult of Christian Trumpism." A handful were neutral, presenting arguments for and against some Trump policy or another. None were positive. Not one. Not even after the fall of *Roe*.

In fact, none of the nine articles *The Gospel Coalition* ran about *Roe*'s downfall in the month after the *Dobbs* decision came down even mentioned the former president. An essay released on the day of the ruling, titled "Why We Should Celebrate the *Dobbs* Decision," gave credit to the justices who voted with the majority, but not to the man who had fought fierce political battles to keep his word in appointing three out of five of them.[40] This meant, by extension, that *The Gospel Coalition* was also refusing to give credit to the evangelical voters who had propelled Trump to victory.

Prior, at least, acknowledged that the *Dobbs* decision would not have happened had evangelicals not cast their ballots for Trump. But she called it a "shortcut" to the "right way" of ending *Roe*[41] and said that it had not been worth electing him.[42] "It was like some O. Henry short story," she told the *Washington Post*. "We got what we wanted, a quote-unquote pro-life president and this was not what I wanted. I thought: I'm not willing to pay this price."[43] She then, rather ironically, accused the pro-life Christians who had pragmatically decided they *were* willing to vote for Trump despite his flaws of making an idol of politics. It did not seem to occur to her that those who cling more tightly to their political ideal than to actual human lives might be doing some idolizing themselves.

New York Times columnist David French is frequently an honored speaker at seminaries, Christian colleges, and churches, and his opinions are constantly platformed by institutional leaders. Like Russell Moore, he counts Marvin Olasky among his friends and was widely known as a conservative evangelical voice. (For a while, he used an image of John Calvin as his profile picture on Twitter.)[44]

He also shares the distinction with Wear, Prior, Russell Moore, and a number of other well-known Never Trumpers of being a Trinity Forum fellow (the Christian think tank seems to be assembling a certain type of thought), which comes with its own constant promotion in evangelical spaces. Just before the 2020 election, French argued that there was no reason for pro-lifers to vote for Trump. His three key arguments were (1) "Presidents have been irrelevant to the abortion rate," meaning anything Trump did would be unlikely to have much impact; (2) "Judges have been forces of stability, not change, in abortion law," meaning whomever Trump appointed would probably leave *Roe* unchanged; and (3) "Even if *Roe* is overturned, abortion will be mostly unchanged in the U.S.," meaning that new state laws wouldn't have much effect on abortion.[45]

French turned out to be glaringly wrong on the first two counts and is on his way to being wrong on the third. The Court was indeed a force for massive change in abortion law, making Trump massively consequential to abortion because twenty-four states either had trigger laws (which immediately restricted or banned abortion) or they quickly passed new legislation. While some of those laws were blocked by lower courts, many more have taken effect. And though it's early yet to get any serious understanding of how these changes will impact the abortion rate in the long term, a study from the Institute of Labor Economics has already estimated that 32,000 young lives that would otherwise have been lost were saved by new laws made possible by the Dobbs decision.[46] That's not nearly enough, but new and historic progress has reenergized the pro-life movement for the long, dogged state and federal fights ahead.

When the *Dobbs* decision proved how spectacularly wrong French was, he came up with the bizarre argument that Trump still did not qualify as a pro-life president because he had robbed women of hope, and that had caused them to abort their babies during his presidency. "If we change the metric from abortion law to actual, legal abortions, the picture is considerably different, and begins to challenge our assumptions about what it means to build a true pro-life culture in the United States," he wrote. "If there is one thing that we know, it is that the culture in which we live decisively influences whether men and women possess the hope sufficient to have a child."[47]

Barack Obama, despite supporting abortion up to birth, was actually the most pro-life president, French insisted. Quoting Jeremiah 29:11 on God's plans to give Israel hope and a future, he claimed that women had fewer abortions under Obama because his presidency gave them more hope. Of course, French's tally didn't take into account the decrease in abortions that would immediately occur after *Dobbs*, which, if we stick with our slavery analogy, is a little like saying we can't really credit Lincoln with being antislavery because plenty of slavery occurred during his presidency.

The pro-abortion Guttmacher Institute managed to come up with somewhat more quantifiable explanations for the difference in abortion rates under Trump and Obama than the general miasma of hope that filtered through the air during their respective presidencies.[48] After Trump took office, a number of blue states expanded Medicaid to include abortion coverage, and distribution of online abortion drugs ramped up.[49] Then, in 2018, Republicans lost the House, and Democrats picked up significant power at the state level. They gained trifecta control (House, Senate, and the governorship) in seven states while Republicans picked up only one. French also failed to mention the fact that during the Obama presidency, Democrats suffered their largest loss of power in fifty years, with 13 governorships and 816 state legislative seats turning red.[50] A key priority for most of those conservatives was to enact the most aggressive pro-life policies they could under *Roe*.

Interestingly, before the *Dobbs* decision, French knew that it was red state regulations and not "hope" that drove the abortion rate down during the Obama administration. He wrote in August 2020, "In reality, the astonishing advance of the conservative movement in American states *during the Obama administration* yielded more concrete pro-life gains than anything the Trump administration has accomplished" (emphasis his).[51] Perhaps he forgot that he knew this, or perhaps something about his new gig at the most elite secular media outlet in the country had triggered abortion-specific amnesia.

French has transformed over the past eight years from a stalwart conservative favorite with a somewhat niche audience at *National Review* to the heights of the *New York Times* precisely because of his opposition to his fellow evangelicals over Trump. Certainly the Gray Lady would not have come calling if he were still warning (correctly) that same-sex marriage would lead to attempts to "drive Christianity out of public life"[52] rather than arguing that Christians should now support it as a matter of law.[53]

To illustrate just how quickly French's rocket has climbed, when a group of neocons floated his name as a possible independent candidate in 2016, the popular left-wing political site Vox responded, "If your reaction to that is, 'Who?' then congrats, you nailed it. David French is exactly as obscure as you think he is."[54]

Arguably no other figure so represents the ideological and theological fault lines Voddie Baucham wrote about in his 2021 book of the same name. The vast majority of French's writing during that meteoric rise has been devoted to savaging his fellow Christians for making a pro-life devil's bargain in voting for Trump. *Dobbs* meant they might have known something he didn't, might have been in possession of some moral faculties he wasn't. Rather than consider this, French joined Prior in insisting that any lives saved weren't worth it.

There was no political or legal reality that could convince them that evangelicals had made the right or even reasonable call when they chose Trump over Hillary Clinton or Joe Biden. If Trump was going to go down in history as the most consequential pro-life president, it would mean they were wrong to constantly attack and denigrate their fellow Christians who had elected him. To allow them to go on attacking while credibly claiming to be pro-life, they would have to redefine the term.

The Pro-life Kitchen Sink

To be fair, the redefinition of pro-life began years before Trump, initially picking up steam in mainstream evangelicalism in the 2010s with the creation care movement. Environmental activists tried to piggyback on the moral authority of saving babies in the womb by arguing that their cause was about saving lives, too.

"We're not adverse [sic] to government-mandated prohibitions on behavioral sin such as abortion," Richard Cizik told the New York Times in 2005. You'll recall Cizik was then the vice president of governmental affairs for the National Association of Evangelicals. He added, "We try to restrict it. So why, if we're social tinkering to protect the sanctity of human life, ought we not be for a little tinkering to protect the environment?"[55]

Under the banner of "pro-life," the NAE held a "National Day of Prayer for Creation Care" in 2010 with the scientifically dubious premise that coal-burning power plants release mercury that impacts the unborn. The Evangelical Environmental Network reportedly classified thirteen political leaders as "sensitive to pro-life concerns" even though they had perfect pro-abortion voting records.[56]

The following year, Ben Lowe, a former Democratic congressional candidate and co-chair of the left-wing group Christians for Social Action, built on this tortured logic in Relevant magazine,[57] which presents itself as evangelical and enjoys a wide circulation among younger Christians.[58] He argued that evangelicals should vote for Obama not in spite of their pro-life convictions, but because of them. "We remember that being fully pro-life means caring about the whole of life, in all its fullness and diversity," he wrote. "The same Bible and the same Savior that call us to protect the unborn, call us also to care for the poor, the immigrant, the sick, the aged, others who are socially marginalized, and all of Creation."

Transforming the definition of pro-life to mean everything—and thus nothing—would become a standard line among progressive evangelicals like Wear and the AND Campaign. But with the advent of the Trump candidacy, it found its way into conservative evangelicalism.

When Beth Moore was challenged on Twitter about her abortion convictions given her vociferous opposition to evangelical Trump voters, she deflected with her own version of those progressive talking points: "I believe in pro-all-of-life from conception to the grave, including every ethnicity," she said.[59]

Prior echoed this, arguing in the *Washington Post* that pro-life could mean anything from "supporting sex abuse victims" to "helping start and run an inner-city high school in Buffalo."[60] So, essentially, just doing good deeds. One has to ask, would she say that "#MeToo" should also applied to someone denied a job because of their race? Or does the force of the phrase stem from the specificity of its intent?

Eventually, Prior devalued the term "pro-life" to such a point that even as medical experts were casting serious doubts on the effectiveness of Covid masking,[61] she insisted that a person could not credibly claim to be pro-life unless he continued wearing them anyway.[62] She also repeatedly argued that those, like Cross, who had spent years working in pregnancy centers and fighting to overturn abortion laws, couldn't claim to be pro-life if they weren't willing to get the vaccine.

Such attempts at moral equivalency infuriated Cross. "What we're talking about is one person's quality of life and another person's actual right to life. We can't equate the two, they're not in the same plane at all," she told me. She worried that this trend to throw anything Christians might support into the pro-life basket would exhaust evangelicals and make them complacent about supporting the work she and her center do. "Every pregnancy center is different, but we're all donor funded. So, we're more likely to act based on the desires of the churches and Christians that support us. So, if people are hearing, 'We like to make sure that you're providing for all of these different kinds of needs' rather than laser focused on stopping abortions, then the organization itself can become subject to mission drift."

Defining so many issues outside of abortion as "pro-life" also ignores the fact that there is not a legislative intent to kill human beings with other causes now being identified as part of the movement. Whatever one's feelings on the legitimacy of systemic racism, there is no lobby arguing for a right to murder black people. No one fought mask or vaccine mandates with the goal of killing old people. The purpose of abortion is to destroy babies, and nearly every one that is carried out achieves that goal.

That hasn't stopped the redefinition from spreading. There are now few progressive causes that evangelical leaders are not insisting Christians accept as part of the pro-life movement. Russell Moore has argued that amnesty for illegal immigrants qualifies.[63] In 2023, Brent Leatherwood, the man who replaced Moore as ERLC president, lobbied for gun control under a pro-life banner.[64] So did *The Gospel Coalition*'s senior editor Brett McCracken, who tweeted after a school shooting, "We've utterly failed our children when: They can be brutally killed in the womb because enough adults clamor for abortion rights. They can be brutally killed in the classroom because enough adults clamor for gun rights. A child's life is more precious than our rights."[65]

McCracken's use of pro-life language to argue against the Second Amendment overlooks the fact that whatever debate Christians have about gun reforms, nowhere is it legal to shoot children, and no one is advocating for that position. As Christian podcaster Josh Daws responded to McCracken, "The right to murder your child is in no way analogous to the right to own a device that is primarily used for self-defense or sport. The only way this analogy works is if pro-lifers were trying to ban forceps."[66]

These attempts to name anything and everything a pro-life issue only serve to minimize the unique horror of abortion, which has taken more than fifty million lives in the United States since 1973—three times the number killed in the Nazi, Soviet, Rwandan, and Cambodian genocides combined. There is no moral equivalent.

Even if one were to agree with progressive Christians that racial inequities should be the Church's greatest concern, no other race-based injustice can compare to what is being done under the auspices of "reproductive rights," something Professor Carl Trueman ably highlighted in *First Things*. "Police actions in 2018 accounted for the deaths of fewer than three hundred African Americans, while in the same year abortions of African-American babies accounted for more than 117,000 of the same," he pointed out. "One would think this extreme difference (390 to one) would make abortion the centerpiece of Christian critiques of racism."[67]

The only reason it wouldn't is if those drawing such equivalencies do not, deep down, see those 117,000 babies as equally human as the 300 adults.

Prior, French, Keller, and both Moores have taken to the pages of the most elite media outlets in the world to incessantly disparage average Christians who felt it was worth voting for Donald Trump for a chance to dismantle the most wicked practice this nation has ever known. Let's be clear, no one cast a ballot for Trump because he committed adultery or because he bragged in 2005 about grabbing women's private parts. Nor was the legal protection of adultery or lechery a feature of the Trump campaign's platform.

In contrast, Clinton and Biden *did* promise voters that electing them would allow the butchery to continue. They did make it a part of their platforms, and a significant number of voters cast ballots for them based on those promises. Given this, which vote is more morally compromising for the Christian—the one that places power in the hands of those who promise to allow the innocent to be put to death or the one that vests power in those who promise to make a way to rescue the innocent?

Which group of Christians do these celebrated evangelical leaders accuse of defaming the name of Christ with an untoward interest in political power, and which do they excuse and even promote?

What they forget is that while using power for the wrong reasons is sinful, wielding it for the right reasons is a biblical command (Isaiah 1:17). All throughout the Bible we see commendations of good rulers who use power to do justice. In a self-governing society, it is ultimately citizens, not the president or other representatives elected, who rule. It is we, the people, who elect them. To use that power, that rule, to put in office proxies who pledge to sentence the innocent to death by the hundreds of thousands every year is to participate in their wickedness.

Thanks to the single-issue voters who cast ballots for Donald Trump, tens of thousands of babies are alive today who otherwise would have been fed to the abortion machine.[68] And the way has been made so that many millions more may yet find rescue. Those who used their power to bring about those rescues have nothing to apologize for. The same cannot be said of the church leaders who heap censure on them for the approval of our death-desensitized cultural elites.

CHAPTER 4

Christian Media and the Money Men

Your rulers are rebels, partners with thieves. Everyone
loves a bribe and runs after gifts.

—Isaiah 1:23

Like every subculture, evangelicalism has its own publications, personalities, and thought leaders that address their audience's particular interests. Evangelical media may cover many of the same topics as secular news outlets and culture journals, but they ostensibly do so through the lens of biblical doctrine, Christian history, and evangelical outlook. Thus, if the *Washington Post* is covering the Biden administration's push to legalize marijuana at the federal level, *The Gospel Coalition* might review how church leaders are gearing up to minister to pot-numbed teens in their youth groups.

Many, if not most, average people in the pews don't read these publications regularly, but their leaders not only read them, but also publish in them, appear on the associated podcasts, and participate in the related seminars. More important, they often look to them for social cues to determine what topics they should be discussing and the polite boundaries for discussing them. Just like with mainstream media outlets, powerful secular interests recognize that these outlets are tools for shaping public conversation, and they're leveraging them to disseminate certain narratives—in this case, what God requires from Christians when it comes to participating in the political system.

I'll give you an example.

Not long ago, I received a text from my childhood pastor Randy Brannon, wanting to know what had happened to *Christianity Today*. Brannon had retired some years earlier from his large Southern Baptist church, and it had been awhile since he'd picked up a copy of the magazine Billy Graham founded in 1956. The character and emphasis of its coverage has ebbed and flowed over the years, as all publications tend to do under the leadership of different editors, but it had generally reflected the broad outlook of a traditional pastor like him. Or, at least it had the last time he'd paid attention to it. What he'd read while leafing through a couple of back issues early in 2023 shocked him—so much so that he began to poke around the *Christianity Today* website to see if perhaps he had just stumbled on one or two outlier months. He quickly discovered he hadn't.

In one interview, a self-professed Christian psychology professor bemoaned the fact that states had been banning transgender medications and surgeries for children because these are "complex clinical issues."[1] A highly racially divisive essay, titled "White Churches, It's Time to Go Pro-Life on Gun Control," said "alt-right racism" was responsible for making Donald Trump president.[2] The author demanded that white pastors lobby their governors for gun restrictions. Then there were the dozens of reports promoting lax border policies with no counterbalance to show the harms of unfettered illegal immigration (a topic Brannon knew well as a California resident of some forty years).[3] It was all far more political than he'd ever remembered and *far* more progressive. Recalling that he had a family friend familiar with the inner workings of evangelical media, he texted me. "Is *Christianity Today* going woke?!"

I texted back a laughing emoji. "How long has it been since you read it?" I asked. He confessed that he couldn't remember—a long time. When I told him *Christianity Today*'s progressive slant was nothing new, though it had become more overt since 2016, he wondered how the magazine could stay afloat when it was so obviously out of step with the mainstream of evangelical views. Didn't it need to serve the interests of its readers?

What he didn't realize was that these days, a significant portion of the magazine's funding doesn't come from readers, or even Christians.

Unequally Yoked

In 2016, evangelicalism's "flagship" publication began receiving substantial support from one of the wealthiest private foundations in the world, the Lilly

Endowment,[4] a charitable institution founded in 1937 by the Eli Lilly family of pharmaceutical fame. After evangelicals propelled Donald Trump into the presidency, Lilly awarded, for the first time, a sizable grant to *Christianity Today*—just over $2 million for a project to "[Create] a Future for Christian Thought."[5]

That same year, Lilly gave the outlet a separate grant for $750,000 as part of a "faithful pastors" project. Combined, it was a substantial sum for the magazine—nearly the total amount of grant money it received that year and more than six times the funding it had received the previous year.[6] It was also well over the magazine's net income for the year.

There might be nothing worrying in that, if the endowment's interest were to promote biblically sound "Christian thought," but a glance at its other grantees makes it clear that this was not the case. For instance, another recipient of $750,000 under the pastors project was North Park University,[7] an ostensibly Christian college that touts its "Queers and Allies" student organization.[8] The school is so committed to excising traditional biblical beliefs on sexuality from its campus that it once pretended to shut down an entire department to rid itself of a tenured professor who had had the bad manners to believe out loud what Jesus teaches in Matthew 19—that marriage is meant for one man and one woman for life.[9] Nor was North Park an exception. Most of the project's participants (largely seminaries and colleges) fall on the liberal side of the ledger.

And that was just the beginning of the Lilly Endowment's patronage of Billy Graham's magazine. Between 2019 and 2022, it would award the outlet another $1.6 million, with more than $1 million earmarked for a "compelling preaching" initiative to create new content to help "educate" preachers.[10] As the magazine explained in a press release, Lilly had expressly invited it to apply for a grant to help "equip preachers in bringing their message to life."[11]

Protestant organizations have understandably accepted funding from secular foundations in the past to minister to the homeless, poor, and sick and for any number of other related humanitarian projects. The issue with the Lilly grants is that they're specifically going to evangelical institutions for pastoral and ideological efforts, and they appear to have no commitment to orthodoxy. To wit, the endowment's Thriving in Ministry Initiative is so overtly left-wing that its participants promote abortion, reparations, illegal immigration amnesty, and LGBTQ ideology.[12]

Of course, it doesn't necessarily take financial incentives to shift the nature of an organization if the worldview of the staff has already shifted. As Jesus observes, "Where your treasure is, there will your heart be also" (Matthew 6:21). And a quick look at public campaign records shows that when it comes to political donations, *Christianity Today*'s heart is most certainly with the party of abortion and the LGBTQ agenda.

Between 2015 and 2022, the outlet's staff and board members made seventy-four political donations. Every single one went to Democrats.[13] That tally includes *Christianity Today* president and CEO Timothy Dalrymple who in 2020 donated $300 to failed Georgia Senate candidate Sarah Riggs Amico, who ran on a platform of protecting abortion "without exception" and of repealing the Hyde Amendment, which prevents federal tax dollars from funding abortions.[14] Amico also declared herself a "staunch LGBTQ ally," promising to support the Equality Act, a radical bill that would, as the Heritage Foundation has detailed, threaten parental rights over children who claim to be transgender, decimate conscience rights for medical workers, and "cancel religious freedom."[15] Theologian and Southern Baptist Theological Seminary president Albert Mohler put the Equality Act in even starker terms, saying it "represents the greatest threat to religious liberty in the United States in our lifetimes" and would "totally transform the United States as we know it."[16] Yet the man at the helm of evangelicalism's most recognized and influential publication twice donated to the campaign of a Senate candidate pledging to vote for it.

Nor is the issue just that a number of *Christianity Today* staffers donate to Democrats. It's also *which* staff have done so. It might not make much difference if the IT guy or the woman who sells advertising places some chips on blue before an election, but when the CEO, a board member, and a vice president do so, and no one in the executive ranks appears to counterbalance their views, there's a question of how much that's influencing the content of the magazine. Even worse is when the editorial staff are making campaign donations. Then it's not just a question of a political outlook that's wildly out of step with the audience the magazine purports to serve, but also of a violation of professional ethics.

How serious a breach is it for journalists to donate to candidates? Serious enough that back in 2010, MSNBC suspended host Keith Olbermann over three campaign donations even though his show was clearly marketed as opinion.[17] The *New York Times,* the *Los Angeles Times,* the *Washington Post,* NPR, and just about every other major secular newsroom do not allow editors or reporters to contribute to campaigns, and they've suspended journalists who got caught doing so.[18] According to the Society of Professional Journalists—which also says, "No. Don't do it," by the way—one Denver newspaper publisher wouldn't even let mailroom employees attend a concert whose proceeds "were being donated by the band to a candidate for the U.S. Senate."[19] Yet *Christianity Today* staffers have not only flouted this convention, but have done so on behalf of those who would further entrench practices God hates.

Five different editors at *Christianity Today* contributed to Democrats (and only Democrats) between 2015 and 2022, including news editor Daniel Silliman. He gave to five different pro-abortion candidates, among them, Elizabeth Warren, who is so committed to the cause of death that she has pushed to shut down all crisis pregnancy centers across the country.[20]

After he left the magazine, former editor in chief Mark Galli admitted in a since-deleted essay that the staff is driven by a deep desire for the approval of secular elites:

> Elite evangelicalism (represented by CT, IVPress, World Vision, Fuller Seminary, and a host of other establishment organizations) is too often "a form of cultural accommodation dressed as convictional religion." These evangelicals want to appear respectable to the elite of American culture . . .

Part of the reason for this, Galli explained, was because these members of the evangelical media fancy themselves as elite:

> For the longest time, a thrill went through the office when Christianity Today or evangelicalism in general was mentioned in a positive vein by The New York Times or The Atlantic or other such leading, mainstream publications. The feeling in the air was, "We made it. We're respected" . . . [21]

Galli acknowledged that this hunger for worldly respectability drives *Christianity Today*'s editorial decisions as well, not just in what editors cover, but also in what they choose not to cover.

> We said, for example, that the magazine did not take a stand in the com-
> plementarianism or egalitarianism debate. But we rarely if ever pub-
> lished an article that endorsed complementarianism; we did offer many
> that assumed egalitarianism in family and church life (not to mention
> the many women pastors who [sic] we published).

It was also no coincidence, Galli said, that *Christianity Today* has not run an article in the last 30 years that "argued for or assumed six-day creation." Instead, it publishes writers who take the respectable secular position that the Earth is a billion years old.

Before I came across Galli's essay, I noticed this same kind of selective coverage, though over issues that demonstrate cultural accommodation in far more glaring fashion.

At the same time that *Christianity Today* is putting out the progressive-slanted reporting that my old pastor Brannon noticed, the magazine offers virtually *no* coverage of the dozens of laws being passed across the country that ban transgender surgeries and treatments on minors, or of states out-lawing drag queen performances in front of children, or of bills mandating that schools keep gender indoctrination out of the classroom. As I write, the existence of such bills is briefly mentioned in only one interview and as a one-sentence aside in an article about an intermural denominational battle, but the magazine has not devoted a single article to covering this massive legislative trend.[22] Yet few cultural topics have been more important to evan-gelicals in recent years. For *Christianity Today* to all but ignore it speaks vol-umes about the value it places on the views of ordinary believers and with whom it prefers to align.

Finally, there's the judgment of its leadership, which chooses to part-ner with Religion News Service, a wire service supported by the aggressive LGBTQ grant maker the Arcus Foundation (more on this in a later chap-ter). In 2014, Arcus directly stated that its purpose in funding RNS was to "recruit and equip LGBT supportive leaders and advocates to counter rejection and antagonism within traditionally conservative Christian churches."[23]

This aim shows up regularly in RNS stories that overtly push LGBTQ affirmation in the Church as a question of civil rights rather than biblical doctrine. Just one example of many, in an August 2021 story titled "Young Evangelicals Are Leaving Church. LGBTQ Bias May Be Driving Them Away," RNS reports, "White evangelical denominations such as the Southern Baptist Convention, the Presbyterian Church in America, the Anglican Church in North America and dozens of others have *resisted offering gay people equality*" [emphasis mine].[24] So, according to RNS, denominations who choose to adhere to Scripture rather than current cultural opinion are anti-equality.

Occasionally, the magazine's use of RNS, with its consistently secular, progressive framing of social issues, has caused a bit of awkwardness with well-known Christians who, like my childhood pastor, missed the memo that it's a new day at *Christianity Today*. In November 2022, Babylon Bee CEO Seth Dillon took note of an article that characterized his satire site's jokes the same way the left would.[25] He sounded off on social media, quoting from the magazine: "Christianity Today says the Babylon Bee 'has run a number of anti-trans jokes—mocking both particular transgender people like [assistant secretary for health Rachel] Levine as well as fictional trans people.' Our jokes are not anti-trans. They're pro-truth. The idea that men can become women is false (and funny)."[26]

Dalrymple responded quickly, clarifying that it was actually a Religion News Service story. His outlet had just chosen to rerun it. But he failed to explain why he was using a wire service with a worldview so in conflict with the Bible in the first place or what made the magazine publish that article in particular, given that it selects only some RNS content. After the dustup, in which Dalrymple had no choice but to admit that his Christian magazine had published a story that accepted the premise that to question biological reality (and God's created order) was "anti-trans," *Christianity Today* went right on using RNS.[27]

What has happened to *Christianity Today* is a story common to any number of once-faithful evangelical institutions. Part of it is, no doubt, organic, as predicted by the famous "First Law" coined by British political pundit

John O'Sullivan: "All organizations that are not explicitly right-wing will over time become left-wing." Hebrews 2:1 warns of a similar tendency when it comes to theological matters: "Therefore, we must give the more earnest heed to the things we have heard, lest we drift away."

Nothing in the world comes so naturally to a Christian as putting away his oars of resistance and floating off on the cultural tides. This is especially true when you know that the firm ground of Scripture you're standing on is increasingly becoming a deserted island.

But another part of what is happening at some high-profile evangelical media organizations and think tanks is being quite intentionally orchestrated. Young Christians on social media have developed something of an edgy corollary to O'Sullivan's law that describes the phenomenon: "Progressives will hollow out your trusted institutions and wear them like a skin suit." That is, from the outside, those institutions will still use the lingo and the symbols of the Christian faith. But look at them a little more closely, and you will discover something newly alien within.

Champagne Ministry

In 1991, author and social critic Os Guinness proved that the entrepreneurial spark that had led his great-great-grandfather to found one of the most successful brewing companies in history ran in his veins as well. After immigrating to the United States in the mid-eighties, Guiness noticed that the Aspen Institute, a sort of secular salon that brings together intellectuals, artists, and journalists to discuss ideas at public events, had left one monumental element largely out of its discourse: Christianity. He and businessman Alonzo McDonald decided to launch Trinity Forum as a corrective that would allow speakers and attendees to consider "how the gospel and the Bible as a whole is the leading voice in the western conversation."

The events proved so popular that Guinness and McDonald were soon facilitating five or six around the country every year, eventually expanding into Europe. They drew not just scholars, but businesspeople, lawmakers, nonprofit leaders, and more to explore "permanent things"—that is, the larger questions of meaning that unite us all. Guinness had anticipated that, as with Aspen, lively conversation would take place. But what he hadn't anticipated was the element of fellowship that would develop as a result of what he called the "Christian openness" of the events. He remembered one early forum, held at a resort hotel over the course of a weekend, that ended with half the group in tears at the things they'd heard and shared. "It was quietly apologetic, although I don't know if people thought of it quite like that," Guinness, who described himself as an "unashamed evangelical," told me in his plummy English accent. Many believers were deepened in their faith, while many nonbelievers, he said, came to Christ after attending a forum.

He particularly recalled the skill with which his late friend, philosophy professor Dallas Willard, charmed the audience. Another unashamed evangelical, Willard had a tremendous gift for speaking to his listeners at whatever level of education and understanding they possessed. "He could put very heavy philosophical concepts in language fit for a five-year-old or a PhD student and would graciously shift his presentation to meet them. So, he was perfect with our businessmen," Guinness chuckled, "because many of them are either afraid of academics or would come believing that kind of thing was irrelevant. Dallas was able to change their perspective." That was a good thing, because at that time, Guinness told me, funding for the forums came mainly from people who attended them.

Over the next thirteen years, as Trinity Forum grew and developed a fellowship program, its fellows became sought after by national news outlets looking for a religious perspective on any number of topics. By the time Guinness officially stepped down in 2004, handing over the reins to a new generation of leaders, Trinity Forum had managed the rare feat of earning respect from both serious Christian thinkers and open-minded secular intellectuals. It would eventually become clear that the new leaders had somewhat different ideas about the purpose of the organization.

In February 2008, they decided the time had come for Trinity to host a different sort of event—a high-profile battle of wits on the existence of God, to be held at the Edinburgh International Festival. They reached out to Larry Alex Taunton, an author and apologist known for both participating in and arranging vigorous debates with the world's foremost atheist thinkers—men like Christopher Hitchens and Richard Dawkins, who loomed large on best-seller lists and in the pages of Vanity Fair. Trinity Forum had already secured Hitchens for the debate, but they were surprisingly at a loss to identify a suitable Christian sparring partner for him. They'd hoped that Taunton, who had a wide network of connections throughout the United Kingdom, could help them pinpoint the right person.

As I've gotten to know Taunton a bit over the last couple of years, he's come to represent something of an Indiana Jones figure in my mind, though the hat he favors is a wide-brimmed Panama rather than a fedora. He is equal parts scholar and globe-trotter, with his social media accounts offering a window into the winding trails he has taken—from Nigeria to Greece, Rome to Egypt—in his pursuit of his next story, next interview. As Taunton told me with a hint of Alabama drawl during a car ride to some airport or another, he believed he had the perfect person to oppose Hitchens: a prominent professor able to put complex ideas into language ordinary people could understand. As Taunton described his friend, he sounded very much like Guinness sharing recollections of Dallas Willard.

Taunton had no doubt this professor had the steel and mind to take on one of the world's most renowned intellectuals, so he was surprised when Trinity seemed less than enthusiastic. They suggested other names with higher social pedigrees, whom Taunton also knew well—well enough to know they would be no match for Hitchens. They were brilliant men, but not brilliant debaters, yet Trinity persisted in pressing for them. Taunton couldn't understand why they would seek out his expertise and then not trust it. After further discussion with Trinity leaders, he got the sense they weren't interested in his professor friend because the friend was, in their view, "too evangelical"—which for the new Trinity meant "unsophisticated."

"They liked his educational background, but they weren't keen on the fact that he was, for them, just a little too 'man of the people,'" Taunton said. "I got the sense they didn't want too much Jesus, too much Bible. They wanted somebody whose faith had a respectability with the world. A Christian that the world would love."

After the event, it would strike him that Trinity's new president Cherie Harder hadn't even seemed to care much whether Christianity was well defended during the debate. What she seemed most interested in was meeting Hitchens and socializing with the dignitaries in attendance. "As I stood back and watched, it seemed to me that [Trinity Forum's new leadership] longed for acceptance from the secular social elites," Taunton remembered. "And it appeared they had it. But at what cost? It kind of left a bad taste in my mouth because I could only feel like, ideologically, we were not the same. I thought we were, but weren't. And I came away with the feeling that this is a group that likes to fashion themselves as very posh and very intellectual."

Taunton has seen a lot of that kind of thing under the guise of Christian ministry. He calls it "champagne ministry," and it, naturally, requires plenty of funding. Though Taunton wasn't aware of it, Trinity's new leadership, like *Christianity Today*, has turned to secular foundations that have not demonstrated the slightest commitment to orthodox Christian beliefs but have shown an outsize desire to shape society. One of Trinity's biggest backers today is the man researchers who track the intersection of money and politics call "the new George Soros."[28]

The Political Evangelicals

Born in Paris to Iranian parents, Pierre Omidyar immigrated to the United States with his family as a child. A degree in computer science from Berkeley was the right education, a few years working for Apple was the right place, and the mid-1990s was exactly the right time to join the Silicon Valley gold rush with gusto. Omidyar's vision was to create the perfect online marketplace for person-to-person commerce, and in late 1995, he wrote the code and launched an auction site. Two years later, as the company began to host hundreds of thousands of sales a day, Omidyar gave it a new name: "eBay."

Like several multibillionaires before him, once Omidyar rose to the ranks of the world's richest people, he developed a strong interest in shaping society. He would soon launch his own grant-making foundations and partner with Soros (who called Omidyar a "core partner")[29] and the Bill and Melinda Gates Foundation[30] in various left-wing causes like vote-by-mail initiatives, socialized health care, and gun control.[31] Between 2004 and 2020, his nonprofit network doled out more than a billion dollars, which led Capital Research Center to name him "a quiet but potent player on the nation's political battlefield."[32] He has taken a particular interest in influencing media.[33] One of his first major philanthropic ventures was backing the progressive news outlet the Intercept. However, the man Omidyar tapped to oversee it, Pulitzer Prize–winning journalist Glenn Greenwald, left when the site would not allow him to publish an essay critical of then-candidate Joe Biden.

Greenwald later said of Omidyar, "One's funding sources are relevant to one's mission. Liberal billionaires will only fund groups that advance liberal causes."[34]

And suddenly, Omidyar was interested in funding Trinity Forum.

Between 2018 and 2021, his foundation, Democracy Fund, gave the group nearly four hundred thousand dollars to research the "role of Christian leaders in political life" and "how their followers engage in politics."[35] In 2020, an election year, Trinity Forum tapped former Democratic strategist and Obama administration official Michael Wear to cowrite a report on the topic that argued, in essence, that it would be best for the nation and the Christian faith if evangelicals embraced pluralism—meaning they must show less interest in seeing their own beliefs enshrined in American law and more willingness to accommodate the policies of the left.[36]

In its conclusions, the report cited numerous Christian leaders who have emerged as progressive influencers—like Duke Kwon and Christine Edmondson, both strong proponents of the notion that the country systemically oppresses racial minorities and must be restructured to achieve justice. Wear quoted Kwon offering this advice: "I think Christians more than anyone should be willing to vote for or labor towards interests that might actually come at the cost of their own because that is the basic cruciformity of life, bearing the cross and loving others, even at the cost of ourselves." To go along with the idea that Christians must vote against their interests and beliefs to follow Christ's command to crucify the self, the report immediately stressed that evangelicals as a whole have become overly political. "I find American Christians to be primarily discipled by their political agenda . . . [using] theological justifications for their predetermined, reflexive, intuitive, political, tribal beliefs, that's the biggest problem I run into," said Gospel Coalition editor Collin Hansen. He didn't explain which "tribal beliefs" he found biblically unsupported.

This report was far from a one-off. Trinity Forum's new fellows have made the notion that the American Church has become far too politicized and far too right-wing a favorite theme. *Christianity Today* editor in chief Russell Moore and *New York Times* columnist David French, both recently minted Trinity fellows, have become famous for castigating evangelicals for their engagement in the public sphere.

In his 2023 book, *Losing Our Religion: An Altar Call for Evangelical America*, Moore approvingly quotes Robert P. Jones, president of the left-leaning research organization Public Religion Research Institute, who has accused "white Christian churches" of being "responsible for constructing and sustaining a project to protect white supremacy." The quote Moore references is similarly about white churches. Moore, through Jones, says, "Their greatest temptation will be to wield what remaining political power they have as desperate corrective for their waning cultural influence. If this happens, we may be in for another decade of close skirmishes in the culture wars."[37]

But what is wielding political power besides making use of the same constitutional remedies—freely speaking, freely associating, and electing candidates who promise to enact their preferred policies—that secularists do? And what is Moore's alternative to engaging in "culture wars"? To passively submit to the left's program of subjecting confused children to surgeries that permanently deface their God-given bodies and drugs that rob them of their fertility? To cease the long struggle to protect babies in the womb now that we have seen the most significant victory in fifty years? Wielding power through the political process is exactly what a representative democracy is designed to offer.

French, meanwhile, called conservative Christians "dominionists" who want not just "religious freedom, [but] religious authority," as demonstrated by their efforts to "purge . . . books off school library shelves."[38] He didn't bother mentioning that the books in question were in *middle school* libraries and that they depicted, among other pornographic images, boys performing oral sex on one another.[39] He has also counseled evangelicals to give up the ghost on traditional marriage as a matter of law, writing in several essays that accepting the *Obergefell* decision as permanent is how "pluralism is supposed to work" and that gay couples "now enjoy more rights to form their own famil[ies]."[40] He doesn't explain why LGBTQ activists shouldn't have accepted the law of the land in the name of pluralism before *Obergefell*. Nor does he grapple with the moral implications of the booming surrogacy trade that is providing children for these, by nature, fruitless families.[41]

Nevertheless, this is the Christian political wisdom that thousands of pastors may be bringing into their churches.

In January 2024 (another election year), Trinity Forum partnered with French, Moore, and Duke Divinity consulting professor Curtis Chang to launch the After Party, a Bible study curriculum that would bring their ideas on politics into churches to help "reframe[e] Christian political identity from today's divisive partisan options."[42] Their pitch: "As nationally trusted evangelical voices, local leaders do not have to take all the fire by themselves. They only need to sponsor this curriculum into their small group communities, and let us make the case."[43]

The question was: Just whose case would they be making?

During the After Party's germination phase, the project hit a roadblock. Evangelical donors had little interest in funding an explicitly political Bible study. Thus, to get it off the ground, the trio turned to what Chang admitted were "predominantly progressive" "unbelievers." In fact, they turned to secular left-wing foundations.[44]

In May 2022, Rockefeller Philanthropy Advisors announced that the After Party would be one of the thirty-two beneficiaries of its New Pluralists project, which is investing ten million dollars to "address divisive forces."[45] Rockefeller stressed that the curriculum would launch in the "battleground" of Ohio, though none of the After Party founders call that state home.

You need only glance at other projects Rockefeller deemed worthy of investment to have serious concerns about its interest in bankrolling Bible studies. In the same grant round as the After Party was a group seeking to promote the "leadership of rural LGBTQ+ people." Another was committed to "keeping the remaining fossil fuel resources in the ground" in the name of "climate justice." In 2019, the After Party's benefactor gave one hundred million dollars to the Collaborative for Gender and Reproductive Equity, an initiative that funds efforts to safeguard abortion rights and to ensure that "youth" have access to "gender-affirming care."[46]

And Rockefeller's wasn't the only progressive purse with strings attached to the After Party. When I pressed the group about its funding, it admitted that the Hewlett Foundation, the second largest private donor to Planned Parenthood, was also a backer. Other groups the After Party lists as partners on its website hardly inspire more confidence in the curriculum's biblical soundness. The board of the ecumenical group One America Movement, for example, includes the leader of an LGBTQ-affirming synagogue[47] and a cofounder of Black Lives Matter of Greater New York who excuses rioting as self-defense and has called Jesus a "black radical revolutionary."[48]

As for what the After Party teaches, while it claims to be nonpartisan, the thrust of its message for evangelicals is that politics is very complex. If anyone tells you they know how you should vote when it comes to an issue like abortion, the training advises you to "run from that person." Yet there is one issue the After Party frames as unequivocally clear—the idea that America is systemically racist and that Christians should vote to ensure racial justice. If voting on the issue of abortion is complex but voting on the issue of racial injustice is clearcut, it seems fairly obvious for which party the ostensibly nonpartisan After Party curriculum is encouraging Christians to vote. It's even more obvious when considered alongside David French's March 2024 *New York Times* column urging Nikki Haley supporters to vote Biden and Chang's participation in a February 2024 conference for the Never Trump political action committee, Principles First.[49][50]

A week after it launched, the After Party was already booking pastors' conferences.[51] But even months before that, in October 2023, the Council for Christian Colleges and Universities sent out an email prepping its 185 member schools, including many in swing states, to adopt the curriculum upon its release. The email suggested, on Chang's behalf, that the school presidents "offer the small group course through student development or student life, whether through chapel services, discipleship groups, residence life, or student orientation." Another suggestion: "Integrate the curriculum into political science, theology, or pastoral ministry courses."

Who's Political?

Leaving aside the tremendous irony that creating a Bible study curriculum devoted to teaching Christians how to be less political is, in itself, inappropriately politicizing Scripture—that is not, after all, what Bible studies are for—there's a funny little data point Wear, French, Moore, Hansen and other voices promoted in Trinity Forum material never talk about. Evangelicals *aren't* all that political. The claim is, to use a term the Trinity Forum employs regularly, misinformation.

Sure, you see lots of stories in the *New York Times* and *The Atlantic* claiming they are (often via quotes from French, Moore, and other Trinity fellows), but research shows they're pretty solidly in the middle of the pack. Agnostics, atheists, Jews, and mainline Christians are all far more partisan (and far more liberal) than evangelicals.[52] They donate more money to candidates, they contact legislative offices more often, and they are far more likely to attend protests and marches.

If you drill down on the subgroups of Christians alone: research shows that those who self-identify as progressive are not only *much* more politically active than those who identify as conservative, but they have stronger political loyalty and are less tolerant of other political views.[53] Yet after much searching, I've never found evidence of Omidyar funding reports or Rockefeller bankrolling Bible studies to convince progressive evangelicals that *they* need to be less partisan or more willing to embrace conservative policies for the sake of pluralism or crucifying the self.

At the launch of French and Moore's curriculum, Moore argued that young people are leaving the Church because "atheists and agnostics are demonstrating more peace, joy, gentleness, righteousness, [and] self-control" than evangelicals, particularly in the political sphere. One friend closely connected to Trinity Forum, who has attended many of their events over the years, was present for the launch. He told me he came away "absolutely appalled." "I don't consider myself a populist," he said, "but certainly one of the problems in America is this growing gap between populists and elites. And the evening was an hour and a half of Christian elites criticizing evangelical populists. Our Lord would have been horrified to see it. I was angry."

His comments were eerily reminiscent of something Taunton told me as he reflected on his experience with Trinity. "I'm fully convinced that much of this conflict that we're seeing isn't actually political at all. I mean, it has political outworkings, but it isn't actually about policy. It's sociological . . . Because they see themselves as very much above the quote-unquote populists. And populism is just a grassroots movement. It's just ordinary, decent, hardworking American people who are black, white, Hispanic, Asian, all across the political spectrum. But Trinity Forum doesn't want anything to do with those people. And it's why I always say the way to identify leftists is that they love humanity in the abstract, but not in reality."

Ironically, while bolstering the narrative that conservative Christians compromise their faith by participating in the political process, Trinity Forum, whose aim under Guinness was to encourage intellectual discussion of heavenly ideas, has become explicitly partisan. President Cherie Harder also spoke at the summit for the Never Trump PAC, Principles First, alongside Wear and Chang, where she called Trump a "frankly, evil and nihilistic leader" with "tendencies of cruelty and belligerence and dishonesty."[54] Her think tank's most famous fellows frequently appear in the usual prestigious secular media outlets like the *Washington Post*, the *New York Times*, and *The Atlantic*, assuring their readers that they're quite right to despise ordinary evangelicals because of their choice in political candidates. French and Moore have occasionally cast themselves in the role of Old Testament prophets, suggesting that such columns and interviews are merely a case of their calling their fellow Christians to repentance.[55] Among the many significant points this overlooks: The prophets did not go to the pagans to rebuke the Israelites. They did not go to Nebuchadnezzar's court and assure him that he was well justified in attacking the Jews. They did not receive the wealth and honor of the pagan world for doing so. Inasmuch as they were aware of Him at all, the Roman powers reviled Jesus just as much as the Pharisees. They didn't offer Him a privileged place in their social and professional circles to heap scorn on His people.

■ ■ ■

Christianity Today and Trinity Forum are only two examples of how the institutions evangelicals built are now being used to besmirch them and work against their interests. The money from the billionaires of the left flows to any number of such groups. Though the Democracy Fund is Trinity's biggest progressive backer, the forum also takes hundreds of thousands of dollars from Rockefeller foundations[56] and from the Fetzer Foundation,[57] which in turn gets money from Bill Gates, who has used his own nonprofits in recent years to shape public perception through media.[58]

The Southern Baptists' legislative lobbying arm, the Ethics and Religious Liberty Commission, is a fellow beneficiary of Omidyar's largesse, to the tune of some $150,000. The Fetzer Foundation, likewise, has gifted the ERLC $220,000. Facebook's Mark Zuckerberg was good for another $90,000—and all this between 2018 and 2021 alone. After thoroughly reviewing all these donations, as with Trinity, I could not find any that were not earmarked for convincing average churchgoers that faithfully following Jesus means holding less tightly to conservative positions or disengaging from politics.

Do rank-and-file Southern Baptists have any idea how much money is coming from progressive billionaires who do not share their faith, to produce patronizing reports that purport to teach Christians "what healthy democratic participation looks like" and how to "love our neighbors politically"?[59]

■ ■ ■

Since he stepped down, Guinness, for his part, has carved out a very different position from that of Trinity Forum. During a recent podcast interview, he said that Christians who buy the line, oft peddled by *Christianity Today* and current Trinity Forum fellows, that to be faithful believers means "keeping their heads down" as the early Christians did under Rome are "dead wrong." "The early church were faithful, yes," he said, "but they were under an imperial dictatorship. . . . [We] are in a Republic, where every citizen is responsible for the health and vitality of the Republic." Guinness added that *not* to contend for God's laws in the political sphere would be a "failure of citizenship."[60]

As Proverbs 29:2 confirms, the common grace of just laws benefits everyone in a society, whether they know it or not. Christ did not command us to be sure to respect pluralism or to be careful not to polarize the political debate by having too much certainty in our views. All things must be said and done with graciousness and love, of course, and fulfilling our duties as citizens should never become an excuse not to serve our families, churches, and communities in other ways, as well. But we are commanded to be salt and light (Matthew 5:13–16). We are commanded to disciple the nations, including our own nation, teaching them to observe all that He has commanded (Matthew 28:19–20). We can't do that if we let elite voices moving in haughty packs, promoting and promulgating one another's work, convince us to stay quiet and ashamed of what we believe.

CHAPTER 5

Gracious Dialogue

How the Government Used Pastors to Spread Covid-19 Propaganda

Only what God has commanded in his word should be regarded as binding; in all else there may be liberty of actions.

—John Owen, seventeenth-century theologian

In February 2021, a day after the *Daily Wire* published my viral report on how evangelical leaders had helped National Institutes of Health director Francis Collins (also known as Dr. Anthony Fauci's boss) spread false Covid-19 narratives to Christians, an invitation appeared in my inbox.

It was an opportunity to interview Dr. Collins one-on-one over Zoom about a grade school curriculum he had helped develop on the intersection of faith and science. Two people can cover a lot of conversational ground in fifteen to twenty minutes, and the umbrella of that topic left plenty of room for getting into questions of ethics on things like government transparency and public coercion.

For a reporter, it was like God was giving me an early birthday present. I immediately replied, "Yes please!"

During the few days between that invitation and my appointment with Collins, I expected at any moment to receive a cancellation, especially as my *Daily Wire* story was blowing up in a way I had never anticipated. In fact, I hadn't even told my editors I was working on the piece before I turned it in. It had started out as personal curiosity born of irritation. I'd watched the ER-LC's December 2020 webinar with Collins and come away incensed at how the Southern Baptist Convention's lobbying arm had lent him its influential platform as a propaganda vehicle.[1]

The interview consisted entirely of Russell Moore, then ERLC president, setting Collins up to shame Christians for not questioning his highly questionable Covid-19 claims. When Moore asked how pastors should respond to church members' resistance to getting the vaccine, Collins answered that they should tell their congregants, "If you believe that God gives us the opportunity to act as His agents to try to relieve suffering and death . . . and if we are trying to model ourselves after Christ, who spent so much of His time on this earth in healing activities, it seems like [we] could take advantage of what science, through God's grace, has given us as a means of ending this terrible pandemic."

This bit of spiritual manipulation, like the rest of Collins's answers, received zero pushback. Not only that, but throughout just about all his responses, Moore murmured agreement, giving the impression that the NIH director's claims shouldn't be opposed by any reasonable Christian.

"We need to be just absolutely rigorously adherent to things that we know work. But they don't work unless everybody actually sticks to them faithfully without exception," Collins said when Moore asked him about churches that were holding services in person again. "Churches gathering in person is a source of considerable concern . . . So, I think most churches really ought to be advised if they're not already doing so, to go to remote, virtual kinds of services."

Remember, this was nearly a *year* after the initial lockdowns. Moore, representing the largest Protestant denomination in the United States, didn't even bother to ask the ostensibly committed Christian Collins how he squared this advice with biblical commands not to give up meeting together (Hebrews 10:25). Nor did either man acknowledge that isolated, vulnerable people (the depressed, the addicted, the plain old lonely) desperately needed churches to open their doors. Both men seemed not to know such people existed or that churches had a responsibility to minister to them, something they couldn't do if they were closed.

Moore and Collins concluded their interview with a bit of guilting over masks. Moore smiled, chuckled, and nodded his agreement as Collins held

up a basic, over-the-counter cloth square and lectured, "This is not a political statement. This is not an invasion of your personal freedom. . . . This is a
lifesaving medical device." Even in late 2020, this claim was highly debatable
among medical experts, with many international studies showing by then
that such masks were pointless at best.[2] Eventually, the most rigorous and
comprehensive study to date concluded the masks accomplished nothing—
except, that is, to increase the rate of dyslexia and speech impairment in
young children.[3]

But Moore didn't ask Collins why many public health officials supported
public gatherings for Black Lives Matter while opposing public gatherings
to worship Christ as the Bible commands.[4] He didn't ask why Collins and
the NIH were setting different masking policies for the United States from
those endorsed by the World Health Organization and the European equivalent of the CDC, requiring masks on children above two years old while the
other two organizations recommended ages six and twelve, respectively.[5] He
just finished by telling Collins, "Well, I need to let you go back to saving the
world."[6]

It might have been one thing for the ERLC to offer this kind of promotional event to a theologian promoting a new book. But this was a federal
official—a representative of the state—arguing that churches needed to remain closed and that pastors needed to use their offices to convince their
congregations to comply with government orders that violated their First
Amendment rights. Instead of using its institution for the purpose for which
it was created—to represent the interests of Southern Baptists (whose tithes
pay their salaries) to the government—the ERLC was instead representing
the interests of the government to Southern Baptists.

After hearing that interview, I decided to check if Collins was talking to
any other Christian leaders or outlets and to see what those conversations
sounded like. The next thing I knew, I had a notepad covered in quotes and
time stamps from the many, many podcast interviews, reports, and essays
that resulted from Collins's Christian media circuit. Later, I would learn
that, just as Fauci's role was to pressure secular media outlets to carry the
government's water, Collins had been specifically dispatched to leverage
his relationships with evangelical leaders to get Christians to fall in line.
"While Fauci has been medicine's public face, Collins has been hitting the

faith-based circuit toting his 'favorite pet rock,' a baseball-size 3-D printed model of a spiked protein, and preaching science to believers," *Time* magazine reported in February 2021.[7] That "pet rock"—a blue lump covered in what looked like bits of glued-on popcorn, like a kindergarten art project—was the illustration Collins would use to convince Americans, but especially Christians, that they weren't allowed to debate "the science."

■ ■ ■

The day of the interview, I steeled myself for the notification that Collins was canceling on some vague scheduling pretext. But the cancellation didn't come.

I arrived early to the Zoom waiting room, internet connectivity and recording apparatus triple-checked. When the clock ticked five minutes past our meeting time, I still held out hope. These sorts of round-robin promotional press schedules always run over, and I happened to know that the guy who had the slot before me was a self-important run-at-the mouth type. Collins was probably barely getting a word in edgewise.

When the time reached fifteen minutes past our scheduled appointment, and I was still in the waiting room, I started to get the sinking feeling that Collins wasn't coming. I texted my contact at the PR company who had arranged the interview. He assured me everything was fine, our appointment was still a go.

Suddenly, my Zoom waiting room blinked out. In its place was a notification that the meeting had indeed been canceled.

The PR company then texted to tell me there had been an issue on their end, but they gave no other explanation and made no offer to reschedule. I called to inquire, and after about a half an hour, my contact called me back: Collins, it turned out, had recognized my name and was concerned that I would not stick to the topic. "Dr. Collins has to have federal clearance to talk about certain issues," he said.

This, of course, did not wash. Collins had no way of knowing what I was going to ask (and, for the record, all my questions were in some way related to the curriculum, though they were by no means softballs). And if there had been a topic he could not address, he could simply have said so during the interview. *I apologize, Ms. Basham, I need federal clearance to answer that.*

What else would you like to ask about? It's a maneuver that government officials like the head of the NIH know how to mouth in their sleep. I'd seen Collins, Fauci, and CDC director Rochelle Walensky proffer answers like this in front of enough Senate hearings—why wouldn't Collins have been able to say it to a suburban mom talking to him from her slightly untidy kitchen?

I relayed my lack of buying it to my contact. The next day, his boss, the owner of the PR company, sent me an email:

> Hey Megan,
>   We'll be straight. We hadn't seen your piece "How The Federal Government Used Evangelical Leaders To Spread Covid Propaganda To Churches" when we invited you to do the interview. The tone and claims of this article are inconsistent with the gracious dialogue [Collins's organization] is seeking to promote. . . . You're still welcome to pursue the interview through the NIH press office.

She didn't bother to note what, specifically, about my 100 percent accurate, fact-checked, and run-through-Legal reporting Collins had found lacking in grace. But I, along with the rest of the world, would soon discover that Collins's idea of "gracious dialogue" included suppressing the opinions of medical experts who disagreed with him and using his friends in the media to paint those experts as "fringe."[8] This was to say nothing of his previous "gracious dialogue," which included spreading false narratives about the origins of the virus, or his suggestions for future "gracious dialogue," which included bringing "to justice" people who spread "misinformation" about "the science."[9]

A major part of the reason Collins and Fauci were able to get away with so much gracious dialoguing was because the media they spoke to did not ask tough questions, including, especially, Christian media. Obviously, today we know well how that lack of integrity has hurt so many in our nation, but pastors and ministry leaders had an even higher obligation not to use the roles with which they'd been entrusted to act as vassals of the state.

"Love Your Neighbor, Get the Shot"

Collins's crusade to leverage churches for his Covid-19 campaigns actually began before the bulk of his Christian media tour.

In late August 2020, BioLogos, a faith and science organization Collins founded that merges Darwinian evolution with Scripture, released a public statement titled "Love Your Neighbor, Get the Shot" in favor of vaccines, masks, and lockdown orders. Its signatories included celebrated theologian N. T. Wright, bestselling author Philip Yancey, then-*Dispatch* editor David French, *VeggieTales* creator Phil Vischer, *Christianity Today* CEO Timothy Dalrymple, NAE president Walter Kim, Baker Publishing Group president Dwight Baker, and several seminary presidents.[10]

The statement opened with the dubious claim that "Scientists said stay-home orders would reduce cases, and thankfully those measures worked. Scientists predicted that ending quarantine too soon would increase cases, and that has been the case."

Among the pledges the signers took "because of [their] faith in Jesus Christ":

- "Wear Masks" because "Mask rules are not experts taking away our freedom, but an opportunity to follow Jesus' command to love our neighbors as ourselves (Luke 6:31)."
- "Get vaccinated" because "Vaccination is a provision from God."
- "Correct misinformation and conspiracy theories when we encounter them in our social media and communities." Because "Christians are called to love the truth; we should not be swayed by falsehoods (1 Corinthians 13:6)."

That last promise was especially noteworthy, because the signatories weren't just pledging to shush their crackpot QAnon neighbors or the organist from their church who posted anti-mask memes on Facebook. Elsewhere, the document got a lot more specific, and it suggested that the signers were agreeing to treat medical opinions that didn't align with those of Collins and Fauci as conspiracy theories as well.

They promised, for instance, to "actively promote accurate scientific and public health information from trustworthy, consensus sources" and to counter "misinformation" and "conspiracy theories" from "non-consensus" sources. "When Dr. Fauci, the nation's leading infectious disease expert, tells us what scientists have learned about this infectious disease, he should be listened to," the document explained in a tone that suggested its target audience was made up of second-graders rather than the Christian intelligentsia. The statement also warned, "One can always find dissenters, but scientists working together are far more accurate than one person's theory on YouTube."

The wording of this was striking, as only a few months before, other respected experts—like Stanford professor of medicine and health policy Dr. Jay Bhattacharya—had begun to argue in viral YouTube videos that the United States' approach to Covid-19 was too extreme.

Bhattacharya and some of his "non-consensus" colleagues—like biostatistician and Harvard professor of medicine Martin Kulldorff and Oxford infectious disease epidemiologist Sunetra Gupta—opposed pandemic policies like lockdowns, and they questioned conventional scientific wisdom about the severity of the virus. They were beginning to advocate publicly for a different approach, one that didn't require everyone to isolate and social-distance but instead focused on protecting vulnerable populations, like the elderly and the immunocompromised. This non-consensus group would eventually release their public proposal for herd immunity as the Great Barrington Declaration, and tens of thousands of epidemiologists and public health scientists, including a Nobel Prize winner would sign it. As the pandemic progressed, they also spoke out against mask and vaccine mandates and called for more serious consideration of vaccine injuries and risk.

In the end, more than eight thousand people, many pastors and ministry leaders among them, signed on to the "Love Your Neighbor, Get the Shot" statement, promising to work against the evidence and arguments Bhattacharya and his colleagues were presenting in order to promote Collins and Fauci's policies instead. As *National Review*'s Michael Brendan Dougherty told me, "The signers were basically saying, 'We need to treat the Church as a mission field for the Establishment.'"

Which is not to say Collins and Fauci were content to leave it to Church leaders to combat scientific "misinformation." They also got busy behind the scenes to make sure that the public viewed Bhattacharya and any other experts who questioned their opinions as purveyors of conspiracy theories. In private emails in October 2020, Collins deemed the Great Barrington authors "fringe epidemiologists" and worried that they were "getting out of control, and getting too much traction."[11] He urged Fauci to make sure the work of the Great Barrington doctors faced a "quick and devastating take-down."

This didn't mean seriously engaging with the scientific arguments presented in the Great Barrington Declaration—neither Collins nor Fauci ever did that. It meant relying on media connections to ensure the declaration was dismissed as quackery. Within a few days, the two federal officials were taking victory laps by email, sending each other various articles discrediting Bhattacharya and his colleagues.[12] There was a story from the *Washington Post* that said the Barrington proposal "appalls top scientists."[13] One from *Wired* titled "There is no 'scientific divide' over herd immunity," simply rejected the notion that the nearly 3000 scientists signing onto a different position represented any sort of second opinion at all.[14] A journalist for *The Nation* called the declaration a "deadly delusion," then emailed Collins to let him know how much he agreed with and admired him.[15] From there, the ball really got rolling.

U.S. News and World Report published an article calling the Barrington scientists "ill-advised and arrogant."[16] NBC's headline: "Why experts say we need to stop talking about herd immunity," as though the Barrington doctors weren't experts.[17] The *New York Times* framed the advice in the declaration as a "Viral Theory . . . Draw[ing] Fire from Scientists," again, as though those who proposed it weren't also scientists.[18]

All this took a terrible toll on Bhattacharya's professional reputation. At the height of the frenzy to suppress "misinformation," posters with his picture were plastered around Stanford's campus alongside Florida's Covid-19 mortality numbers. The implication was that because Florida governor Ron DeSantis followed his advice to resist most restrictions, Bhattacharya had caused excessive deaths in that state. Since then, age-adjusted statistics have proved that Florida, in fact, came out in the middle of the pack, behind states that employed much more severe measures.[19] And Florida fared much better economically. During the time he was publicly arguing against lockdowns and mandates, Bhattacharya's fellow faculty members circulated petitions against him, claiming his divergent (but correct) opinion that masks didn't stop the virus from spreading was "putting lives at risk."

And he was hardly the only physician who weathered reputational damage due, in part, to Christian leaders warning their flocks to stay away from views that ran counter to those of Collins and Fauci. Dr. Kirk Milhoan, a pediatric cardiologist and a pastor himself, in Maui, had his medical license put under review because he questioned the wisdom of administering vaccines to children.[20]

What not one of the signatories to the "Love Your Neighbor, Get the Shot" statement seemed to consider was whom they might be slandering in making these pledges. Born to a Hindu family in Kolkata, India, Bhattacharya became a believer after arriving in the United States for college. He's been a member of First Presbyterian Church in Mountain View, California, for twenty-seven years and has served as both a deacon and an elder. We can hope that if they had been aware of how Bhattacharya's biblical convictions helped form his scientific outlook, fewer prominent evangelical pastors, theologians, writers, and seminary heads would have been so willingly promised to "counter misinformation" from "fringe" sources like him.

When I asked Bhattacharya about efforts church leaders undertook to shut down debate, he answered from the perspective of both a doctor and a follower of Christ. "Scientists and scientific leaders should allow debate to happen, not misrepresent that the debate is already settled and then essentially trick Christian churches into following them," he told me. In response to the idea that "get[ting] the shot" was synonymous with "lov[ing] your neighbor," he said this was always gaslighting: "From a basic scientific perspective, for a church to say that [Covid-19] vaccination is an act of love because you're protecting other people is just not factually correct." Eventually, revelations would emerge that federal officials knew early on that the vaccines did not prevent transmission, vindicating Bhattacharya on that point as well.[21]

He stressed that the argument Collins made, which so many pastors and theologians parroted, that official Covid-19 polices reduced harm to the "least of these" was also always deeply flawed.

"The lockdowns essentially were a policy that privileged the rich laptop class," he said. "The BioLogos statement had it exactly backward. It was the policies pushed by Francis Collins that destroyed the poor, destroyed the vulnerable, destroyed the working class." To Bhattacharya's point, a UN report in March 2021 estimated that 228,000 children died from starvation in South Asia due to lockdown disruptions.[22]

"There's millions of people who have starved as a consequence of economic dislocation caused by the lockdowns," Bhattacharya explained. "And the World Bank issued reports suggesting that almost 100 million additional people were thrown into poverty due to loss of income. That's what I call trickle-down epidemiology. The idea is you protect the rich, and somehow that'll trickle down and help protect the poor. But, in fact, it's the opposite. It devastated the poor, and that was deeply immoral."

Bhattacharya told me that while he had long admired Collins before the pandemic, today he believes the former NIH director abused his position both as a public health official and as a trusted Christian voice: "[Collins] said, 'Look, because I have this authority, not only can I render a verdict on science, but I can also use that verdict to guide the morality of the Church and the moral teaching of the Church. I think it's just an extraordinary position for one man to take on himself.'"

As for the Church leaders who signed the BioLogos statement and platformed Collins, the Stanford professor is bewildered that they ever could have thought it was a responsible decision. "It's one thing to have a public health campaign to help people know *how* to get vaccinated," he said. "But to tie that to moral behavior—to say, 'If you don't get vaccinated, you're a bad guy, you're sinning . . .'" He sighed, struggling to find words. "I mean, that, that's really . . . that's really dangerous."

And he didn't even know the half of it.

Conspiracy Theorists

The BioLogos vaccine pledge was just the beginning of Collins's campaign to use churches to convince average people in the pews to comply with government orders. He also leveraged the relationships he had with key church leaders and relied on herd respectability to cow the rest. As is frequently the case with evangelical institutions, few wanted to be on the wrong side of the consensus; few were willing to risk being classed among the kooky. Soon, parachurch executives and Christian website editors too far down the food chain to have any direct connection to Collins were peddling his line on everything from masks for all ages to vaccines for all ages to lockdown compliance to church closures. He even got them to help cover his and Fauci's obfuscation regarding the NIH's funding of gain-of-function research in Wuhan, China by teaching their followers that it was a sin to question whether the virus had natural origins.

In an interview with Fox News in June 2021, anchor Martha MacCallum did what Christian news outlets never did: she asked Collins some tough questions and refused to let his "golly gee," Ned Flanders persona sway her from getting answers.[23] By then, emails had leaked showing that Collins and Fauci had, despite their claims, known since the very beginning of the pandemic that it was not just plausible but probable that Covid had come from the Wuhan Institute of Virology.[24] MacCallum asked why, then, they had tried to wave the media and the American public off the lab leak hypothesis. Collins insisted that neither he nor his famous subordinate had ever done so, even though he'd referred to the hypothesis as a "conspiracy theory." He claimed he was referring to other conspiracy theories connected to the lab leak idea:

> There were a lot of conspiracy theories and other ideas floating around at that point. One of them was that actually Covid had been a bioengineered bioweapon . . . But then there was this other idea that maybe it was an accident, a lab leak, that the Institute had been studying this virus that had happened somehow in nature, and it got loose. I never rejected that one . . . So when we talk about what happened, let's try to clarify the difference between those various statements or various options . . . I deny that you were waved off of that by me.

As MacCallum proceeded with admirable steel to cross examine Collins about his claim that there was "no evidence to support" the lab leak hypothesis, a distinct whine entered the NIH head's voice. He tried to shame the journalist for not instead treating their interview as a public relations opportunity to urge more Americans to get vaccinated.

"So you know, I am a little disturbed, Martha, we're spending all this time on this issue. Here we are today, we should be talking about how to put Covid-19 behind us, not going back to January 2020," he said. "And meanwhile, people are still dying from Covid-19. And we didn't even talk about the ways to get to an end of this with vaccines. So, please, could we have a bit more of that focus on how we're going to save lives?" (Watching Collins's complete inability to respond to MacCallum's tough but more-than-fair questioning helped explain why he might have been so wary of subjecting himself to interviewers who did not look likely to be sycophants.)

Had MacCallum known of them, she could have played for Collins his own comments from an April 2020 Q&A cohosted by *Christianity Today* that would have proved he wasn't being truthful with her.[25] During that livestream Collins unequivocally characterized the lab leak theory on its own, quite apart from any question of it being a bioweapon, as both misinformation and conspiracy theory. His answer is lengthy but—aside from a couple of superfluous references to his blog, which I cut—worth reading in full:

Question: How do we know this virus wasn't manufactured in a lab in China and released either intentionally or maybe accidentally, instead of the story we get through the news?

Collins: There have been a lot of those conspiracy theories around, and you know, it was not a crazy idea when this first burst onto the scene to say, "Where did this come from?" And particularly because there is a virology lab right there in Wuhan, some people wanted to jump to the conclusion "There must be a connection there!" Of course, there's virology labs in other places, too. But I can tell you . . . because now we have the complete RNA sequence of this virus, we can compare it to every other similar virus that has ever been described. And it turns out, initially, it was most similar to a virus from a bat in a cave in China. More recently, it's closer to a virus in a pangolin, which is a fascinating little mammal in China. And it does look like it's very plausible that this virus has been floating around in other animal species and jumped into humans.

Now, if you look at the details, if you were trying to design a more dangerous coronavirus, you would never have designed this one. Because it has some properties that make it look like, from everything we knew before, [that] it wouldn't work. It wouldn't be very infectious at all. Turns out, it's really infectious, but you would not have known that.

So I think one could say with great confidence that in this case, the bio-terrorist was nature, which has been going on for centuries as viruses jump from species and occasionally into us. And that's often where serious trouble starts, whether it's influenza, or whether now it's Covid-19. But humans did not make this one, nature did.

He threw out a somewhat tangential reference to "bioterrorist," but other than that, he clearly discounted any possibility of a lab origin, right down to dismissing the proximity of the Wuhan Institute of Virology as a coincidence and concluding that "humans did not make this one, nature did." To believe otherwise was to traffic in conspiracy theories. And that was just the line that Collins's influential evangelical friends echoed.

In an April 2020 *Christianity Today* essay titled "On Christians Spreading Corona Conspiracies: Gullibility Is not a Spiritual Gift," Ed Stetzer, author and director of the Billy Graham Center at Wheaton, said that evangelicals who entertained the lab leak hypothesis needed to "repent" and to "consider taking Christian off [their social media profiles] so the rest of us don't have to share in the embarrassment."[26]

Joe Carter, editor at *The Gospel Coalition,* took an almost identical tack. He gave as an example of sinful Covid conspiracy mongering, "the virus is a human-made bioweapon created by Bill Gates," and claimed this idea was connected to QAnon. After I wrote in my *Daily Wire* story that Carter had linked to QAnon "the reasonable hypothesis that the virus might have been human-made," he took umbrage with me on Twitter. Like Collins with Mac-Callum, he claimed he was characterizing the entire package of beliefs as a conspiracy, not the isolated idea that the virus could have leaked from a lab.

It's funny, though, that Carter didn't note that the lab part was plausible, and his juxtaposition of it alongside outlandish ideas seemed tailored to discrediting it. One also wonders what he does now with a bombshell June 10, 2023, report from the United Kingdom's *Sunday Times* revealing that the Wuhan Institute of Virology *was* working in collaboration with the Chinese military and that internal records show they may very well have been motivated by the virus's use in biowarfare.[27] Or what he does with a story from the *Jerusalem Post* more than two weeks later about a former Wuhan Institute engineer who said he and his colleagues were tasked with isolating the most contagious strain of coronaviruses for the purpose of developing a bioweapon.[28]

Even the Bill Gates element turned out to have a grain of truth. Kentucky senator Rand Paul said this of the Microsoft billionaire on Fox News in June 2023: "Bill Gates is the largest funder of trying to find these viruses in remote caves and bring them to big cities. So what happened to China is, they went eight to 10 hours south of Wuhan, 200 to 300 feet deep into a cave, found viruses, and took them back to the city of 15 million. There are many, many scientists who think that Bill Gates is wrong in funding this."[29]

So, unless two long-established, highly reputable international newspapers and a sitting U.S. senator are also QAnoners, maybe Carter and Stetzer are the ones who need to repent for suggesting Christians who had very valid questions about a still-developing public health crisis were guilty of sin. And maybe they should ask themselves why they felt their publications needed to formally weigh in on the subject at all. Though it was only a very small part, they might also consider how their articles potentially helped a government official, in the words of the House Oversight Committee, "suppress truth" and cover his tracks over "fund[ing] gain-of-function research at the Wuhan Institute of Virology [that] fell below recommended bio-safety markers."[30]

Other ways high-profile Church leaders helped Collins spread federal Covid-19 dogma had more immediate impact on ordinary Christians. When Stetzer interviewed the NIH director on his *ChurchLeaders* podcast in September 2021, the two focused primarily on why Christians who wanted to obey Christ's command to love their neighbors must get the Covid vaccine and submit to mask mandates.[31] During that discussion, Collins and Stetzer were hardly shy about asking clergy to act as the administration's go-between with their congregants. "I want to exhort pastors once again to try to use your credibility with your flock to put forward the public health measures that we know can work," Collins said. Stetzer replied that when he heard from ministers who didn't feel comfortable preaching about Covid-19 vaccines, he advised them simply to promote the jab through social media. "I just tell them, 'When you get vaccinated, post a picture and say, "So thankful I was able to get vaccinated,"'" Stetzer said. "People need to see that *it is the reasonable view*" (emphasis mine). At one point, when Collins insisted that even very young children needed to be masked for seven to eight hours at school and chided Christians for being resistant to the idea, Stetzer offered no challenge or follow-up questions based on views from other medical experts. He simply agreed.

Stetzer's efforts to help further the NIH's preferred coronavirus narratives went well beyond giving Collins a softball venue to rally pastors to his cause. He ended the podcast by announcing that the Billy Graham Center would be officially partnering with the Biden administration. Together with the NIH and the CDC, it would launch a website, Coronavirus and the Church, to provide clergy with resources they should then convey to their congregations.[32]

While then-Southern Baptist President J.D. Greear never interviewed Collins, he did reveal in an April 2021 Facebook post that he had "been asked several times by government leaders to give a 'this is your Christian duty' presentation" to his multi-campus megachurch that would convince his congregation to get the jab. Greear did not identify the government leaders but said he declined their request. Ironically, though, in that very post he *did* use his influence to urge members of the country's largest Protestant denomination to submit to vaccine mandates in the name of Romans 13's directive to be "subject to governing authorities." He then linked to a *Washington Post* op-ed from then-ERLC head Russell Moore and NAE president Walter Kim titled "Not the mark of the beast: Evangelicals should fight conspiracy theories and welcome the vaccines."[33][34]

Tim Keller platformed Collins as well. In a joint interview in May 2020 (hosted by BioLogos and *Christianity Today*), Keller and Collins agreed that churches like John MacArthur's Grace Community Church, which defied Covid lockdowns and resumed meeting after two months, represented the "bad and ugly" of good, bad, and ugly Christian responses to the virus.[35]

During Saddleback pastor Rick Warren's special broadcast with Collins on behalf of the U.S. Department of Health and Human Services, he mentioned that he and Collins had first met when both were speakers for the billionaires and heads of state who gather annually in Davos, Switzerland, for the World Economic Forum. In fact, Warren has been a guest of the WEF several times, and has urged international leaders to use the "Christian church" as a means of "universal distribution" for various government programs because churches have a "built-in credibility with local residents."[36]

Collins and Warren reconnected sometime after the start of the pandemic, Warren revealed, at an "off-the-record" meeting between Collins and "key faith leaders." Warren did not say, but one can make an educated guess as to who convened that meeting and for what purpose, given the striking similarity of Collins's appearances alongside all these Christian luminaries.

As with Stetzer and Moore, Warren spent the interview lamenting along with Collins about the unlovingness of Christians who questioned the efficacy of masks, specifically framing it as a matter of obedience to Jesus. "Wearing a mask is the great commandment: love your neighbor as yourself," the bestselling author of *The Purpose-Driven Life* declared, before insisting that religious leaders had an obligation to convince religious people to accept the government's narratives about Covid-19.[37]

"Let me just say a word to the priests and pastors and rabbis and other faith leaders," Warren said. "This is our job, to deal with these conspiracy issues and things like that. . . . One of the responsibilities of faith leaders is to tell people to . . . trust the science. They're not going to put out a vaccine that's going to hurt people." In fact, the government *does* have a record of putting out vaccines that hurt people. A polio vaccine that infected forty thousand children with the disease in the 1950s is just one example. It wasn't until months after the rollout of Covid-19 jabs that health officials began to receive reports of myocarditis in young men, leading a number of European countries to restrict the use of the Moderna vaccine in younger people.[38] A community of Americans—many of whom were initially proponents of the vaccine—has sprouted up sharing anecdotal evidence of vaccine injuries.[39]

But leaving aside debates about the safety and efficacy of various Covid policies, we have to ask: Is it clergy's job to tell church members to "trust the science?" Is it a pastor's place to slyly insult other pastors who chose to handle shutdowns differently, as Warren did when he quipped that his "ego doesn't require" him to "have a live audience to speak to."

And still the list goes on.

Around the same time that MacArthur's church was in the news for resisting California governor Gavin Newsom's orders to keep houses of worship closed, Collins participated in an interview with celebrated theologian N. T. Wright.[40] The pair warned against conspiracies, mocking "disturbing examples" of churches that continued meeting because, according to Collins and Wright, these churches were of the belief "the devil can't get into my church" or "Jesus is my vaccine." Lest anyone wonder whether Wright experienced some pause over lending his reputation as a deep Christian thinker to Caesar's emissary, the friends finished with a guitar duet.

Collins even made time for *Relevant* magazine, whose readers had likely never heard of him. That story also quoted women's Bible teacher Beth Moore insisting that masking and getting vaccinated were proof that one was "follow[ing] Jesus."[41]

It's hardly surprising, given that the biggest names in evangelicalism were passing Collins their mics, that numerous Covid-19 articles in Christian news outlets cited him as their sole medical authority. Meanwhile, he continued to bring his message to the faithful through their preachers and leaders. "God is calling [Christians] to do the right thing," Collins said of his Covid-19 policies. And none of the preachers and leaders questioned whether his "right thing" and God's "right thing" were necessarily the same thing.

Why not? As Warren said of Collins during their interview, "He's a man you can trust."

A Man You Can Trust

With his concrete record, Collins should have been a strange ambassador to spread the government's Covid-19 messaging to theologically conservative congregations. Other than his proclamations that he is, himself, a believer, the former NIH director has espoused nearly no public positions that would mark him out as any different from any extreme-left-wing bureaucrat.

He has not only defended experimentation on fetuses obtained by abortion, but he has also directed record-level spending toward it.[42] Among the priorities the NIH funded under Collins before he retired at the end of 2021: a University of Pittsburgh experiment that involved grafting fetal scalps onto lab rats and projects that relied on the harvested organs of aborted full-term babies.[43] Some doctors even charged Collins with giving money to research that required extracting kidneys, ureters, and bladders from still-living preborn infants up to 42 weeks of development. So, beyond full term.[44]

He further endorsed unrestricted funding of embryonic stem cell research, personally attending President Obama's signing of an executive order to reverse a previous ban on such spending. When *Nature* magazine asked him about the Trump administration's decision to shut down fetal cell research, Collins made it clear he disagreed, saying, "I think it's widely known that the NIH tried to protect the continued use of human fetal tissue. But ultimately, the White House decided otherwise. And we had no choice but to stand down."[45]

When it came to pushing an agenda of racial quotas, Collins was a member of the left in good standing, speaking fluently of "structural racism" against minorities in America's institutions.[46] He put his money (or, rather, taxpayer money) where his mouth was, implementing new policies that required scientists seeking NIH grants to pass diversity, equity, and inclusion tests.[47]

To the most holy of progressive sacred cows, LGBTQ orthodoxy, Collins was happy to genuflect. He declared himself an "ally" of the gay and trans movements and said he "[applauds] the courage and resilience it takes for [LGBTQ] individuals to live openly and authentically," pledging his support to them as an "advocate."[48] These were not just the empty words of a hapless Christian official saying what he must to survive in a hostile political atmosphere. Collins's declaration of allyship was deeply reflected in his leadership.

He initiated a new NIH program to specifically direct funding to "sexual and gender minorities."[49] On the ground, this translated to awarding millions in grants to experimental transgender research on minors, such as giving opposite-sex hormones to children as young as eight and mastectomies to girls as young as thirteen.[50] Another project, to which his initiative awarded eight million dollars in grants, included recruiting teen boys to track their homosexual activities, like "condomless anal sex," on an app—without their parents' consent.[51]

Other than his assertions of his personal Christian faith, there is almost no public stance Collins has taken that would mark him out as someone of like mind with the orthodox believers to whom he was appealing. So, how did he overcome all this baggage to become the go-to expert for millions of Christians? With a little help from his friends, who were happy to stand as his character witnesses.

Keller, Warren, Wright, Moore, and Stetzer all publicly lauded Collins as a godly brother, as did *Christianity Today* and *Relevant*. When presenting Collins to Southern Baptists, Moore gushed over him as the smartest man in a book club he attends that also includes, according to *Time* magazine, such leading members of the "Christiantelligentsia" as *Atlantic* editor and former George W. Bush speechwriter Pete Wehner and *New York Times* columnist David Brooks.[52] *Christianity Today*'s livestream had the audacity to introduce Collins as a "follower of Jesus, who affirms the sanctity of human life."

In October 2021, even after Collins's funding of the University of Pittsburgh research had become widely known, Moore continued to burnish his friend's religious reputation, saying, "I admire greatly the wisdom, expertise, and, most of all, the Christian humility and grace of Francis Collins."[53] That same month, evangelical pundit David French deemed Collins a "national treasure" and his service in the NIH "faithful."[54] Another former Bush speechwriter, Michael Gerson, struck the most poetic tone, claiming in the *Washington Post* that Collins possesses a "restless genius [that] is other-centered" and is a "truth-seeker in the best sense."[55]

Except, apparently, when those others are aborted infants or gender-confused children or when that truth pertains to lab leaks or gain-of-function funding.

When news began breaking that Collins and Fauci had intentionally used their media connections to suppress the lab leak theory, not one of these men who had incessantly accused evangelicals of hypocrisy over Trump corrected their records or asked Collins publicly about his previous statements (though Stetzer's article disappeared without comment and now lives only on Internet Archive).[56] Nor did any of them ever address revelations that Collins had, at best, misled the public about the NIH funding gain-of-function research in Wuhan.[57] They likewise said nothing after my *Daily Wire* story came out and there could no longer be any plausible deniability that they hadn't known what Collins believed or what he had taken part in.

Well, they said nothing directly.

In a March 2021 Twitter thread that was widely taken to be a response to my reporting, Keller said this:

Can Christians be leaders in publicly-owned corporations or government agencies that are committed to many non-Christian values? Some say "No." They say, "If you are the CEO of a secular space you must impose Christian moral values on all of it—or else not take the job."

I believe this is often behind the guilt-by-association attacks made at Christians[,] making them responsible for every action, program, and directive that company or agency enacts. "You allowed THAT kind of movie to be produced? How could you?"

This is short-sighted. Obviously, they can be 'salt and light' there, making those places better through their faithful presence . . . Daniel refuses to worship anyone but God (Daniel 6) and conducts his own work and life with the love, integrity, and faithfulness of a believer, but while he serves high up in the pagan hierarchy he also doesn't appear to use his power to force others beneath him to worship and obey God's law.

Joseph's career is similar. It is hard to lead and even harder to do it in secular spaces. Let's give Christians the grace to do so.[58]

In nearly every respect, Keller's argument falls apart with even a casual review of Collins's legacy and beliefs. He didn't just "allow" anti-life policies to be enacted because he had no choice. By his own admission, he pushed for more fetal tissue research when "Nebuchadnezzar" was shutting it down.[59] Hard to imagine faithful Daniel declaring himself an LGBTQ "ally" or being "proud" of launching a program that provided grant money for experimental transgender research on children. And the outrage over Collins wasn't because Christians expected a self-professed brother to "force others beneath him to obey God's law," but they *did* expect him not to support the creation of human-animal chimeras from discarded baby parts.

Exactly what part of Collins's presence did Keller find faithful? What salt and light was Collins providing in the halls of power as he not only participated in gross immorality but voiced approval for it as well? Collins's clear support for what was occurring on his watch, as well as his hubris and contempt for ordinary Americans, would become even more evident at a private event with Russell Moore in 2022.

"A Devil's Bargain"

All through his handling of Covid-19, Collins consistently maintained that his role in helping to set federal Covid policies was nonpartisan. He told NPR that he and Fauci were "not political figures," and he expressed frustration over criticism directed toward them as being driven by "a very strong political overtone."[60] Their recommendations, he insisted, were based solely on scientific data.

But a leaked audio recording I obtained after my initial report was published blew apart any claims Collins had to political neutrality.[61]

Perhaps it was because he was soon to retire and feeling relaxed that during a private forum at the University of Chicago in October 2021, Collins wandered far afield of medical opinion. He and Moore noted that they were enjoying an opportunity to speak freely because the event was not being recorded. Collins, especially, let his personal views fly. He blamed Trump for Covid-19 deaths that occurred early in the pandemic and said it was wrong for Trump to make good on promises he'd made to his evangelical supporters. He also admitted to greenlighting the University of Pittsburgh's research that relied on organs harvested from aborted infants.

Moore hosted the event on behalf of the Institute of Politics, an organization founded by senior Obama adviser David Axelrod. After Moore introduced Collins to a select group of students he described as "future elected officials, diplomats, [and] economists," Moore explained that he and his friend were there to describe the efforts they had made "separately and together to deal with evangelical resistance to the vaccine," and to discuss "some of the controversies we've had over masking and government mandates."

Though the Supreme Court would eventually hand the White House a humiliating defeat in its attempt to force employers with more than one hundred employees to mandate Covid-19 vaccinations, at the time, it was still a live issue, and Collins's convictions shifted with the political winds. Four months earlier, in a June 2021 interview with Moore, he had assured evangelical audiences that there would not be "any mandating vaccines from the U.S. government."[62] But by September 2021, the Biden administration had shifted toward an aggressive policy of coerced jabs under threat of unemployment.[63] Collins made it clear in the October seminar with Axelrod's select group of students that his views, too, had altered in support of the new agenda.

Speaking from a legal rather than a medical standpoint, Collins responded to a question regarding the wisdom of federal vaccine mandates by pointing to the 1905 Supreme Court case *Jacobson v. Massachusetts*, which had dealt with the much deadlier smallpox virus.

In a summary for the American Enterprise Institute, legal scholar Sean Trende called the ruling a "previously obscure 116-year-old precedent [that] barely warrants a footnote in most constitutional law treatises." But he noted that nonexperts had taken to citing it "whenever anyone questions the legality or constitutionality of vaccine mandates in response to the Covid-19 pandemic." Collins referenced it in just that fashion, telling the students that because of *Jacobsen*, "There's no question in my mind that the mandates are legal." (Thankfully, the Supreme Court felt differently.) He then argued that intimidation tactics should be used to motivate the resistant to take the vaccine.[64]

"The US government does have the authority to mandate vaccinations if there is an outbreak that is threatening people, because it's not just about you, it's about the people you're going to infect," Collins claimed, even though science journals were already reporting by that point that vaccinated people were just as likely to spread the then-dominant Delta variant as those who were unvaccinated.[65] Collins went on to ask rhetorically, "Do [mandates] convince people who otherwise wouldn't get them?" He gave a cynical little laugh as answered himself, "Oh yeah, especially if it means losing your job."

As evidence, he described how effective the threat of unemployment had been at persuading vaccine-hesitant NIH employees and contractors to submit. When Collins made it clear to the 2,000 out of 46,000 workers who had declined to take the jabs that they were "in serious danger of being fired in the next month if they [didn't] do something about it," Collins chuckled and said that he got a "big response."

"Reality [was] sinking in," he explained, so that even the "pretty darn resistant" elected to get vaccinated. He chuckled again. "You get the feeling that their resistance was not maybe quite that deeply seated," he said before speculating that deep down, many unvaccinated people may actually want to get the vaccine but resist doing so out of peer pressure. "They're sort of thinking to themselves, you know, maybe I really should do it, but if I do, I lose my credibility with my peeps."

Mandates, he argued, can give such individuals a way to save face because they can tell their social circle, "'Well, my employer made me do it. I didn't really want to get them.' They get, you know, bonus points, because they're now a victim. But they've also gotten the mandated vaccine that they kind of wanted anyway."

As a pastor friend put it to me at the time, there was something of the rapist's logic in Collins's argument: deep down the victim really wanted to be forced and was tacitly asking for it.

Collins felt that evangelicals were especially to blame for resistance to vaccine mandates, saying they overemphasized notions of individual liberty and had so "wrapped themselves in the flag and wrapped themselves in this concept of personal freedom, that public health just grates on them."

"[Evangelicals] have forgotten many times that freedom is not just about rights," he said. He then employed a mocking caricature of a southern accent, asking the students, "How many times have you heard, 'Muh freedom means I got rights'?"[66] The pretense he had put up in all those webinars and podcast interviews, that he was just a regular ol' average Joe evangelical himself who was simply trying to do his job without taking political sides, had completely fallen away.

Arguably the most politically pointed portion of Collins's remarks came when Moore asked for his views on his fellow Christians. Collins answered by referencing an *Atlantic* article that argued evangelicals have "embraced the worst aspects of our culture and our politics" and that "churches [have] become repositories not of grace but of grievances, places where tribal identities are reinforced, where fears are nurtured, and where aggression and nastiness are sacralized."[67]

Building on this theme, Collins claimed that the Trump administration uniquely violated norms of separation of church and state in reaching out to white, Protestant voters. "[Separation of church and state] all got pretty muddy under the Trump administration. There was clearly a heavy effort to try to build political alliances with particularly white evangelicals. And it worked," Collins said.

But in fact, former Presidents Obama and Bush both had more extensive records of relying on faith-based initiatives to support their agendas, while Trump erected new barriers to state interference with religious organizations.[68]

Then, contra his public claims of political neutrality, Collins disparaged Trump personally and evangelicals generally. "Every aspect of that President's character seems to be the opposite of what evangelical Christians would admire," he said. He called evangelicals' overwhelming support of Trump in the 2016 and 2020 elections "divisive" and a "devil's bargain" that did "great damage to the credibility of the Church," though what he felt they should have done instead—vote for Hillary Clinton and Joe Biden or not vote at all?—he didn't say.

At one point, Moore brought up Collins's work with Fauci, asking how they could have "somehow ended up the controversial figures." Collins, naturally, didn't mention his or his colleague's collusion to suppress medical viewpoints they disapproved of or their ongoing push for Covid-19 restrictions or the underwhelming success of the vaccines at stopping the spread of the virus in his answer. Instead, he replied that his and Fauci's increasing unpopularity was a result of Trump shifting blame to deflect from the massive loss of life Trump ostensibly caused in the early stages of the pandemic.[69]

"Great harm was done to the people in this nation by a very, very self-involved and misguided president in the previous administration. Hundreds of thousands of people have died who should not have had to do so," Collins told the Institute of Politics students, adding, "And so there was an effort to try to distract from that dreadful circumstance by finding somebody else to blame."

In truth, by December 2021, more Americans had died of Covid-19 under Biden's administration than Trump's, despite the fact that Biden inherited multiple vaccines and other federal infrastructure to help mitigate the spread of the virus.[70] In August 2020, near the end of Trump's tenure in office, the United States boasted an excellent case fatality ratio in comparison to other countries, ranking twenty-fourth for the percentage of deaths arising from Covid-19 cases.[71] Yet, after extensive searching, I've never been able to find any instances of Collins criticizing Biden's handling of the pandemic or placing any blame on him for Covid deaths that occurred during his presidency.

The Horns of the Dilemma

When one of Axelrod's students asked Collins about the NIH having funded the University of Pittsburgh experiments, Collins didn't deny knowing about or approving such projects. He also didn't say that he opposed abortion. Instead, he said that he was "troubled" by abortion, and he made a case for the morality and efficacy of research based on aborted tissue. "After all," he said, "pregnancy termination is, at the present time, legal in the United States. Whether you're in support of it or not, it's happened. . . . The material from those elective abortions is discarded. There are aspects of fetal tissue that can be extremely valuable in understanding how life works, how development happens, and how to treat certain diseases like Parkinson's disease, for instance."

Collins then continued to press the argument that research derived from fetal tissue could be ethical. "Which of those two choices is more ethical—discard all the tissue or use a small part? . . . Can you in fact, in some circumstances, even with actions that you consider immoral, derive something from it that might actually be moral and beneficial? That's the horns of the dilemma upon which I have been resting here for these 12 years as NIH Director . . ."

For his part, Moore gave no indication that he was not aware of Collins's background or his views that diverged sharply from those of most pro-life activists and the mainstream evangelical Christians who made up Moore's primary following. Instead, he told the student, "I don't have to agree with every Christian on everything in order to see the fruit of the Spirit in that person."

What Collins never grappled with in his sanitized discussion of "pregnancy termination" and "material" collected from abortions was how quickly black markets form in a society that commoditizes killing. He acknowledged no connection between the demand he was creating by funding such experimentation and the supply Planned Parenthood has been all too happy to offer.[72] In 2014, for example, the federal government spent $76 million on research using aborted baby parts.

Just a reminder of the cold reality of what abortion medical research bartering sounds like, this was what Dr. Deborah Nucatola, senior director of Planned Parenthood's Medical Services Department, said when she didn't know *she* was being recorded: "I'd say a lot of people want liver. And for that reason, most providers will do this case under ultrasound guidance, so they'll know where they're putting their forceps. The kind of rate-limiting step of the procedure is calvarium. Calvarium—the head—is basically the biggest part.... We've been very good at getting heart, lung, liver, because we know that, so I'm not gonna crush that part, I'm gonna basically crush below, I'm gonna crush above, and I'm gonna see if I can get it all intact."[73]

Collins was an especially successful envoy for the Biden administration, delivering messages to an audience of mostly Republican Christians who would otherwise have been reluctant to hear them. In their presentation of Collins's expertise, Moore, Stetzer, Warren, and the rest suggested that questioning his explanations as to the origins of the virus or the efficacy of masks was not simply a point of disagreement but sinful.

Former *Rolling Stone* editor and independent journalist Matt Taibbi is a well-known liberal, but he's been unflinchingly honest about the devastating loss of credibility the government has sustained due to its handling of Covid-19. "Once people see an institutional malfunction on this scale, it's like walking in on a cheating spouse, they can't unsee it," he wrote of the revelations about the lab leak cover-up. "That's what these scientists were risking when they played around with a lie this big: everything . . . [their] inability to find their consciences under pressure in the first months of 2020 might end up having lasting consequences, for society and science."[74]

The same can be said for evangelical leadership and the Church. Perhaps more than any other issue in the last decade, the pandemic crystallized for average Christians, many of whom had been feeling vague misgivings for years, how compromised the people at the top had become. And not just because of Collins.

New York City's Redeemer Presbyterian, the theologically conservative church founded by Tim Keller, segregated its church body based on vaccine status, allowing the "fully vaccinated to sit on the main floor of the sanctuary." The announcement posted to the church's website said that unvaccinated kids under sixteen would be allowed to sit with their vax-compliant parents. The unvaccinated, it said, were "welcome to sit in the balcony."[75]

It had already been established at the time that Redeemer set the segregation policy that both vaccinated and unvaccinated could transmit the virus. If it was just about science and not shaming parishioners into getting the jab, why allow unvaccinated children to sit in the vaccinated section? It was also well known by then that children got and spread Covid just as often as adults, even if it didn't make them as sick.

No one could accuse Calvary Church in Charlotte, North Carolina—one of the largest nondenominational evangelical churches in the country—of leaning left politically or theologically. Yet it announced that for the safety of preschoolers, employees in its Child Development Center would be required to get the vaccine. The memo informing employees of the policy (that a source shared with me) showed very little grace, saying, "For those who choose not to comply with the vaccine requirement and those who refuse to disclose their decision by October 8, we will consider that you have voluntarily resigned." Despite the fact that children faced extremely minimal risk from Covid-19 exposure,[76] Calvary offered no exceptions for the young, female day care teachers who made up approximately half the staff, some of whom had objections based on the new vaccine's still-unknown long-term impact on fertility and pregnancy.[77] The result of this thrown-down gauntlet? Dozens of families who relied on Calvary for childcare were left in the lurch due to caregivers who quit rather than comply.[78]

In a move even their much more liberal counterparts in the United Methodist Church resisted, in September 2021, the International Missions Board of the Southern Baptist Convention mandated vaccination for any missionary or member of a missionary family over age sixteen.[79] Protests from the many who did not want to get a new vaccine that had not gone through the typical trial process—particularly as it was well established that myocarditis was a particular risk for younger males—fell on deaf ears. (Originally, the policy included children twelve and up, until outcry prompted IMB leadership to raise the threshold.)

Then there were the downright bizarre analogies. In his *Washington Post* op-ed, Moore equated believers who got vaccinated with the friends of the paralyzed man in the Gospel of Luke who drops his bed through the ceiling by ropes. "Similarly," he argued, "evangelical Christians should join with other Americans in holding the ropes for those who are in danger of serious illness or death."[80]

What Moore's metaphor didn't grapple with was the fact that if ropes (the vaccines) were effective, the rope holders (the vaccinated) faced no additional danger from the ropeless (the unvaccinated). Nor did it address the fact that, as with breakthrough infections (which were well established at the time), having a rope in your hand wouldn't necessarily prevent you from falling through the roof onto someone else's head (i.e., spreading the virus). It just meant *you* likely wouldn't hit the ground as hard.

But Moore's tortured analogy was positively mundane compared to the biblical contortions his associate, Duke Divinity professor Curtis Chang, employed on a federally funded section of his website with the header Christians and the Vaccine. Chang, who has since co-developed the After Party (with Moore), the Bible study curriculum designed to teach Christians to be less partisan that we discussed in chapter two, argued that believers concerned about the fact that the vaccines were developed using cell lines initially derived from an abortion should view it as "an image of God's redemption."[81] Using something of the elementary school teacher's singsong cadence and exaggerated expression, Chang explained (emphasis mine):

> The Bible tells us that in His death and resurrection, Jesus redeemed human sin, the very human line . . . That is what it means to be 'made alive in Christ.' That is redemption. Now, this idea that what began in death could be reworked into life. Well, it's hard for the human mind to grasp.
>
> This is why *we need images of redemption in the world . . . Yes, the vaccine may have a distant origin story in abortion, but that past has been reworked and redeemed into something that saves life.*
>
> *We can point to the vaccine and say, 'Jesus' redemption is kind of like that.'* . . . So, my invitation to pro-life Christians who may distrust the Covid vaccine currently is this: please remember that *the Christian story is the story of redemption . . . The vaccine is ultimately a redemption story, so let's be part of that story.*

At least Moore and Chang offered positive, albeit spiritually manipulative, pressure. French played the bad cop, leveling vicious accusations at his fellow believers who, for a variety of reasons, were hesitant to get the shot. Somewhat echoing Collins's "muh freedom" line, French accused them of "pursu[ing] the 'freedom' to make their neighbors sick." "Anti-masking further exposed [their] darkness," he railed. "It's such a small thing to show love of neighbor, but that small thing was and is too much for all too many who claim to be pro-life."[82]

In a separate essay, he wrote that the only reason "white evangelicals" were resistant to getting the vaccine was because of "partisan politics" and because "millions of self-described Evangelicals don't have much clue about any of the teachings of the church."[83] Naturally, he offered no evidence that vaccine-hesitant Christians were any more political or guilty of scriptural ignorance as compared to those who were vaccine promoters.

Later, when studies began to find that the vaccinated were as infectious as the unvaccinated, French didn't bother to apologize for heaping legalistic guilt on his brothers and sisters.[84] Nor did he offer any mea culpas once major studies were unable to prove that the masks ever accomplished much of anything.[85]

During the three years that witnessed massive social upheaval, unprecedented isolation, and increasing economic uncertainty, how many non-Christians might have suddenly heard a still, small voice in the back of their minds reminding them of a long-forgotten Sunday school lesson? Perhaps a lesson about the one who offers a peace that passes understanding? And when they came to the church doors in search of balm for their bruised and battered souls, should the pastor's response to them have been "Show me your papers"? Of course, that's if they found the doors open at all.

Thank God one desperate sinner, at least, did.

In January 2022, a video of Jennifer Scott from Waterloo, Ontario, went viral. It was of her baptism. After years of living as a functional drug addict, Scott found her habit kicked into overdrive by the virus that brought society to a screeching halt. Isolated, and with the rest of life's distractions put on hold, she increased her usage, which ballooned to seven grams of cocaine a day. "I was a slave to darkness," she said. Canada's lockdown measures were even more stringent than the United States', leaving nearly all churches closed. In early 2021, as the pandemic was still in full force, Scott's son begged her to go with him to a prayer meeting at one church that was keeping its doors open in defiance of government orders. She went, and a small group prayed for her to overcome her addiction.

The pastors at Trinity Bible Chapel continued to minister to Scott.

"[They] tracked me down and called me to pray for me and to encourage me to keep coming to church. I did," she said. They then helped her find a place at a sober living facility, and she kept attending Trinity in the meantime. At the time of her baptism, she had been clean for over seven months and had moved into her own apartment. The church helped furnish it. "None of these things would have happened if Trinity closed its doors and was solely online," she explained through tears. "I know for a fact that I'd be dead right now if God had not used this church in my life."[86]

Wear your masks. Make your kids wear theirs. Shut down your churches. Take the vaccine. Shut up about your employer demanding you take a vaccine. And do it all to show you love Jesus and your neighbor. Was Jennifer Scott not our neighbor, too?

The manipulations and accusations so many in the evangelical leadership class leveled at ordinary Christians who saw debatable matters differently than they did exposed a callousness and elitism that caused deep wounds. Even their attempts at reconciliation today have been high-handed and demanding, as in a *Christianity Today* essay published in June 2023 that called for "amnesty."[87] Titled "It's Time to Forgive Each Other Our Pandemic Sins," it framed unnamed ministry leaders who promoted mask and vaccine mandates as merely mistaken, while tagging average Christians who questioned "the science" and resisted authoritarian overreach as "unwise" and "grossly insensitive."

"Some church members were a burden, not a blessing, to their spiritual leaders by turning their church's stance on Covid-19 into a litmus test of spiritual faithfulness," wrote author Paul D. Miller. He made no note of the tests the leaders required congregants to pass to prove they loved their neighbors. No passing mention of the judgment and hectoring heaped on them. Predictably, the reaction online was ferocious. As Joel Berry, managing editor of the Babylon Bee, quipped, "I can't help feeling this is like an abusive husband telling his wife to 'get over it.'"[88]

■ ■ ■

Moore, Stetzer, Keller, Warren, Wright, and many others stood by while Collins demonized and promoted discrimination against the unvaccinated, twisting the Bible to do so, while others, like David French, actively fanned flames of hatred against them. Real people were hurt by these policies. Without acknowledgment that what happened went far beyond mistakes, sentiments like Miller's are the bitterest of gall. We should all desire reconciliation after the strife Covid-19 brought into the Church. Those hurt *do* need to be willing to offer forgiveness. But a plea to sweep all that happened under the rug seems more like a bid to avoid accountability than to restore unity.

I believe if those who used their positions of influence to unjustly burden and malign other evangelicals would acknowledge the hurt they caused, they'd be surprised to discover how many of their brothers and sisters are eager to at last put away resentment and anger. These leaders acted with utmost certainty. Yet they know now that they were wrong, while those they were accusing of being unloving were right. Refusing to say so suggests they have learned nothing and would do it all over again.

CHAPTER 6

Critical Race Prophets

Here there is not Greek and Jew, circumcised and uncircumcised,
barbarian, Scythian, slave, free; but Christ is all, and in all.

—Colossians 3:11

I appeal to you, brothers, to watch out for those who cause divisions and create
obstacles contrary to the doctrine that you have been taught; avoid them.

—Romans 16:17

On June 30, 2020, Julie Bell opened up an email from the elders of her large Charlotte-area PCA church and felt a familiar weight of discouragement settle over her. It was an apology letter addressed to the entire congregation. In it, the "non-black leaders" sought forgiveness for being "blind to [their] privilege" and "complicit in perpetuating systemic racism." Though the leaders didn't have any specific prejudices or bigoted acts to confess themselves, the letter explained that this was not necessary, because racism is "more than the racist beliefs and actions of individuals. It is a system of advantage based on race. It involves cultural messages, misuse of power, and institutional bias." The non-black leaders had been passive about the "pattern of systemic racism we see in our nation," and so, they were repenting.

The letter then gave special instructions to the "non-black" members of the church, whom they were calling on to repent with them. As those in the "majority culture," they exhorted the white members to "resist defensiveness" and not to "run away" from this "hard conversation." The elders and deacons who signed the letter noted that, going forward, the church would "commit to [being] antiracist," and thus the first week of every month would be dedicated to "collectively repenting of our complicity in racism." For the nonwhite members, the church reaffirmed the importance of the "affinity groups where," they said, members with a "common cultural background" can "safely meet to grieve." In other words, in the name of repenting of racism, Christ Central Church had started racially segregating some of its gatherings.

Julie, a soft-spoken mom of two, was disturbed by what she read, but she wasn't surprised. Though the death of George Floyd a month before had precipitated this particular letter, her church had been having these "hard conversations" for about two years by then. The repenting had been pretty constant. Most of the time, Julie was fuzzy just what she was supposed to be repenting of. If this was what passivity looked like, she didn't think she could handle a more active approach.

Christ Central hadn't always been like this. Julie and her husband had been members for eighteen years, ever since they first got engaged. It had been founded by a black senior pastor and a white associate pastor. And part of what the Bells had liked about it, what had made them willing to make the thirty-minute drive there at least once a week, was that it was organically multi-ethnic, attracting a cross section of the metropolitan population.

But in 2018, that comfortable sense of community began to change. That fall, the women's ministry hosted a mini-conference with the hosts of *Truth's Table*, a religion podcast that bills itself as "for black women, by black women."[1] The key theme for this event, however—the white colonization of American Christianity—seemed targeted for a different audience: women like Julie Bell. White women. The idea that there was something deeply oppressive in her faith as she'd always practiced it upset Julie immensely, but she told me later she trusted her leaders and was committed to working on whatever spiritual issues they believed important.

"The point of the conference was that white Christians were making black Christians fit into a particular mold. So we needed to"—she paused to read from her conference notes—"decolonize discipleship from whiteness. I remember I came away feeling really guilty about that. Just really ashamed." Even as she described it to me three years later, there was still something of the confused mewl of a struck puppy to her voice.

Whatever its stated objective, that first conference definitely didn't seem to introduce a new sense of understanding or camaraderie within the women's ministry. For the first time, Julie felt timid with her black church friends and nervous to speak, for fear of offending or imposing her white preferences on them. But she assumed this was part of the "work" she was being called to do, and she pushed ahead with her leaders' plans for monthly ladies' luncheons dedicated to ongoing discussions of racism. One of the first books they would study was Robin DiAngelo's *White Fragility*, the bestseller that teaches, among other things, that "a positive white identity is an impossible goal. White identity is inherently racist; white people do not exist outside the system of white supremacy"—a Kafka trap in which saying you are not racist is proof of just how racist you are.

But Julie was committed, and she read the book diligently and tried to apply it to her life. When her husband, alarmed at some of the ideas she was beginning to espouse, picked the book up and declared it unbiblical, Julie believed this was a manifestation of *his* white fragility. "It became a real point of contention between us," she told me. "Because I was like, David, you're doing exactly what it says you would do. You're not open to seeing your unconscious bias."

Meanwhile, the women's meetings were getting harder. They were supposed to be about lament, and Julie certainly cried in many of them, but that seemed the wrong thing to do, too. A black woman she didn't know well told her, a little harshly, that black women had been crying for years and that "white women's tears" were a manipulation tactic to avoid responsibility.

Julie also couldn't help noticing that as a pre–K teacher in the Charlotte-Mecklenburg public school district, it was all very similar to the training she was going through at work, except with ill-fitting Bible verses wedged in. "I remember one Sunday we had a message from First Samuel about King David. The passage had nothing to do with race, but it was sort of forced to teach a racial lesson. It was so weird, and it just became really obvious that the pastors were making Scripture fit with, you know, the theme they wanted to preach. It just began to feel like everything—the sermons every Sunday, the book studies, the Wednesday night Bible studies, the get-together discussions—everything was just race, race, race, race."

By then, critical race theory had become enough of a public debate that David Bell believed that's what they were being taught. He and Julie scheduled a meeting with an associate pastor to share their concerns. The pastor acknowledged that, yes, the church was intentionally utilizing some lessons from CRT, but they believed it could be a useful tool if selectively applied alongside the Bible. David forcefully disagreed. "He said, 'I'm not a racist. I'm tired of being called a racist, and of my wife being called a racist,'" Julie remembered. "And he told them that he didn't see any of this stuff bringing us together. And I think that's when it hit me that we did not feel that we had sinned or that there was something on our consciences that we needed to address. And I felt like, you know, they were not leaving room for individuals to bring these things before God. It felt like our pastors were, like, trying to be the Holy Spirit for us."

Still, the Bells stayed—David because he felt a responsibility to offer some argument against what they were seeing and Julie because this had been her church family for so long. Painful as the previous two-plus years had been, she didn't want to start over.

The final straw came when the Bells received an email announcing that Christ Central had hired a new youth pastor. The Bells' oldest daughter was just going into the sixth grade and had been excited to advance from the children's ministry to the youth group. When Julie saw the announcement, she knew she would never let her go. "It listed some goals for what he wanted to accomplish with the teens and tweens, and one of them was to see the 'racism discipled out of them.'" Julie had no desire for her eleven-year-old, who had never thought it was anything but natural to have church friends of various ethnicities, to experience the guilt, shame, and tension that she and her husband had been feeling.

They left.

It's a common story by now, one that cuts across denominations. A woman from Phoenix described the misgivings she felt when her nondenominational church sent out an email for parents of kindergartners through fifth-graders offering suggestions for how they could talk to their kids about their white privilege. A couple from Illinois recalled their congregation being led in a prayer of confession for their complicity in white supremacy.

When I asked these people when this particular focus on racism had started in their churches, some mentioned racial reconciliation efforts going back decades, though they described those in positive ways. They all agreed that the much harsher teachings about power and privilege began sometime in the previous few years. None could remember hearing before 2015 any sermons or Sunday school lessons about decolonizing from whiteness. And all felt that such teaching wasn't something arising organically from specific faults within their particular church bodies. They felt it was being imposed on them from the outside.

Tool or Trojan Horse?

In August 2020, then-Southern Baptist Convention president J. D. Greear took part in a panel discussion on the subject of racism.[2] It has become rare in mainstream evangelicalism to hear in-depth theological teaching. Megachurch pastors of Greear's variety wear not suits and ties, but checked sport shirts, the sleeves rolled up at the wrist, with maybe a fleece Patagonia vest in the fall. Their sermon style tends to be similarly informal, rarely taxing attendees' attention by delving into theological terms like *soteriology* or *hypostatic*. Yet, in recent years, a new form of spiritual jargon—words like *hegemony* and *cultural representation*—has peppered their preaching. Out of the pulpit, many have taken up the same social activism that saw New York's City Hall remove its statue of Thomas Jefferson and school boards across the country rename junior highs so as to disassociate from the likes of Patrick Henry and Francis Scott Key.

National outlets like PBS and the *Washington Post* had fawned over Greear as just such an antiracist reformer. Among his highest priorities for the SBC in 2020—retiring the 150-year-old presidential gavel that had belonged to Robert E. Lee's chaplain and the founder of the first Southern Baptist seminary, John Broadus, a man Charles Spurgeon once called the "greatest of living preachers." Broadus's repudiation of slavery in 1882 (he called it "impossible to justify" and denounced it as a product of greed) and his preaching to his fellow white Southerners, "You look with incredulous contempt or horror upon the worship of many negroes. Perchance the angels have a rather poor opinion of your worship," were not enough for Greear to retain the artifact. That same year, Greear also made a heavy push to change the SBC's name to "Great Commission Baptists" as part of what the media called as a "racial reckoning" that would give the denomination a "global" identity.[3][4][5]

In this particular discussion, Greear explained that because white people had been in power for so long in the United States, the systems of law and governance they had put in place still benefit them at the expense of minorities. Civil rights reforms, he argued, have not done enough to ensure that the "scales of justice [are not] out of balance."

Greear went on to give a definition of "systemic laws" as part of his argument that racism is not primarily an issue of individuals harboring sinful bigotry in their hearts, but an all-encompassing problem throughout American life. Squinting at an iPad, he quoted this clunky academic passage:

> [It's] a system in which public policies, institutional practices, cultural representations [here Greear ad-libbed "like movies and books"] and other norms work in various, often reinforcing ways to perpetuate racial group inequity. It identifies dimensions of our history and culture that have allowed privileges associated with "whiteness" and disadvantages associated with "color" to endure and adapt over time. *Structural racism is not something that a few people or institutions choose to practice. It has been a feature of the social, economic, and political systems in which we all exist* [emphasis mine].

Greear said he was quoting political pundit David French. In fact, he either made a mistake on his source or didn't want to accurately identify it. His definition actually came from "Dismantling Structural Racism/Promoting Racial Equity," a glossary put out by the Aspen Institute, the left-leaning think tank funded by progressive grant makers like the Bill and Melinda Gates Foundation.[6] The same document is used in Ivy League schools and government DEI (diversity, equity, and inclusion) departments throughout the country.

The glossary provides a few other definitions for readers to use in their pursuit of antiracism—which, as most people know by now, is a very different thing than just being against racism. It actually requires you to embrace bias by considering race in nearly every aspect of life:

- *Racial Equity: . . . In a racially equitable society, the distribution of society's benefits and burdens would not be skewed by race . . . It demands that we pay attention not just to individual-level discrimination, but to overall social outcomes.*

- *National Values: Certain values have allowed structural racism to exist in ways that are hard to detect. This is because these national values are referred to in ways that ignore historical realities. Two examples of such national values are "personal responsibility" and "individualism" . . .*
- *White Privilege: . . . [This term] refers to whites' historical and contemporary advantages in access to quality education, decent jobs and livable wages, homeownership, retirement benefits, wealth and so on. The following quotation from a publication by Peggy Mcintosh can be helpful [for] understanding what is meant by white privilege: ". . . White privilege is an invisible package of unearned assets which I can count on cashing in every day. . . ."*

There's no denying that the term *critical race theory* has sometimes been thrown around too cavalierly and applied with too little understanding. But that was not the case with the document Greear was quoting. Whether he knew it or not, "Dismantling Structural Racism/Promoting Racial Equity" didn't just borrow from CRT; it *was* CRT, right down to citing McIntosh, an antiracism scholar who in 1989 popularized the concept of "white privilege," a key element of CRT.

The major CRT tenets are represented in the Aspen Institute glossary: Racism permeates our society's systems and institutions, and disparities between racial groups are the result of racist oppression even if no individuals are acting with racist intent. Values like punctuality are actually the dominant culture of "whiteness" maintaining its advantages. Regardless of the circumstances of their birth or upbringing, white people possess these advantages just by virtue of being white. Therefore, American life must be radically restructured, and equity of outcome must replace equality of opportunity.

I won't go into extensive exploration of CRT's well-documented roots in Marxism here.[7] But it doesn't take much study to recognize that if individualism and personal responsibility are racist, then collectivism (the Marxist political theory that prioritizes the perceived good of the group over the liberty and private property rights of the individual) is the solution to racism.

If white people are the oppressors and minorities are the oppressed, the struggle between racial groups takes the place of Marx's class struggle. And if white people gain various kinds of wealth and opportunity through their privilege, then that wealth and opportunity must be compulsorily redistributed at mass scale to achieve racial justice (equity).

If anything is directly analogous to the Soviet Comintern's successful efforts in the 1930s–1950s to smuggle socialism into American churches, CRT, which unequivocally has socialist origins and objectives, is it. It is for this reason that, as of this writing, sixteen states have blocked CRT from being used in public schools to teach that some students are more privileged or more oppressed because of the color of their skin, and twenty more are considering doing so.[8] While Greear may have been the most prominent SBC leader promoting the ideology, he was hardly alone.

In 2019, concerned over rumors that CRT had "infiltrated some Southern Baptist churches and institutions" and caused "unbiblical division," California pastor and U.S. Army Reserve chaplain Stephen Feinstein submitted a resolution for the denomination's annual convention.[9] His intent was to give delegates from local churches all around the country the opportunity to vote to reject CRT because it was "founded upon unbiblical presuppositions descended from Marxist theories" and "inherently opposed to the Scriptures as the true center of Christian union."

But the SBC's process allows a committee to amend submissions before they're put to a vote. When the committee, which included at least three SBC seminary professors, had finished amending Feinstein's resolution, it had completely transformed the wording. Instead of asking the delegates to reject CRT, it prompted them to *approve* it as an "analytical tool that explain[s] how race has and continues to function in society." So long as its use was "subordinate to Scripture," the new resolution said, CRT could "aid in evaluating a variety of human experiences."

At the time, few non-academics had much understanding of CRT, and the committee's new resolution stressed that "evangelical scholars who affirm the authority and sufficiency of Scripture have employed selective insights from critical race theory." In other words, the committee's version of Feinstein's resolution, in direct opposition to the original, reassured the delegates that CRT could be valuable. Yet their rewrite included none of the condemnatory language the original had. There was no mention of Marxism, no mention of "unbiblical presuppositions." Anything in CRT that contradicts Scripture was put down to *"appropriation by individuals with worldviews that are contrary to the Christian faith"* [emphasis mine].

This last claim regarding "appropriation" was either supremely mistaken or supremely dishonest, given that when they developed critical race theory, Richard Delgado and Jean Stefancic were transparent about being confirmed Marxists and that CRT was an outgrowth of Marx's conflict theory.[10] Their purpose, as they explained very clearly in their foundational text, *Critical Race Theory: An Introduction*, was to create a new "theory of civil rights" that would be incorporated into virtually unlimited disciplines, including theology.[11] But the SBC delegates were given zero information about this background.

With such "unbalanced scales" (to borrow from Greear), little wonder the resolution passed.

Theologian Owen Strachan, then director for the Center for Public Theology at the Midwestern Baptist Theological Seminary, was there for the vote and told me he doubted the delegates (mostly ordinary working folks visiting from their rural and suburban home churches) had any idea what they had passed. "It's not easy to understand these issues in a full semester of discussing them. You know, different kinds of terminology that we consider and address alone." He blew out an exasperated breath and continued: "On the floor of the convention, in front of thousands of people, trying to sort things out as the session's nearly over—I think tons of people were confused over what was happening."

If the committee hadn't framed CRT as a positive tool, Strachan had little doubt the voters would have rejected it.

Feinstein, who was commendably charitable, agreed that the redraft caused confusion, but he told me he later went to the members of the committee to find out what had happened and came away convinced that they weren't trying to undermine his intentions. He believed they were only trying to explain an issue that was becoming a hot cultural topic. He doubted they would have addressed CRT at all if he hadn't submitted the resolution.

This raises a question, though: If the committee felt the concept of CRT was so unfamiliar that it required them to almost entirely rewrite Feinstein's resolution, why not simply choose not to bring it forward for a floor vote, something they had every right to do and had frequently done in the past? When I asked this of committee co-chair and SBC seminary professor Keith Whitfield a short time after the vote, he said it was because they had "taken note of where we are culturally" and admitted that they thought they needed to "address [only] the application of the ideas, not the origination of the ideas." They had brought the amended resolution forward, he told me, because they wanted to help pastors and ministry leaders evaluate *how* to use it, not *whether* to use it.

A Christian philosophy professor at the denomination's flagship seminary, Southern Baptist Theological Seminary, who had previously served on the resolutions committee, thought there was another reason they chose to rewrite Feinstein's resolution and bring it to the floor for a vote. He alleged that it was meant to provide cover for SBC professors who were already teaching CRT.

"Some folks are pretty keen on [CRT], and they've been catching heat (well-deserved in my opinion)," Dr. Mark Coppenger wrote on Facebook. "So, they managed to craft a long resolution to provide some cover and leverage. A good many [delegates] had little or no idea of what was going on but they didn't want to be difficult. So they went along."[12]

And that, Strachan told me, was a very bad idea, because CRT is not a neutral ideology. "It is no more an analytical tool in a positive sense than Marxism or nihilism or existentialism or any non-Christian worldview is," he said. "Are there fragments and elements of the truth in many different worldviews? Yes, there are. Critical race theory looks at a real problem, the problem of racial division, ethnic division in our society, and it posits a solution . . . [But] in terms of how it understands the human condition and the solution that it posits, neither is Christian."

Where Christianity teaches that mankind's greatest need is salvation from his sin, CRT teaches that it is power over his oppressors. The two groups in CRT are not, as in the Bible, sinners and saints, but victims and oppressors. CRT encourages collective grievance in the first group and collective guilt in the second, without ever dealing with the individual heart. Rather than embracing unity through Christ, it encourages division through ethnicity, pitting groups against one another. Rather than goodwill, it instills suspicion and bitterness, encouraging its devotees to read bias and secret aggression where none may have been intended. Dr. Gerald McDermott, the Anglican chair of divinity at Samford University's Beeson Divinity School, rightly called it a "new religion" that "encourages people to practice what Jesus condemned, judgment of another person's thinking and character . . . This is racism by another name. It is also sinful judgment."[13]

Yet these very unchristian ideas have been echoing all across evangelicalism over the last several years. Matt Chandler, the dynamic, youthful-looking megachurch pastor and head of the enormously influential Acts 29 church-planting network, was an early adopter. His 2017 video on "How to Understand and Address White Privilege" drew on McIntosh's original definition (the one reprinted in the Aspen glossary) almost to the point of plagiarism. "I have grown up with this invisible bag of privilege," Chandler said, "a kind of invisible tool kit that I can reach in there [sic] at any given moment and have this type of privilege . . . White privilege isn't overt racism. Instead, it's just this unique kind of experience of life and predominant culture."[14]

In 2019, Pastor Bryan Loritts, board member at Biola University and vice president for the Send Network, another major church-planting ministry, cited How to Be an Antiracist author Ibram X. Kendi at a conference for the Council for Christian Colleges and Universities. One the most prominent prophets of CRT today, Kendi has argued that the "job" of Christians should not be to "bring [sinners] into the church . . . and heal them and save them" but to "revolutionize society . . . to liberate society from the powers on Earth that are oppressing humanity." Quite a contrast from "My kingdom is not of this world" (John 18:36) and "Go ye therefore and make disciples" (Matthew 28:19).

"Antiracists," Kendi has said, "fundamentally reject Savior theology."[15]

Kendi's embrace of liberation theology, which mainstream evangelicalism has long acknowledged to be both heretical and Marxist,[16] hadn't stopped Loritts from recommending his work in various places for years by the time of his CCCU speech, so there was little doubt he was well familiar with it.[17] Yet Loritts offered no caveats when he endorsed Kendi. "He argues in his book that the opposite of racist is not, 'I'm not racist.' That's not the opposite. That's neutral passivity," he told the conference. "The opposite of racist is anti-racist." The "Christian worldview," he added, holds that commitment to antiracism is an "indicator light of the Gospel," suggesting that those who subscribe to the biblical model of showing no partiality to any group, no matter their color (Leviticus 19:15, Galatians 3:28, James 2:9), should question whether they're even in the faith.[18]

A year after making this speech, Loritts would take a position as the teaching pastor at Greear's church.

Racial Ed

Loritts had plenty of help in encouraging Christian colleges to embrace CRT and the antiracist movement. Following George Floyd's death, evangelical campuses quickly began to catch up to their secular counterparts. In June 2020, Azusa Pacific University, long trusted as doctrinally conservative, sent out a notice to teachers asking them to make a "commitment to read, watch, or listen [to]" resources on "Allyship and Anti-racism." The recommendations read like an enthusiastic endorsement of CRT, including radical texts from Kendi, DiAngelo, and the *New York Times*'s revisionist history series "The 1619 Project," which posits that every aspect of the American founding was steeped in racism.[19] As Rod Dreher noted in *The American Conservative*, "If this were a list at a secular university, it would still [have been] startlingly unbalanced."[20]

Linda Livingstone, president of Baylor University, a Baptist school, followed suit with a letter commending "5 Tips to Cultivate Cultural Humility and Antiracism," from the school's associate dean for diversity, equity, and inclusion.[21] If one were setting out to create a parody of CRT propaganda, her suggestions wouldn't have looked much different.[22] She recommended that recipients familiarize themselves with a list of characteristics that demonstrate a "white supremacy" culture, which included having a sense of urgency, engaging in logical thinking, and for some inexplicable reason, writing memos.[23] (One wonders how the suggestion that the written word is more taxing for black people than white is not racist.)

Not to be outdone, in 2021 Billy Graham's alma mater, Wheaton, held a racially segregated graduation ceremony for minority students,[24] calling it a "Racial and Cultural Minority Senior Recognition Ceremony."[25] It also removed a nearly seventy-year-old plaque honoring one of its most famous sons, Jim Elliot, a 1950s missionary who was martyred while witnessing to an Ecuadorean tribe, because the inscription described his murderers as "savage."[26]

Even the small-town Pennsylvania Grove City College, known as one of the most theologically and politically conservative religious schools in the country, became a CRT battleground. Many GCC parents and alumni were surprised in 2020 when they heard that the president's office was launching a diversity council, given that the famously independent school accepts no federal funding, so it need never wriggle under the thumb of Uncle Sam's ever-expanding discrimination regulations. That surprise turned to alarm when they discovered what developments were emerging from that council. Students were coming home describing resident assistant training that sounded, as parent Scott Klusendorf (himself an author and educator) put it to me, like "racial struggle sessions," with the director and his wife pressuring students to admit their inner racism and white guilt.

A chapel series on racial justice included[27] antiracist scholar and Kendi protégé Jemar Tisby, who contended in the *New York Times* that "white Christians have to face the possibility that everything they have learned about [their] faith has been designed to explicitly or implicitly reinforce a racist structure."[28] Tisby's sermon under the stained glass of Grove City's vaulted chapel followed much the same theme and was not just activist but political in nature. "Freedom, justice, and democracy, especially for black people and other people of color, are in imminent danger," he thundered from behind the hand-carved pulpit, his words reverberating off the stone walls with ecclesiastical solemnity. He finished by exhorting the students not to "refuse to get involved in the struggle," not to be "white moderates." "What if God brought you to this college at this time and this place in an election year to demonstrate courage to fight against racism?" he asked.

The problem, as one professor told me, wasn't hosting a talk by Tisby. That would have been fine in the context of a classroom, where his ideas could have been cross-examined. It was that the ideas he and similar speakers for the series presented were delivered in the chapel, where they carried the imperative of religious instruction. Nor were any speakers with different views on how Christians should pursue racial justice ever invited.

The real tipping point came when the education department introduced a new course titled Cultural Diversity and Advocacy, which promised to teach students "how to become actively antiracist." The course was advertised around campus with posters showing raised black Power fists, and the reading listed in the syllabus, including Kendi and DiAngelo, consisted entirely of antiracist texts. On top of that, the final exam required students to create a racial reconciliation community project, with the express hope that they would carry the projects out, putting the class in the realm of activism, not scholarship.

Several faculty members I spoke to felt the course endangered Grove City College's reputation for high academic and intellectual standards. "Those are kind of pop texts, rather than scholarly argumentative texts," one told me. "But if you look at Grove City's mission, it talks about 'examining texts of enduring values.' Well, a *New York Times* bestseller published in 2019 does not fit that bill to me!"

Klusendorf was bewildered that GCC would have felt the need to jump on a secular bandwagon of diversity councils and CRT-driven training in the first place. "If the council [was] simply wanting to figure out how to help minority students feel welcome on campus, you can do that without the campus embracing critical race theory," he said. "You don't have to talk about white privilege and intrinsic racism. You can [do that] in a targeted way within a biblical worldview."

But while the Christian colleges and universities that began adopting worldly trends of antiracism, DEI departments, and CRT-led policies were legion after 2015, GCC may have been the only school to significantly course-correct and own the mistakes publicly. After a petition circulated by concerned parents and alumni drew significant media attention, the board of trustees initiated an investigation.[29] They would later acknowledge that inviting Tisby had been a mistake, that the RA training did include inappropriate race-based activism, and that the education course did promote CRT, which the board said the school unequivocally rejects.[30]

It is one thing, though, when individual Christian schools embrace CRT, but quite another when an extensive evangelical ministry, welcomed on just about every campus across the country, does so in the name of Christ.

Once upon a time, the organization established in 1951 as Campus Crusade for Christ inspired hope for the future of evangelical Christianity, as thousands, if not millions, of students were saved thanks to its ministry. Cru, as it became known in 2011, eventually grew to 19,000 staffers in 190 countries, one of the most successful evangelistic efforts in history.

In November 2020, however, a group of whistleblowers came forward alleging that the organization had drifted away from the Great Commission it had always zealously pursued in favor of "an agenda of social justice, liberal theology, and CRT." A 179-page report presented detailed and well-documented evidence that Cru had begun importing CRT-derived teachings in 2015, "embracing a secular system of ideas that divides humanity into victims or oppressors."[31]

Events in the report sound disturbingly similar to what Julie Bell experienced in her Charlotte church. During a 2019 seminar, it said "one Cru national leader was recorded 'shaming' a fellow staff woman to tears because she benefited from white privilege." In one reprinted letter, a couple who had worked with Cru for more than thirty years said they finally decided to leave after attending a conference in which a speaker enjoined them to "stand, hold hands, and repent/lament of our racism (whether we have been racist or not)."

"The accusations made about white privilege are often nothing more than veiled racism," said one longtime prison ministry worker. "We are being judged because of the color of our skin. . . . With this brand of social justice, I'm just an old white man, which gives me no right to speak out at all."

The aspect of the report that drew the most headlines, however, was a secretive training program called Lenses. In CRT, a lens is commonly used as an analogy, referring to interpreting culture and history through an entirely racialized paradigm, and you will often hear Bible teachers who have been imbibing vast doses of CRT literature refer to lenses.[32]

The ostensible purpose of Cru's five-day Lenses immersion program was developing "cultural competency," but staffers said it operated more like a reeducation camp. According to the report, "staff [were] required to disclose nothing about the teaching content outside of the training. Independent thinking [was] discouraged." Assigned and recommended reading included, once again, Kendi and DiAngelo. As to the training itself, attendees said it "involved shaming most of the majority culture in the room. . . . Ethnic minorities are encouraged to view themselves as the 'oppressed' and whites are automatically defined as the 'oppressors.' . . . There is no practical path for unity. . . . I left the training with a tremendous amount of guilt and no way to deal with the blame that was heaped on me just for being in the white majority."

Cru said it shut down the Lenses program in 2021 due to the "toxic" climate, but some staffers have told me morale is still low and that there's lingering wariness among coworkers.

Even more alarming than Cru—with all its access to Christian higher education—are the seminaries that train pastors and ministry leaders in CRT, so that they will then teach it to their congregations, employees, and volunteers. No one would be surprised to find antiracist activism at those seminaries that are outright liberal and graduating outright liberals (Duke Divinity) or even soft progressives (Fuller). But what about the system of seminaries recognized as the most theologically conservative in the United States that also just so happens to educate the plurality of Protestants who go into ministry work? Surely, they would have avoided this worldly bandwagon, wouldn't they? Unfortunately not.

The Southern Baptist Theological Seminary is the second largest seminary in the country, only recently losing the title of number one to Liberty's Rawlings School of Divinity. Though its president, Dr. Albert Mohler, along with the other five SBC seminary presidents, signed a statement in late 2020 repudiating CRT as unbiblical, the move came only after widespread outcry from the rank and file.[33] But even now that Mohler and his fellow SBC seminary presidents have waved off the CRT smoke, there's no question the fire was real.

Though average Southern Baptists may have been confused about what CRT was when they voted for it at the behest of their leaders at the annual convention in the summer of 2019, by the fall of 2020, like many Americans, they had a much clearer picture of what the ideology taught. And they didn't like it. When word got out that Dr. Jarvis Williams, a New Testament professor at SBTS, had, during an interview with *The Gospel Coalition* a few years before, recommended *Critical Race Theory: An Introduction* as the book "every evangelical should read," it raised a few eyebrows.[34] But that didn't necessarily mean he was endorsing CRT as it is generally a good idea for Bible teachers to stay abreast of the major ideologies impacting culture. Then social media users unearthed a 2018 video of Williams, wearing a shirt with the SBTS logo, insisting that seminaries needed to decolonize their theology curriculum from whiteness. It left no question that he *was* teaching major tenets of CRT.[35]

"White supremacy is an ideological construct that believes that whiteness is superior to non-whiteness. How this shows up in part is in curriculum," Williams said in the clip, which came from a conference at pastor John Piper's Bethlehem College and Seminary. He then argued that "whiteness becomes the standard by which all good theology is judged, so that if it's right theology, it is written by a white scholar, who is conceptualizing that theology for white audiences." Williams offered no examples of which theologians, pastors, or seminaries were guilty of doing this or what characterizes theology that has been conceptualized for white people. But he argued that not having a "regular requirement of black and brown authors" is a form of white supremacy. Though they could not be just any black and brown authors, Williams said. They had to be those who have proven they haven't been "colonized to whiteness." We have to ask, what constitutes a colonized minority theologian? A penchant for the Puritans, a reliance on five-point Calvinism, publication of a bestselling anti-CRT book like black theologian Dr. Voddie Baucham? Again, Williams didn't say. Yet like the pastors at Julie Bell's Presbyterian church, he was unequivocal in characterizing "whiteness" as a form of unrighteousness in need of repentance:

That, in part, is the way in which white supremacy works in a socially sophisticated way. When you have whiteness as the priority . . . to privilege that whiteness, and then to require those who are non-white to culturally colonize to whiteness, the solution is not more black and brown faces in white spaces who are colonized to whiteness. The solution is fundamentally—yes, the Gospel, the cross, the resurrection, and the blood of Jesus—but also dethroning white supremacy in all of the forms in which it shows up in Christians spaces, folks.

Leaving aside the circular nature of Williams's argument—whiteness is bad because it colonizes, and the way you know it colonizes is because of its whiteness—it came perilously close to putting "dethroning white supremacy" on par with the sanctifying work of the Cross in terms of resolving the sin of racism. So, it was hardly surprising that it sparked some backlash that left SBC seminaries rushing to quash rumors of CRT peddling, especially because it wasn't an isolated incident.

Soon, other videos turned up of Williams making comments like "whiteness isn't about your biology but your ideology," a common CRT slogan.[36] Theoretically, this separating of whiteness from actual skin shade could offer an escape hatch from race-based guilt for those whites willing to embrace CRT's Marx-based redistributive ideology. But other SBTS faculty and administrators, who were likewise espousing CRT tenets and making similar (or, in the case of the biology-ideology rhyme, identical) comments, demonstrated that there was no escaping blame for whiteness.

Then-provost Matt Hall insisted, in the vein of DiAngelo's *White Fragility*, that all white people are guilty of intrinsic racism, including him.

During a 2018 interview that began to get attention after the 2019 CRT convention vote, Hall confessed, "Guess what, I am [a racist]. I'm going to struggle with racism and white supremacy until the day I die and get my glorified body and a completely renewed and sanctified mind. Because I'm immersed in a culture where I benefit from racism all the time."[37] Similar remarks he made during a 2019 presentation offered no more clarification, but he reiterated his position that white Americans suffer from an irremovable stain of racism that will not be alleviated this side of Heaven.[38]

Scripture, of course, knows nothing of particular classes of sin from which there is no freedom or repentance. Either Hall was saying that God is not capable, as He promises in 1 John 1:9, of cleansing us from all unrighteousness, or that racism is not really unrighteousness.

Again, it's important to remember that in the case of SBTS, we are not talking about one rogue professor, but the seminary's chief academic officer. In yet a third interview on the subject, held at his own school, Hall gave the textbook CRT definition of racism, calling it a "system built upon allocating privileges, power, and opportunities in inequitable ways." In that same panel, one of Hall's colleagues commented that what he especially appreciates about him is that he is "well versed in critical race theory."[39] One wonders if Hall's new colleagues at Biola University, where he is now the Chief Academic Officer, are similarly appreciative of his commitment to CRT.

■ ■ ■

In recent years, entertainment companies like CBS and Disney, as well as Fortune 500 corporations and even the NASDAQ, have instituted diversity mandates as part of a bid to redistribute wealth and opportunities and address America's structural inequities.[40] Far from differentiating themselves from secular culture in this regard, much of evangelical academia has hurried to keep pace with it. In 2013, Southeastern Baptist Theological Seminary, a sister school of SBTS, launched a similar initiative with a spiritual twist, called Kingdom Diversity.[41] Instead of setting identity-based quotas on acting parts or board seats, SEBTS pledged to make a certain percentage of faculty hires and scholarship awards based on race and gender. But whatever other aims, stated or unstated, this program has had, it also soon began to proselytize for CRT.

In a six-part series titled "Is Critical Race Theory 'UnChristian [sic],'" published on the dedicated Kingdom Diversity website, associate dean and English professor Matt Mullins not only answered "no," but also unequivocally extolled the virtues of the ideology.

He began, in Part 1, by either dishonestly or ignorantly suggesting that critics connect it to Marxism only to "[accuse] people of exchanging the gospel of Jesus Christ for a commitment to solving social problems . . ."[42] At no point in any of the six parts did he acknowledge that CRT arose from the Frankfurt School's critical theory, a new social application of Marx's conflict theory. The history is much more in-depth and complex, of course, but Mullins didn't even pretend to allude to it.

Calling CRT "just a theory" (which minimized its overtly activist aims), he said its purpose was to "call attention to and redress the subtler forms of racism that replaced the overt racism made largely unacceptable by the civil rights movement of the 1950s and 1960s." What decent person wouldn't sign on to that? He never mentioned that its method of "redress" was, as Kendi has explicitly stated, to replace our capitalist system with a more socialist one. "Capitalism is essentially racist; racism is essentially capitalist," Kendi, whose ideas are broadly representative of CRT proponents, has said.

Of CRT's founders, in Part 2, Mullins said only that Delgado and Stefancic's work was a "natural reaction to the aftermath of the Civil Rights

Movement of the 1960s." And he insisted that Christians associating it with "something bad ... suggest[s] that CRT must not be well understood in evangelical circles."[43] That is, if some Christians think it harmful and unbiblical, it is only because they don't really know what it is.

Mullins then spent three installments covering the basics of CRT, but with a rose-colored, grade-school-level tone. "Racism is ordinary," he wrote. "It's just the normal, everyday order of things." Most unintentionally amusing was his Part 5 list of just what it was that critical race theorists did. Painting them as something of a cross between Mother Teresa and Atticus Finch, he said they merely wanted to do things like "[tell] a more complete story of United States history" and "advocate for voting rights." He even offered Black Lives Matter as a positive example of CRT activism.[44]

In the conclusion, Mullins revealed what had no doubt been clear to his readers all along—that he's a fan of CRT and believes it "provides Christians with helpful lenses through which to view the problem of racism." As to his main question, he noted that because CRT didn't adhere to "doctrines of sin and salvation," it was "not *strictly* Christian" [emphasis mine]. But, he added, "neither is a strong belief in the free market." He finished by recommending that Christians "take what is beneficial from CRT and discard what is not," which, by then, really didn't include anything. In Mullins' presentation, it was all beneficial.[45]

It's important to remember that this series on CRT was not on Mullins's personal blog or class page, nor was it merely one of several CRT views offered by SEBTS. It was the *only* uncontested view presented by the seminary's Kingdom Diversity program, which came with the imprimatur of a righteous DEI cause. It took pride of place on a landing page for press releases and boilerplate pitches to prospective students, not a page of resources for scholarly debate.

Somehow the school's president, Danny Akin, managed to maintain a straight face when he insisted after this with "crystal clear clarity", "We do not advocate at Southeastern Seminary Critical Race Theory." He went on to say, "There's a difference between advocating something and educating you about something," and yet, the in-depth article series was so *un*educational that it included no information about the ideas that gave rise to CRT,[46] no background on its progenitors, and no serious critique of CRT from either a

Christian or a secular perspective, though volumes upon volumes have been written on the subject. The series was, at best, grossly ill-informed and, at worst, propagandistic, something Akin or someone else at Southeastern apparently realized, as the articles later disappeared from the website and live today only on Internet Archive.

It's worth mentioning that Mullins was using CRT as the "lens" for at least one of his English classes as well. A leaked syllabus for his Multiethnic Literature of the United States course stated that the class would be exclusively focused on "the interdisciplinary fields of Critical Race Theory, whiteness studies, and ethnic studies to consider how these theoretical frameworks might add dimensions to [students'] reading of literature." The texts included Delgado and Stefancic's foundational work, along with a series of novels by minority authors. The syllabus included no texts critical of CRT.[47]

■ ■ ■

As I've noted, this is not a book of political or theological argument. But you don't have to read more than a couple of paragraphs of serious CRT critiques to strongly question if not explode Mullins's premise that "on the structural level, racism has produced dramatic inequalities in our society that will not disappear even if everyone begins to love each other."

As the highly respected black economist Thomas Sowell points out in *Discrimination and Disparities*, while we can all feel righteous anger at the racial discrimination of America's past, the idea that it must be the cause of racial disparities today is often belied by the evidence. Just one data point: the black poverty rate fell from 87 percent in 1940 to 47 percent in 1960, even while Jim Crow, redlining, and other racist policies still held sway. After the Johnson administration began to address inequities through its vast welfare expansion specifically targeted toward black communities, the growth was much slower. "There was a far more modest subsequent decline in the poverty rate among blacks after the [Johnson's] massive 'war on poverty' programs began," Sowell writes.[48]

As for how to address racial disparities today, Sowell highlights one institution that CRT proponents like Greear, Mullins, and Hall rarely (if ever) discuss in relation to black well-being: marriage. While the poverty rate for blacks overall is high, for black married couples, it's a very low 7.5 percent—3.5 percent *lower* than for whites as a whole. "Apparently," Sowell concludes, "individual lifestyle choices have major consequences for both blacks and whites."[49] The white-versus-black marriage gap sits at about 30 points right now.[50] If equity across races is what these churchmen are really committed to, why not launch programs to encourage marriage across demographics, but especially in those communities where the institution is most imperiled? Of course, that would mean having to stake out culturally unpopular positions rather than marrying Christianity to trendy Marxism in racial reconciliation's clothing.

Perhaps if their promotion of this brutal, unforgiving, and divisive new religion were at least limited to their church staffs, the cost would be theirs alone to bear. But just as in secular academia and the corporate world, these leaders have demanded that real, ordinary people in the pews pay devastating prices to indulge their fashionable preoccupations.

Quotas and Their Discontents

In 2018, Akin argued in an ERLC video that ministry heads may "need to be willing to surrender leadership" to black candidates "if we're really going to make progress."[51] (He has never, notably, offered to resign under these conditions himself.) That same year, Chandler said that he had told a church hiring firm if they brought him an "Anglo" candidate ranked as an eight out of ten and an African American candidate ranked as a seven, he would hire the African American as a way for white church culture to "give power away."[52] He also told the white people in the audience that if they had black friends who disagreed with that approach to addressing racism, it was probably because "that African American [is] trying to win approval or position."

Greear, however, as president of the SBC, was in the best position to fundamentally transform American evangelicalism with a DEI-based hiring philosophy. In May 2019, he delivered a sermon in which he outlined one of his tasks as the national leader of the denomination: appointing people to committees who make further appointments that "end up shaping the institutions," (those institutions being the SBC seminaries that educate a plurality of pastors of all Protestant denominations; the North American

Mission Board that plants churches, provides pastoral training, and supplies chaplains all across the U.S.; and the International Mission Board that sends American missionaries throughout the world). Greear noted with some pride that he took pains to ensure that "two thirds of them [were] either women or they [were] people of color" because "we need their wisdom."[53]

There are many wise black pastors and women in positions of influence from whom the church benefits, of course, but Greear (in contradiction to Galatians 3:28 and Romans 2:11) was suggesting they had a special wisdom *because* they were black or *because* they were women. Theologian Voddie Baucham, himself black, addressed this well with his coinage of the term *ethnic Gnosticism.* "[It] is the idea that people have special knowledge based solely on their ethnicity," he wrote in *Fault Lines,*[54] a book on CRT's devastating impact on the Church.

But give Greear this much—his were no empty words.

Six months after he made this speech, a disturbing headline ran in the Religion News Service, a wire service used by a number of secular news outlets, including the *Washington Post* and the Associated Press. It read, "Southern Baptist Church: Racial Prejudice a Factor in Rejection of Black Pastor."[55] The source of this acknowledgment was a leaked letter from First Baptist Church Naples's pastoral staff. Someone had passed it along to Southern Baptist blogger Ben Cole, a political operative whose past activities included running interference for disgraced former congressman Aaron Schock (R-IL) just before Schock was ousted from office in 2015 for spending one hundred thousand dollars in public funds to decorate his office like Downton Abbey.[56]

It was an alarming allegation, especially as this was not just any church. FBC Naples was Chuck Colson's church. Colson, Richard Nixon's onetime "hatchet man," went to prison over his role in Watergate and emerged a saved sinner who would go on to become one of the most influential Christian thinkers of the modern era, beloved for his prison ministry.

Curiously, for a wire service regularly utilized by the ostensible best and brightest papers in the country, RNS's story did not include any details of the racism—no examples, just the fact of it. And the fact was this: Some members of the church had chosen not to vote for a black candidate named Marcus Hayes to replace the recently retired senior pastor. This had prevented

Hayes from meeting the 85 percent threshold necessary to get the job. The leaders of the church, as detailed in the leaked email, announced that a "portion of the 19% that voted against Marcus Hayes did so based on racial prejudices." It then called on "anyone who took part in such divisive and sinful actions to immediately confess and repent."

Strong condemnation indeed.

What did these racists have to say for themselves? Religion News Service didn't say. In fact, its reporter didn't even mention asking them. The only sources she quoted were SBC leaders angry about the racism. Former SBC president and Texas megachurch pastor Jack Graham accused the church members of slander and lies, along with racism, but RNS apparently didn't press for any particulars about what the slander or lies were, because Graham didn't offer any. He simply said, "You can only conclude that sin, in effect, disrupted this whole process and the call of a good and godly man to be the pastor."

Normally, a story like this would have been catnip for secular outlets, particularly the *Washington Post*, which not only covers the SBC extensively, but has a particular fondness for Baptist scandals. Yet the *Post* must not have been interested. No outlets of note picked up the story. Two days after RNS published it, the SBC's house organ, *Baptist Press*, boosted the story again, with an article on an open letter the pastoral staff had released addressing the "disgruntled people" whose "racial prejudices" had "exposed a sickness" and "cancer" within the First Baptist Church Naples.[57]

It is curious that while the story mentioned that the racism had been introduced to the voting process through social media, texting, and emails, *Baptist Press* failed to provide any records from this long digital trail. Nor were First Baptist's remaining pastoral staff willing to offer them to any other news outlets. *Christianity Today*'s coverage noted that "First Baptist declined to share further details about its allegation of racism," which seemed rather incongruent with its efforts to ensure that as much of the public as possible heard about them. The *Naples Daily News* wasn't able to obtain any specifics, either. First Baptist told its reporter that "it would not be proper for us to share that content openly even though it had certainly shared the accusations readily enough."[58] When asked for details on the racist messages, Hayes himself also failed to return journalists' calls.

But lack of evidence didn't stop Greear and other big names and influential leaders from trumpeting the "bold gospel-witness" of the open letter condemning these holdouts for their bigotry. Greear shared the letter with his one hundred and fourteen thousand Twitter followers, calling for his denomination to "lament that any vestige of this kind of sinful prejudice remains in our churches." Dwight McKissic, a prominent black SBC pastor, tweeted out his thanks to the church for "amputating the racists." Akin went the positive route, calling the letter a "strong and redemptive word." Hall shared it with the comment "Sin flourishes in the dark."[59] Future SBC president Bart Barber, who was at that point a trustee in one of the seminaries, advised the church to kick the "miscreants" out and hold the vote again.[60]

In short, an awful lot of high-profile men in the SBC wanted to make sure everyone was aware that racists had thwarted the hiring of a black pastor. Following Barber's advice, the church did indeed kick the miscreants out. There then commenced a lot of self-congratulating among Southern Baptist pastors on social media for a job well done moving on from the racists.

The "racists," as it turned out, were happy to tell their side of the story and provide records.

Bob Caudill his wife, Katy, both in their eighties, were members of First Baptist Naples for thirty years, during most of which Bob served as a deacon. He was appointed to the pastoral search team after their pastor, Hayes Wicker, made plans to retire. During his years shepherding the church, Wicker (who several former members told me has a passive, trusting demeanor) grew FBC Naples into one of the largest and most prosperous congregations in the denomination. Naturally, he expected his staff pastors, a number of whom were relatively recent hires who came recommended by national SBC executives, to consider his input on his replacement. He was wrong. The well-connected staff pastors brought in Auxano, a church consulting firm whose founder also happens to serve as a director of the SBC's national publisher, Lifeway. Auxano advised against Wicker's involvement in the pastoral search. In short order, Wicker was banned from the process and then, in a move that shocked everyone, forced out of the door earlier than he had wanted to go.

Bob Caudill and a group of about eight hundred other members were alarmed by this treatment, so, in accordance with the church's bylaws, they petitioned the church's remaining leadership for a business meeting to address what had happened. Not only was this special meeting not granted, but other planned meetings were canceled. When Caudill objected, he was removed from both the pastoral search team and his deacon role. A new search team was constituted, consisting of those aligned with the effort to push Wicker out. None of this, a number of the dissident group's members told me, was done in accordance with the church's bylaws. As one of the members put it, "It was like they were executing a hostile takeover of our church."

A lot of complex infighting was going on, to be sure, but none of it hinged on race, and feelings were running high by the time the new pastoral search committee all but announced that it had hired the next pastor and would introduce him to the congregation in two weeks. When the time came, Marcus Hayes was presented with unprecedented fanfare. A special recommendation letter from Greear was read aloud from the stage. In it, Greear introduced himself as SBC president and said that it was "with great joy" that he commended Hayes to First Baptist Naples; he particularly cited Hayes's service as a former member of the SBC's executive committee. As if that weren't enough, before Hayes came out, national SBC leaders acted as hype men in a specially produced video.

"Hey, Naples family! This is Kevin Ezell, president of the North American Mission Board," chirped one of the most powerful and feared men in the SBC. His winning smile flashed through filtered light on the giant LED screens, and he spoke vigorously with his hands in classic C-suite style as he said of Hayes, "He genuinely cares and relates to all ages! You have been very blessed by God that He sent you a guy like Marcus Hayes!"

Interspliced with footage of Ezell was that of self-help author and Nashville megachurch pastor Robby Gallaty, whose edgy, MMA vibe balanced out Ezell's corporate sport coat pitch. Sitting in front of a shiplap backdrop, Gallaty, his body builder biceps straining the bounds of his striped polo sleeves, beamed through a pointed goatee: "It is a privilege of mine to be able to recommend my friend Marcus Hayes!"

Much of the church was dazzled by this production from what one called "the beautiful people of the SBC," but dissident members of First Baptist Naples were nonplussed. "We didn't know who J. D. Greear was, for the most part," Teri, another member who would later be excommunicated told me.

"We just thought, *If you say he's the president of the Southern Baptist Convention, that's probably a big deal, right?* But that's not how Southern Baptists do things. It felt like it was being dictated from on high who our pastor would be. I had never heard of anything like that."

Few Southern Baptists would have. The SBC's casual, independent association is part of what allowed it to become the nation's largest Protestant denomination in the first place. Its loose structure appeals to those who don't want a top-down hierarchy or centralized authority. For that freedom, congregants are happy to contribute to the billion-plus dollars in unrestricted funds that go to the national entities to pay for things like missions and seminaries. But there have been signs that the centralized authorities are no longer so content with this arrangement and would prefer to exert greater control—to, as Greear put it, "shape the institutions."

First Baptist Naples, with its storied past and wealthy congregation, would have made an ideal model to show how it could be done. But there was still that little formality of a vote, and fanfare notwithstanding, 19 percent of the members decided they didn't care what the national leaders wanted and voted against Marcus Hayes.

Some of their reasons were based purely on qualifications. The initial search committee criteria included someone who had been a senior pastor of a church of at least 1,500 for a minimum of five years. Hayes checked neither of those boxes. He had worked only three years as a teaching pastor at a larger church's "satellite campus" (meaning messages from the senior pastor would sometimes be streamed via satellite). In fact, Hayes's white senior pastor had been up for the Naples job, and he had not met the qualifications, either. Hayes also had no experience overseeing a multimillion-dollar budget or building program.

Then there was the fact that the dissident group, which had formally rallied around the name "Concerned Members of FBC," had sent Hayes a warmly addressed and complimentary email detailing what had happened with Wicker.[61] They'd hoped to get his input on how he would manage to overcome these internal divisions. He never answered. It was an inauspicious beginning to a job interview.

That said, some of their concerns did center on racial politics. Some of the Concerned Members group noticed that Hayes had posted a number of progressive-leaning items to his Twitter account, including retweeting praise of Vice President Kamala Harris for a publicity stunt press conference announcing that lynching had finally been made a federal crime. As a few members of the group noted, lynching had already long been outlawed by any number of statutes, and they were dismayed to see their potential pastor cheering a pro-abortion, pro-LGBTQ politician. They also found it concerning that Hayes had promoted the book *Woke Church*, by author Eric Mason, who has argued that "whiteness causes blindness of the heart."[62] Also, several members of the church who work in law enforcement were dismayed to see that Hayes had shared a tweet that said of a police shooting, "It seems all cops ever see is black."[63]

This is not to say that Hayes might not have offered persuasive responses to all these concerns, but was it racism for the members of the church to suggest in an email to other members that he should be asked about them at the all-church meeting before the vote?[64]

The dissident group has been more than willing to share these documents with the public and let people decide for themselves whether they had racist motivations when they chose not to vote for Hayes. First Baptist Naples's leadership, along with Greear, Akin, Barber, Hall, and the other national SBC leaders, has never offered the slightest explanation for why they felt comfortable publicly naming these people guilty of the gross sin of racism. When Bob Caudill emailed Greear and Akin, pleading with them to meet with him and retract the accusation, Greear did not respond, and Akin would only acknowledge receipt of the message.

"I just said, 'Please, before you start criticizing us, or in any way demeaning us and calling us racist, please come and talk to us,'" Bob told me. "Those people [Greear, Akin, and Barber] were never in our church. They sent videos, and they played them on Sunday, but they themselves seemed to just be of the mind-set that we need some black pastors in the convention and thought [First Baptist Naples] would be a good place to start, regardless of the qualifications, you know?"

Many of those who were excommunicated for their refusal to vote for Hayes had been members of First Baptist Naples for decades, serving in ministries, even teaching in the associated school. Some not only lost their church home but their jobs. Is this what racial justice looks like—kicking old people and longtime faithful members out of their church because they were naïve enough to think they were entitled to have a say over who their pastor would be? As one of the group, who was afraid to use her name, told me tearfully, "When the church calls you racist, people believe it."

It wouldn't be the last time Greear would attack his sheep for failing to see the issues of CRT and antiracism as he did. During the same 2021 SBC national convention sermon where he claimed that closet racists and neo-Confederates were sitting in Southern Baptist pews, he added, "The reality is that if we in the SBC had shown as much sorrow for the painful legacy that racism and discrimination has [sic] left in our country as we have passion to decry CRT, we probably wouldn't be in this mess." He did not specify what "mess" he was talking about.

The comments received plenty of cheering in the major press outlets, none of whom apparently thought to ask Greear who the racist Southern Baptists were or how he knew of their bigotry if they were closeted. If Greear truly was aware of neo-Confederates sitting in pews under his leadership, surely he had a duty, under Matthew 18:15–19, to inform their pastors, so that bigotry could be addressed, or even to look into the matter himself along with two or three witnesses. If the racists did not repent, then was he not obligated to tell this publicly to the church, to name them so that they might even be put out for the purpose of producing godly sorrow that leads to repentance (2 Corinthians 2:5–8)? Are neo-Confederates beyond forgiveness and redemption? Is their sin so great that no shepherd should sully himself by going after them?

The more disturbing implication of such generalized accusations without evidence is that Greear was broad-brushing the sheep under his care as racists in order to bolster his own antiracist image before a secular culture.

■ ■ ■

Racism is real, it is ugly, and it should be opposed wherever it is found. I have seen the hateful messages my friend Samuel Sey, a black Christian essayist, receives when he posts photos of himself with his white wife on social media. When a draft of the Supreme Court's *Dobbs* opinion leaked showing that *Roe v. Wade* would be overturned, pro-abortion actress Amanda Duarte tweeted,

"I do wonder how these white supremacist lawmakers would feel if their little white daughters were raped and impregnated by black men."[65] The immense backlash Duarte received from people across the political aisle who called her remarks "racist" and "vile" was well-deserved. The fact that white supremacist leaders like Nick Fuentes and Richard Spencer are attracting a large audience of young men is a legitimate crisis. It takes no special knowledge for Christians of any color to look at these issues in light of Scripture and recognize them as an abominable affront to the image of God stamped on every human being equally.

But there is evidence that making every aspect of American life serve a narrative of racial oppression is inciting bigotry, not reducing it. In 2021, the year after millions of Americans in all regions of the country participated in Black Lives Matter protests (and riots), and after countless churches preached and practiced repentance for their alleged racism and embraced CRT, hate crimes surged 12 percent, largely driven by racial animus.[66]

More broadly, Americans' views on white-black relations are now at their lowest point in twenty years. In 2005, 72 percent of Americans rated race relations as very or somewhat good. By 2020, this was down to only 44 percent. As pollster Gallup noted, "until 2015, large majorities of both [blacks and whites] thought relations were generally good."[67] We are being trained in fear, suspicion, bitterness, and resentment. Why would the Church ever want to synthesize such ungodly lessons with the Gospel that reconciles men to each other by reconciling them first to Christ?

As Sey put it, antiracism and CRT are, in fact, *pro*-racism. "Professing to be wise, Robin DiAngelo became a fool. Professing to be antiracist, she became a racist," Sey wrote in his review of *White Fragility*.[68] The fact that so many white Christians, like Julie Bell and the staffers at Cru have been willing to subject themselves to shaming rituals and struggle sessions demonstrates the grief most white Christians feel over America's racist sins.

Craig Mitchell is a black Christian ethicist and former professor at Southwestern Baptist Theological Seminary. In 2020, he was among those sounding the alarm over CRT's incursion into SBC seminaries. Speaking to a group of Louisiana college students, he stressed that just like the Marxism from which it sprang, CRT promises an earthly utopia without God.

"If you're looking for perfect justice—if you're looking for perfect righteousness—you're not going to find it until Christ comes again," Mitchell told them. "The best thing you can do is share the Gospel of Jesus Christ with this fallen world. To the degree that you share the Gospel with others and they come to Christ, and they strive for justice and righteousness, we will have a more righteous society."[69]

CHAPTER 7

#MeToo, #ChurchToo, and an Apocalypse

The one who states his case first seems right, until
the other comes and examines him.

—Proverbs 18:17

In November 2019, just as polls showed the public mood toward the MeToo movement was beginning to sour, comedian John Crist's career imploded in a storm of abuse allegations.

At that moment, Crist had been about to break into the mainstream in a way few Christian-branded performers ever had. The pop singers Debby Boone and Amy Grant managed it in the 1970s and '80s, the rock bands Lifehouse and Skillet in the 1990s and 2000s. But no stand-up comedian had ever gone from telling jokes in churches to the comedy big time. As one of the top one hundred touring artists in the world that year, and mere months away from the release of a Netflix comedy special, Crist was on the cusp of making Christian entertainment history.

But revelations laid out in the Pentecostal magazine *Charisma* put an end to all that.[1]

The article that broke the Crist sex scandal included a number of melodramatic disclaimers that would seem difficult for a non-omniscient reporter to assert as fact, such as "These women have testified out of a desire not to ruin Crist's career but to warn other young women not to fall for his manipulations." Yet the story was surprisingly light on journalistic details.

Taylor Berglund reported that Crist had initiated sexting relationships with a number of female fans, some married, but failed to present a single direct quote to illustrate the tone of Crist's messages or whether they had ever contained threatening or abusive language. Nor did the reporter, even once, hint at the tenor of the women's side of the exchanges, something that would presumably have revealed their level of willingness to participate.

Were all Crist's messages so explicit that the editors of *Charisma* felt they could not in good conscience reproduce any of them? Did Berglund ever ask to see the women's replies to Crist or only the messages Crist sent the women? We don't know, and that missing context is relevant, as we'll see in a moment.

What specifics the story did offer alleged that, while skewering evangelical culture with highly shareable social media skits like "Road Rage in the Church Parking Lot" and "Guy in Your Bible Study Who Ain't Even Christian," Crist was using his fame to solicit sexual favors. The five women who told their stories to *Charisma* detailed a method of pursuing conquests that, though carried out over Snapchat and Instagram, is as at least as old as Molière's seventeenth-century lothario Dom Juan.

According to *Charisma*, the majority of the interactions were virtual—Crist would initiate flirtatious exchanges with the women via direct message before requesting explicit photos. He and the women would exchange dirty texts, and sometimes he would drunkenly call them late at night. Why did the women say they complied? Because like Molière's libertine philosophy, Crist strung the women along with declarations of affection and hints that he wanted to marry them.

There was one accuser, though—the only one of the five who says she told Crist "no"—whose interactions with him took place almost entirely IRL. (That's "in real life," for my readers over forty.)

Though *Charisma* didn't provide the ages of any of the women, it did note that the one at the center of the most damning account was a college senior, putting her presumably between twenty-one and twenty-three years old; Crist at the time was thirty-three. After the woman and her boyfriend met up with the comedian in Las Vegas so she could interview him for her podcast, Crist asked for her phone number, which she gave him. Later, he began sending her messages on Snapchat, which she answered. He then invited her out one evening, which she agreed to. Once she arrived at his Los Angeles apartment, he suggested they go Rollerblading on the boardwalk and offered her vodka in a water bottle to take along, which she accepted and drank. As they rolled along, Crist quipped that he wanted to skate behind her to "enjoy the view."

The woman told *Charisma* that she thought the cliché comment was "kind of weird." But because Crist was a Christian celebrity, it didn't register with her as a pickup line, even though he said it in the context of what, from these bare details, can only be described as a date. Nevertheless, at some point, the two took off their Rollerblades and ran into the ocean. There, Crist "grabbed" the woman and attempted a kiss.

What unfolds at that point depicts Crist as a lecher who certainly could have used a punch in the mouth. Whether it makes him guilty of something more serious is difficult to determine, given the vagueness of *Charisma*'s account.

After the woman rebuffed the kiss, Crist "told her in crude terms how much he wanted to have sex" with her. (*Charisma* doesn't recount specifically what he said—again, that lack of journalistic detail.) The woman says she pushed him away and informed him that she was interested in him only as a mentor, and they headed back to his apartment. Once there, *Charisma* reports that Crist "grabbed" her again, though the story doesn't identify what part of her he grabbed (a hand, a shoulder, something more intimate that would have put his actions in the realm of sexual assault?) or with what manner of force or menace. It says only that he again "crudely propositioned her for sex and begged her to stay."

The woman left. In her own words, she found Crist "creepy," but she never describes herself as a victim of abuse. Yet that is exactly how every major evangelical media outlet and public figure that commented on the Crist case described *all* the women, not just the one who refused him.

Charisma noted that it decided not to publish the accusers' names because it didn't want to foster "criticism and shame against the women Crist manipulated." At no point in the article or in a follow-up editorial statement about *Charisma*'s decision to publish the allegations did the outlet suggest that any of the women did anything wrong. Indeed, when Berglund mentions that one of the women was married, he seems to intend the detail to add to *Crist's* guilt, not to impute any to the woman for cheating on her husband.

As to the only case where abuse could be a factor if we read between the lines, Berglund apparently avoided any probing questions that could have cleared up the matter definitively. Did the woman clarify before she accepted an invite for a one-on-one evening out that it would be purely platonic? Not that this would have made Crist's alleged sexual propositions any less egregious, but it would at least have resolved the question of whether he had deliberately deceived her.

Berglund gives no indication that he asked. Did the woman fear for her safety in any way? The phrase "begged her to stay" carries the connotation of pleading rather than threatening, implying that both Crist and the woman understood that she retained the power to give or withhold sex, to leave or remain. But again, Berglund doesn't seem to have probed this highly relevant point—he just mentions that she felt "disgustingly let down by a role model"—certainly an appropriate reaction. But feeling disgusted and disillusioned is a long way from feeling that one has experienced abuse. And again, this was the only woman of the five who did not willingly enter into an immoral sexual relationship with the comedian.

The reactions to the Crist story were my first inkling of how deeply the worst excesses of the MeToo movement, which at that point had been dominating the national discourse for two years, had taken root in the Church.

Power Plays

In a since-deleted joint essay about the Crist revelations, the Billy Graham Center's Ed Stetzer and Laurie Nichols wrote, "Our first concern should be for the victims, and we must stand with and help their voices be heard."[2]

Karen Swallow Prior recommended a student op-ed about the case that opined, "Finding forgiveness for Crist and reconciling ourselves with the ugliness of human depravity require first looking the sin of sexual abuse square in the face . . . for the sake of its victims."[3]

Two years after the scandal, when Crist returned to the club circuit—he publicly acknowledged that it would no longer be appropriate for him to perform in churches—*Christianity Today* worried what impact his continuing to tell jokes for a living would have on "victims and their advocates."[4] At no point in any of these essays or social media posts did any of the Christian notables suggest that the women who willingly sexted with Crist were anything *other* than victims. At no point did they suggest the women had committed

sins as well. In fact, some took pains to insist they hadn't, as Christian radio host Bekah Eaker did in an open letter in which she assured the women,
"This isn't your fault."[5]

Really? Even the woman who violated her marriage vows to sext with
Crist? It certainly wasn't all their faults, but with the exception of the one
who says she refused Crist, wasn't at least *some* of it?

At first, I thought perhaps the uniformity of the comments was a matter
of self-selection—the people who were choosing to write about Crist were
doing so because they were eager to signal their alliance with the most zeal-
ous tenets of the MeToo movement. But when I brought up the issue with
several high-profile Christian authors and speakers, I found that was not the
case. For instance, during a casual conversation with a bespectacled ERLC
executive, I mentioned that I didn't see any reason to characterize four of
the women as abuse victims when, by their own admission, they had entered
into sexual relationships with Crist of their own accord. He frowned at me,
clearly ruffled by such an unorthodox opinion. I pressed him for an explanation of how it could be abuse when there were no threats, no force, no intimidation. Exasperated, he replied, "Because he held power over them."

At that point, I'll admit, I might have chuckled. Crist wasn't anyone's employer. He wasn't anyone's pastor. He held no authority over these women in
any way. He was a stand-up comic, and none of the women had even claimed
to have comedy aspirations. What power of Crist's were they supposed to
have feared? The exec explained to me slowly, as if I were a dull child, that
fame is a sort of power and that Crist had used his to convince women to
send him nude photos and reply to his explicit texts. That power inequity, the
ERLC exec insisted, made it abuse.

For a brief moment, it flitted through my head that beauty is a sort of
power, too. (If you doubt it, reread the story of Samson and Delilah.) My
guess was that, on that score, these women probably outranked Crist, whom
I'd describe as an average-looking schmo. But I held my tongue. My charitable interpretation was that the balding, portly, sweater-vested man in front
of me was a pretty average-looking schmo himself, so perhaps a little naïve
about women's ability to focus that power in the direction of famous and/
or wealthy men when they've a mind to. Later that same night, however, I
discovered that I was wrong again and that "fame creates a power disparity

that renders women helpless" *was* apparently the official party line for this ministry.

That evening, during a podcast panel, I asked the executive's coworker, Bible study author Trillia Newbell, about the Crist scandal. In particular, I asked how a church could balance caring for women who've been hurt by consensual but sinful relationships with holding them accountable for their own transgressions. Newbell looked slightly stunned at my question but conceded that when women have sinned, they should be encouraged to confess and repent. However, she was unwilling to concede that any of the women in the *Charisma* story qualified as sinful.

"In many of these cases, we are talking about someone abusing their power, abusing their role, abusing their celebrity, even," she said. "I think when we look at these unfortunate, sobering situations, we have to be able to distinguish [between] what is actual sin and what is a crime. What is sin and what oversteps the boundaries of what becomes abuse. In this case, I do think he confessed that there was some abuse."

Crist had never confessed this. What he admitted to in a statement to *Charisma* was that his behavior had been "hurtful to [the women]." He confessed to treating "relationships with women far too casually, in some cases even recklessly." As to crime, no one in the story alleged any. In fact, Berglund, who was surely in possession of more details than he offered to readers, explicitly stated that the women's allegations were *not* criminal.

What the article accused Crist of, fairly, was emotionally manipulating and harassing women. (Though harassment is usually defined by whether the sexual attention is reciprocated. And in the *Charisma* story, there was only one account where it wasn't.) I pointed out that if *I* had sexted with Crist, my husband would be pretty angry with me regardless of how emotionally manipulated I'd felt or how powerful I'd found Crist's celebrity.

Newbell was not persuaded. "Yeah, so, I think if we are called to love our neighbor, we won't manipulate them, right," she said in a slightly clipped tone. "And I do think that people can, I mean, we have no idea the state of [the women's] minds. They're weak; who knows. I know that in a case of power, we can be given to fear and allow fear to lead us."

Were the women afraid of Crist? None said so. Not even the college senior. And what of Newbell's contention that loving your neighbor means not manipulating them? Surely one can stipulate that this is true without agreeing that Crist's failure to love his neighbor must also make him guilty of abuse and render the women wholly innocent. This blasé conflation of different degrees of offense—that if a man is clearly guilty of doing one bad thing, it gives Christian leaders license to publicly name him guilty of things degrees of magnitude worse—is now a pattern in the Church.

The evangelical media's case that Crist was not just immoral but an abuser rested entirely on assumptions about the fearfulness and naïveté of women who were not named, whose responses to Crist were not described, and whose ages were not provided. Yet none of those outlets sought out more information before airing their verdicts.

Once the comedian began putting new stand-up specials on his YouTube channel (the Netflix offer never rematerialized), one of the women *Charisma* repeatedly characterized as a "young" victim identified herself on Instagram and YouTube.[6] Melissa Hawks was two years *older* than Crist, and thirty-seven at the time of the article's publication, a detail the magazine could have offered while still maintaining Hawks's anonymity. Ashlee Rohnert, another accuser who later revealed her identity, was only a year younger than him.[7] A third, whose identity I confirmed privately, was thirty at the time the story was published.

Yet, while Crist was around the same age of at least three of the five of the women, *Charisma* never described him as a young man; nor did any of the evangelical commentary that labeled him an abuser of "young women."

None of those who cited power imbalances created by Crist's celebrity notice that three of the five women had said their relationships with Crist took place in 2012–2013, when he was still a far-from-famous local club act and long before he had put a single video on social media, let alone had one go viral. The abuse commentators also missed that three of the women had said they met Crist not because of his comedy, but because they were all members of a Facebook group started by motivational speaker and author Jon Acuff.

The responses to the Crist scandal might not matter at a broader level if they weren't indicative of how deeply the Church has imbibed MeToo's dogma that any nebulous definition of power that can be ascribed to men erases agency (and thus responsibility) on the part of women. *Christianity Today, The Gospel Coalition,* and other evangelical publications and websites have run numerous articles analyzing whether sexual interaction between adults is sin or abuse based not on consent, but power imbalance. The Southern Baptist Convention's abuse task force website has recommended videos, books, and articles that do the same.[8] The Church's response is even coloring our understanding of Scripture, with prominent abuse activists like Rachael Denhollander arguing that due to "power dynamics," the story of David and Bathsheba must be understood as a story of rape and that pastors must describe David as a rapist or else they will fail to "handle Scripture properly."[9]

The most important question we must ask when we hear such arguments: Is this a biblical standard?

Jesus encounters several women who are involved in sinful sexual relationships throughout *The Gospels*. Given the kind of culture they lived in and the low social position they occupied, it's reasonable to assume the women are at a power disadvantage. Yet He doesn't tell the adulteress of John 8 or the woman at the well to "go and be 'emotionally manipulated' no more." He doesn't scold the religious leaders of Luke 7 that the "certain immoral woman" who washed His feet should be categorized as a victim because her illicit acts occured within a system in which the power disparity favors men above women, though it very much does. He acknowledges these women's transgressions and forgives them, because though the men with whom they transgress have sinned as well, those are not the hearts Jesus is concerned with at that moment. He is concerned with freeing the women from their burden of guilt for *their* sinful acts, which could only happen if He and the women acknowledge that sin.

But perhaps the best biblical example is Joseph, whose physical beauty makes him a target of the wife of one of the most powerful men in Egypt. Though favored above all Potiphar's household servants, Joseph is still a foreign slave. So, when the mistress of the house seeks to entice him to bed, does Joseph assume the power imbalance between them means he should acquiesce because the offense will be hers alone? No, he answers, "How then could I do such a wicked thing and sin against God?"

The idea that a lack of power excuses willful, knowing sin is found nowhere in the Bible. Quite the opposite.

It is not Scripture but Karl Marx who taught that guilt is based not on the intent of an individual heart but on class distinctions between oppressors and oppressed. This poisonous ideology is drifting into ministries and churches not simply via cultural osmosis, but is also being intentionally introduced by church leaders through the creation of formal bureaucracies. And it's bringing with it a host of other destructive ideas that come straight from the political left.

Numbers Too Bad to Be True

In almost every respect, the abuse reforms being instituted in the largest Protestant denominations in the United States mirror the Title IX policies that have unleashed a storm of false allegations and unjust investigations on college campuses.

It began in 2011, when President Obama, Vice President Joe Biden, and education secretary Arne Duncan began to give hyperbolic speeches decrying the campus "rape culture" that had given rise to a "plague" of sexual assaults and an "epidemic of sexual violence." To justify the bureaucratic power grabs that would accompany these pronouncements, they cited statistics that claimed that one in five college women are sexually assaulted and that only 2–8 percent of rape allegations are false.[10] These were shocking numbers, and they should have shocked, given the fact they had almost no grounding in reality.

The one-in-five claim, for instance, is based on deeply misleading surveys like one the *Washington Post* conducted that asked college women if they'd experienced anything from a "forced kiss" to being ground on while dancing, to engaging in sex while intoxicated, to forcible rape.[11] What did it not ask the women?[12] If *they* characterized these incidents as assault. Given that rubric, it's staggering the *Post* came up with only 20 percent.

By contrast, a 2014 Bureau of Justice Statistics study that directly asked female students if they'd been the victims of sexual assault found an incident rate of 0.61 percent. (It's odd that the White House website dedicated to the campus rape crisis didn't bother citing research conducted by a department in its own administration.)[13] Then there's the hard statistics reported under the Clery Act, a federal statute that requires colleges and universities to submit annual tallies for reported campus crimes. As with the *Post* survey, the

Clery Act's definition of sexual assault includes fondling over clothes and does not require physical force, only that the act is committed against the victim's will. It also includes cases where the defendant is eventually cleared. Yet, in 2012, the Clery Act sexual assault rate for female students was 0.03 percent—a tiny fraction of the Obama administration's claims.

The statistic regarding the rate of false rape allegations is no sounder. In *Unwanted Advances*, a book about sexual abuse hysteria in higher education, Northwestern professor Laura Kipnis traces the origins of the statistic that only 2 percent of reports aren't true. She finds that this claim stemmed from a quote in feminist activist Susan Brownmiller's 1975 manifesto, *Against Our Will: Men, Women and Rape*, a book that defines rape as "a conscious process of intimidation by which all men keep all women in a state of fear."

Brownmiller's source was an appellate court judge's 1974 speech. But as to where the by-then-deceased judge had gotten it, a legal scholar who tried to track the figure in 2000 eventually had to conclude that the origins had been "lost to antiquity."[14] Keep in mind, Kipnis is a self-described left-wing feminist, hardly someone given to taking up for frat boys or protecting predators (the usual sort of invective that gets thrown at people who dare question abuse statistics).

The reality is this: Studies showing that 10 to 12 percent of rape allegations are false are often as flawed as those finding that 25 to 41 percent are.[15] Former Denver chief deputy DA Craig Silverman built a reputation for vigorous prosecution of sexual assaults and today represents rape victims in civil trials. Yet he has noted that false allegations occur with "scary frequency."[16] And it's important to remember, these statistics refer only to rape, not to the much more elastic category of assault.

During her ten years as supervisor of San Diego's Sex Crimes Unit, Sgt. Joanne Archambault oversaw investigations into approximately one thousand felony sexual assaults every year. When she retired in 2003, she used her expertise to launch a nonprofit dedicated to improving police sensitivity to those who report such crimes. After explaining why the statistics most activist groups cite are unreliable, Archambault's training documents conclude simply, "We have no knowledge of what percentage of sexual assaults are false on a national level."[17]

But ultimately, even if the Obama administration had been able to pin-point a legitimate rate of false allegations, it would have been irrelevant. All this research is based on claims provided to the police, where lying carries the risk of felony charges. Campus Title IX offices (or Southern Baptist hot-lines, which we'll get to in a moment) offer no such deterrent.

Standards of Evidence

Of course, the fact that the administration's statistics could be easily dis-credited did not stop the *Washington Post*, the *New York Times*, *The Chronicle of Higher Education*, or countless other outlets from repeating them ad nauseam. Buoyed by the media support, President Obama's Office of Civil Rights (OCR) sent a letter to more than seven thousand colleges and univer-sities across the country informing them that, under the auspices of the Title IX Civil Rights Act prohibiting gender discrimination, there would now be a federal policy addressing all forms of sexual abuse. Today, that missive is referred to as the infamous "Dear Colleague Letter."

Any school that did not conform to the letter's centralized policies risked losing their federal funding. And to ensure the opportunity for further bu-reaucratic meddling, the OCR instituted a White House task force that would issue periodic recommendations to strengthen "compliance."

The first indication that the reforms would spur campuses to throw out the few vestiges of due process they maintained when it came to sex-ual misconduct claims was what Kipnis described as a "slippage" in rhetoric. Where once students who made allegations were "accusers" or "complain-ants," OCR missives (and, following their example, Title IX investigators) now referred to them as "survivors" and "victims," without even an "alleged" thrown in to maintain the appearance of objectivity. These biased descrip-tors were accompanied by a new burden of proof.

Criminal cases, as everyone knows, require an evidentiary standard of "beyond a reasonable doubt." But many campuses had been using a lower threshold known as "clear and convincing"—which translates to roughly 75 to 80 percent probability of guilt. The OCR demanded that campuses apply a much lower burden, known as "preponderance of evidence," which requires that likelihood of guilt be only above 50 percent. In other words, if a Title

IX tribunal looks at the evidence and puts the odds of an accusation's being true at 50.01 percent—barely better than a coin toss—the accused is judged guilty.

Of course, because these investigations are taking place outside the legal system (no one ever seems to wonder why the women complain to their Title IX offices and not to the police) the accused doesn't face risk of jail time or fines. But there are still plenty of life-altering punishments schools can mete out, including expulsion and code-of-conduct violations that not only ruin these men's reputations, but often make it impossible for them to move on to comparable schools (if they are students) or jobs (if faculty).

The Obama administration defended the preponderance standard by arguing that the same burden was used in civil court. This conveniently ignored four facts: First, accusers and witnesses in civil court are subject to perjury charges and financial penalties for lying—a threat they don't face from schools (or Protestant denominations). Second, unlike in civil court, Title IX's single-investigator model allows a single person to act as investigator, prosecutor, and judge. There is no check or balance on that person's judgment, and no one is tasked with the job of dispassionately reviewing the evidence with fresh eyes. Third, civil cases are public and, therefore, transparent—much of the work of the investigator, prosecutor, and judge is laid open to public scrutiny. Fourth, and finally, civil cases afford defendants many of the same due process protections found in criminal cases, like the ability to review the evidence, cross-examine witnesses, and be judged by a jury of one's peers.

Due to a little trick known as "trauma-informed investigations," none of that features in the Title IX process.

Trauma-Informed Tyranny

American jurisprudence is built on a cornerstone known as Blackstone's ratio, named for the eighteenth-century British jurist William Blackstone, who famously wrote that "it is better that ten guilty persons escape than that one innocent suffer." Benjamin Franklin upped the ante, saying that it was better to let one hundred guilty go free than risk injustice against one blameless man.

This philosophy finds its expression in the presumption of innocence, which in turn finds it's grounding in biblical principles. In Genesis 18, for example, Abraham bargains with God over the destruction of Sodom, correctly arguing that the Lord is too righteous to destroy even ten innocents to justly punish a city so wicked that practically every man in it was a violent, would-be gang-rapist of Lot's angelic visitors. Meanwhile, Deuteronomy 19:15 sets the standard that "one witness is not enough to convict a man accused of any crime . . . a matter must be established by the testimony of two or three witnesses."

Today, DNA or other forensic evidence may stand in for witnesses, but now, as then, such stringent standards inevitably mean that guilty people sometimes get away with their crimes. Part of what makes the Day of Judgment so sweet to Christians is knowing that every wrong will be righted and every misdeed answered for.

The Title IX approach inverts Blackstone's ratio, implicitly operating on the principle that it is better for innocent men to be caught in the sexual abuse net than for any abusers to escape it. It presumes that the accused is guilty and demands he prove his innocence, in the name of not retraumatizing victims.

If a preponderance standard with no deterrent for lying seems like stacking the deck, trauma-informed (also known as "victim-centered") investigating is like getting to play your opponent's cards for him as well. It contends that sexual abuse can cause severe neurobiological trauma such that victims' brains scramble details and time lines and may leave them unable to verbalize or retain certain memories. Of course, no one should expect a victim of rape or assault to perfectly recall every aspect of their ordeal, and there can be gaps in recollection of any event, especially with campus assault allegations where alcohol is often a factor. But trauma-informed theory goes far beyond that.

If an accuser's explanation of where, when, or how an assault took place doesn't align with the evidence or her story changes, trauma-informed investigating holds that the investigator should not suspect it's because the accuser is not telling the truth. They should assume it's because her brain is reordering and repressing memories. But Title IX investigators often don't scrutinize allegations closely enough even to get to the point of detecting conflicting details because standard courtroom cross-examination, too, is judged to be trauma triggering.

Trauma is also used to explain why an accuser might not have resisted or even said no to her abuser—it holds that she may have entered "tonic immobility," a catatonic state wherein the victim "freezes" for an extended period, unable to voice or signal any distress or displeasure during an assault. It may even seem like consent.

Except, this is all junk science.

Quite a bit more than preponderance of recent neurological and psychiatric research has found that traumatic memories are no more fragmented or elusive than any other type of memory.[18] In fact, studies on Holocaust victims and soldiers suffering from PTSD show quite the opposite. Trauma actually *heightens* memories—the recollections stay sharper, becoming intrusive and hard to forget, even though subjects wish they could. As Richard McNally, director of clinical training in Harvard's psychology department and an expert in the field of memory, once put it, "The notion that the mind protects itself by repressing or dissociating memories of trauma is a piece of psychiatric folklore."[19]

As for tonic immobility, while fear or shock may cause people to freeze for a second or two, as they are caught in indecision over how to respond, the notion of being unable to react for a prolonged period simply has no scientific backing. In an *Atlantic* article debunking the idea that trauma triggers neurobiological disruption that can cause immobility, one of the foremost disseminators of the theory was forced to admit that there were "very valid questions" as to whether it exists in humans at all.[20] Yet Title IX attorneys who represent male students say most accusers' formal complaints now include claims of being frozen throughout much of the incident.

Eventually, campus officials dismissing exculpatory evidence due to a trauma-informed approach became such a problem that, in 2019, the Association of Title IX Administrators was forced to publish an unprecedented statement. They warned that investigators relying on "trauma science" were overlooking a lack of evidence and that claims regarding trauma and memory were "far more conjectural than empirical." They stressed that research has not definitively demonstrated that sexual assault significantly impacts memory. Finally, they chided some school officials for being "politically motivated to extrapolate well beyond any reasonable empirical conclusions currently supported by the science."[21]

While it seems incredible that vast swaths of abuse activists could be held under the sway of a theory that has almost no empirical basis, it would hardly be the first time. One need only look back at the equally specious recovered-memory craze of the 1980s. Then, undiscerning therapists and fad books convinced tens of thousands of women that they had repressed memories of being molested as children.[22] Thousands of women even believed the abuse had been part of Satanic rituals. As a result, innocent people were charged, some were even jailed, and families across the nation were torn apart until common sense reasserted itself and the moral panic retreated. Today, entire rows of libraries are devoted to analyzing the recovered-memory hysteria that led people to become convinced they had forgotten traumas lurking in the recesses of their psyches.

If activists' only interest is in seeing abusers brought to justice, why would they continue to insist that discredited theories inform the investigation process? As *Reason* magazine put it, "the 'neurobiology of trauma' movement seems to have become popular because it plays so nicely into progressive ideology."[23]

Harvard Law professor Janet Halley, who reviewed her school's Title IX training, said that the trauma-informed portion was "100% aimed to convince [investigator trainees] to believe complainants precisely when they seem unreliable and incoherent."[24] And history professor KC Johnson and journalist Stuart Taylor said that the university training materials they reviewed seemed intended to prompt investigators to "consider virtually any accused student guilty and virtually any accuser truthful, no matter the impression each party gives."[25]

That's exactly what happened in *Doe v. Purdue*, a 2019 Seventh Circuit Court of Appeals case that held that the university's Title IX panel had violated a young man's due process rights. Future Supreme Court justice Amy Coney Barrett wrote in that decision, "Fairness can rarely be obtained by secret, one-sided determination of facts. . . . The majority of the panel members appeared to credit [the accuser] based on her accusation alone, given that they took no other evidence into account."[26]

MeToo activists have often complained that conservatives deliberately exaggerated their slogan "Believe Women" and made it "Believe *All* Women" as a tactic to discredit the movement. But trauma-informed investigations provided a pseudo-scientific framework to demand exactly that. Add to this a low standard of evidence, a single-adjudicator model, and the absence of basic due process rights like the ability to cross-examine your accuser (which the Supreme Court has called "the greatest legal engine ever invented for the discovery of truth"), and you have a process that could not be farther from what civil liberties and the Bible require for justice.

As one U.S. district judge said after reviewing a typical Title IX investigation, "It's closer to Salem, 1692 than Boston, 2015."[27] Yet it is exactly this system that is driving the abuse reforms being introduced into America's churches.

Title IX Goes to Church

When it comes to implementing abuse reforms, there is not a step on the Title IX path that the largest Protestant denomination in the United States has skipped, though it has added quite a number of its own particularly theatrical flourishes.

Joe Cohn, policy director for the Foundation for Individual Rights and Expression, quipped in the *Wall Street Journal* of the over-the-top rhetoric that accompanied the new campus regulations: "It's tough to strip people of basic rights without fanning moral panic."[28] And as with the Obama administration, that is exactly where an offshoot of the MeToo movement known as ChurchToo started.

It should go without saying that any sexual assault or molestation is an offense against God, and the church must not only condemn it but take all measures that accord with due process to bring the perpetrators to justice and prevent it from recurring. We know from James 1:27 that Scripture especially calls on Christians to care for vulnerable women and children, who are usually the targets of predators. We know from Psalm 72:13 that the Lord has compassion for the weak and needy, and thus, so should we. We also know that because we live in a fallen world full of sinners, no human institution is entirely spared from the wages of fallen human nature, and that includes abuse. All church workers, but especially pastors, must be held legally accountable and face church discipline for committing or covering up abuse.

Yet no institution long in existence is likely to have a perfect record of addressing the issue, given that our ideas of what constitutes abuse have evolved over time. It is simply a fact that a church today is going to view a nonforcible sexual relationship between a seventeen-year-old student and a twenty-two-year-old youth pastor differently than it would have in 1970 or even 1990. Even today in most states, this scenario would not be illegal. Churches in all eras would (or should) judge it a disqualifying sin, but it is only in the last decade that many churches have begun to view it as sexual abuse. We cannot justly evaluate the response of a 1970 or 1990 church with post-2015 standards when the Bible itself does not draw clear lines on when sexual sin becomes sexual abuse where no force is involved and where both parties are above the age of consent.

Likewise, the same fallen nature that prompts predators to sometimes seek prey in churches can also prompt the power-hungry to seize on a legitimate issue and inflate it as a way to amass control, as Obama did with campus rape. Sexual assaults do, of course, happen in higher education. But the frequency the former president claimed prompted even the left-wing outlet *Slate* to scoff that his "assertion would mean that young American college women are raped at a rate similar to women in Congo, where rape has been used as a weapon of war."[29]

In the Southern Baptist Convention, those who wanted to seize power and settle scores did not have dubious abuse statistics they could point to within the denomination, but they did have a report they could describe in the most hyperbolic terms. The storm of intrigue and infighting that led to the commissioning of what came to be called the Guidepost Report[30] would have made even the writers of the HBO political drama *House of Cards* blush. Russell Moore, then-head of ERLC, played the role of calculating political operative Frank Underwood, maintaining cozy relationships with major media outlets, who, in turn, just happened to keep up a running stream of coverage that savaged his enemies while lionizing him. (An essay in the *New York Times*, for example, literally named Moore a "dissenter trying to save evangelicalism from itself,"[31] while *The Atlantic* said he was "fight[ing] for the soul of the Southern Baptist Convention."[32])

But the incessant Trump bashing that earned Moore Beltway plaudits was considerably less popular with rank-and-file Southern Baptists. That, along with his tendency to use the ERLC to pull the denomination to the left on issues ranging from immigration to ostensible racial injustice, had earned him no friends on the much more conservative SBC executive committee. But all-out war ensued when Moore unexpectedly changed the theme of the ERLC's 2019 conference from "Gospel Courage" to what he claimed was the SBC's "Abuse Crisis" and welcomed a star speaker who attacked the committee from the stage.[33]

Rachael Denhollander made history in 2018 as the first woman to speak out about former Olympic doctor Larry Nassar's sexual assault of young gymnasts. Her image, delicate, slight but with a spine of steel, was splashed across news outlets as she courageously faced down her abuser and asked the court at his sentencing, "How much is a little girl worth?" Denhollander rightly became a hero to many, winning *Glamour* magazine's Woman of the Year award. Afterward, she became a well-known abuse activist, and Moore drafted her to help the ERLC create a curriculum to deal with abuse in Southern Baptist churches.

At the close of the newly rethemed conference, Denhollander savaged the SBC executive committee from the stage. Her complaint? It had failed to label a publishing executive who had been involved in a twelve-year relationship with a married professor an abuse survivor in the SBC house organ, *The Baptist Press*.[34] To be fair to the committee, it was a curious case.

The relationship began in 2004, when Jennifer Lyell was a twenty-six-year-old student at the Southern Baptist Theological Seminary. Lyell had struck up a friendship with the Sills family and began some sort of sexual relationship with Dr. David Sills. (Sills does not recall that Lyell was ever in one of his classes; nor has Lyell ever asserted that she was.) After two years, she accepted a publishing job in another state and began to contract books from Sills. He even thanked her in some of his acknowledgments. Eventually, Lyell rose to become the highest-paid woman in the SBC, occupying an executive job at the denomination's publisher, Lifeway. Their long-distance involvement carried on for another ten years until Lyell was thirty-eight, finally ending in 2016. She says it was because she grew strong enough to stop being Sills's victim. Sills says it was because he had repented.[35]

Two years later, at the height of the MeToo movement, Lyell went to the seminary's administration and alleged that she had never consented throughout the entirety of the twelve years, even during the ten years she had to travel to meet with Sills. Sills was summarily fired,[36] and about a year after breaking her silence, Lyell provided her story to *Baptist Press* as an SBC-specific example of the "cultural moment" taking place throughout the country.[37]

The SBC executive committee, which included a number of lawyers, got a look at the first draft of the story naming Lyell as a certain victim and balked, reasonably fearing that Sills would have grounds to sue. Instead of pulling the story altogether, they amended "abuse" to read "morally inappropriate relationship," though they retained a quote wherein Lyell accused Sills of "grooming and taking advantage" of her. This led Denhollander to make her much-publicized conference accusation that the committee had "trampled" on a "precious survivor," after which she promptly threatened them with a defamation suit on Lyell's behalf. To avoid further bad press (and against the advice of its insurance company, which felt Lyell did not have a strong case), the committee settled with Lyell for a reported one million dollars.[38] But the bitter infighting had barely begun.

The executive committee then commissioned an investigation into whether Moore's progressive politicking had led SBC churches to give less to the national entities.[39] As strike backs go, it was rather dull. The same could not be said, however, of Moore's next move.

Just before the SBC's June 2021 convention, Moore, who had become so unpopular among many rank-and-file Southern Baptists, ERLC sources told me he would often hide out in his office to avoid having to engage with any hoi polloi at the SBC's Nashville headquarters, announced that he was resigning.[40] Lest anyone wonder why, within days, a letter he had sent to his ERLC trustees ostensibly a year before, in February 2020, was leaked to the press.[41] And it was no read-between-the-lines, corporate-speak complaint, either. Moore leveled lurid accusations at the committee, accusing them of wanting him to live in "psychological terror" and claiming that they told him to stay quiet about threats he'd received from "white supremacist" and "neo-confederate" SBC members involved in "groups funded by white nationalist nativist organizations."

I'll let readers judge whether the words Moore puts in the committee's mouths sound plausible or more akin to what one would expect to hear from soap opera villains: "One of these figures told me in the middle of the 2017 debacle: 'We know we can't take you down. All our wives and kids are with you. This is psychological warfare, to make you think twice before you do or say something.'"

The key accusation Moore made in his letter, though, which Religion News Service thought was of such high public interest that it published it in its four-thousand-word entirety, was that the committee had turned a blind eye to abuse. (Moore threw in a plug for himself for "ministering" to "that mistreated young woman," by whom he meant Lyell, who was by then over forty.)[42]

Yet none of the many major media outlets that amplified the letter— like the *Washington Post*, MSNBC, and CNN—evinced the slightest doubt about his claims. None apparently thought to ask him to provide any evidence of the neo-Confederates or the white nationalist, nativist funding, let alone hard proof that the committee had "disparag[ed]" and "mistreated" Lyell. Still, Moore was not done.

Three days later, a second four-thousand-word letter was leaked; from Moore to then-SBC president J. D. Greear, the date at the top asserted it had been written only days before.[43] It centered almost solely on abuse and seemed obviously crafted for public consumption, given that nearly all its contents relayed information Greear would already have known. (In fact, Moore prefaced his statements with some variation on "as you know" about twenty-five times.) Moore frequently provided résumé details Greear would not have needed—for example, describing Denhollander as an "Olympic gymnast, attorney, and advocate for survivors of sexual abuse," even though both men had been consulting with her on abuse reforms for two years by then. He also repeatedly referred to people obliquely with terms like "one SBC entity president," though he would have had no reason to conceal these identities from Greear.

One passage seemed to throw caution of betraying an overt agenda to the wind entirely, simply stating, "What most Southern Baptists do not know, but you and I do know, is how the issue of sexual abuse lurks just below the surface of so much of the controversy of the last few years." (Apparently Moore had never heard the axiom "Trust your reader.") He then spent six paragraphs addressing the only specific account of abuse mishandling he would mention in the letter: Lyell's, acknowledging that he had given Denhollander his blessing to blast his colleagues from the stage because of the great offenses they had committed against the publishing executive:

> [Lyell] had granted permission for Rachael to mention her story as long as I approved of her doing so. I said that I would not at all censor anything that she had to say. That would have been true about anything, but certainly true about this survivor, a person [my wife] and I love and have walked alongside as she has experienced not only the sexual abuse of her past, but the disparagement and then bullying and intimidation by the SBC Executive Committee. This survivor attempted to tell her story of abuse, through the channels of the Executive Committee, and her own words were altered by Executive Committee staff to make it seem as though this horrifying experience had been a consensual affair . . .
>
> In fact, as I knew then and know far better now, if anything, Rachael downplayed the horror this survivor had experienced, and later would experience, at the hands of the Executive Committee. She relayed through tears her experiences of bullying and intimidation by figures all the way up the org chart at the Executive Committee . . .

But even though this letter, too, received massive amplification throughout legacy media, Moore had not finished. The explosion of leaks finally came to an end five days later, when Moore's former chief of staff, Phillip Bethancourt, released secretly recorded audio from two abuse reform meetings with executive committee leaders.[44] He claimed these recordings proved the committee was callous toward victims' suffering and cared only for defending the SBC. The catch was the total meeting time was around five hours, but Bethancourt released only six minutes, broken up into five brief clips. Each clip directly corresponded to a claim Moore had made in the May 31 letter supposedly intended only for Greear, though none contained anything especially scandalous.

There were no dastardly threats of psychological warfare, no mention of neo-Confederates. No one raised their voices or even seemed particularly ir-ritable with Moore in the meeting whose purpose was to air grievances about Denhollander's conference comments. Committee CEO Ronnie Floyd only asked Moore, with a bit of a whine, how he was supposed to soothe bruised feelings over Moore's not giving Denhollander tighter "parameters." One clip featured a boring administrative complaint about a bylaws group feel-ing "thrown under the bus," though it's impossible to discern the context, as those comments are only nine seconds long. Rather than provide longer and more clarifying recordings that listeners could judge for themselves, Bethan-court helpfully wrote up summaries of the context.

But given how he failed to accurately represent the most controversial clip—the one that made its way into *Washington Post*, *New York Times*, and *Houston Chronicle* coverage—there's reason to doubt his framing of all the snippets. A close listen shows that Floyd actually expressed the exact *oppo-site* sentiment to which Bethancourt claimed.

In accordance with Bethancourt's synopsis, the *Post* and the *Houston Chronicle* both reported that the executive committee did not want to hear feedback from survivors.[45] As proof of this, they both offered the same Floyd quote: "I am not concerned about anything survivors can say."

In fact, what Floyd actually said was "I'm not *scared* by anything the sur-vivors *would* say" [emphasis mine]. The subtle difference becomes even more significant when one hears Floyd's conciliatory tone, which even with the extremely limited context, suggests he wanted victims to have the freedom to express their opinions, but *at the same time*, he was asking Moore, "As you think through strategy, do everything you can to remember the base"—a reasonable request from one institutional leader to another as they are dis-cussing reforms.

Given that both the *Chronicle* and the *Post* happened to mistranscribe the same two words in the exact same way, one has to doubt that both did, in fact, listen to the clip. The best-case scenario is that one reporter did, and the other cribbed off him. Nor did any of the media reports mention that toward the end of the clip, it became even clearer that Floyd was *not* saying that the SBC should focus only on protecting its reputation. Moore and Bethancourt (who knew they were being recorded and would have taken pains to cast themselves in the best light) replied to Floyd that the best way to "protect the credibility of the convention" would be to make a "concerted effort on abuse." To this, Floyd murmured his agreement *six times*.

Maybe the media missed all that concurrence because Bethancourt didn't include it in his summary. The *Houston Chronicle* and the *New York Times* didn't even bother to mention that the audio had been released in clips, never mind that it represented only six minutes out of three hundred. Both gave the impression that the full recording had been released.

But there was one more little detail about Moore's leaked letters that did not attract the media's attention, perhaps because Moore would not have wanted it to. Jon Whitehead, an attorney from St. Louis, wondered why he had never seen Moore's February 2020 letter to the ERLC trustees.[46] He was one of those trustees, and he not only would have remembered a letter like that, but would have taken steps to see if he could help Moore address whatever was causing his "psychological terror."

Ironically, long before that letter, Whitehead had noticed that Moore seemed to be isolating himself from his colleagues and constituents, and he made a motion to survey ERLC morale and see if anything needed to be done to help Moore and his staff better relate with other Southern Baptists. This suggestion was rebuffed by the trustee board chair David Prince, whose relationship to Moore was so close that it was "like a suckerfish to its host," as one ERLC source told me and another confirmed.

Prince had assured Whitehead that Moore had a good working relationship with the executive committee. So, one can imagine Whitehead's shock when Moore's first leak hit the press. Prince later told Whitehead the reason he hadn't forwarded the June 2 letter to the board was because he believed "Dr. Moore had written it in the heat of the moment." He thought Moore had "got over it" in a few days. As Whitehead wrote later, "The blatant deception admitted by this response leads me to conclude that the letters were not designed for action by the ERLC Board; they were written and leaked to shake [voter] trust and confidence at an SBC annual meeting."[47]

That is exactly what they did.

In June 2021, in the midst of the media tsunami Moore had created around the narrative that he had been persecuted for confronting an abuse crisis, nearly sixteen thousand attendees descended on the annual meeting of the Southern Baptist Convention. The Church delegates were so eager to show the world that the SBC *did* care about abuse that they approved all three of the abuse reform motions that Denhollander, who is not a Southern Baptist, had helped draft. An abuse task force was created, and Denhollander was appointed to advise it. Guidepost Solutions—the for-profit, third-party investigative company that Denhollander recommended—was hired to investigate and produce a report. At Denhollander's urging, the SBC executive committee was directed to waive attorney-client privilege so that all communications between committee members and the denomination's legal counsel could not be kept confidential.[48] A number of attorneys with no connection to the SBC told me that such a thing should not have been necessary for fact-finding and that they would never have advised an entity to agree to it. But it had to be done, Denhollander and other reformers insisted, so that everything could be laid bare in the Guidepost Report.[49]

When the report came out a year later, the press coverage surrounding it made Moore's letters sound as staid and mild as the classifieds.

Apocalypse

NBC and *USA Today* called the Guidepost Report a "reckoning."[50] CNN labeled it "explosive."[51] The *Washington Post* went with "bombshell."[52] The *New York Times* said it "stun[ned] from pulpit to pews."[53] David French, writing for *The Atlantic*, characterized it as a "horror" that proved the SBC was not suffering from a few bad apples but was a "diseased orchard."[54] And, most curious, within an hour of the nearly three-hundred-page document's being released, Moore published an essay in *Christianity Today* in which he claimed to have read the report in detail and found it revealed an "apocalypse . . . far more evil and systemic than I imagined it could be."[55]

Naturally, this raises a question: What does an apocalypse look like in hard numbers? In this case, it meant that over the course of twenty-one years, the investigators identified 409 accused abusers who had at one point been associated with one of the SBC's approximately 48,000 churches. Note that this did not mean that all the abuse occurred in connection to the Church or that the accused individuals were involved with an SBC church at the time of the alleged abuse, just that the 409 had had SBC associations at some point.

Conservatively estimating five paid staffers per church (knowing that some churches will have only one and some many more) would create a pool of around 235,000 people. Except that this accounts only for staff, and some of the alleged abusers were volunteers. If we (again conservatively) estimate 10 volunteers per church, knowing that the largest SBC churches could easily have hundreds serving in various capacities, the pool from which the 409 were drawn from would be over 700,000. Except, this assumes a static number of staff and volunteers, and of course people drift in and out of churches all the time. So, being extremely cautious with numbers would easily put the pool at over a million people serving or working in SBC churches over the course of those twenty-one years. Four hundred and nine out of a million—even assuming that every accusation is true (and there's no reason not to assume that nearly all are), this is, in truth, an astonishingly low rate. And it was roughly the same figure a team of reporters at the *Houston Chronicle* came up with after six months of investigation in 2019.[56]

By comparison, Chicago Public Schools is made up of 39,000 employees. Yet students lodged 470 complaints of sexual abuse against school staffers in 2022 alone.[57] For some reason, rates of sexual abuse in the public school system are not often investigated by the media, but the most recent Department of Education report found that by the time they graduate from high school, 10 percent of all American public school students will have been the victim of sexual misconduct by a school employee.[58]

I asked Lyman Stone, a demographer at the Institute for Family Studies, who has no affiliation with the Southern Baptist Convention, about the media's coverage of Guidepost's findings. He was bemused. "Statistically speaking, there were not that many cases," he told me. "This is not actually that common of a problem in this Church body. If you wanted to argue that based on this report that executives of the SBC mismanaged the cases that were brought to them, then fine. But if you want to say this shows that [the SBC] is corrupt, hypocritical, and rife with sexual abuse—the report doesn't demonstrate that."

What surprised Stone the most, however, was the number of *current* cases Guidepost investigators had turned up: two. In the entire country, only two alleged abusers were found to be currently serving in Southern Baptist churches. "I mean, if I had been betting beforehand," Stone told me, "I would have bet for a couple of hundred. Just your baseline rate of sex offenders tells you you should have gotten a couple thousand sex offenders in there just by random chance." He concluded that while the Guidepost Report may have shown the need for reforms in responding to allegations, it did not show an endemic problem of sexual abuse.

But even on proving the need for reforms, the report had little to offer. Moore and media outlets ranging from NPR to *The New Yorker* were quick to characterize a list of accused abusers that a committee staffer had assembled as "secret" evidence of a "coverup."[59] In fact, it had been created to give the committee an idea of the feasibility of an abuser database and was culled entirely from Google Alerts and newspaper clippings. Every accusation it contained was already in the public domain. How does one cover up public information? Eventually, Bart Barber, who won his bid for the SBC presidency largely by promising to right the wrongs the executive committee had committed regarding abuse, conceded that claims of a cover-up were false.

"After looking hard to see if they could find a time when the convention or the executive committee knew about abuse and failed to report it, or facilitated an abuser being able to continue to abuse, [investigators] didn't find any instances where the convention or the executive committee did that," Barber said during a recorded interview at a Florida church in January 2024. "We know the Southern Baptist Convention has never made a mistake in terms of not reporting abuse."[60] But by then, with the media's help, the cover-up narrative was already deeply entrenched in the public mind and nobody paid any attention to Barber's admission that flew directly in the face of the impression he had given during an interview with CNN anchor Anderson Cooper.

The other surprising element of Guidepost's investigation was that while those 409 alleged abusers certainly included some serious cases in local churches, Guidepost had devoted the bulk of its report to murky allegations from two adult women. The most prominent case by far? Jennifer Lyell's.

Just as with the many media reports featuring Lyell's allegations after the 2019 conference, Guidepost didn't explain what acts of abuse David Sills had committed, and SBC abuse reformers insisted that no one should be allowed to ask.

After I began asking questions of just about everyone connected to the case for a *Daily Wire* story, SBC president Bart Barber put out a public statement, saying, "[Lyell's] claims have been investigated by [Guidepost Solutions], and whatever you think of their political positions or positions on social issues of the day, they are experts in this subject matter [of] investigation of sexual abuse claims."[61] On another occasion, when a Twitter user, in response to an SBC leader urging rank-and-file Baptists to support Lyell, mildly asked what the abuse was, Denhollander popped up, seeming to threaten the man with a lawsuit:

> @FarmerIsidore: Is there somewhere that outlines what the abuse specifically was? I can only find publications saying she was abused but can't find any specifics.
>
> @R_Denhollander: I am one of Ms. Lyell's attorneys. . . . Ms. Lyell's abuse has always been confirmed to be criminal assault and was confirmed as such [by] multiple SBC entity heads. . . . As a result we settled a very significant defamation suit against the Executive Committee of the SBC for deliberate defamation of Ms. Lyell. Please cease and desist from this line of questioning at this point.[62]

But the questioner was right. No one had ever offered the slightest detail about the nature of Lyell's abuse. And Lyell had never filed charges against Sills, so no court or legal authority could have "confirmed [it] to be criminal assault." She had claimed in an interview that both she and the school had contacted the authorities and that the police had gone to Sills's house to "track" him, out of fear he might attack her. Yet when I checked, I found that no local police department had any records pertaining to her or Sills, and SBTS president Albert Mohler said he could not answer any questions about Sills due to legal constraints.

Nevertheless, at several points in the thirty-five-plus pages that argued that the SBC executive committee had mishandled Lyell's abuse claims, Guidepost investigators insisted that Lyell's story had been "corroborated." By this, the consulting firm appeared to have meant only that SBTS administrators (who had asked Denhollander to help them properly respond to Lyell's accusations[63]) had decided that Lyell was credible.

I asked Guidepost Solutions to clarify what they meant by "corroborate," but they declined to answer. However, Lyell's boss was one of the supposed corroborators and the first person to whom Lyell had revealed the alleged abuse in 2018. He told me that Guidepost had never spoken to him.[64] Another source the company cited for corroboration was a SBTS professor who also happened to be Sills's pastor. He told me he had told the investigators only that he believed Lyell, which is hardly to be wondered at, given that his employer was publicly taking that stance. He had provided Guidepost no additional evidence, and he explicitly told me that Sills had *not* confessed to sexual abuse, something Guidepost investigators never noted, any more than it noted Denhollander's role in advising the seminary.

Guidepost defended its choice to present Sills as a certain abuser by noting that it hadn't found any evidence that "indicated that the interactions between Ms. Lyell and Professor Sills was [sic] anything but sexual abuse." Perhaps that's because they weren't looking for any. It took me only a couple of phone calls to track down a former coworker of Sills; he recalls seeing him and Lyell together and feeling that their relationship looked very much consensual: "The two of them [were] eating and laughing with their heads very close together in the lunchroom at Southern Seminary," Old Testament professor Russell Fuller remembered. "They were so public, you almost thought, *Well, guilty people wouldn't be that public. They would be more careful.*" Other colleagues and longtime friends of the Sills family told me they could have never conceived of Sills being violent.

There was one other source I spoke to that Guidepost didn't: Sills himself. He flatly denied the abuse and said that, as far as he knows, Guidepost has never tried to contact him. After Sills filed a lawsuit against Lyell, the SBC, and Guidepost Solutions for defamation, Guidepost told the court it had never investigated whether Lyell's allegations were true. It had only investigated whether the SBC executive committee had mistreated her in refusing to allow *Baptist Press* to name her a definitive victim of abuse. But, of course, Guidepost's finding of mistreatment hinged on the truth of Lyell's claims. If the committee wasn't certain her claims were true, then how could it have mistreated her in declining to print that they were?

The correspondence reprinted in the report that Denhollander, Moore, and Guidepost cited as proof that the committee had "trampled" on Lyell simply showed that it had been unwilling to label her a victim because it had no specifics concerning the nature of her accusations and no firm basis on which to form a judgment. As one of the executive committee's attorneys wrote in response to a draft of the *Baptist Press* article:

> What age is Jennifer Lyell? Her story uses the term "sexual abuse," but it is not clear to me whether she means child sexual abuse, abusing a relationship of trust, or some type of power differential abuse . . . I think we need to be careful about those distinctions. Does this article cast Sills in a "false light" as a sex offender? . . . What has [Baptist Press] done or what can it do to corroborate this story if you decide to run it? Will Dr. Mohler say that Sills confessed to "sexual abuse"? The author never indicates what the abuse was.

Such was the tenor of all the discussion surrounding Lyell's MeToo article. In hindsight, it probably would have been better for the committee to spike the article, but internal correspondence shows that its members feared being accused of "attempting to silence a victim" if it did. It was a no-win situation—thus, the tortured discussions over how to phrase her accusations. Yet at no point in their correspondence with one another or with Lyell did they so much as hint that she wasn't telling the truth. Every piece of communication reproduced in the report showed that the committee members and their legal counsel were responsive to her emails and discussed her and her wishes respectfully. Even as Lyell began to join Denhollander in publicly bashing the committee, its members emailed one another comments like "I want [Ms. Lyell] to be whole again. I want her to experience healing and happiness, but what she is doing [online] isn't the way to attain that."[65]

So, where did Moore get his claims, amplified through media megaphones, that the committee had subjected Lyell to "bullying," "intimidation," and "horror"? How did Denhollander justify publicly accusing them of "casting [Lyell] away"? Not a single reporter seemed to feel that this rhetoric, which they quoted from liberally, should be backed up with specifics. And just as in the case of campus adjudications, Guidepost investigators seemed perfectly willing to preside over one-sided proceedings. That might explain why, in 2022, Lyell posted her own statement praising the report and encouraging people to "read the reflections of Dr. Russell Moore," by which she meant his "apocalypse" essay.[66]

The second most prominent case in the Guidepost Report also involved adults. An anonymous pastor and his wife approached the investigators to tell them that former SBC president Johnny Hunt had sexually assaulted the wife in 2010 when she was staying in a Florida vacation rental adjoining the Hunt family's. Hunt said it was a consensual encounter that involved groping, kissing, and removal of clothing that stopped short of intercourse. Guidepost investigators reported that Hunt had "groomed" the couple with "flattery and promises of help in ministry." They stressed that Hunt was twenty-four years older than the woman and had "daughters close in age to [her]." Yet, for some reason, they didn't mention that Alisa Womack, whose identity was revealed when her attorneys failed to redact her name in court filings, was thirty-five at the time and her husband, Rusty, was around forty. Also worth noting, though Guidepost didn't: Hunt held no authority over either of the Womacks.

A few days after Hunt returned home, he confessed to a consensual extramarital encounter to the counseling pastor at his church. The counseling pastor then scheduled a meeting between Hunt and the Womacks. The Guidepost Report's description of the meeting and explanation for why Alisa Womack didn't resist Hunt was eerily similar to the trauma-informed framing common to campus allegations:

> [She] felt frozen . . . [The counseling pastor] said that in his expert opinion an inappropriate relationship had developed, and that based on his information it was consensual. [The woman] states that at the time she believed that, even though she did not consent to what Dr. Hunt did to her, she was made to feel it was consensual because she did not fight back.

And, in fact, the Womacks told the *Houston Chronicle* that they themselves came to characterize what had happened as abuse only during trauma counseling ten years later, well into the MeToo era:

> [Rusty Womack] enrolled in a non-SBC seminary, where he was introduced to scholarly work on abusive systems and deception techniques.
>   Suddenly, it all clicked. Through counseling with experts, including with the firm of renowned religious trauma scholar Diane Langberg,

the couple said they came to understand what they could not quite articulate for a decade.

They decided to talk to Guidepost, hoping that their story would help illustrate how power dynamics—combined with a lack of trauma-informed counseling—can be weaponized against the vulnerable.[67]

As corroboration of assault, Guidepost investigators cited three separate past conversations Rusty Womack had had with friends about the encounter, though all three conversations would have taken place before Womack himself admits he came to see the encounter in that way, and none of the friends characterized it as assault in the report. Nevertheless, new SBC leadership then publicly named Hunt guilty of sexual abuse and assault. Hunt is also suing the SBC and Guidepost for defamation.

Meet the Church Bureaucracy, Same as the Government Bureaucracy

This does not mean that Sills could not have been abusive or that Hunt could not have committed assault. But these were the most prominent cases in the Guidepost Report that were used to argue that Title IX–style reforms were needed in the country's largest Protestant denomination, yet neither involved so much as a police report, let alone charges or a guilty verdict. And that's to say nothing of the process Guidepost followed, which was far from what would have been included in a police investigation or a civil or criminal trial.

When the dust settled after the report's release, almost the entirety of the old conservative executive committee was pushed out. The only issue remaining for the SBC was how to implement Guidepost's recommendations.

The question of how to better protect children was uncontroversial, centering largely on background checks, training in protective processes, and education in reporting to the police. But as with Title IX regulations, the truly transformational reforms involved allegations of encounters between adults.

Though the SBC had previously operated as a loose federation of churches whose national leadership, by design, had little power over individual congregations, the reformers, like the Obama administration, said the revelations in the Guidepost Report demanded a new "administrative entity." This new body would be empowered to carry out ongoing investigations into abuse allegations between adults that would follow a single-investigator process running parallel to, but apart from, the American legal system.

An independent third party would be brought in to adjudicate. Names of the "credibly accused" would be added to a public database of those judged guilty not just of sexual immorality but also *abuse*—meaning they would find it difficult to land comparable employment outside the ministry. Guilt would be based on the >50.01 percent preponderance-of-evidence standard. Just as with the Obama administration, the SBC's abuse task force promoted this as being the same as the standard used in civil court, without explaining that the single-investigator model doesn't provide the due process protections of civil trials.[68]

The task force also stressed the need for state and national SBC entities to engage firms "professionally trained in trauma-informed investigative techniques and practices."[69] Denhollander made it clear in interviews that the task force's definition of "trauma-informed" was no different from that which the Association of Title IX Administrators had been forced to repudiate.

She spoke on Twitter of the "neural damage" trauma causes, in which victims' "memories are fragmented, not linear."[70] She told the *Houston Chronicle* that "mental neurobiological injury often make[s] it impossible for survivors to fully remember what's taken place."[71] In an interview with a religious think tank, she adhered to the same unfalsifiable acceptance of allegations that Title IX critics warn about, saying that when someone responds to abuse claims with questions about "why the abuse couldn't have happened the way [the accuser] described," it's because they "don't understand trauma responses."[72]

There is no question that Denhollander is passionate about protecting the vulnerable. Her heroic efforts to bring Larry Nassar to justice for molesting children stands as a testament to her courage and compassion. Her bravery is even more impressive given that she herself was a Nassar victim, at fifteen. But it would be difficult for anyone given extraordinary influence over one topic, without the benefit of checks and balance, not to grow myopic.

The SBC could not have failed to recognize the conflicts of interest inherent in its arrangements with Denhollander. Yet its leadership was either too cowed, too cowardly, or too incompetent to acknowledge them.

Denhollander advised the SBTS on how to respond to Lyell's allegations, then recommended Guidepost, the company that cited those responses (and those responses alone) as proof of Lyell's claims. She represented Lyell in a defamation settlement against the SBC executive committee and then helped draft the convention motions that both demanded an investigation into that committee and directed the committee to waive privilege. After this, she accepted an appointment as the chief adviser to the investigators. Finally, when the SBC awarded Guidepost a pricey contract to create an abuse hotline,[73] she took on the role of caller advocate. Acting as advocate to one party and adviser to another that had opposing legal interests was ethically questionable enough. But to make matters worse, in two leaked texts, Denhollander admitted that she was "quietly" using her hotline role to connect callers to a "truly solid legal team" so they could "potentially sue" the SBC.[74]

Even after the revelation that Denhollander was both advising the SBC on abuse reforms while facilitating lawsuits against the denomination, no one in SBC leadership raised so much as a peep about ethics. It's hard to imagine anyone would let such a situation stand if it were not tied to such an emotionally loaded subject.

At the very least, it should raise doubts about Denhollander's judgment when it comes to abuse, which has at times been more than questionable. For instance, she accused Republicans of "community protectionism" when they were unwilling to take Christine Blasey Ford's assault allegations against Justice Brett Kavanaugh at face value because of Ford's lack of evidence, corroboration, or consistency.[75]

Denhollander blithely waved away the fact that Ford could not prove that she'd ever met Kavanaugh or that the party where he allegedly assaulted her had ever taken place. Denhollander was similarly unbothered by the fact that Ford had changed her recollection of the year of the party and couldn't recall basics like how she got there or got home. Writing for Vox, Denhollander, once again, put it all down to trauma. "The 'evidence' wielded against Ford, such as gaps in her memory, was easily explainable by anyone who understands the impact of trauma," she said.[76] The fact that Ford's own witnesses did not back up her claims, or that Kavanaugh had contemporaneous calendars to support his innocence, didn't seem to register in Denhollander's thinking at all.

She has even seemed to suggest that the American justice system, with its bedrock right to be judged by one's peers, cannot be trusted to adjudicate abuse claims and that some new arrangement is needed. When the jury and the vast majority of Americans decided, after weeks of listening to testimony and reviewing evidence, that they did not believe actor Johnny Depp had abused his ex-wife Amber Heard, Denhollander tweeted that it was because "Jurors have none of this [trauma] training, and are simply part of our society."[77]

It might be one thing if Denhollander's influence were limited to the SBC, large as it is, with its millions of members, seminary networks, and vast church-planting ministries. But she is now guiding abuse reform in other large evangelical denominations and parachurch ministries.[78] She and Guidepost investigator Samantha Kilpatrick helped implement a mandatory abuse course at Southeastern Baptist Theological Seminary, one of the largest seminaries in the country, which trains pastors in every Protestant denomination.[79] In one session of the course a source provided to me, Kilpatrick describes sexual abuse between adults as being based on a "power differential" between someone who is an "oppressor" and someone who is "oppressed." (The course uses the oppressed/oppressor model in a number of sessions). Her description of how to identify the oppressor in a given scenario would seem to encompass just about anyone on a bad day:

> Some use aggressive tactics, some use passive tactics. . . . So the core beliefs of those who feel entitled, oftentimes you will see an attitude of it's all about me, you will see an attitude that the person is always right. They will also see other people's opinions or other people's disagreement as attacking . . . they will feel that the rules do not apply to them, that they're above the rules, but the rules actually apply to others, and

they will use the rules for their benefit. You will also see an attitude that their anger is always justified, they will turn themselves into the victim and accuse the true victim or the true survivor of being the one attacking, attacking.

This abuse curriculum Denhollander helped develop is being promoted across the evangelical landscape, including in Presbyterian denominations.[80]

One prominent SBC leader I spoke to started out as a vocal supporter of Denhollander's reforms. But over time, as he got to know her views better, he began to have misgivings—not because he doubted her honesty or commitment, but because he felt she had developed a sort of tunnel vision.

"There is a righteous cause there," he told me. "But I use the illustration of Inspector Javert from Victor Hugo's great work *Les Misérables*. You know, he's a fascinating character because he's one hundred percent committed to justice. And justice is a good thing, a great thing, in balance. But his commitment to justice becomes distorted because it's devoid of grace and mercy and even understanding of the point of justice. I'm not suggesting Rachael is a villain like Javert, but she's a little Javert-like in that she demands submission on this issue, and to disagree with her is to excuse abuse. And that's all she sees."

Under Denhollander's guidance, SBC leaders seemed unable to identify claims that demanded further scrutiny and unwilling to acknowledge gradations of offense when it came to adults, placing assault, mutually sinful relationships, and unwelcome sexual overture into one catchall category—abuse. The penalty for all, as well as for the unlucky innocent man who could so easily be caught in the credibly-accused net, is to end up a name on a public list, not just a sinner but an abuser.

As to why so many of the SBC leaders who have quietly messaged me about their concerns have gone along with all this, one puts it this way: "If you don't, you know the hounds of hell are going to be unleashed on you. And you have in your mind that other, better men than you have fallen because they didn't handle an allegation of sexual abuse in just the way [the Church-Too activists] wanted. We all know we're dealing with dynamite here."

Of course, there's also the SBC pastors who have clearly calculated that they can ride the abuse wave to larger national platforms. They have tended to make spectacles of themselves at the annual convention, towing alleged victims up to microphones when they make abuse motions, conspicuously weeping over the issue on the stage, turning down no chance to make hyperbolic condemnations to the media. One pastor, Todd Benkert, became so overt in this kind of brand building—plastering his survivor ribbon–themed convention booth across social media, organizing unofficial break-out sessions in which he positioned himself as an expert, leaking to the press complaints he was supposed to be investigating—that he had to be removed from the abuse task force altogether.[81]

His biggest error was that he wasn't smart enough to be as subtle in his machinations as others.

Laura Kipnis, the feminist Northwestern professor who wrote the book about campus abuse panic, said this about the ways the Title IX process has been used in academia to settle scores and target rivals:

> There are often shadowy players and issues behind the scenes: departmental rivalries, personal grudges, even scheming exes. It's not unheard of for professors to urge students to press charges against other professors, or otherwise play the process to their advantage. In some cases, an older generation of feminists have proved adept at using vague misconduct allegations to knock off ideological foes, including loathed younger male professors. And what a great opportunity for payback over tenure disputes. . . . The retaliation factor figures in undergrad student-student cases, too, especially in romances gone wrong. . . . Given weak evidentiary standards and credulous investigators, the Title IX process is extraordinarily available to manipulation.[82]

Similarly, the internecine tangles, power plays, and competing agendas that were rampant all through the run-up to the SBC's abuse reforms are too long to tell even in this very long chapter.

Many activists and media figures have implied or outright stated that the SBC's abuse "crisis" delegitimized conservative theology.[83] They leveraged this narrative to demand that evangelicalism "interrogate its own hetero-patriarchal white supremacy" or, at the very least, join the secular world in prioritizing female power.[84] That's to say nothing of leaders in the SBC seminaries who used the issue to oust their ideological opponents from key positions over claims that abuse accusations were mishandled. Those same claims failed to withstand the close scrutiny of the court and were later dismissed.[85]

Other conversations Moore and his team secretly recorded were initially mentioned in Guidepost's report but quietly removed when it came out that the remarks were entirely unrelated to abuse.[86] Then there were the two serious allegations of abuse cover-ups involving close Moore allies that Guidepost strangely did not mention in its report, even though, unlike many of the claims that *did* make it in, both were substantiated by police and court records.

To give just a brief sense of them: According to witnesses, after his brother-in-law was caught secretly recording women and children in church bathrooms, Pastor Bryan Loritts decided to handle the matter internally rather than call the police.[87] The witnesses allege that Loritts disposed of video evidence contained on a cell phone and silenced victims before the brother-in-law went to work at another church, where he was eventually caught and convicted. When former SBC president J. D. Greear hired Loritts as an executive pastor at his church, victims say they told Greear about the alleged cover-up. In response, they say Greear (the same Greear who positioned himself as an abuse crusader and who had been the recipient of Moore's second leaked letter) called in Guidepost to carry out a show process meant only to clear Loritts.[88] The witnesses—who, unlike the "corroborators" in the Sills case, had direct knowledge of events—say Guidepost investigators ignored Loritts's conflicting statements, used his sister as a key witness, and overlooked glaring holes in his story.

The other case involved Kevin Ezell, the powerful head of the SBC's North American Mission Board and a close associate of Moore's. In 2004, while he was the pastor of a church where Moore served as elder, a grand jury subpoenaed Ezell regarding charges of molestation against one of the church's former employees.[89] Though the SBC does not practice Catholic-style confessions, Ezell successfully invoked clergy-penitent privilege to avoid testifying. The former employee was eventually convicted of having molested seven boys.[90] In 2018, when Baptist journalist Joni Hannigan brought up the case (which was in the public record) in regard to SBC abuse reforms, a member of Ezell's team threatened her with libel, something she told me she shared with Guidepost.[91]

Yet not a word of either of these cases made it into the Guidepost Report.

The entertainment industry was scandalized when it was revealed that Time's Up, a Hollywood splinter group of the MeToo movement, had given a pass to political ally and New York governor Andrew Cuomo over allegations that he'd harassed staffers.[92] Time's Up's advisory board was dissolved so as not to further embarrass A-list members Reese Witherspoon and Natalie Portman.[93] When average Southern Baptists began to point out that Guidepost and the abuse task force were similarly using unequal weights and measures, SBC leadership shrugged.

What We Lose

There is no question as to what these reforms will do to the SBC and other denominations. We have already seen what they have done on campuses. But one interesting footnote suggests that at least a few of the Southern Baptist leaders building their public platforms promoting these policies may be savvier than the college administrators who simply had the policies foisted upon them.

Predictably, once the trauma-informed, single-adjudicator, preponderance-of-evidence process was entrenched in academia, colleges and universities began to face a tsunami of lawsuits from young men who'd had their educations derailed by false allegations. In the majority of these cases, the courts later sided with the young men against the schools.[94] And a study from a university insurance group revealed that the vast majority of settlements schools are paying over Title IX cases have gone to accused men, not to abused women.[95]

But one Southern Baptist leader hit on a way to have his cake as a courageous abuse reformer while avoiding eating any liability.

SBC president Bart Barber drafted legislation that shields churches and ministries from lawsuits should they wrongly list someone on their planned abuser database (again, the database operating without oversight or involvement from our actual legal system).[96] So, if an innocent man in the state of Texas ends up on that *public* list and it damages his career prospects or harms him financially or emotionally, he will have no legal recourse. He will not be able do what many college students have done and sue for restitution in court.

And if Barber and the other reformers have their way, this will eventually roll out across the nation. In light of the many verses that tell Christians to make restitution when they have wronged someone, is this biblical? No. But it *is* smart.

But other costs to these reforms will have to be paid, and not all of them will be paid by wrongly or overly accused men. I'm speaking of the serious, spiritual cost they will exact from many women.

When I was posting some of my objections to the ongoing labeling of all the women in the John Crist case as victims, I received the expected criticism (which should be read as searing verbal lacerations) from various reformers, including a number of SBC pastors (who, it turns out, can be astonishingly pugilistic with the right kind of woman).

I was a rape apologist. (Never mind that I've been a victim of rape and would never have it in mind to apologize for my rapist.)

I was shaming victims. (I did not want to shame anyone. And certainly, if these cases had not been held out with a demand for my assent, I would not have had reason to speak about them.)

I was a "pick-me girl." (I had to ask my teenage daughter to explain this one to me. Turns out, it's a girl or woman who, in a bid for male approval, tries to show she is "not like the other girls.") This one didn't make much sense, as most of the people hurling epithets at me were men.

And then I received a text from a professional acquaintance well known in the evangelical media world. My heart sank. I liked and respected this woman and wanted her to like and respect me. I did not relish receiving even mild condemnation from her. But when I clicked on the body of the text, condemnation was not what I found. I reprint her note here with only a few alterations, to protect her anonymity:

> Megan, I have seen some of your tweets about #ChurchToo, and I have been silent. . . . I have written this very text a number of times, but I could never hit send.
>
> When the #MeToo movement was strong and loud, I was silent

then, too. While I could commiserate with the women harassed by men in powerful positions who used that power for evil, I couldn't wholly get behind the movement.

The Holy Spirit has been using your tweets and your questions to stir up 20-year-old emotions and memories I have buried.

Let me encourage you to keep asking questions. Yes, women like me and I believe you as well, who have been propositioned, should tell their stories, and #MeToo isn't a bad tagline. But as I go back and read the painful prayers I recorded in prayer journals from the time in life when I might have been tempted to join their movement, I can say "me too" for another reason. I sinned, too.

It's so easy to fall into line with the culture's narrative because part of it is valid. I was under the authority of someone I admired and trusted. That man was a predator in a suit and a church robe. But the part of #Me Too that isn't talked about is the painful, embarrassing, and regret-filled part that admits, in the end, I could have chosen differently and did not. I sinned too.

I trust and cling to 1 John 1:9. If we confess our sins, he is faithful and just to forgive us our sins and to cleanse us from all unrighteousness.

How thankful I am for that promise.

I called my friend, and she told me more of her story. She was in her early thirties, and her husband had left her. It was a uniquely vulnerable time in her life. She wasn't even particularly attracted to the pastor at the church she had started attending, but as he continued to pursue her, she was flattered. Her divorce had shattered her self-confidence, and the attention went some way toward restoring it. For a very brief time, the two engaged in a sexual relationship, until she ended it and left the church.

When I asked my friend if she viewed this pastor as an abuser, she hesitated. "I can say that he abused his authority because I respected him. The first time he attempted [to kiss me], I immediately left. And I could have stayed away. But I came back. I lingered. So, I would say that in the beginning, he sexually harassed me. But then, it wasn't sexual harassment, because I went back. Then it was consensual. And then I left."

She similarly vacillated when I asked if she would identify as a victim.

She didn't like that word. "It's so easy to be the victim," she sighed. "It really absolves you almost of your part. Because you tell yourself, I didn't make the first move. He did. And it makes us feel better about ourselves when the focus can be on this other person, who *is* a bad guy. No doubt. And you're not saying that he isn't a bad guy. But you do need to acknowledge your part so that you can accept God's forgiveness, because he will forgive. He has forgiven me. And when the adversary reminds me of it, I remember that."

My friend's story was messy, and challenged some of my own thinking on this issue. Did I believe this man's name deserved to go on a public list? I did. And if I could ensure that only men like him or worse would end up on such a list, I would be hard-pressed to find an argument against it. I was angry that someone who should have been ministering to her in her weakness instead took advantage of her.

But I also considered the woman she is today. She has always evinced to me a sense of godliness and wisdom that I at first found a bit intimidating, if I'm to be honest—the sort of person whose spiritual depth is evident almost immediately. I wondered if I would still have had that sense of her if she'd been encouraged to tell herself a different story about what had happened, one that was easier and less complex, one that gave her refuge from personal responsibility.

Certainly, there *are* clear-cut cases of abuse between adults. But there are also many messy entanglements where exploitation runs in two directions. And we are trying to force those stories into neat "victim" and "villain" boxes, because that is what nice people, good people, respectable people do today. They pretend there are no messy stories in the Church.

Yet, as many examples as there are of bad men, Solomon would not have had to warn his son so often in Proverbs to beware seduction if there were not bad women as well. To acknowledge these things is not to absolve men from guilt over sins they have committed, but to ensure we do not leave women in theirs. I wonder whether these pastors, who crusade as compassionate reformers as they insist we dare not ask even the most obvious questions about some allegations, consider the state in which they may be leaving some women's consciences.

I have thought of events in my own past—one where I could unequivocally say I was a victim, others where I was not a victim, because I consented, but where, nonetheless, I should have been protected, and instead my own vulnerability was seized on and exploited. Where I have since sat quietly with my God, who knows I was wronged but also in the wrong. Where I, like my friend, prayed MeToo and me too.

CHAPTER 8

None Dare Call It Sin

LGBTQ in the Church

... For certain individuals whose condemnation was written about long ago have secretly slipped in among you. They are ungodly people, who pervert the grace of our God into a license for immorality and deny Jesus Christ our only Sovereign and Lord ...

In a similar way, Sodom and Gomorrah and the surrounding towns gave themselves up to sexual immorality and perversion. They serve as an example of those who suffer the punishment of eternal fire.

—Jude 1:3–4, 7

In 2021, Ben and Sasha Hughes grew concerned about how moody and withdrawn their fifteen-year-old son was becoming. The year before, they'd caught Aaron, first, searching for porn on his phone and then buying oxycodone from a classmate. Between that and their public school district's Covid-driven "hybrid" model, which mandated learning online from home several days a week, they decided his freshman year offered a good opportunity to enroll him in a Christian high school. The family also made a commitment to attend church services weekly. Though Ben and Sasha had both been believers their entire married life, they'd become nominal churchgoers since their sixteen-year-old daughter, a talented volleyball player, made a competitive club team a few years earlier. That meant a lot of weekend travel to out-of-town tournaments. Sasha estimates their church attendance had been averaging about once a month, if that.

But the developing crisis with their son outweighed their daughter's scholarship prospects. They might have to pay for her college rather than keep her skills sharp enough for college recruiters through weekend tournaments. But if that meant short-circuiting the spiral of secrecy and self-destruction threatening to engulf him, so be it: they would be in church every week.

In a bid to make church as appealing as possible, the family switched to a start-up Saturday night service that had rock-style worship and preaching from a young staff pastor. Though Aaron dragged his feet at first, to Ben and Sasha's delight, he seemed to fit in quickly. It helped that he played drums—an ability the church band made use of regularly. He also hit it off with the other members of the worship team, two of whom went to his high school. They and several other students from the school would often hang out after church. Ben, a medical sales executive, was starting to see more of himself in his increasingly outgoing son. What impressed him more was that Aaron seemed to be thinking seriously about his faith for the first time, to the point where he was initiating friendly debates at dinner.

"He'd start with, 'Hey, Jesus wasn't a Republican or a Democrat, Dad,'" Ben recalled. "And you know, that's right; he wasn't. So, I was fine with that. I mean, I just thought, *This is the kind of thing boys do, right?* They challenge their fathers, and that's part of growing up. I was like the original Rush [Limbaugh] baby, so I thought he was just kind of needling me." Even if Ben disagreed with his son's burgeoning views on things like gun control, he was mostly delighted to see him interested in spiritual things and engaging issues with confidence.

About six months after the family had begun regularly attending church, toward the end of the academic year, Sasha got a call from the school asking her and Ben to come in for a meeting. The headmaster told them Aaron and a group of other kids had been, in effect, proselytizing for the position that homosexuality and transgenderism were compatible with Christianity. This went against the school's statement of faith, which their family had signed. The headmaster showed them an essay Aaron had submitted in his Bible class.

"It was just a few paragraphs, and it wasn't the most sophisticated thing," Sasha told me, "but it basically argued that Jesus didn't say anything about being gay or trans, so Christians shouldn't, either. And it said Christians are causing gay and trans people to commit suicide and are sacrificing them to their theology, when love should come before theology. Stuff like that. [The headmaster] told us he didn't want to make too big of an issue out of it, but he thought we should be aware of it. Also, Aaron and some of his friends had been sort of debating other kids about it. And some parents were upset."

Ben and Sasha assured the school that their convictions were in line with the school's statement of faith and that they'd talk to Aaron. Though they'd never seen any sign of it, they left the meeting worried that he was struggling with same-sex attraction. Of course, they would assure him of their unconditional love, but they also knew they would not budge on their biblical beliefs, and the thought of the strife this might introduce to their home left knots in their stomachs. But that wasn't the issue. Aaron liked girls. In particular, he liked one of the older girls on the worship team who was also among the students espousing these ideas at school.

After a bit of probing, they discovered that the Saturday night worship leader appeared to be the primary influence behind the burgeoning progressive views of most of the students. He was where the proselytizing had started. After some conferring with the other parents, they discovered that the leader had recommended the kids listen to LGBTQ-affirming podcasts like *The New Evangelicals* and *The Bible for Normal People*.

Ben, Sasha, and another couple went to the church leadership and were told they'd known nothing about the young leader's views. Unlike the Sunday morning worship pastor, he was still only a volunteer. If he'd officially come on staff, even part time, they would have probed farther. Sasha says the church expressed how sorry they were and asked for forgiveness. "They seemed kind of shaken by it too, to be honest. I think we all just kind of assumed that if your church is transparent about the fact that it believes a certain thing, people will respect that."

■ ■ ■

Even until the late twentieth century, if there was one subject on which most Protestants, be they mainline or evangelical, were in clear agreement, it was sexuality. The cautionary tale of Sodom and Gomorrah confused no one, and when Paul wrote in 1 Corinthians 6:9 that those who practice homosexuality will not, along with drunkards and swindlers, inherit the kingdom of God, everyone took him at his word. It's surreal now to reflect that the Episcopalians, who today drape their historic cathedrals in rainbow-hued flags, as recently as 1998 approved a resolution asserting that homosexuality was "incompatible with Scripture."[1]

Yet, in 2003, the Episcopal Church consecrated its first openly gay bishop. In 2012, it approved transgender ordination. The other six sisters of the mainline held no firmer. The United Church of Christ, the Evangelical Lutheran Church in America, the Presbyterian Church (USA), the United Methodist Church, the American Baptist Churches USA, and the Disciples of Christ—today, not one still adheres to orthodoxy when it comes to sexuality and gender. And the Catholic Church is hardly doing better.

Pope Francis may have held off condoning gay marriage (while nonetheless making ambiguous statements media outlets cheer as proof of affirmation), but at 69 percent approval of same-sex marriage, rank-and-file Catholics are nearly as supportive of it as mainline Protestants.[2]

Religious academics and intellectuals attempt to justify this shift with tortured interpretations of Scripture that conveniently align with every power center in the United States from the Fortune 500 to the NFL. But most Americans who call themselves Christians today don't even bother with that. They make no appeals to serious theology; they have simply traded God's creational wisdom for a "Love Is Love" bumper sticker mentality and shifted their allegiance from Jesus Christ to Harvey Milk.

Evangelicals alone remain holdouts, and now they, too, are teetering.

Sift through *Washington Post* or *New York Times* coverage of the views of various evangelical subgroups on topics like immigration or entitlement programs, and you'll notice the reporters often take pains to separate out black or Hispanic evangelicals from their white counterparts. It's a curious thing, though, that you will rarely see the same differentiation when it comes to homosexuality or transgenderism. This is because, while there may be variations in degree, on this topic evangelicals of every ethnicity are in unanimous agreement.

According to a 2022 survey conducted by Lifeway Christian Resources, fully 72 percent of black evangelicals believe the Bible's condemnation of homosexual behavior still applies today, as do 56 percent of Hispanic evangelicals and 67 percent of white evangelicals. (Note that Asian evangelicals represent such a small subgroup, their sample size is not large enough to produce reliable results.)[3]

It is hardly surprising, then, that an all-out effort is being made to break down this final citadel of orthodoxy. While the frontal assaults of LGBTQ activists demanding full inclusion have garnered the lion's share of attention, more transformational efforts are being made by well-known megachurches using their dominance on the evangelical landscape to quietly influence smaller congregations to compromise.

Influence for Error

In September 2019, Mesa, Arizona, pastor Ryan Visconti was thrilled to find himself at a private dinner with Andy Stanley, pastor of what was then the largest church in the United States.[4]

On any given weekend, Atlanta's North Point sees roughly 31,000 attendees across eight campuses.[5] Stanley is also the author of dozens of books, and his sermons are distributed through a vast digital ministry that includes not only podcasts and YouTube videos, but also traditional broadcasts on NBC, CBS, and radio stations across the country. His late father, Rev. Charles Stanley, was a pioneer in Christian media and a leading figure in the Moral Majority movement of the 1980s, making Stanley generationally prominent. Little wonder, then, that *Preaching Magazine* ranked him number eight on its list of the twenty-five most influential preachers of the last twenty-five years, behind giants like Billy Graham, Chuck Swindoll, and John MacArthur.

But perhaps over no group does Stanley hold more sway than other pastors, with a number of his titles, like *7 Practices of Effective Ministry* and *Next Generation Leader*, specifically targeted toward that demographic. Phoenix had been a stop on Stanley's "Irresistible" tour, a conference that promised to teach church leaders how to "expand [their] influence." Visconti was excited for the opportunity to pick Stanley's brain, though, at thirty-four, he would be the youngest at a table of about fifteen men and expected to spend the majority of the meal quietly soaking up wisdom from Stanley and the more seasoned leaders. "I was mostly just planning to be a wallflower," he told me.

At some point in the evening, though, that plan went off the rails when the discussion turned toward homosexuality and how the men's ministries were confronting increasing cultural pressure to compromise on clear biblical teaching. Stanley shocked the room by arguing that they shouldn't so much confront it as accommodate it. "He said he would encourage any gay couples in his congregation to commit to each other," Visconti recalled.

That was the proverbial record scratch moment. "Like, everybody in the room just went, 'Wait. What?'" Visconti said. For the next hour and a half, he listened as Stanley went on to contend that modern pastors must make allowances for gay and lesbian couples to be married in their churches because "that's as close as they can get to a New Testament framework of marriage." Visconti remembered Stanley likening same-sex attraction to a disability, something that can't be helped. "Telling gay people they have to stop being gay to follow Christ is like taking a wheelchair away from a guy who can't walk." An expectation of celibacy, he argued, would be unfair.

Finally, Stanley revealed that while he had never officiated a same-sex wedding, he could see himself doing so eventually, especially for a family member. "If my granddaughter asked me someday, maybe I would," he told Visconti and the others, adding, "I know I shouldn't let experience dictate my theology, but I have. Maybe I'm wrong."

Visconti was dumbstruck: "I remember thinking to myself, if his church knew what he was saying right now, half of them would probably leave overnight." He joined several pastors in arguing with Stanley as others "squirmed in their chairs, muttering, 'That's not right.'" Host Joel Thomas, then pastor of Mission Community Church, had gotten his start in ministry under Stanley's tutelage, first as a North Point intern and, later, as campus pastor of one of the church's satellite locations. When the dinner was over, he moved swiftly to protect his former boss's reputation. "It was just basically like Joel kind of went into damage-control mode," Visconti recalled. Thomas asked the pastors to "honor" Stanley for being willing to "be vulnerable" in front of them. By this he meant they were not to speak of Stanley's views to anyone else.

Visconti felt torn. It *had* been a private event, which meant there was an expectation of confidentiality. But another part of him felt plagued by the knowledge that a man with so much influence on his fellow teachers was encouraging them in error. "I just thought, *This is bad. People need to know about this*." He prayed and pressed several of his mentors about it, trying to decide how to address someone as famous as Stanley. Should a group of men try to call him? Should they send a letter?

The mentors didn't think confrontation was the right approach, even though two weren't surprised by what Visconti had told them. Stanley had already preached messages about needing to "unhitch from the Old Testament," seeming to suggest he was laying the groundwork for more liberal theology. And a sermon illustration in which he reproved a husband in his church for committing adultery with another man but not for the homosexual acts involved had raised eyebrows as far back as 2012.[6]

In short, Visconti, who wasn't very familiar with Stanley's ministry, discovered that the fact that he might have heretical views had been whispered about for years. Yet this had not prompted the doctrinally sound pastors in Stanley's circle to warn churches not to host his conferences or to caution Christians not to buy his books or entertain his teaching.

Visconti held out hope that those witnesses who were on more equal footing with Stanley might be the ones to call him to account. He also hoped the famous pastor might just have been processing his ideas out loud.

"I was trying to give him as much benefit of the doubt as possible," Visconti said. "And, you know, pastors need pastors, too, sometimes. So I thought maybe I could equate it to someone sharing their own personal struggle with a temptation or with a faith issue that they might be wrestling with. I thought as long as it was a question Andy was trying to work out in his own mind, it wouldn't really feel right to publicly blast it out to the world."

Yet, as the months went by, there was no evidence that any of the more senior pastors who knew Stanley better had addressed the issue with him. Then, in 2022, clips of Stanley from his biennial Drive Conference—another event specifically targeted at pastors and ministry leaders—began to make the rounds on social media. In one, he heaped praise on LGBTQ individuals, saying their desire to come to church despite receiving judgment from Christians showed they had more faith than heterosexual church members. "A gay person who still wants to attend church after the way they've been treated—I'm telling you, they have more faith than I do," he said. "They have more faith than a lot of you." He went on to call 1 Corinthians 6, Leviticus

18, and Romans 1 "clobber passages," echoing a phrase common among gay activists when referencing Bible verses that address homosexuality. At no point did he indicate that homosexual acts or desires were sinful.[7]

When Stanley's remarks had given rise to similar questions in 2012, a North Point spokesperson claimed he was being taken out of context, though the representative did not clarify Stanley's views.[8] It would have been difficult for the church to offer the same defense this time, however, as it quickly took down the sermon that was the source of the clip, preventing it from being viewed in full. Now that Stanley was being asked again to explain whether he believed, as the Bible teaches, that homosexuality is a sin, his church declined to respond entirely.

Amid all the speculation about Stanley's meaning, another clip from the Drive Conference especially pricked Visconti's conscience. In it, Stanley seemed to encourage pastors to lead their congregations carefully and strategically toward acceptance of homosexuality. He contrasted those who abruptly announce their church is shifting its standard on the issue to those who "nudge" their congregations in a new direction:

> Pastors who get up and announce, "We're affirming." And the congregation is like, "We are? I don't even know what that is. Now I can't come back to my church." Whether the person is right or wrong is irrelevant. You're pastors and you're leaders. Don't take people's church away from them unnecessarily. It was terrible leadership [to announce they're affirming] because they skipped discipleship, teaching, preparing, and nudging. They played the role of a prophet and not a pastor.
>
> You are not a prophet. You are a pastor—very different role. Prophets drop in and drop truth bombs, and then they get on their chariot and go to the next place and drop truth. That's not what we're doing. We are leading people.[9]

Visconti feared that further silence would allow Stanley to use his platform to sow error and confusion in many churches across the country. Fifteen men knew. Fifteen *pastors* knew in which direction Stanley was trying to nudge evangelical churches. And for more than three years, none of them had said anything. Visconti decided enough was enough. He posted an explosive thread on Twitter revealing what Stanley had said and naming his views "overtly heretical."

Two other pastors who had been at the dinner that night confirmed that Visconti's account was accurate, fulfilling the Matthew 18 requirement of two to three witnesses. But that was as far as they were willing to go. When it came to issuing any more substantial warning, as the younger pastor had, both backed away.

One told me he didn't feel comfortable providing details because the dinner had been private. The other shared this concern about confidentiality but added, "[I'm] not sure I want to get into a political battle on this." He did indicate he'd be up for a book interview if I was interested in "speak[ing] to a pastor who is holding fast to Scripture with grace and truth."

He seemed like a nice guy, and I appreciated his initial impulse to back Visconti. But I wondered how his view of himself as one holding fast to Scripture held up in the light of the Bible's mandate to confront a brother who is in sin and tell the Church if he continues in it unrepentant.

The most unsettling thing about my exchange with this man was the implication that because Stanley's unbiblical stance centered on homosexuality, raising any alarm about it would have been "political." A highly influential pastor was compromising the Word of God and encouraging other church leaders to do likewise. If any matter could be classified as ecclesiastical rather than civil in nature, this was it. Especially as it turned out there was a lot more going on at North Point to spread LGBTQ ideology through America's churches than just Stanley's pastors' conferences.

The Other Big Church

In 2000, Jon Stryker, gay heir to a one-hundred-billion-dollar surgical supply conglomerate, kicked off the new millennium by launching the Arcus Foundation, a grant-making institution that soon became the largest funder of LGBTQ initiatives in the United States.[10] But after legislative defeats like the passage of a 2008 California law banning gay marriage, it realized its efforts to break down America's last remaining vestiges of traditional sexual morality were continually running into the same formidable roadblock—Christianity.[11] As the journal *Inside Philanthropy* put it in 2013, "In recent years, it has become clear in the US, at least, that the only real opposition to LGBT equality is moral opposition based on religious beliefs. It seems Arcus is committed to combating this argument at its very source."[12]

The source, of course, was churches.

Stryker's foundation began devoting tens of millions of dollars to, in its words, "challenging the promotion of narrow or hateful interpretations of religious doctrine" within every major Christian denomination.[13] Between 2013 and 2018, for instance, it gave over two million dollars[14] to the Reconciling Ministries Network[15] to "secure the full participation of people of all sexual orientations and gender identities in the United Methodist Church," the last of the mainline denominations still resistant to full affirmation of the entire rainbow panoply. How did RMN go about this? According to Arcus's own reports, by training "faithful Methodists at all levels to become advocates for LGBTQ persons in the full life of the church."[16] Given that the UMC went through a schism in 2022 over LGBTQ ordination and gay marriage, it seems Stryker's money was well spent.

While evangelicalism's decentralized and independent nature makes any wholesale attempt at reshaping doctrine rather like trying to herd a field of darting rabbits, it, too, came in for the Arcus treatment, albeit with more scattered outlays of cash. One particular expenditure proved strategic, as it managed to harness the influence of both North Point on the Eastern Seaboard and another internationally famous megachurch in the West, Rick Warren's Saddleback.

Between 2014 and 2018, the Reformation Project, a brand-new organization led by twenty-three-year-old Harvard dropout Matthew Vines,[17] received $550,000 in grants.[18] The purpose of the funding, according to Arcus, was to "reform church teaching on sexual orientation and gender identity among conservative and evangelical communities."[19] This phrasing was borrowed directly from the fledgling nonprofit's website, with one addition. The Reformation Project's initial "About" page said only that it was committed to "reform[ing] church teaching on sexual orientation and gender identity."[20] Arcus's press release about its new grantee inserted the bit about "conservative and evangelical communities." It understood what it was buying.

On the surface, the Reformation Project would have seemed an unlikely vehicle for making inroads with the most stubbornly resistant strain of

American Christianity. Vines was not only young, but with his slight build and elfin face, he looked even younger. Anyone watching the viral 2012 YouTube talk[21] in which he argues that God does not condemn loving, gay relationships, only same-sex rape and orgies, might have guessed he was a high-schooler and a nervous, swallowing-between-sentences (though clearly bright) high-schooler, at that.

But youth and inexperience were only the first obstacles Vines faced as an ambassador to conservative Christians. The second was his overt branding as a "Side A" evangelical. While the views of their counterparts on Side B can be, by design, slippery (something we'll delve into in a moment), Side A activists are fairly transparent. The straightforward title of Vines's book, *God and the Gay Christian: The Biblical Case for Same-Sex Relationships*,[22] exemplifies their beliefs as well as anything. Nor do they make any bones about their goal, which is to convince the Church to set aside the passages in both the Old and New Testaments that prohibit LGBTQ behavior and identities. In fact, Vines has called affirmation of homosexual unions "a requirement of Christian faithfulness."[23] So, not exactly the type of teacher most doctrinally sound churches are going to welcome in the front door to set up ministries and Bible studies. For Vines and the Reformation Project to have any hope of fulfilling their mission, they needed partners who looked and sounded like the conservative Christians they were trying to convince but whose teaching was equally committed to the project of undermining Scripture.

Peruse the speakers lists for the Reformation Project's past conferences or visit the recommended Resources page on its website, and you'll find an array of authors and organizations who are as forthright about their LGBTQ agenda as secular groups like the Human Rights Campaign or GLAAD. All wear their commitment to full inclusion and affirmation in the Church on their sleeve—except one.

As they explain in their book of the same name,[24] Greg and Lynn McDonald founded Embracing the Journey,[25] an organization for Christian parents of LGBTQ children, in 2015, at the urging of North Point's executive director, Bill Willits.[26] They had recently relocated to the Atlanta area and had begun attending services at the church. Over a breakfast meeting with Willits early in the year, Greg happened to share that his son had come out as gay in 2001, and he described how his and Lynn's process of acceptance eventually led them to become informal counselors to other parents of gay and transgender kids. Willits was "captivated" by their story and revealed that North Point had already begun exploring new ministries in that vein. He asked if he could follow up with the McDonalds and, during a series of meetings over the ensuing months, became their "mentor, good friend, and kindred spirit in ministry." His first bit of mentoring was urging them to film a video for Stanley's Drive Conference that May.

As Stanley introduced the McDonalds' video to approximately two thousand church leaders from all over the country, he urged those leaders not to view homosexuality through a "political" lens.[27] Like the pastor who declined to speak to me on the record about the 2019 dinner, he didn't specify what he meant by political. Perhaps more noteworthy, given the audience, he also didn't suggest that ministers use the Bible as their foremost frame of reference. (In fact, he made a joke about *not* citing any Scripture.) Instead, he urged the audience to approach the issue through a "relational lens." His example for relational was the McDonalds' story.

Even before the camera pans across old photos of Greg and Lynn from the early days of their marriage, it's easy to picture the couple as the high school sweethearts they once were. A tall, broad-shouldered marketing executive, Greg still shows vestiges of big man on campus as he flashes a toothy grin at his pretty, blonde wife. Lynn, a homemaker, busies herself about an expansive kitchen of high-end custom finishes, putting the final touches on a charcuterie tray. Between their teasing interplay and the backdrop of what is (given real estate prices in metro Atlanta) easily a million-dollar home, they present an attractive and aspirational image. Then their voice-over tracks begin to play over soothing music.

They talk about their two children, especially their son, whom we glimpse at various ages smiling shyly from gilt-framed photos that decorate the tastefully furnished living room. Greg Jr. came out to his parents when he was seventeen, after Greg found gay porn on his computer. The couple share how the news changed them. Greg describes developing a new sensitivity to gay jokes; Lynn tears up as she remembers worrying that if she "chose to love her son, would that mean [she] would have to abandon God."[28] She explains that her fears were based on her conservative upbringing, because that was "how verses of the Bible were taught to [her]." But over the years, the McDonalds met dozens of their son's LGBTQ friends, who told them that the deepest hurts they experienced came at the hands of the Church. What the context or substance of those hurts were, Greg and Lynn don't explain. But eventually, they learned not to care what their church friends thought.

Toward the end of the video, the camera pans across a new family photo, lingering a bit on the smiles of Greg Jr. and his male partner. The music swells as Greg grips his wife's hand and says, "We're not interested in trying to change people; we're just interested in trying to love them." A few final images show a laughing Lynn flirtatiously feeding her husband a snack off the tray just after the camera rests on a decorative sign that reads, "Welcome Friends."[29]

Though the video is too brief and too vague to offer much clarity on the McDonalds' views about sexuality, its not-so-subtle implication is that conservative churches that are clear on what the Bible teaches have little to offer the same-sex-attracted beyond condemnation and trauma, certainly not love. This is a theme developed much more explicitly in the McDonalds' book. While they never offer their opinions on whether the Bible permits LGBTQ behavior and identities, it's obvious they think it does and that they believe other Christians should as well.

At the outset, they encourage readers not to focus on whether Scripture prohibits gay sex, writing, "In our experience, as soon as someone says sin in a conversation about LGBTQ issues, battle lines are drawn." From there, the only time they bring up the question of sin is to cast doubt on the idea that homosexuality qualifies. They share that they *once believed* gay acts were sinful [emphasis mine]. And they contrast churches that "publicly [support] including the LGBTQ community" and "[make] every person feel welcome in God's kingdom" with churches that "double down on six verses in Scripture that seem to condemn homosexuality."[30] Again, according to the McDonalds, the verses only *seem* to do this. They lament the fact that denominations have chosen to split over this issue when they could just agree to disagree.

Nor are they content simply to encourage skepticism of orthodoxy. They also promote heresy, teaching that parents cannot know what God wants in regard to their son or daughter's homosexual behavior. "Only God knows how and whether your child should change," they write. This is a theme the book returns to again and again as they reflect with embarrassment on the simplistic mind-set they once had—as when Lynn recalls once telling her son's gay friend, "God wouldn't bring you into a homosexual relationship. That's never what God wants for you." She then adds in her present voice, "As if I had any idea what God wanted for a young man I'd just met."

Note that Lynn cringes not just at the timing or phrasing of her comments, but at their meaning. Whether she conveyed her message in the most tactful way or not, biblically her statements were correct. God does not bring us into homosexual relationships, as James 1:13—"When tempted, no one should say, 'God is tempting me'"—makes plain. Likewise, Genesis 19, 1 Timothy 1:10, and the other verses the McDonalds (like Stanley) dismiss as "clobber passages" make it unquestionably clear that it is *not* what He wants for us.

As they present themselves as the model for growing in grace and love toward the LGBTQ community, Greg and Lynn explain that they eventually bought a condo in a gay neighborhood of Chicago where they allowed their son to live with his partner. When Greg Jr. visited home with boyfriends, Greg and Lynne stopped requiring the men to sleep in separate bedrooms, because they realized it would be hypocritical given that they didn't require heterosexual singles to sleep apart. It apparently didn't occur to them that the biblical standard would have been to have a separate-bedrooms policy for all unmarried visitors, gay or straight.

Nowhere do the McDonalds feature any Christians who have chosen to turn away from LGBTQ sin to follow Jesus, but they characterize quite a number of practicing homosexuals, including their son, as faithful disciples of Christ. When describing a Bible study hosted by two "married" men, they even suggest that LGBTQ individuals are *more* spiritually mature because of their unrepentant sin, echoing what Stanley said in the viral video clips:

> Up to that point, Greg and I hadn't had many opportunities to sit down
> and connect personally with devout Christ followers who also hap-

pened to be LGBTQ. . . . There were two dozen folks gathered in a living room, and the first thing I noticed was how excited they all were to dig into the Bible. Here was a group of people who had been told over and over that they were abominations, and that God doesn't love them. Famous Christians publicly said that being gay was enough to send them to hell. And yet they were not dissuaded or discouraged. In many ways, just the opposite happened. They pursued God with passion. The depth of their knowledge humbled me, as did their desire for building a supportive, Christ-centered community.[31]

The book doesn't spend much time on the issue of transgenderism, but there, too, it is clear the McDonalds are fully affirming, especially when they describe their success at counseling a Christian couple to embrace their daughter's belief that she is a man:

> For many years, they'd struggled with the idea that their daughter was gay, but that was nothing compared to the confusion that came when their child sat down with them and explained that he was actually transgender. Over time, and with a lot of love, prayer, and community support, their fear turned to surviving, and then eventually thriving. They eventually supported their child's transition and built a new, stronger-than-ever relationship with their son.[32]

Arguably the most insidious counsel the McDonalds offer to vulnerable Christian parents coming to them for help is to encourage them to dismiss the idea that a lack of repentance in this area destines their child for Hell. Yet it's impossible not to have some sympathy for Greg and Lynn as they recount facing this chasm of fear themselves. The discerning reader gets the sense it may have been this that ultimately caused them to reject what is clearly revealed in Scripture.

While they confess that they once feared for their son's soul, they later rejoiced that while he continued to pursue homosexual relationships, he never denied Christ, and he assured them he "would never turn away from God." This they took as evidence that his salvation was secure. Today, their curriculum assures readers that "my child will go to Hell" is among the "irrational fears" Christian parents sometimes experience after a son or daughter discloses their homosexuality or transgenderism.

We would do well to pause for a moment to remember the words of the author of Hebrews that it is "a fearful thing to fall into the hands of the living God," as well as those of 1 Corinthians 6:9–10, which directly contradict the McDonalds' casual assurances: "Do you not know that wrongdoers will not inherit the kingdom of God? Do not be deceived: Neither the sexually immoral nor idolaters nor adulterers nor men who have sex with men nor thieves nor the greedy nor drunkards nor slanderers nor swindlers will inherit the kingdom of God."[33] Thankfully, the Apostle Paul goes on to remind his readers "such were some of you." But they were washed and sanctified and justified. That is why they are what they were no longer. And that is why they have the hope of Heaven.

Author Rosaria Butterfield left a life of lesbianism when she became a Christian. She has described her process of dying to self to live for Christ in several books, but in her latest, *Five Lies of Our Anti-Christian Age*,[34] she offers a haunting rebuke to anyone peddling false peace in these matters: "How sad indeed for someone who is already weighed down by sin to be denied the true remedy for the problem. That is what gay Christianity does. It denies the sexual sinner repentance." Without repentance, there is no salvation. Without salvation, Hell is not just possible; it is inevitable.

In October 2022, I received a direct message on Twitter from a young man who'd been involved with the Log Cabin Republicans, a political advocacy group that represents LGBTQ conservatives. The man was raised in an orthodox evangelical home and even attended a doctrinally sound Bible college. Shortly after graduating, though, he came out as gay and spent the next eight years in an exclusive relationship with another man. When they broke up, he engaged in many relationships, describing himself as a "modern-day gay Mary Magdalene. . . . my faith never dead but shoved into the recesses of my mind and heart."

It was while attending a gay wedding ceremony in the summer of 2022 that he said, "Jesus broke me." Seeing the two men bless their wedding in Christ's name pierced his dormant conscience. "It was the final chink in my armor," he shared. "I was brought to repentance." He went home and immediately resigned from his gay-related job and no longer describes himself as a gay man. "I'm completely sold out on Jesus," he told me. "It's as if all the amazing biblical knowledge and doctrine I learned in school has been renewed and given life again. It's quite amazing."

Without the groundwork laid in his childhood and college years, where would this man be today? *How, then, shall they call on Him in whom they have not believed? And how shall they believe in Him of whom they have not heard? And how shall they hear without a preacher?* (Romans 10:14).

But perhaps the clearest evidence of the McDonalds' agenda comes from Amos 3:3—"Can two walk together, except they be agreed?"

Vines (along with his backer Arcus) has unabashedly stated his aim of "chang[ing] every Christian church worldwide, no matter how conservative their theology," to become fully affirming of same-sex relationships and gender transitions.[35] While theologically conservative churches might conversely say they would like to see every affirming church embrace biblical standards on sexuality, gender, and marriage, they're not training activists to infiltrate affirming denominations in order to transform them from within. Instead, again and again, they have done what the Bible commands us to do when we find heresy and immorality in our midst: they have warned and, when those warnings were not heeded, they have separated (Matthew 18:15–17, 2 Thessalonians 3:14, 1 Corinthians 5:9–10).

As might be expected, given how seriously he takes his mission, Vines's courses are far more rigorous than the kind of light, Wednesday night discussions the typical evangelical church offers on such subjects, if it offers them at all. Over a period of three months, the Reformation Project requires participants of one program to spend twelve to fifteen hours *a week* reading "dense and scholarly" materials in preparation for written homework and online discussions. In other words, they complete the equivalent of an advanced college course, all for the purpose of preparing to subvert the faithful churches Vines has called "the last stronghold of homophobia."[36]

If Vines is not willing to let churches and denominations to which he has no connection continue in their biblical beliefs without interference, it's not likely he's going to team up with ministries that might undermine his goals.

In 2020, the Reformation Project (which, again, had received Arcus funding specifically to subvert doctrinally sound churches) began partnering with the North Point–backed Embracing the Journey, bringing in the

McDonalds not only to speak at events, but also to help design conferences and lead their "parents-in-process" program. Embracing the Journey, in turn, began recommending Vines's book and other content as "Bible-based" resources and directed Christians wrestling with how to respond to a gay or transgender child to Reformation Project events.[37]

Nor was the Reformation Project the only fully affirming, Arcus-backed group with whom Embracing the Journey locked arms. The Gay Christian Network (now called Q Christian Fellowship) also engaged the couple as conference speakers. The McDonalds' book described GCN's mission benignly as "advocat[ing] for stronger relationships between the church and the LGBTQ community."[38] The Arcus Foundation had a slightly different way of putting it when it funded a GCN program called the "Evangelical Education Project."[39] Similar to the Reformation Project, it was designed to "develop, test, and refine a pilot program that prepares young adult evangelicals to support pro-LGBT dialogue within evangelical communities."[40]

Of course, if these were simply affirming "Christian" organizations working together, that would hardly be newsworthy. The issue was that the McDonalds, following in Stanley's footsteps, were careful to play coy about their views in front of mainstream evangelical churches and ministries. Greg McDonald's Embracing the Journey bio, for instance, doesn't mention that it "simply breaks [his] heart when people are told they can't be a Christian and LGBTQ." No, this is from his bio at Renovus, an openly affirming organization where he serves as a board member. Meanwhile, North Point began providing Embracing the Journey concrete support that went well beyond advice and encouragement, allowing it to maintain the illusion that it was a conventional Christian organization.

The megachurch helped with "branding strategy to make sure [Embracing the Journey] didn't veer off message," and a staff pastor recorded an endorsement video sharing what "big fans" the church was of the McDonalds and how the church "completely" trusted the couple "to lead [parents of LGBTQ children] towards a better relationship with God."[41] Though the amount was not disclosed, Embracing the Journey's 2021 financial records list a "record donation" from North Point.[42]

Leveraging Stanley and North Point's influence, Embracing the Journey was well equipped to make inroads with the biggest names in the evangelical landscape. After an interview with the McDonalds in 2019, popular faith and family authors Mark and Jill Savage recommended Embracing the Journey to their audience.[43] If the Savages' names don't ring a bell, some of the organizations they're associated with probably will: Crosswalk, Family Life, and James Dobson's Focus on the Family, all among the best-known and most-trusted Christian media platforms in the country. The Savages are frequent contributors to each, meaning the McDonalds were within striking distance of having access to the best-known and most trusted Christian media platforms in the country. Then, in 2020, the McDonalds landed a whale: Rick Warren's Saddleback.

With thirty thousand weekly attendees spread across fourteen Southern California campuses, not to mention international campuses in Hong Kong, Germany, the Philippines, and Argentina, plus online extension groups around the world, Saddleback was in the best position to boost the McDonalds' bona fides among average churchgoers. Founding pastor Warren had not only authored The Purpose Driven Life, one of the bestselling books in American history (coming in at number three), but he'd beat Stanley by five spots on Preacher Magazine's influential pastors list—though, given that major media outlets dubbed him America's most influential spiritual leader, perhaps he should have been number one. In other words, compared to Warren, Stanley was practically a piker.

Equivocating, Dodging, and Remaining Silent

In April 2019, two longtime Saddleback members flew to Atlanta to learn more about Embracing the Journey.[44] Shauna Habel had been engaged in efforts to subvert church teaching on sexuality since attending a Reformation Project conference in 2016, where she said she "saw the Holy Spirit and knew that God was in that place."[45] Only a month before meeting with the McDonalds, she openly described her mission with another Arcus-funded group, FreedHearts, as working "with conservative parents to help them become affirming."[46] When her stepdaughter came out as a lesbian, she was able to bring her husband, Doug, into the enterprise, and they began exploring options for launching a ministry for parents of LGBTQ kids at their church. Embracing the Journey fit the bill for both of Shauna Habel's goals.

Upon returning home, the Habels spent the next few months meeting with Saddleback pastoral staff until longtime counseling pastor, Chris Clark, and his wife, Elisa, agreed to help them in the venture. In early 2020, the four launched the first Embracing the Journey support group at Saddleback. By the end of 2021, they had added three more, plus an ongoing small group.[47] Saddleback was apparently so pleased with the ministry that it provided the McDonalds an endorsement video. It's possible the church later added more groups, but after I reported on its involvement with Embracing the Journey in the spring of 2023, Saddleback took down all web pages associated with the group. Its endorsement video also disappeared from Embracing the Journey's website, though the original web page with a now-dead link to it can still be found on Internet Archive.

The question is whether Saddleback got duped by Embracing the Journey or whether it, like North Point, understood what kind of organization it was partnering with and was hoping to gradually "nudge" its members in an affirming direction. I reached out to Saddleback about these questions but never received a response. But the best-case scenario is it had a shockingly poor vetting process and an equally shocking lack of discernment. The worst case is that Warren and, certainly, the husband-and-wife team he hand-selected to take over pastoring duties in August 2022 knew exactly whom they were letting in the door.

One would assume that any church as large and prosperous as Saddleback would have plenty of available staff to check a website or read a book (never mind invest a couple of hours in internet sleuthing) before handing its members over to a new ministry. The barest due diligence would immediately have revealed the true nature of the McDonalds' beliefs. And certainly the Habels' involvement with the Reformation Project should have been a matter of church discipline. If Saddleback failed to do this, why not simply acknowledge the mistake and issue an assurance that it had been corrected? Instead, other than deleting the web pages associated with Embracing the Journey, it has stayed completely silent. Sources close to the church tell me Saddleback is still using the ETJ program, though it is no longer posting meeting times on the "Support Group" and "Events" pages of its website.

Then there is the fact that Saddleback didn't seem concerned with the engagements its counseling pastor was accepting under its name. Within a year of launching the Embracing the Journey chapter, Chris Clark was speaking at a Reformation Project conference himself.[48] At some point, he and his wife joined Embracing the Journey in a more official capacity, as counseling group leaders. And North Point's September 2023 conference to help ministry leaders "discover ways to support parents and LGBTQ+ children in their churches" included Clark in the lineup alongside a number of openly affirming speakers.

The Saddleback name, which featured prominently in promoting Clark's involvement with these groups, helped legitimize them as sound resources for evangelical audiences. Could it have been a case of a rogue pastor taking liberties with his title? Perhaps. But after I inquired with Saddleback about the nature of Clark's activities, his name and photo also mysteriously disappeared from the website with no explanation. Before Clark's LinkedIn page similarly disappeared, it revealed that one of his pastoring responsibilities at Saddleback is teaching lay counselors, which would, presumably, include training them in how to respond to congregants dealing with homosexuality or transgenderism. One can't help but wonder how many trainees came under his tutelage and what exactly they learned.

The couple Warren chose to replace him as the main pastors of Saddleback appear rather muddled on the Bible's stance on homosexuality themselves. During a Q&A segment of a podcast a few years ago, Andy and Stacie Wood were asked wheter a gay "married" couple should continue their relationship after becoming Christians. Andy Wood responded by saying that the question may not have a "black-and-white answer." Citing no Scripture, the Woods then said they would encourage the couple to consider how they "feel the Holy Spirit is leading them."[49]

Finally, there is Warren himself. During an interview with him in May 2023, *Premier Christianity* reporter Megan Cornwell asked if same-sex marriage could be considered a secondary matter over which churches in the same denomination could agree to disagree.[50] It was a fair question, given that Warren appears not to have talked about the issue since the year before the Supreme Court's 2015 *Obergefell* decision that legalized gay marriage. At first, Warren avoided mentioning homosexuality at all, but he seemed to suggest that it *could* be a debatable question:

I believe in the inerrancy of scripture. A fundamentalist believes in the inerrancy of their interpretation . . . I don't believe in the inerrancy of my interpretation of it, which is why we have to come humbly to scripture. Paul talks for an entire chapter on the secondary issues. Go read Romans 14—it teaches us how to deal with what Paul calls "disputable matters." He talks about eating meat, or drinking wine . . . they have nothing to do with your salvation. And it basically says: keep these between yourself and the Lord and don't divide over them [ellipses part of original interview].

Cornwell asked again, directly: "To come back to that issue of blessing same-sex marriage, because that's a huge topic right now in the UK. Would you say it's a secondary issue?" Warren again dodged, replying that sins like racism, sexual abuse, and sexual immorality were justifiable reasons to expel a church from an association, but he then gave an example that once again shifted the focus away from homosexuality. "If we are endorsing a sinful lifestyle, [for example,] we've got a pedophile as a pastor, then that church should be kicked out," he said.

The intrepid reporter soldiered on, pointing out that she hadn't asked about pedophilia; she'd asked about gay relationships. This time Warren explained that "gay relations are not God's best." It took four attempts before Cornwell at last pinned Warren down enough that he tepidly admitted LGBTQ affirmation is a justifiable reason for schism. But even then, he did not directly name homosexuality a sin. He said only that blessing same-sex civil unions "[strays] too far from Scripture." (Kudos to Cornwell for her dogged interviewing technique.)

This is not to suggest that, like Stanley, Warren may be secretly affirming. It is only to point out that the Bible's standard for marriage and sexuality are no longer issues he speaks about with conviction and that he will engage in some verbal gymnastics to avoid addressing them at all. He also doesn't seem especially concerned to see the church he founded, which he still serves in an advisory role, maintain sound doctrine on these issues.

The McDonalds like to highlight quotes from well-known pastors as relevant to Embracing the Journey's work. They have quoted Stanley, saying: "If your theology gets in the way of your ministry, there is something the matter with your theology." It sounds spiritual, but it's not biblical. Or, as the Apostle Paul puts it in 2 Timothy 3:4–5, it has a form of godliness, but it denies its power. Theology is the study of God. It is doctrine. Within a Christian framework, it is the study of truth. While we may have to consider how we're presenting truth to make sure it is not in violation of other parts of Christian theology, we don't measure its soundness by whether we feel like it's "getting in the way" of our ministry. If we're following Christ in the truth and in how we speak it (with love but with clarity), and it is still being received by the world as hatred, bigotry, or homophobia, we are, in fact, commanded *not* to change our theology. We are to hold fast to the sound teaching presented in Scripture (2 Timothy 1:13). Ultimately, Stanley's statement is a prime example of pragmatism—using the ends to justify the means. And in churches, pragmatist logic can be used to justify just about anything.

The McDonalds also found a certain Warren quote relevant to Embracing the Journey. "We don't need to see eye to eye to walk arm in arm." On tertiary matters, Warren is right. We need not agree on end-time theology or styles of worship to work together. We can debate these things in a collegial, respectful way (though Romans 14 forbids being quarrelsome or judgmental about them), because it is possible to argue from Scripture for different positions and because these are often matters of personal conscience. Sexual immorality is not one of those issues. We are of course to be welcoming to lost sinners regardless of which sins characterize their lives, but if someone claims to be a brother or sister in Christ, we are commanded to separate:

> I wrote to you in my letter not to associate with sexually immoral people—not at all meaning the sexually immoral of this world, or the greedy and swindlers, or idolaters, since then you would need to go out of the world. But now I am writing to you not to associate with anyone who bears the name of brother if he is guilty of sexual immorality or greed, or is an idolater, reviler, drunkard, or swindler—not even to eat with such a one. For what have I to do with judging outsiders? Is it not those inside the church whom you are to judge? God judges those outside. "Purge the evil person from among you"—1 Cor[inthians] 5:9–13.

It is to the American Church's shame that it has not followed this command consistently when it comes to adultery and fornication. Yet, even there, you'd be hard-pressed to find ministers in even the most liberal denominations arguing that cheating on a spouse or having sex before marriage is acceptable. The answer to this failure is not to exponentially multiply it by condoning homosexuality, in all its forms, simply because our culture and laws now have.

In his 2021 book, *Hope in Times of Fear*, theologian Tim Keller explains why sexual morality cannot be dismissed as an issue on which Christians of good faith can agree to disagree:

> The Christian sex ethic was understood by the apostles to be a nonnegotiable part of orthodoxy, one of the core beliefs of Christianity. What Christians taught and practiced about sexuality was as much a necessary implication of the gospel and the resurrection as were care for the poor and the equality of the races. This makes it impossible to argue, as many try to do, that what the Bible says about caring for the poor is right but what it says about sex is outmoded and should be discarded.

Keller's insight here is helpful. Ironically, though, he was far less discerning when the camel's nose of gay and transgender affirmation pushed its way into the tent of his own denomination.

Side B and a New Kind of Christian

The Side B approach to the LGBTQ issue takes its name from the flip side of a vinyl record. Vines's claim that God blesses homosexual unions is Side A—popular with the masses, easy to hum. Side B is the tune less played. Because the record company doesn't think it'll sell, it's where artists often find a home for what they view as their most authentic, complex work. As a metaphor for professing Christians who claim they're committed to honoring the letter of the Bible's prohibition against homosexual acts while they violate the spirit by embracing the trappings of gay culture, it says a lot about how its adherents view the authority of Scripture.

If Side B Christians are differentiating themselves from full-blown affirmers, they are also distancing themselves from that old-time religion, with its simple prescriptions of repentance *from* and mortification *of* sin through the ordinary means of grace. They identify themselves as gay, queer, and trans Christians and sometimes celebrate their sexual proclivities, just as their Side A counterparts do, by attending Pride parades and marking National Coming Out Day.[51] Choosing to identify by their attractions isn't just a question of terminology, either. The movement's leading figures have argued for the Church to accommodate certain kinds of gay relationships like "spiritual friendships"—a sort of celibate marriage that involves committed, covenantal unions between same-sex partners. And both partners in the arrangement need not be homosexual. One example that sparked controversy in 2020 involved a gay PCA youth ministry director discussing the commitment he made to his straight male best friend and roommate, a young adult pastor for an Alliance World Fellowship church. Even if a wife enters the picture, the two men vowed, they will still find a way to live together and "function as a household."[52]

You will often hear Side B proponents liken these relationships to the commitments made between Ruth and Naomi and David and Jonathan. But there is a significant difference in those examples—those pledges were purely platonic, made to demonstrate loyalty in moments of extreme duress, not to sublimate homosexual desire. In Ruth and Naomi's case, Ruth's promise shows that she is permanently grafting herself into her mother-in-law's family as they return to Naomi's homeland as impoverished widows. Jonathan and David's commitment centers on the fact that Jonathan's father, Saul, plans to murder David to prevent him from taking the throne. Jonathan's pledge shows his loyalty lies with David and God.

The Side B notion of spiritual friendship is something very different. Author Gregory Coles (whose book *Single, Gay Christian* received a rave review from *Christianity Today*[53]) and other leaders in the movement have revealed that just because these typically cohabitating partners don't have sex, it doesn't mean romance is off the table.[54] Coles explained in a 2022 paper for his nonprofit, the Center for Faith, Sexuality and Gender, that such partners may be "physically affectionate in ways that include cuddling, kissing, and holding hands."[55] He then suggested these behaviors would be sinful only if they became a source of temptation. "While there are important questions to be asked about the wisdom of specific behaviors, those questions are best asked in the context of a personal relationship built on trust, knowing the unique experiences, struggles, and giftings of the people involved," Coles wrote, adding that "not everyone experiences sexual temptation or responds to physical behaviors in the same way."

It's worth stressing that Coles's organization is hardly on the evangelical fringes. High-profile pastors like J. D. Greear have credited its president, Preston Sprinkle, with shaping their thinking on transgenderism.[56] And among its endorsers, you'll find Acts 29 president Matt Chandler, bestselling author and pastor Francis Chan, and columnist and former seminary professor Karen Swallow Prior.[57]

To see just how far the spiritual friendship concept can stretch, Catholic writer Eve Tushnet, who has been an intellectual leader in the Side B movement, openly describes herself as part of a lesbian couple and waxes poetic about her deep love for her same-sex partner.[58] She argues that spiritual growth can lead to stronger same-sex attractions. "I went from 'mostly gay but also bisexual???' to just lesbian, because of an extraordinary experience of healing and rescue that I received from the Lord," she wrote in 2023.

One can't help but see a certain cruelty in *not* clearly rebuking these kinds of partnerships, just as one would counsel a heterosexual friend to walk away from a self-destructive relationship that tormented yet drew her. In choosing not to give full rein to their sexual desires while at the same time entangling themselves in deeply emotional relationships, the movement's adherents call to mind the famous Rhett Butler line about his romantic rival Ashley Wilkes: "He can't be mentally faithful to his wife and won't be unfaithful to her technically." The point of the quip was that Wilkes was causing heartache to everyone involved, including himself. However, Side B ideology does not simply impact those who buy into it, but also makes demands on the Church and how it responds to homosexuality and gender dysphoria.

Side B advocates, like *Christianity Today* and Gospel Coalition contributor[59] Nate Collins and Keller-endorsed[60] author and pastor Greg Johnson, have contended that homosexual desire is not a disordered temptation as

Romans 1:26–27 tells us, but rather, no different from heterosexual attraction outside marriage. This ignores the fact that there is a God-given, creational purpose for heterosexual desire—how else would husbands and wives get together and make families? Both men have argued that using biblical language and standards when it comes to sexuality amounts to spiritual and emotional abuse,[61] and both borrow from the secular LGBTQ movement in likening gay temptations to race-based civil rights.[62] They refer to those with same-sex attractions and gender dysphoria as "sexual and gender minorities" and insist that sexual "orientation" is immutable and inborn, meaning sanctification provides little to no hope for lessening sinful same-sex attraction.

In one particularly telling passage from Collins's book *All but Invisible*, he wonders not how a person who comes to Christ can find victory over gay desires, but "what does gayness look like when it is redeemed?"

> Christians have traditionally used terms like sin, temptation, and healing to answer these questions, all of which are found in various texts of Scripture. My suspicion, however, is that we could provide more specific and potentially more meaningful, answers to these questions if we broaden our search for descriptions of gay people's experience beyond terms explicitly found in Scripture.

One might look at this as a modern twist on the Serpent's question in the garden. Rather than "Has God really said," Side B asks, "Is what God said really more important than what we have to say?"

For his part, Johnson has written that "to be all about Jesus" means that we have to "repent of our complicity in North American society's idolization of marriage and romance. And we have to be ready to learn. We have to learn from the LGBTQ community in a way that does not threaten their safety within the queer spaces they create."[63]

The unbiblical ideas that were growing under Side B came to wider evangelical notice when Collins founded a formal organization to promote these views. The first Revoice conference was held in 2018 at Greg Johnson's church, then part of the Presbyterian Church in America (PCA), one of the largest theologically conservative denominations in the United States. The name was symbolic. In the past, Revoicers argued, evangelicalism's voice on LGBTQ issues had focused on saying no.[64] They wanted to rethink the issue with a new voice—a voice that would find ways to say *yes*.

As soon as some of Revoice's ideas for saying yes became known, prominent evangelical leaders like Southern Baptist Theological Seminary president Albert Mohler, ecclesiastical historian Carl Trueman, and Council on Biblical Manhood and Womanhood president Denny Burk began sounding the alarm. And for good reason: Revoice's first conference included lectures on the "queer treasure" gay Christians might take into Jesus's millennial kingdom.[65] The talk's presenter, Grant Hartley, later offered examples, equating gay clubs to the "homecoming" celebration the prodigal's father throws for his returning son, and correlating coming out of the closet to the Resurrection. That first year, Collins gave a speech that likened "gender and sexual minorities" to the prophet Jeremiah, come to "call to the church to abandon idolatrous attitudes toward the nuclear family." This claim—that a church culture experiencing crashing birth and marriage rates right along with the rest of America is guilty of overemphasizing these institutions—is especially popular among Side B.

From there, Revoice conferences grew even more overtly aligned with Side A, from which its attendees were supposedly differentiating themselves. By 2022, the event featured all the typical Pride trappings and nomenclature, like passing out name tags that included selections for pronouns and referring to sex as "assigned at birth."[66] Presenters wore T-shirts emblazoned with trans flags and the words "Imago Dei"—the implication being that trans identity is another way God reflects his image in humanity. Breakout "affinity" groups offered conferencegoers the chance to socialize with fellow bisexuals, pansexuals, asexuals, and aromantics, among other sexual subgroups. Meanwhile, some conference leaders, like keynote speaker, author, New Testament professor, and former *Christianity Today* columnist Wesley Hill,[67] were beginning to acknowledge openly that they weren't sure that Side B was correct in its understanding that homosexual acts are inherently sinful.[68] Both he and Collins have no compunction labeling Side A fellow Christians, in direct contradiction to verses like 1 Corinthians 6:9–20.

The first two years of Revoice became a hot point of contention within the PCA, made more heated because not everyone found it alarming. Mainstream figures like Keller's protégé and Nashville megachurch pastor Scott Sauls, endorsed the conference,[69] as did Karen Swallow Prior.[70] Author Rachel Gilson, a Cru leader, and Gospel Coalition regular,[71] led a Revoice workshop in 2019.[72] And no less an authority than celebrated New Testament scholar D. A. Carson lavished praise on a book by Coles that classed gay marriage among the issues on which "sincere Christians" might disagree. "To say [Single, Gay, Christian] is important is a painful understatement," Carson wrote. "It is not to be read with a condescending smirk, but with humility."[73]

In 2019, when Greg Johnson, who had previously presented himself solely as an ally, came out in the pages of Christianity Today as a Side B celibate gay man himself, the PCA's formal authority structure could no longer ignore the Revoice issue.[74] While discussions about how to handle Johnson were barely under way, news broke that he had played host to an even more controversial event. The Chapel, a dedicated arts building his church owned, welcomed the collaborative exhibition Transilluminate, a "short-play festival and celebration of transgender, agender, non-binary, genderqueer, and genderfluid artists."[75]

Efforts were already being made at that point to oust Johnson from the denomination for teaching that which conflicted with PCA doctrine, but the Church's judicial commission cleared him by one vote. Those who hoped to shore up the denomination's ramparts against the incursion of LGBTQ ideology instead turned their attention to buttressing orthodoxy. First, they endorsed the Nashville Statement, a 2017 declaration outlining basic Christian beliefs regarding sexuality whose early signers included such evangelical luminaries as J. I. Packer, R. C. Sproul, and Wayne Grudem. Then, the 2019 PCA General Assembly took the further step of appointing a committee to study homosexuality, same-sex attraction, and transgenderism in light of Scripture and to submit a report. Naturally, the seven men appointed included the PCA's best-known theologian, Keller.

There were legitimate concerns over whether Keller should have been included among the report's authors, given the fact that he had welcomed Revoice leader Wesley Hill to speak at his church only a few years before. And in 2018 he'd agreed to speak at a conference for Living Out, an organization that endorsed Revoice and has distributed audits for churches to measure how "biblically inclusive" they are of "sexual minorities."[76] [77] But given Keller's towering reputation, it wasn't surprising the General Assembly went forward with having him on the committee anyway.

The report he and the other authors returned,[78] which Keller later confirmed *was* intended to address Side B, was received as thorough, clear, and biblical by most of those who had expressed concerns over the heresies the movement and its Revoice conference were introducing into the PCA.[79] There were some remaining worries regarding the report's pledge not to police language and its drawing a moral equivalence between heterosexual and homosexual attraction outside of marriage.[80] But the main objection was that it was only an articulation of principles, with no mechanism for enforcement. The next logical step to many PCA elders was to introduce two amendments to their governing documents that would give the report the weight of law, so to speak. If those amendments passed, it would have then been possible to eject officials like Johnson who identified not as struggling with a particular sexual temptation but as proudly and immutably gay. In other words, people who denied the clear command of Ephesians 4:22–24 to put off the old sinful self and put on the new, increasingly sanctified self.

When it came to put flesh to the words of the report, however, Keller suddenly began to lobby against an enforceable standard. The thrust of his position was that he felt it would be unwise to create new pastoral qualifications based on "identity" without a study on what "identity" meant.[81] This understandably perplexed many of his fellow PCA elders, given the fact that he had just helped author a study that included this clear statement: "To juxtapose identities rooted in sinful desires alongside the term 'Christian' is inconsistent with Biblical language and undermines the spiritual reality that we are new creations in Christ."

Keller had had no problem understanding the definition of "identity," then, nor recognizing why gay or transgender identity was incompatible with the identity of Christian. And it wasn't his only incongruity. Less than two years after the report, he insisted that Side B did not pose a serious risk to the PCA. "As far as I know, there is not one PCA court—not one session, presbytery, or agency—that has ever endorsed Side B Christianity," he wrote.[82] In this, he was being more than a little slippery. No ecclesiastical entity had endorsed it, but its establishment and growth within the PCA was well documented. It was founded by a gay-identifying member of the PCA. The first Revoice conference was hosted by a PCA church and promoted by a Side B PCA pastor who had been one of its most prominent speakers and promoters since the beginning. And several well-known Side B and Revoice leaders, including Collins and Hill, had graduated from a PCA seminary. The real issue seemed to be, as Carl Trueman put it, that Keller had intended for the report to be only "pious advice," with no power behind it.

Then came Keller's most inscrutable move of all. In April 2022, a month after insisting that Side B and Revoice had made no serious inroads into the PCA (despite the fact that he'd agreed to help author a report with the understanding that they had), he promoted them himself with an endorsement of Johnson's book about coming out as a gay man. "*Still Time to Care* provides a good history & critique of the older ex-gay movement which was a form of the 'prosperity gospel,'" Keller posted on Facebook. "It's important that we know its history and, in light of its implosion and [sic] ask: now what?"[83]

It wasn't a rhetorical question. Johnson's book specifically provides an answer to "now what." The "now what," which he lays out clearly in the conclusion, is Side B and Revoice! If Keller disagreed with Johnson's "now what" but felt he could commend his work in other respects, the only responsible thing to do would have been to note where their views parted ways. He didn't. With Keller's help, the overtures that would have constrained soft-LGBTQ affirmation in the PCA were defeated.

Becket Cook is no pastor, no celebrated theologian, but he is a former Hollywood production designer who became a Christian and repented of his former homosexuality. After coming to a better understanding of the beliefs of Side B, he retracted his own endorsement of Johnson's book, saying, "A person's 'gayness' cannot be sanctified. This idea is in violation of the Creation Ordinance (Genesis 1:27) and the biblical understanding of personhood. We are not our desires."[84]

He explained in an interview with *The Gospel Coalition* that he would never call himself a "gay Christian" because his former gay identity has been crucified with Christ: "Why in the world would I use a sinful adjective—gay—to describe my new identity in Christ? I wouldn't and I don't."[85] Though she never signed on to Revoice or Side B, Rosaria Butterfield did once argue—as they do—that Christians should use transgender pronouns, though for her it was as a show of kindness, not to affirm their identity. She later publicly repented for promoting this view, saying that, among other things, using transgender pronouns "cheapens redemption, and it tramples on the blood of Christ."[86] She has called gay Christianity "a different religion."[87]

Given the fight with pancreatic cancer that ultimately took his life in May 2023, we can hope that Keller might also have eventually thought better of his commendation of Johnson's book, which was inextricably bound up with Revoice and Side B. But his Gospel Coalition partner Carson never retracted his endorsement of Coles's book (though in 2019, two years after he praised Cole's book, Carson explicitly wrote that it is "deceptive and idolatrous" to claim we cannot know for sure that the Bible condemns homosexuality. So perhaps Carson endorsed Single, Gay Christian without carefully reading it)[88]. Nor did Keller's protégé Sauls ever withdraw his for the Revoice project as a whole. Prior distanced herself from the conference, saying she disagreed with some of the speakers' views, but she likewise never retracted her endorsement.

Shepherds or Hired Hands?

Here's the truth—the examples I have laid out in this chapter barely scratch the surface of the countless tentacles of gay and transgender ideology that have invaded evangelical institutions. To even begin to cover it would take a very lengthy book of its own. These are presented as representative examples.

Though public outcry later forced it to reverse, in 2014 the humanitarian charity World Vision announced that it would start hiring "married" gay Christians as a symbol of "unity."[89] No amount of fierce criticism was enough to stop Bethany Christian Services, the largest Protestant adoption institution of its kind, from deciding in 2021 to begin placing children with same-sex couples, even though heterosexual married couples already often have to spend years on waiting lists before they're given a child.[90] It would be much faster to list the formerly faithful Christian colleges and universities who have *not* capitulated to LGBTQ demands than to try to cover those who have, but Baylor, Azusa Pacific, Wheaton, and Calvin University are just a few who offer some level of accommodation, including allowing LGBTQ clubs and same-sex student romances and retaining faculty who reject orthodoxy on this issue.[91]

Beth Moore, whose Bible studies shaped a generation of Christian women, removed passages from her book *Praying God's Word* that described homosexuality as "another deadly assault of the evil one in our society" and encouraged those struggling with the issue that "God indeed can deliver you" and "complete transformation is possible."[92] She later said those passages had "overshot Scripture by a mile."[93] In 2012, three years before *Obergefell* created a right to same-sex marriage, Timothy Dalrymple, now the CEO of *Christianity Today*, paradoxically argued that in order to protect our Christian witness, believers should consider whether it's time to "stop opposing same-sex marriage as a matter of law."[94] Among his reasons were that marriage is merely a "secondary issue" and that, whatever our convictions, we have to "humbly acknowledge the limitations of our knowledge, and recognize the possibility that we are mistaken."

No posture of humility is more pernicious than the one we assume at the expense of what God has clearly said. Perhaps that's why, since Dalrymple assumed leadership of *Christianity Today* in 2019, when it runs articles about homosexuality at all, it runs them from Side B-friendly pastors and commentators like Greg Johnson. Its news team has avoided the issue of transgenderism almost entirely. Of the many laws red states have passed in recent years to protect children from LGBTQ indoctrination in the classroom and to ban doctors and parents from permanently mutilating children's bodies and destroying their reproductive systems, evangelicalism's flagship magazine has covered exactly none—not few, but zero, even though the magazine frequently covers legislation pertaining to immigration, gun control, and other progressive priorities.

The reason for so much compromise is obvious. Today, this is the point of pain where orthodoxy falls away for those who are not truly committed to picking up their cross. For the most part, our current culture will not fault you, as liberals did in J. Gresham Machen or Francis Schaeffer's day, for having orthodox beliefs about the resurrection or the inerrancy of Scripture. They will often not even fault you for saying Jesus is the only way to Heaven, but simply brush the belief off as an antiquated oddity. The thing that could shut you out of careers, cost you social standing, and even land you in a years-long legal struggle—as happened with the Colorado baker Jack Phillips—is a refusal to capitulate on what the Bible says about sex, sexuality, and marriage.

Yet even though, of any class of Americans, pastors risk the least in speaking about these issues forthrightly, many of them, if they address it at all, whisper. And they counsel other Christians to whisper about it, as well. Literally.

Baptist Equivocation

Though he reversed his position after two years of pushback, North Carolina megachurch pastor J. D. Greear, while president of the Southern Baptist Convention, encouraged his congregation to minimize speaking about sexual sins like homosexuality, saying they should not "shout about what the Bible whispers about"[95]—as if the destruction of Sodom and Paul's description in Romans 1 of the progression of societal depravity were mere murmurs. Greear was also a prominent proponent of what he called "pronoun hospitality." First popularized by Sprinkle and Coles,[96] it soon came in for widespread derision as an example of therapeutic double-speak.[97] It means simply using pronouns that don't align with a gender-dysphoric person's sex in order to show compassion.

In 2019, he'd said on his podcast, "If a transgender person came into our church, came into my life, I think my disposition would be to refer to them by their preferred pronoun."[98] When I pressed Greear on the issue, he doubled down, telling me, "What leads a young person to get deceived and then mutilate themselves is confusion. It's not the pronoun use."[99] He then compared Christians who oppose using preferred pronouns to the brother of weak faith in Romans 14. Later, again after much controversy, Greear softened his position, saying his thinking had "matured" and that "part of [a believer's] calling is to speak to culture when culture does not align with what God has said." But he still allowed for using preferred pronouns provided a Christian had "been clear about the truth on the front end and the back end" of a conversation.

While leaders like Greear have been whispering, a veritable army of trained wolves has been sneaking in among the sheep. In 2016, Vines told the gay news outlet *The Advocate* that at the end of its first two years of operation, his organization had trained about a thousand people in affirming theology.[100] Extrapolating out six more years, and taking into consideration the Reformation Project's financial growth—which saw its annual revenues going from one hundred thousand dollars to more than nine hundred thousand—it would be a conservative estimate to guess he has now trained at least ten thousand. Ten thousand activists carrying out Arcus's mission of reforming conservative evangelical churches so that they will no longer teach their "narrow" doctrine.

In recent years, Vines has turned his attention to Pastors in Process, a confidential program that secretly trains pastors to stealthily "move the conversation on LGBTQ inclusion forward in [their] congregation[s]."[101] Faithful American Christians could soon be facing—if we're not already— thousands of Andy Stanleys. And the Reformation Project is only *one* of the many organizations carrying on this work. That's to say nothing of the courses and extracurricular groups at ostensibly Christian colleges and seminaries dedicated to the same effort.

Many pastors, doctrinally sound but unaware of the boot camp efforts that have been under way for years, have, out of a desire not to appear judgmental or overly focused on one sin to the exclusion of others, been successfully shamed into barely mentioning homosexuality, transgenderism, or the rest of the LGBTQ array. When they do mention it, it is only briefly and in the vaguest terms, so as not to be accused of being unwelcoming or unloving. Given this imbalance in commitment to our respective beliefs, faithful Christians can hardly wonder at the fact that the LGBTQ movement is chewing up ground and claiming new converts as quickly as evangelical churches are meekly ceding the field.

These shepherds should recall the warning of John Calvin: "Ambiguity is the fortress of heretics." Well, the heretics are here. They are all around us, and their numbers are growing. Pastors need to remember that while evangelism is important, it's not their first responsibility. Their first responsibility is to feed the sheep, to equip the saints. For too many pastors, concern for showing compassion to the lost means they're not protecting the sheep from false teaching. They are, in fact, starving the sheep to appease goats. John 10:12–13 has a word for them: "The hired hand is not the shepherd and does not own the sheep. So when he sees the wolf coming, he abandons the sheep and runs away. Then the wolf attacks the flock and scatters it. The man runs away because he is a hired hand and cares nothing for the sheep."

Shepherds who aren't teaching their sheep to understand in depth what the Bible teaches about sexuality and why God has prohibited homosexuality are creating sitting ducks for Reformation Project wolves.

I have heard from many parents who excitedly launched their sons and daughters into middle school and high school ministries expecting them to have experiences that would mirror their own from that period of their lives. They expected that it would be a time of tremendous growth for their children, thanks to friends who would spur in them, in a way that only an adolescents' peers can, a zeal to follow the Lord. At the very least, they expected the youth leaders to reinforce the biblical standards they'd carefully taught at home. Instead, their kids came back from Wednesday night youth groups muddled and questioning—at best, encouraged to stay quiet about their convictions regarding sex and marriage; at worst, no longer sure they should *have* convictions.

One couple, newly relocated to Austin, Texas, in 2022, chose to attend a large nondenominational church, rather than the kind of small Baptist congregation they'd left specifically so their two children would have the best opportunity to make strong Christian friends. The couple eagerly signed up their seventh-grade daughter for an overnight lock-in. When she returned home the next morning, she told her parents that perhaps a third of the kids at the event had shared that they were uncertain whether they were boys, girls, or something in between; nor were they sure which sex they were attracted to. That would have been fine if the leadership had lovingly taken the opportunity to teach truth to these lost tweens and teens, but they hadn't. The daughter told her parents the leaders "just kind of listened and said they weren't there to judge."

At a weekend retreat a few months later, when the situation repeated itself, their daughter said she had found herself alone in her boldness. "She told us she kind of stood up and said, 'I don't understand what the confusion is—God's Word says this,'" her father told me. "And the vibe we got from her, that was later confirmed by her small-group leaders, was that she was kind of left out on an island." He didn't want to be critical. He appreciated that these mostly college-age leaders were taking time out of their lives to "love on these kids." But what is youth ministry for if not to bring Scripture to bear on such situations? When the father inquired, the sheepish ministry director told him the youth leaders did have orthodox beliefs, but that the directive coming down from the top—from the senior pastor—was not to address homosexuality or transgenderism at all in group settings.

The LGBTQ community is correct in saying that many evangelicals are treating homosexuality and transgenderism different from how they treat many other sins. They're much softer and shyer in addressing it. Organizations like Embracing the Journey are exploiting this embarrassment. Even if we grant the motive of evangelism, it's nonsensical to believe that sinners are more likely to be won to a truth we take pains to obscure. This is not to say that when we meet a teenage girl suffering from gender dysphoria, we're to launch harshly into the reasons we won't use male terms to address her. But we shouldn't, because of her presence, withhold the truth from our own people or from her. We understand, as Jesus demonstrated, that some "hard sayings" will cause the crowds to leave grumbling. And He may call on us to divide even from children, siblings, and parents to follow Him.

The week Tim Keller died, one of his former church members, *USA Today* columnist Kirsten Powers, wrote a memorial for him titled "My Complicated Feelings About Tim Keller."[102] Powers had risen to the heights of worldly success as an author, former White House staffer, and political commentor on CNN, but she had been left searching for more after the successive deaths of her father and beloved grandmother. She ended up at Redeemer Presbyterian, Keller's New York City church, and was soon "all in on Christianity."

Much of her essay was laudatory, detailing the qualities that had drawn so many Christians to Keller's teaching. She noted Keller's kindness, his sharp intellect, and how he had been able to contextualize the Bible for his urban professional congregation through illustrations from philosophy, art, and pop culture. So why, then, did she also resent him? She explains:

> When I say I signed up for Tim Keller's brand of evangelicalism, I mean I signed up for what I heard from the pulpit, which never included teaching about homosexuality or abortion being a sin. . . . But as I became more involved in the church, I learned that these were in fact core teachings. It was more through peer pressure than any sermons that I started to conform to teachings that left me feeling unsettled and confused. Slowly, I lost myself as I attempted to conform to a theology that

had the effect of disempowering me and alienating me from myself and many important people in my life.

She does not seem to know it, but the doctrines Powers encountered are a feature, not a bug, of following Jesus. He tells us in passages like Mark 10 and Luke 14 that if we don't love Him so much that we're willing to be alienated from the most important people in our lives, we're not worthy to be His disciples. Conforming to His teachings can be unsettling, painful even. But that is what sanctification is. He increases, we decrease.

Powers no longer calls herself a Christian, and she is clear she resents Keller somewhat for not being more up front about the biblical beliefs that, for her, after years in his church, would prove to be a bridge too far. It would have been better, she implies, if he had told her from the outset that the Lord would require from her agreement with ideas that were in direct opposition to our culture's most sacredly held beliefs. If Keller had preached about homosexuality when she first began attending his church, she might have counted the cost early on and known it was not one she was willing to pay.

Keller's fellow PCA pastor Todd Pruitt put it well when he argued for his denomination to provide biblical clarity when it came to sex, sexuality, and marriage. "A simple scan of the history of denominations in the United States tells the tale [of how once-faithful Christian institutions have fallen to LGBTQ heresy]," he wrote. "It is a tragic story of denominations once committed to sound doctrine and a biblically defined mission which, because of increasing latitude, found themselves on the garbage heap of apostasy. This does not happen overnight; it happens day-by-day, over a period of years, one compromise at a time. It happens as those entrusted to be the chief teachers and stewards of the church's doctrinal treasure embrace, for instance, Side-B homosexuality, all the while saying, 'Peace, peace.'"[103]

There seems little doubt that apostasy will be introduced to many ministries and churches through this issue. But woe to those found sleeping, though the alarms have been sounding, and to the those through whom the apostasy comes.

Conclusion

Do you imagine that the gospel is a nose of wax which can be shaped to suit the face of each succeeding age? Is the revelation once given by the Spirit of God to be interpreted according to the fashion of the period?

—Charles Spurgeon, 1887

I felt compelled to write and urge you to contend for the faith that was once for all entrusted to God's holy people . . . These [false teachers] are blemishes at your love feasts, eating with you without the slightest qualm—shepherds who feed only themselves. They are clouds without rain, blown along by the wind; autumn trees, without fruit and uprooted—twice dead.

—Jude 1:3, 12

Late one summer night—or it could have been early morning—while I was in college, I woke up to find myself on the floor of a jail cell.

As one might imagine, I wasn't especially happy about this. But I wasn't especially frightened by it, either. I did start crying, but that was more a matter of self-pity and to prove to myself that I was not like the other women slumped in dark hoodies and stained tank tops along the concrete walls—who, I imagined, from their stoic lack of tears, were probably prostitutes or meth heads. At least, they hadn't had the presence of mind to put on a little blush or get their nails done before getting cuffed, as I had.

Looking back, I find it especially funny that I cast myself as the innocent of the collective, given that this was the third time in five years I had landed myself in the clink, as my friends jokingly called it to take the sting out of my degradation. It was, however, the first time I couldn't remember being arrested. I was wearing a midnight-blue cocktail dress, and a long strip of its tulle hem was torn and hanging loose. I had a vague memory of having had an argument with a roommate and leaving her at a party after washing down two Vicodin, two Xanax, and two Somas with one of several vodka tonics, to take the edge off an amphetamine comedown. Many years later, I would learn that street dealers call this combination "the holy trinity," for its ability to mimic the euphoria of heroin, and that it is a leading culprit in overdose deaths. I had stumbled onto this magic formula after years of experimentation with my grandmother's always-stocked medicine cabinet. That I was in a jail cell and not a morgue is evidence of God's great mercy to me—mercy I would go right back to abusing when my father came to get me out.

I was both high and hungover one Sunday night about a year later while trying to finish an overdue paper on Thomas Malory's *Le Morte d'Arthur*. By that time, the friends I had left had ceased trying to cushion the reality of what I was. Even the old boyfriends I'd thought I could string along forever had moved on to less tiresome pastures. Though I was miraculously still in school (or, I should say, back in school; there were multiple detours), the worn-out welcomes of former roommates meant I was once again living with my parents. All the things that are typically attendant to such a life were attendant to mine—sexual assault, emergency rooms, and car crashes, to say nothing of the steady, humiliating grind of lies and relationship-wrecking scenes.

Any delusion I had that my life was glamourous or enviable or remotely happy had long since worn thin, revived only through more drinking, more drugs. There were times I remember wishing my family would leave me to my sin so I could at last slip away into the gutter.

This was the backdrop as I sat on my parents' couch uncharacteristically attempting to complete my assignment. My outline was simple: regurgitate back to my English 221 professor in essay form his observation that Malory had wisely edited out the religious lectures that a series of hermits gave the adulterous Lancelot in the thirteenth century Vulgate cycle—or as it is titled in the 1969 English translation, *The Quest of the Holy Grail*.

"The unknown author's heavy-handed focus on moralizing obscures the doomed romance that would captivate readers for hundreds of generations," my professor thought. Thus, so would I. (It had been my experience that professors liked seeing their own opinions reflected back at them.)

Then I read the hermit's rebuke: "You stumbled from the path of righteousness and set your feet in one unknown to you till then, the path of lust, the path which degrades both body and soul to a degree that none can really know who has not tried it . . ."[1]

I had tried it. Lust for attention, lust for superiority, lust to feel good. I knew the degradation. My parents were at Sunday evening church service, and their drunken, drug-addicted daughter was writing a term paper at their house because she knew the degradation all too well. A burning lump rose in my throat as I kept reading: "I have told you all these things because of my sorrow at seeing you so abased and shamed that you will meet with nothing but slights and derision from all who know the true account of your fortunes."[2]

At this, Lancelot "wept bitterly," and I wept along with him.

And this time I *was* afraid. I didn't know how to be something other than what I was. I had been raised as a Christian; I had made multiple professions of faith. At more than one church service or youth camp, I had closed my eyes and raised my hand to "ask Jesus to be the Lord of my life" or to "rededicate my life," once after I had graduated from high school. The commitment never lasted longer than the bus ride home or the walk to the parking lot. I never exhibited the slightest sustained interest in spiritual things to suggest I was a true disciple. As the old cliché goes, I knew that if I died one night—as I was pretty sure I had come close to doing a couple of times—I would immediately find myself in Hell.

There is no agony quite like that of the prodigal who has chosen the pigs but still believes in judgment.

Yet, when the hermit offered Lancelot this hope, "None the less you have not so offended but you may find forgiveness" and reminded him that Matthew 22's false follower is cast out of the Lamb's wedding feast, I wanted that forgiveness, too. I did not want to be cast out. Above all, I didn't want my life to go on as it had. With a bit of dramatic flair, to show I really meant it this time—again, I was high—I went into the bedroom, locking the door so no one would come in and catch me, got down on my knees, and prayed.

The following Sunday, I went to church.

I won't pretend that from that day, my battle with substance abuse immediately ended, but it actually became a battle. And one of my greatest weapons in that battle, aside from regular Bible study, was the shepherding and community I found at Christ's Church of the Valley. Within six months, I met my husband, who was a leader of the church's college and young professionals group, and who had never had a drink, let alone touched a drug, in his life. On our first date, he asked how my walk with the Lord was going, and the question didn't make me feel awkward or compelled to come up with a fake, churchy response. I was able to smile at the novelty of being out with such a man and answer honestly, "It's going great."

At points during my wasteland years, my parents tried to help me as best they could. I went to rehab and spent months with "Christian" therapists who had great empathy for the real ways I'd been victimized. They put me on regimens of antidepressants and sedatives and encouraged me to read therapeutic Christian books whose titles I don't recall. We spent a lot of time discussing the traumas I had experienced—not unusual, of course, for anyone who develops such habits. My parents were both barely eighteen when I was born, and would not marry for another five years. Though my home became stable, it didn't start out that way, which leaves a mark.

But focusing on my upbringing and childhood experiences did nothing to help break the stranglehold of my sin. I typically left the counselor's office feeling a different sort of high, the therapy high. Not taking another handful of pills or resisting getting blackout drunk didn't seem as important as figuring out how the wrongs done to me had created my desire to do such things.

It was only when I encountered teaching that challenged me not to focus on how I had been wronged, but to repent for the wrongs I had committed, that I was able to find lasting victory. After my return to church, I stumbled along for a couple months, occasionally giving in to the temptation to take that magic combo from my grandmother's medicine cabinet again. One of my pastors put a book in my hand. *The Vanishing Conscience*, by John F. MacArthur, had very different suggestions for dealing with my "learned behaviors":

> Peter writes, "Beloved, I urge you as aliens and strangers to abstain from fleshly lusts, which wage war against the soul" (1 Peter 2:11). In other words, stop lusting. Abstain from it. Stay away from it. "Flee immorality" (1 Corinthians 6:18). What could be more direct? Do you want to put to death the lusts in your heart? Then stop entertaining them. Peter does not prescribe a program of therapy. He does not suggest that such

sin be treated as an addiction. He simply says to abstain. Quit doing it.
You have no business indulging such thoughts. Put them away at once.
You yourself must do this; it cannot be done for you. There is no point
waiting for some heavenly power to erase this sin automatically from
your life . . .

That is precisely the error Romans 6 refutes. You are free from sin;
now stop doing it. You are dead to sin; now put to death the sin that
remains. How? "Abstain." Reckon yourself dead to sin and don't do it
anymore. "Resist the devil and he will flee from you" (James 4:7).[3]

It was a little like the old *Mad TV* skit where Bob Newhart plays a therapist whose only response to a patient's descriptions of her compulsive behaviors is to shout, "Stop it!"—except MacArthur's rebuke came with biblical
strategies for stopping it.

The rest of the book explains what it means to make no provision for
the flesh (Romans 13:14), why meditating on God's Word is the key to
sanctification (John 17:17), how to buffet one's body and control its desires
(1 Corinthians 9:25–27). I had been immersed in the evangelical subculture
my entire life, but this was all a revelation to me. I had never heard the clarity
of Scripture applied to my habitual drunkenness and drug use, because that
was embarrassing, fundamentalist stuff. It was the kind of stuff that today
would earn long, sneering Twitter threads from Duke divinity professors
and esoteric essays in *Christianity Today* about how such simplistic thinking
fails to account for the evolution of biochemistry in the addict's brain that
requires their reward pathways to be gradually rewired.[4] (That one left me
wanting to yell "Stop it!")

MacArthur's book destroyed all such lofty opinions and—foolish as it
might sound to more nuanced evangelical intellectuals—to me, well on my
way to perishing, it was the power of God. I went away from that book committed to living like the new creation I was. In a very short space of time, I
also stopped caring about how I'd been injured, how I had been oppressed. I
was busy being sanctified. I was busy being grateful. I was free indeed.

That was more than twenty years ago now. And before the last two
years, I've never talked about it publicly with anything more than vague
allusion. I decided I would conclude with it for two reasons. First, because

as soon as I did begin to tell my story—though, with no great degree of specificity—I discovered how many parents out there were desperate to hear testimonies like mine. My word for them: Keep praying, and let any help or counsel you offer adhere to Scripture, not culture. Our God is still a God who brings dead girls to life.

Second, I tell it now because I know the power of faithful preaching and shepherding. They are both so powerful that they can reach across a millennium and pierce the heart of a hopeless sinner in a world the preacher couldn't have imagined, so that other, nearer preachers can help those newly planted seeds to grow. It humbles the heart of the obstinate sheep with the tough but loving truth that change is not only possible, but possible now—if only she will turn her eyes from the tea leaves of her own psyche and grievances and fix them on Jesus. And it's helped me move toward every good thing in my life—my marriage, my children, repaired relationships with my family, rewarding work, all with the promise of eternal glory thrown in. It is what drove me to write this book.

If I had walked into that church and heard the same lessons I was getting in my Feminist Theory class or my therapist's office dressed up in spiritual jargon, I would have had little reason to stay and, if I had stayed, no understanding of how to live my life differently. The pastors might have congratulated themselves for their sophistication, for helping me understand the injustice that had oppressed me, but I would still have been in bondage.

And that, of course, is exactly what the enemy hopes to accomplish.

Many forces are trying to claim American churches for many agendas, but ultimately there's only one force, one agenda. We do not battle against flesh and blood. Satan's wolves in sheep's clothing secretly slip into the church for one reason: to prevent it from snatching more souls out of the fire. But while their number and certainly their advantages can seem overwhelming, we often discover that when we face them with the courage of Christ, it doesn't take much strength or wealth or cunning to overcome them.

Remember New America Foundation, the left-wing think tank funded by George Soros, Pierre Omidyar, and Bill Gates (among others) that released an in-depth report on how progressive groups have tried to co-opt evangelical churches for the sake of climate change? During a presentation about their findings, coauthor Lydia Bean noted with some frustration that millions of dollars and years of effort had availed these groups nothing. The reason, she explained, came down largely to the persistent efforts of one man:

> As things stood in the evangelical climate initiative, a single guy named Cal Beisner was able to pull this coalition together fairly easily. And what's amazing to me is the Cornwall Alliance, for most of the period in question that he was leading this anti-climate-action movement among evangelicals and conservatives, he wasn't even doing it fulltime. He was teaching classes fulltime at a Christian university and doing it as a hobby.
>
> So I don't want you to think that evangelical creation care lost out because the Koch Brothers poured a bunch of money into [stopping it] and they were washed out. This effort wasn't well resourced. It didn't take very much.[5]

This confirms what Beisner told me as well. "The forces on the opposite side are so huge," he admitted. "I mean, if you're talking about the combined annual budgets of the world's top, say, dozen environmental NGOs—that's over thirty billion dollars. And we're going along with our little budget that we hope maybe we can raise up to a total of four hundred twenty-five thousand this year."

It didn't take very much.

If you take away Bean's political jargon of "pulling coalitions together," what you see is just a Christian who, armed with his Bible and common sense, started studying the issue. He then sounded the alarm that left-wing groups were using high-profile evangelical leaders to hoodwink average believers into accepting their agenda.

Without enormous grants being funneled his way from billionaire dark-money fronts, without the fame of bestselling megachurch pastors in his corner or fawning profiles in elite media outlets, without having the ear of heads of state or international governing bodies, he was able to throw a wrench in the machine of evangelical influence peddling—all because he spoke up. And all those who felt deep down that something was off about what they were hearing, but who were too impressionable or embarrassed to say so out loud, were emboldened by his example. Like Moses facing down Pharoah's magicians, or Narnia's Puddleglum stomping his Marsh-wiggle foot on the Witch's fire, the truth Beisner spoke dumped a massive bucket of ice water on the spell that all that Christianese sloganeering was casting.

Like everything in life, there's a verse for this: Beisner destroyed the arguments raised against the knowledge of God by clinging to the Word no matter who might accuse him of being foolish (2 Corinthians 10:5). People woke up. Beisner's courage gave them courage. Beisner's wisdom gave them wisdom.

One more story, from another era.

Not long ago, Larry Taunton devoted an episode of his podcast, *Ideas Have Consequences*, to two men who both lived in London in the mid-nineteenth century and whose worldviews continue to shape human life today: Charles Spurgeon and Karl Marx.[6] While the two did not know each other, there is little doubt, as Taunton explained when I asked him about his research, that each was aware of the other and of the "irreconcilable nature of the messages each proclaimed." Far from resisting the appearance of being political, Taunton told me, "Spurgeon recognized the danger in his day and went after socialism again and again and again. He savaged it."

Over a period of years, the Prince of Preachers unhesitatingly taught that Marx's "religion" desired to "supplant" Christianity.[7] To embrace socialism, he warned, would result in "the real disruption of all society as at present established." It would leave "all society shattered, and men wandering like monster icebergs on the sea, dashing against each other, and being at last utterly destroyed." He mocked those ministers who would abandon "the grand old truths of the gospel" that saw sinners converted and saints edified in favor of preaching the pursuit of a communist utopia on earth:

> They are going to regenerate the world by Democratic Socialism, and set up a kingdom for Christ without the new birth or the pardon of sin . . . To me it seems a tangle of ever-changing dreams. It is, by the confession of its inventors, the outcome of the period—the monstrous birth of a boasted "progress"—the scum from the cauldron of conceit. It has not been given by the infallible revelation of God—it does not pretend to have been. It is not divine—it has no inspired Scripture at its back. It is, when it touches the Cross, an enemy! When it speaks of

Him who died thereon, it is a deceitful friend. Many are its sneers at the truth of substitution—it is irate at the mention of the precious blood. Many a pulpit, where Christ was once lifted high in all the glory of His atoning death, is now profaned by those who laugh at justification by faith. In fact, men are not now to be saved by faith but by doubt. Those who love the Church of God feel heavy at heart because the teachers of the people cause them to err.[8]

At the end of Friedrich Engels's life, Marx's daughter interviewed the coauthor, with her father, of *The Communist Manifesto*. When she asked him who he disliked most in the world, Engels answered with a single word: "Spurgeon."[9] It's little to be wondered at. Engels believed that a counterfeit form of Christianity could be used to advance the cause of socialism, as both ostensibly addressed the interests of what he called the "labouring and burdened."[10] A true shepherd like Spurgeon necessarily stood in the way of such efforts, reminding the world that mankind's greatest need was not a social project, not power over his oppressors, but forgiveness from his sins. True Christianity promotes not grievance but gratitude. There's little doubt Marx and Engels knew this.

Do today's Marxist activists have any reason to say they hate above anyone else in the world the church leaders most celebrated by our cultural elites? Or do they find that these "shepherds" not only don't hinder but even help their cause?

It's the practice of wolves to dismiss the concerns of those who see compromise and false teaching slipping into the Church, to accuse those sounding the alarm of making mountains out of molehills. Yet Scripture never encourages us to minimize or turn a blind eye to such matters. Instead, we are commanded to "contend earnestly" for the faith. The Apostle Paul uses no soft language in Galatians 1 to address those who bring other Gospels into the Church—he calls them "accursed." Jesus does not treat lightly those using the temple to peddle worldly goods for worldly gain—He drives them out with a whip (John 2:15). Christians should, of course, not stir up controversies or dissension over minor or disputable matters, but where clear distortion of Scripture is taking place, we are not permitted to ignore it.

J. Gresham Machen fought a similar battle with liberalism in the 1920s, and he leaves a word of challenge and encouragement:

> The present is a time not for ease or pleasure, but for earnest and prayerful work. A terrible crisis unquestionably has arisen in the Church. Yet there is in the Christian life no room for despair . . . Laymen, as well as ministers, should return, in these trying days, with new earnestness, to the study of the Word of God. If the Word of God be heeded, the Christian battle will be fought both with love and with faithfulness . . . Every man must decide upon which side he will stand. God grant that we may decide aright! What the immediate future may bring we cannot presume to say. The final result indeed is clear. God has not deserted His Church.

Now is our moment—"Laymen as well as ministers"—to stand in defense of the Gospel against foreign doctrines that have come into the Church. It is our moment to pray that the Lord will strengthen our hands and embolden our hearts for the task.

Boniface, Luther, Calvin, Spurgeon, Machen, Schaeffer, and Lewis (not to mention the Apostles Peter, Paul, and Jude) courageously called nonsense nonsense and heresy, heresy. These are our heroes of the faith. The temptation may be to let the reporting in this book cause you to huddle in defeatism, overcome with discouragement that so many in such elevated positions have traded the freedom and victory we should have in Christ for a progressive religion that burdens the faithful with a never-attainable works-based righteousness. (And it doesn't cheer me at all to acknowledge that this book covers only a small slice of what has been happening.)

But the reasons to take heart are numerous. We are finally talking to one another about our concerns. And that talking is leading to action, as we have seen with the Christian institutions and leaders who felt they had no choice but to turn back when the objections to their rough usage of the Church grew too loud.

According to Lifeway research, fully 19 percent of U.S. adults are still, by conviction, evangelical, meaning not merely in how they self-identify but also in how their tested understanding of their faith defines them.[11] That is nearly fifty million people of sound biblical doctrine. Can you imagine the transformation we might see if even a quarter of that number demanded that pastors, professors, seminary administrators, and ministry leaders passionately pursued the cause of Christ and His Word, rather than taking up the preoccupations of billionaires, businesses, and lawmakers? It would be enough to see a new Reformation in the American Church.

Everywhere I go, I see signs that the faithful are ready to battle back the progressive ideologues inhabiting pulpits and high ministry offices. I believe the reason J. D. Greear, Russell Moore, and other progressive-friendly pastors grew so belligerent in secular media interviews regarding ordinary evangelicals is because they are smarting from the disapproval of the large numbers of people who now see what they are about. The message that we will not tolerate the preaching of different gospels is getting through. It should come through even clearer.

Where shepherds and teachers are compromising the Word for the sake of worldly approval, where they are belittling their sheep and defaming the Church for the applause of the important and influential, we should not reward them by remaining in their churches or buying their books.

Protestants in particular do not have a legacy of timidity in the face of heresies. Like Luther, when we find indulgences being sold for white privilege or carbon emissions, we nail to the door our declaration of grace through faith alone and declare, "Here I stand. I can do no other." If the woke preachers torch us as troublemakers and fundamentalists in the pages of the *Washington Post*, the *New York Times*, *The Atlantic*, and so on, let them. They are only setting the blaze of attention higher so the eyes of true believers will turn and see what has been going on for the last few years.

No one, least of all Christians, should welcome civil war in the Church. But too many Church leaders have grown arrogant due to the rank and file's reluctance to seem unpleasant or uncharitable by confronting their deceit and manipulation, and a unity based on acceptance of false teaching is a unity of the damned. As Aragorn says to Théoden, king of Rohan, in *The Lord of the Rings: The Two Towers*, open war is upon us whether we would risk it or not. Or, as Moses says to the Gadites and Reubenites in Numbers 32, "Should your fellow Israelites go to war while you sit here?"

That is where we are. Open war is upon us and has been for a number of years. But we possess a power that no other in the world can rival. Listen to the progressive strategists as they complain that evangelicals have been the toughest nut to crack despite the tens of millions of dollars they have spent promoting elite church influencers who voice their preferred views.

Why is that so? Because unlike any other targeted demographic, we have the objective source of truth. We have a North Star that pulls us back when we wander too far afield, that ensures that we fight the right battles in the right way. We have the Word that is living and powerful and sharper than any two-edged sword (Hebrews 4:12). The time has come to pick up that sword and unashamedly use it against the cunning and craftiness of people who would see us blown here and there by every wind of teaching, and to pursue what our Lord calls us to in Ephesians 4:15–16:

> Instead, speaking the truth in love, we will grow to become in every respect the mature body of him who is the head, that is, Christ. From him the whole body, joined and held together by every supporting ligament, grows and builds itself up in love, as each part does its work.

Acknowledgments

One of the most comforting doctrines of Christianity is the doctrine of Providence—of knowing that God will make a way for any task He would see accomplished.

Tony Daniel first suggested that my reporting on the Church should be a book. Without his enthusiasm for the subject and his expert editorial advice for shaping it, I would never have embarked on the project at all.

From there, a domino-effect of invaluable advice surrounded me, proving that many good counselors are indeed the best means of ensuring successful plans (Proverbs 15:22). Along with other ongoing guidance, on first hearing of the idea, Nick Eicher encouraged me to consult Lynn Vincent. At the top of her list of instrumental advice: "Get a good agent. I know a great one." She certainly did. And I am very grateful to Ian Kleinert for shepherding me through the publishing process every step of the way, especially when that way got bumpy. I'm most indebted to him for guiding me to Eric Nelson, Hannah Long, and the team at Broadside Books, whose insights, suggestions, and cross-examinations made it stronger. If I ever doubted that Providence was directing my steps, this book ending up under the particular oversight of Broadside's James Neidhardt restored my confidence. Not only did his editorial acumen sharpen the work, but his scouring the manuscript for opportunities to share the Gospel more clearly and to encourage readers to join a local church were a neon sign that I was right where I should be.

It can be a fearful thing to entrust your story, your experiences to a reporter. That is exponentially truer when those stories focus on the Church. I am deeply appreciative of all the sources who trusted me with theirs.

Very few journalists plow entirely untilled ground, and by the time I arrived at the subject of infiltration and compromise within the Church, a great many unsung writers and reporters had already done extensive leg work. David Morrill, Alan Atchison, and Jon Harris patiently answered countless questions and unselfishly shared reams of material they had collected over the years, caring more about disseminating truth than protecting their turf. There is a reason Big Eva tries to dismiss you gentleman—you have the goods and they often know it. Michael O'Fallon and Bill Roach were similarly generous and saved me weeks if not months of research with short phone calls.

Kelly Kullberg, my "Dr. Watson," is the true keeper of receipts. This book would look entirely different without her input and passion. It was a providential day indeed when a friend said, "I met someone I think you should know. Let me introduce you to Kelly Kullberg..." I think of this book as only a beginning to our adventures.

The pleasantness of a friend springs from their heartfelt advice, and I've been blessed all through the writing process in friends who offered encouragement, cautions, and wisdom (not to mention shoulders to cry on when the going got rough), including Mary Reichard, Darlene Schmitt (again), Nick Eicher, Bethel McGrew, Georgia Howe, Lisa Bacon, Rosaria Butterfield, Genetta Adair, and Josh Daws.

My employer, the *Daily Wire*, continuously gave me time and support over nearly two years to pursue this passion project.

I don't know if it takes a village to raise a child, but it certainly takes a village for mom to write a book. My mom, Kay, and my sister, Shelby, played taxi and babysitter at a moment's notice. My brother, Travis, kept me laughing on the most frustrating days. My grandmother Marney reminded me often that this book mattered to the wider world and encouraged me to press on in the face of opposition. My dad, Steve, played the role he has played all my life—counselor, coach, and first theological resource. And for two years, my husband and children surrounded me with encouragement that God had given me this task and they were willing to do dishes, run errands, walk dogs, and listen to endless alternately excited and despairing updates on how the work was proceeding.

My husband, further, participated in innumerable conversations about various aspects of the book, reading drafts and offering his unfailing discernment which I have, over twenty-two years of marriage, come to trust more than that of anyone else on Earth. You are the clearest evidence of God's grace and kindness to me.

Notes

INTRODUCTION: How Do You Solve a Problem Like the Christians?

1. Be the Bridge, "16 Bridge-Building Tips for White People," https://bethebridge.com/docs/16Tips.pdf.
2. Kristin Du Mez, *Jesus and John Wayne: How White Evangelicals Corrupted a Faith and Fractured a Nation* (New York: Liveright, an imprint of W. W. Norton, 2020), p. 27.
3. Tim Alberta, *The Kingdom, the Power, and the Glory: American Evangelicals in an Age of Extremism* (New York: HarperCollins, 2023), p. 66.
4. Jessica Martínez and Gregory A. Smith, "How the Faithful Voted: A Preliminary 2016 Analysis," Pew Research Center, November, 9, 2016, https://www.pewresearch.org/short-reads/2016/11/09/how-the-faithful-voted-a-preliminary-2016-analysis/.
5. Paul Kengor, *The Devil and Karl Marx: Communism's Long March of Death, Deception, and Infiltration* (Gastonia, North Carolina: TAN Books, 2020).
6. Ibid. p. 167.
7. Karl Marx, "Introduction," *A Contribution to the Critique of Hegel's Philosophy of Right*, trans. A. Jolin and J. O'Malley, ed. J. O'Malley (1843; Cambridge, UK: Cambridge University Press, 1970), via Marxists.org.
8. Circuit Riders, Inc., *A Compilation of Public Records 20.5%, 1411 Protestant Episcopal Rectors (as of 1955)*, Political Extremism and Radicalism: Far-Right Groups in America (Circuit Riders Inc., 1956), https://books.google.com/books/about/A_Compilation_of_Public_Records_20_5_141.html?id=MsDXzgEACAAJ. See also the *Congressional Record* from March 3, 1960, https://www.govinfo.gov/content/pkg/GPO-CRECB-1960-pt4/pdf/GPO-CRECB-1960-pt4-2-2.pdf.
9. Paul Kengor, "A Group of Communist Clergymen," RealClearReligion, July 25, 2012, https://www.realclearreligion.org/articles/2012/07/25/a_group_of_communist_clergymen.html.
10. Gallup, "Religion," https://news.gallup.com/poll/1690/religion.aspx. *See also* Pew Research, "Party Affiliation Among Evangelical Protestants," https://www.pewresearch.org/religion/religious-landscape-study/religious-tradition/evangelical-protestant/party-affiliation/.
11. Pew Research Center, "Conservatives: Religious Composition of Conservatives," https://www.pewresearch.org/religion/religious-landscape-study/political-ideology/conservative/.
12. *The Atlantic*, "'Evangelical' Is Not a Religious Identity. It's a Political One," *The Experiment* (podcast), Atlantic.com, 2021, https://www.theatlantic.com/podcasts/archive/2021/05/evangelicals-republican-voters/618845/.

13. For the LGBT movement, see Pew Research Center, "Attitudes About Transgender Issues Vary Widely Among Christians, Religious 'Nones' in U.S.," Pew Research Center, 2022, https://www.pewresearch.org/short-reads/2022/07/07/attitudes-about-transgender-issues-vary-widely-among-christians-religious-nones-in-u-s/. *See also* Pew Research Center, "Support for Same-Sex Marriage Grows, Even Among Groups that Had Been Skeptical," Pew Research Center, 2017, https://www.pewresearch.org/politics/2017/06/26/support-for-same-sex-marriage-grows-even-among-groups-that-had-been-skeptical/?utm_source=Pew+Research+Center&utm_campaign=ea3b886144-EMAIL_CAMPAIGN_2017_06_26&utm_medium=email&utm_term=0_3e953b9b70-ea3b886144-400334425. For climate change, see Becka A. Alper, "How Religion Intersects with Americans' Views on the Environment," Pew Research Center, 2022, https://www.pewresearch.org/religion/2022/11/17/how-religion-intersects-with-americans-views-on-the-environment/. For illegal immigration, see Tara Isabella Burton, "The Bible Says to Welcome Immigrants. So Why Don't White Evangelicals?" Vox, 2018, https://www.vox.com/2018/10/30/18035336/white-evangelicals-immigration-nationalism-christianity-refugee-honduras-migrant.

14. Savannah Kuchar, "Ron DeSantis Is Waging a War on 'Woke' in Florida. It's Costing Him Billionaire Donors in the 2024 Race," *USA Today*, August 7, 2023, https://www.usatoday.com/story/news/politics/2023/08/07/desantis-loses-donors-woke-war/70461487007/.

15. Jim Eskin, "Giving While Living Makes Sense: For the Wealthy, Making a Difference Now Offers a Chance to See Lives Touched in One's Own Lifetime," *Dallas Business Journal*, December 20, 2007, https://www.bizjournals.com/dallas/stories/2007/12/24/editorial4.html?jst=pn_pn_lk.

16. The Atlantic Philanthropies, "Investing in a Healthy Future for All Americans: United States | 2006–2015," The Atlantic Philanthropies, n.d., https://www.atlanticphilanthropies.org/subtheme/health-system-reform.

17. Karen Martin, "A Meeting of Queer Minds: Report on a Retreat of LGBTI Leaders and Activists from the Republic of Ireland and South Africa," The Atlantic Philanthropies, March 2010, https://www.atlanticphilanthropies.org/wp-content/uploads/2015/09/Meeting_of_queerminds.pdf.

18. Maggie Severns, "Liberal Megadonors Plan $100 Million Swing-State Blitz to Beat Trump," Politico, May 5, 2019, https://www.politico.com/story/2019/05/05/liberal-donors-trump-2020-1301639.

19. Open Society Foundations, "U.S. Programs Board Meeting," Open Society Foundations, February 13–14, 2012, (source provided hard copy to author).

20. Chris Crawford, "Leap of Faith: Empowering Faith Leaders to Strengthen Democracy," Democracy Fund, September 17, 2018, https://democracyfund.org/idea/leap-of-faith-empowering-faith-leaders-to-strengthen-democracy/.

21. Democracy Fund Inc., Form 990PF for Fiscal Year Ending Dec. 2018, ProPublica, 2018, https://projects.propublica.org/nonprofits/organizations/383926408/201943199349105119/IRS990PF; Democracy Fund Inc., Form 990PF for Fiscal Year Ending Dec. 2019, ProPublica, 2019, https://projects.propublica.org/nonprofits/organizations/383926408/202003219349106935/IRS990PF; Democracy Fund Inc., Form 990PF for Fiscal Year Ending Dec. 2021,

ProPublica, 2021, https://projects.propublica.org/nonprofits/organizations
/383926408/202213199349107641/IRS990PF.

22. Creation Justice Ministries, "From Resilience to Restoration: Keynote by Dr. Rick Spinrad, NOAA Administrator," YouTube video, August 24, 2022, https://www.youtube
.com/watch?v=mdAMhAr4gXM.

23. Here, for instance: Holy Post, "What About Abortion? Should This One Issue Determine How Christians Vote?" YouTube video, October 17, 2020, https://www.youtube
.com/watch?v=RvWD7ykNjCc.

24. For J. D. Greear, see Kelly Williams, "The SBC and Whether God's Word 'Whispers' About Sexual Sin," *The Christian Post*, March 27, 2022, https://www.christianpost
.com/voices/the-sbc-and-whether-gods-word-whispers-about-sexual-sin.html. And for Ed Litton, see Marsha West, "Like Greear, New SBC President Says the Bible 'Whispers' About Homosexuality," Christian Research Network, June 21, 2021, https://
christianresearchnetwork.org/2021/06/21/like-greear-new-sbc-president-says-the
-bible-whispers-about-homosexuality/.

25. Rick Warren, "About Rick Warren," RickWarren.org, March 28, 2023, https://rickwarren
.org/about-rick-warren/.

26. Russell Moore, *Losing Our Religion: An Altar Call for Evangelical America* (New York: Sentinel, an imprint of Penguin Random House, 2023).

27. Mark Tooley, "Contraceptive Evangelicals?," *The American Spectator*, July 12, 2012, https://spectator.org/contraceptive-evangelicals/.

28. Caleb Parke, "Southern Baptist President Calls for Members to Declare: 'Black Lives Matter,'" Fox News, June 11, 2020, https://www.foxnews.com/us/black-lives-matter
-southern-baptist.

29. Francis A. Schaeffer. *The Great Evangelical Disaster* (Wheaton, IL: Crossway, 1983), p. 112–113. Kindle Edition.

30. Timothy Cockes, "Greear Decries Division, Calls False Accusations 'Demonic' in EC Address," *Baptist Press*, February 22, 2021, https://www.baptistpress.com/resource
-library/news/greear-decries-division-repudiates-pharisaical-spirit-in-sbc-ec-address/.

31. Southeastern Seminary, "J. D. Greear | To the Church at Smyrna | Revelation 2," YouTube video, January 26, 2022, https://www.youtube.com/watch?v=WMiWPVBwIFE.

32. David Crary, "Southern Baptists Oust 2 Churches over LGBTQ Inclusion," AP News, December 13, 2023, https://apnews.com/article/race-and-ethnicity-baptist-southern
-baptist-convention-kentucky-louisville-3d117834c18621f0af125f192d4a194c.

33. Ed Stetzer, "Fellow Evangelicals: Stop Falling for Trump's Anti-Immigrant Rhetoric," Vox, November 6, 2018, https://www.vox.com/policy-and-politics/2018/11/6
/18066116/trump-caravan-evangelical-voters.

34. Dalia Fahmy, "7 Facts About Southern Baptists," Pew Research Center, June 7, 2019, https://www.pewresearch.org/short-reads/2019/06/07/7-facts-about-southern
-baptists/.

35. John Gramlich, "What the 2020 Electorate Looks Like by Party, Race and Ethnicity, Age, Education and Religion," Pew Research Center, October 26, 2020, https://www
.pewresearch.org/short-reads/2020/10/26/what-the-2020-electorate-looks-like-by
-party-race-and-ethnicity-age-education-and-religion/.

CHAPTER 1: Climate Change: Sneaking Past the Watchful Dragons

1. World Bank Data Team, "New Country Classifications by Income Level: 2019–2020," World Bank Blogs, July 1, 2019, https://blogs.worldbank.org/opendata/new-country -classifications-income-level-2019-2020#:~:text=The%20World%20Bank%20classifies %20the,calculated%20using%20the%20Atlas%20method.

2. Archana Shukla, "Sri Lanka's Children Go Hungry as Food Prices Soar," BBC News, December 7, 2022, https://www.bbc.com/news/business-63868497.

3. Chad de Guzman, "The Crisis in Sri Lanka Rekindles Debate over Organic Farming," *Time*, July 13, 2022, https://time.com/6196570/sri-lanka-crisis-organic-farming/.

4. Patrick Smith, "How Dutch Farmers Became the Center of a Global Right-Wing Cul- ture War," NBC News, December 12, 2022, https://www.nbcnews.com/news/world /dutch-farmers-emissions-global-right-wing-culture-war-rcna60269.

5. Hugo Struna, "French Farmers' Union Backs Country-Wide Protests in Germany," Euractiv, January 11, 2024, https://www.euractiv.com/section/agriculture-food/news /french-farmers-union-backs-country-wide-protests-in-germany/.

6. Tim McDonnell, "What's the World's Fastest-Growing Economy? Ghana Contends for the Crown," *New York Times*, March 10, 2018, https://www.nytimes.com/2018/03/10 /world/africa/ghana-worlds-fastest-growing-economy.html.

7. The World Bank, "World Bank Approves Largest Ever Guarantees for Ghana's Energy Transformation," The World Bank, July 30, 2015, https://www.worldbank.org/en /news/press-release/2015/07/30/world-bank-approves-largest-ever-guarantees-for -ghanas-energy-transformation.

8. Francesco Guarascio, "EU Split over Fertiliser Plants in Poorer Nations as Food Crisis Bites," Reuters, June 20, 2022, https://www.reuters.com/world/europe/eu-split-over -fertiliser-plants-poorer-nations-food-crisis-bites-2022-06-20/.

9. "Police Disperse Protest over Economic Hardship in Ghana," Reuters, June 29, 2022, https://www.reuters.com/world/europe/police-disperse-protest-over-economic -hardship-ghana-2022-06-28/.

10. Thomas Naadi, "Ghana IMF Loan: Will $3bn Solve the Economic Crisis?," BBC News, May 18, 2023, https://www.bbc.com/news/world-africa-65622715.

11. Dorothy Boorse, "Loving the Least of These: Addressing a Changing Environment," National Association of Evangelicals, 2022, https://www.nae.org/loving-the-least-of -these.

12. C.S. Lewis, "Sometimes Fairy Stories May Say Best What's to be Said," *New York Times*, November 18, 1956, https://www.nytimes.com/1956/11/18/archives/sometimes -fairy-stories-may-say-best-whats-to-be-said.html.

13. Alper, "How Religion Intersects with Americans' Views on the Environment."

14. Influence Watch, "National Religious Partnership for the Environment (NRPE)," Influ- ence Watch, n.d., https://www.influencewatch.org/non-profit/national-religious -partnersip-for-the-environment/#donors-to-nrpe.

15. Gallup, "Religion."

16. Lydia Bean and Steve Teles, "Spreading the Gospel of Climate Change: An Evangeli-

cal Battleground," New America, November 2015, p. 4, https://static.newamerica
.org/attachments/11649-spreading-the-gospel-of-climate-change/climate_care11.9
.4f0142a50aa24a2ba65020f7929f6fd7.pdf.

17. Laurie Goodstein, "Evangelical Leaders Join Global Warming Initiative," *New York Times*, February 8, 2006, https://www.nytimes.com/2006/02/08/us/evangelical
-leaders-joinglobal-warming-initiative.html.

18. Kelsey Kramer McGinnis, "What We Sing as Creation Cries Out," *Christianity Today*, September 6, 2022, https://www.christianitytoday.com/ct/2022/september-web
-only/environment-worship-climate-vigil-songs-portersgate.html.

19. Influence Watch, "New America (New America Foundation)," Influence Watch, n.d., https://www.influencewatch.org/non-profit/new-america-foundation/.

20. Bean and Teles, "Spreading the Gospel of Climate Change."

21. Bean and Teles, "Spreading the Gospel of Climate Change," p. 5.

22. New America, "Global Cooling?," YouTube video, November 24, 2015, https://www
.youtube.com/watch?v=iNTSOGM5rCY.

23. Christine McCarthy McMorris, "What Would Jesus Drive?," *Religion in the News* 6, no. 1 (Spring 2003), https://www3.trincoll.edu/csrpl/RINVol6No1/What%20Would
%20Jesus.htm.

24. Influence Watch, "Fenton Communications," Influence Watch, n.d., https://www
.influencewatch.org/for-profit/fenton-communications/.

25. Laurie Goodstein, "Evangelical Leaders Swing Influence Behind Effort to Combat Global Warming," *New York Times*, March 10, 2005, https://www.nytimes
.com/2005/03/10/us/evangelical-leaders-swing-influence-behind-effort-to-combat
-global.html.

26. Fast Company Staff, "Moving Heaven and Earth: When It Comes to Global Warm-ing, Richard Cizik and Jim Ball Are Hell-Bent on Making Fellow Evangelicals See the Light," *Fast Company*, June 1, 2006, https://www.fastcompany.com/56858/moving
-heaven-and-earth.

27. Clinton Foundation, "Evangelical Climate Initiative (ECI)," Clinton Foundation, n.d., https://www.influencewatch.org/app/uploads/2020/08/Clinton-Global-Initiative
-Grant-to-Evangelical-Climate-Initiative-2006.-08.20.pdf.

28. Acton Institute, "Evangelical Leaders Exploited by Global Warming—Population Con-trol Lobby," Acton Institute, September 29, 2006, https://www.acton.org/press
/release/2006/evangelical-leaders-exploited-global-warming-popul.

29. Vanity Fair, "The Future Is Green," *Vanity Fair*, May 2006, https://www.vanityfair
.com/news/photos/2006/05/green_portfolio200605.

30. Mark Seliger, "The Good Reverend: The Reverend Richard Cizik," *Vanity Fair*, Febru-ary 15, 2006, https://media.vanityfair.com/photos/545e2c4e4d676ce013d68271
/master/w_2580%2Cc_limit/image.jpg.

31. Leith Anderson et al., "Climate Change: An Evangelical Call to Action," The Evangelical Climate Initiative, February 2006, https://www.influencewatch.org/app/uploads
/2020/08/climate-change-an-evangelical-call-to-action.-08.20.pdf.

32. Sheryl Henderson Blunt, "The New Climate Coalition," *Christianity Today*, February

8, 2006, https://www.christianitytoday.com/ct/2006/februaryweb-only/106 -34.0.html.

33. Hayden Ludwig, "'Creation Care,'" Part 3: "The First Crusade," Capital Research Center, December 7, 2020, https://capitalresearch.org/article/creation-care-part-3/.

34. Brian D. McLaren, *A New Kind of Christianity: Ten Questions that Are Transforming the Faith* (New York: HarperOne, 2011).

35. Carol Kuruvilla, "Meet the Evangelicals Who Cheered the SCOTUS Gay Marriage Ruling," *HuffPost*, June 29, 2015, https://www.huffpost.com/entry/evangelical -christians-support-marriage-equality_n_7690408.

36. For more, see E. Calvin Beisner and David R. Legates, eds., *Climate and Energy: The Case for Realism* (Washington, DC: Regnery Publishing, 2024).

37. E. Calvin Beisner et al., "A Call to Truth, Prudence, and Protection of the Poor: An Evangelical Response to Global Warming," Cornwall Alliance, 2006, https://www .cornwallalliance.org/docs/a-call-to-truth-prudence-and-protection-of-the-poor.pdf.

38. Katharine K. Wilkinson, *Between God and Green: How Evangelicals Are Cultivating a Middle Ground on Climate Change* (Oxford, UK: Oxford University Press, 2012), p. 116, https://books.google.com/books?id=DvloAgAAQBAJ&pg=PA116&lpg=PA116 &dq=sbeci+%22national+press+club%22&source=bl&ots=cQu_VGDUJP&sig =ACfU3U2RSt2VogGmX8Y7U1fyQYVPuts-CQ&hl=en&sa=X&ved =2ahUKEwib4vbsh-r_AhXZmmoFHWnmAscQ6AF6BAgXEAM#v=onepage&q =sbeci%20%22national%20press%20club%22&f=false.

39. Associated Press, "Southern Baptist Leaders Sign Environment Vow," NBC News, March 10, 2008, https://www.nbcnews.com/id/wbna23549773.

40. Katharine Hayhoe, "Katharine Hayhoe: Climate Change—Facts, Fictions, and Our Faith," Center for Faith and Culture, April 5, 2021, https://cfc.sebts.edu/faith-and -science/katharine-hayhoe-climate-change-facts-fictions-faith/.

41. Ken Keathley, *Christ and Culture*—"Katherine Hayhoe: the Faith of a Climate Scientist," Center for Faith and Culture, April 16, 2021, https://cfc.sebts.edu/faith-and -science/katharine-hayhoe-the-faith-of-a-climate-scientist/.

42. Lora Kolodny, "Obama, Leonardo DiCaprio, and Scientist Katharine Hayhoe Talk Climate Change at SXSL," TechCrunch, October 3, 2016, https://techcrunch .com/2016/10/03/obama-leonardo-dicaprio-and-scientist-katharine-hayhoe-talk -climate-change-at-sxsl/.

43. Sean O'Grady, "Climate Warrior Leonardo DiCaprio Risks Accusations of Eco-hypocrisy as He Leaves Sardinia from Private Airport," *Daily Mail*, May 30, 2023, https://www.dailymail.co.uk/tvshowbiz/article-12139585/Leonardo-DiCaprio-risks -accusations-eco-hypocrisy-leaves-Sardinia-private-airport.html.

44. LifeSiteNews, "Shaman Performs Pagan Ritual over World Economic Forum Leaders at Davos Summit," LifeSiteNews, January 17, 2024, https://www.lifesitenews.com /news/shaman-performs-pagan-ritual-over-world-economic-forum-leaders-at-davos -summit/?utm_source=most_recent&utm_campaign=canada.

45. Jonathan Moo, "Loving God and Neighbor in an Age of Climate Crisis," L. Russ Bush Center for Faith and Culture, February 13, 2023, https://cfc.sebts.edu/faith-and -science/jonathan-moo-loving-god-and-neighbor-in-an-age-of-climate-crisis/.

46. Adam Groza, "The Kingdom Impact of Seminary Education," California Southern Baptist Convention, May 10, 2022, https://csbc.com/news/the-kingdom-impact-of-seminary-education/#:~:text=Southern%20Baptist%20Seminaries%20educate%20at,ministry%20in%20the%20United%20States.

47. A Rocha USA, "Who We Are," arocha.us, https://arocha.us/whoweare.

48. ProPublica, "The Annenberg Foundation—Nonprofit Explorer," ProPublica, n.d., https://projects.propublica.org/nonprofits/organizations/236257083.

49. Influence Watch, "Annenberg Foundation," Influence Watch, n.d., https://www.influencewatch.org/non-profit/annenberg-foundation/.

50. Ben Lowe, "Why This Election Isn't Just About Abortion," *Ben Lowe* (blog), October 31, 2012, https://www.benlowe.net/updates/2015/1/12/why-this-election-isnt-just-about-abortion.

51. A Rocha International, "Through the Wind and Waves: A Hymn for Climate Change," A Rocha International, August 13, 2021, https://atyourservice.arocha.org/en/through-the-wind-and-waves-a-hymn-for-climate-change/.

52. A Rocha International, "26 Prayers for the Climate and Ecological Emergency," A Rocha International, May 10, 2021, https://atyourservice.arocha.org/en/category/prayers/.

53. Rev'd Jon Swales, "Prayers for the Climate and Ecological Emergency," A Rocha International, April, 2021, https://atyourservice.arocha.org/wp-content/uploads/2021/05/26-Prayers-for-the-Climate-and-Ecological-Emergency-Jon-Swales.pdf

54. Benjamin Lowe et al., "The Generational Divide over Climate Change Among American Evangelicals," Environmental Research Letters—IOP Publishing, October 2022, https://www.researchgate.net/publication/364355784_The_generational_divide_over_climate_change_among_American_evangelicals.

55. *The Gospel Coalition*, "The Keller Center for Cultural Apologetics," *The Gospel Coalition*, n.d., https://www.thegospelcoalition.org/thekellercenter/about/.

56. Truth Unites, " Climate Change: Why Christians Should Engage," YouTube video, March 2, 2022, https://www.youtube.com/watch?v=XRDkBHUXNd0.

57. Colorado State University, "Global Historical Tropical Cyclone Statistics," Colorado State University, n.d., https://tropical.atmos.colostate.edu/Realtime/index.php?arch&loc=global.

58. Geophysical Fluid Dynamics Laboratory, "Global Warming and Hurricanes: An Overview of Current Research Results," National Oceanic and Atmospheric Administration, n.d., https://www.gfdl.noaa.gov/global-warming-and-hurricanes/.

59. E. Calvin Beisner, "Are This Summer's Heat Waves Extraordinary?," Cornwall Alliance, July 29, 2022, https://cornwallalliance.org/2022/07/are-this-summers-heat-waves-extraordinary/.

60. Roger Harrabin, "Climate Change: Young People Very Worried—Survey," BBC News, September 14, 2021, https://www.bbc.com/news/world-58549373.

61. Joseph Bast and Roy Spencer, "The Myth of the Climate Change '97%,'" *Wall Street Journal*, May 26, 2014, https://www.wsj.com/articles/joseph-bast-and-roy-spencer-the-myth-of-the-climate-change-97-1401145980.

62. Patrick T. Brown, "I Left Out the Full Truth to Get My Climate Change Paper Published,"

The Free Press, September 5, 2023, https://www.thefp.com/p/i-overhyped-climate
-change-to-get-published.

63. Anthony J. Sadar, "The Dangers of Challenging the Climate Change Consensus," *American Thinker*, February 2, 2022, https://www.americanthinker.com/blog/2022/02
/the_dangers_of_challenging_the_climate_change_consensus_.html.

64. Ross Clark, "'Climategate' Still Matters—But Not How the BBC Thinks It Does," *The Spectator*, November 6, 2021, https://www.spectator.co.uk/article/climategate-still
-matters-but-not-how-the-bbc-thinks-it-does/.

65. U.S. House of Representatives Committee on Science, Space, and Technology, "Former NOAA Scientist Confirms Colleagues Manipulated Climate Records," U.S. House of Representatives Committee on Science, Space, and Technology, February 5, 2017, https://science.house.gov/press-releases?ID=5A33C440-59E4-4961-8143
-EBF01B0C4EF7.

66. Influence Watch, "Family Planning 2020," Influence Watch, n.d., https://www
.influencewatch.org/non-profit/family-planning-2020/.

67. *The Gospel Coalition*, "Christians and Creation Care—Good Faith Debates," YouTube video, March 5, 2023, https://www.youtube.com/watch?v=vE6ul7qEsbk.

68. Charles W. Colson et al., "A Letter to the National Association of Evangelicals on the Issue of Global Warming," Interfaith Stewardship Alliance, January 31, 2006, https://
www.cornwallalliance.org/docs/appeal-letter-to-the-national-association-of
-evangelicals-on-the-issue-of-global-warming.pdf.

69. Bjorn Lomborg, "Welfare in the 21st Century: Increasing Development, Reducing Inequality, the Impact of Climate Change, and the Cost of Climate Policies," *Technological Forecasting and Social Change* 156 (July 2020), https://www.sciencedirect
.com/science/article/pii/S0040162520304157. See also Indur M. Goklany, "Wealth and Safety: The Amazing Decline in Deaths from Extreme Weather in an Era of Global Warming, 1900–2010," *Reason*, September 2011, https://reason.org/wp-content
/uploads/2011/09/deaths_from_extreme_weather_1900_2010.pdf.

70. Terry Gross, "How 'Modern-Day Slavery' in the Congo Powers the Rechargeable Battery Economy," *Fresh Air*, NPR, February 1, 2023, https://www.npr.org/sections
/goatsandsoda/2023/02/01/1152893248/red-cobalt-congo-drc-mining-siddharth
-kara.

CHAPTER 2: Illegal Immigration: Strangers, Neighbors, and Aliens

1. Samuel Smith, "100 Evangelical Leaders Slam Trump's Refugee Ban in Washington Post Ad," *Christian Post*, February 8, 2017, https://www.christianpost.com/news
/evangelical-leaders-slam-trump-refugee-ban-washington-post-174530/. *See also* Nayla Rush, "Low Refugee Admissions So Far in FY 2022: The Biden Administration Is Prioritizing Those Fleeing Poverty, Not War," Center for Immigration Studies, n.d., https://cis.org/Rush/Low-Refugee-Admissions-So-Far-FY-2022.

2. Julia Ainsley, "Migrant Border Crossings in Fiscal Year 2022 Topped 2.76 Million, Breaking Previous Record," NBC News, October 22, 2022, https://www.nbcnews
.com/politics/immigration/migrant-border-crossings-fiscal-year-2022-topped-276
-million-breaking-rcna53517.

3. Mohammad M. Fazel-Zarandi, Jonathan S. Feinstein, and Edward H. Kaplan, "The Number of Undocumented Immigrants in the United States: Estimates Based on Demographic Modeling with Data from 1990 to 2016," *PLOS ONE* 13, no. 9 (September 21, 2018): e0201193, https://doi.org/10.1371/journal.pone.0201193.

4. U.S. Government Accountability Office, "Criminal Alien Statistics: Information on Incarcerations, Arrests, Convictions, Costs, and Removals," U.S. Government Accountability Office, July 17, 2018, https://www.gao.gov/products/gao-18-433.

5. Baptist Press, "Explainer: ERLC, George Soros and Evangelical Immigration Table," *Baptist Press*, January 9, 2020, https://www.baptistpress.com/resource-library/news/explainer-erlc-george-soros-and-evangelical-immigration-table/.

6. Evangelical Immigration Table, "Evangelical Immigration Table Celebrates Three-Year Anniversary," Evangelical Immigration Table, June 12, 2015, https://evangelicalimmigrationtable.com/evangelical-immigration-table-celebrates-three-year-anniversary/.

7. Victoria Carty, Tekle M. Woldemikael, and Rafael Luévano, eds., *Scholars and Southern Californian Immigrants in Dialogue: New Conversations in Public Sociology* (Lanham, MD: Lexington Books, 2014), 140, https://books.google.com/books?id=8RevAwAAQBAJ&ppis=_e&lpg=PA140&ots=mpaWhED2FZ&dq=Evangelical%20immigration%20table%20National%20Immigration%20forum&pg=PA140#v=onepage&q=Evangelical%20immigration%20table%20National%20Immigration%20forum&f=false. *See also* Influence Watch, "National Immigration Forum (NIF)," Influence Watch, n.d., https://www.influencewatch.org/non-profit/national-immigration-forum/.

8. Dan Merica, "Evangelical Christians Prepare for 'Largest Ever Grassroots Push on Immigration,'" CNN, January 12, 2013, https://web.archive.org/web/20130115030035/http:/religion.blogs.cnn.com/2013/01/12/evangelical-christians-prepare-for-largest-ever-grassroots-push-on-immigration/.

9. Christian Churches Together, "Evangelical Immigration Table Request for Proposals," Christian Churches Together, n.d., https://web.archive.org/web/20140925175355/https:/www.christianchurchestogether.org/evangelical-immigration-table-hiring-part-time-staff/.

10. Trip Gabriel, "Evangelical Groups Call for New Stance on Illegal Immigration," *New York Times*, June 12, 2012, https://www.nytimes.com/2012/06/13/us/politics/evangelical-groups-call-for-new-stance-on-illegal-immigration.html. *See also* Carty, Woldemikael, and Luévano, eds., *Scholars and Southern Californian Immigrants in Dialogue*.

11. Dean DeChiaro and Bridget Bowman, "'Gang of Eight' Revival Unlikely on Immigration Overhaul," *Roll Call*, February 13, 2017, https://rollcall.com/2017/02/13/gang-of-eight-revival-unlikely-on-immigration-overhaul/.

12. NRO Staff, "Sessions: CIS Study Confirms Gang of Eight Bill Would've Caused 'Economic Catastrophe,'" *National Review*, June 27, 2014, https://www.nationalreview.com/corner/sessions-cis-study-confirms-gang-eight-bill-wouldve-caused-economic-catastrophe-nro/.

13. Evangelical Immigration Table, *I Was a Stranger: 40 Days of Scripture and Prayer*, Evangelical Immigration Table, 2013, https://web.archive.org/web/20130825161706

/https:/evangelicalimmigrationtable.com/wp-content/uploads/2013/01/I-Was-a
-Stranger-Bookmark-Text-Message.pdf.

14. James R. Edwards Jr., "False Prophets of Open Borders," Center for Immigration Studies, July 9, 2012, https://cis.org/Edwards/False-Prophets-Open-Borders.

15. ABC News, "Faith Leaders to Obama: 'Time Is Now' for Immigration Reform," ABC
News, March 8, 2013, https://abcnews.go.com/ABC_Univision/Politics/obama-talks
-immigration-faith-leaders/story?id=18684791.

16. The Maddow Blog and Steve Benen, "'Gang of Eight' Unveils Bipartisan Immigration
Plan," NBC News, April 16, 2013, https://www.nbcnews.com/news/world/gang-eight
-unveils-bipartisan-immigration-plan-flna1c9366676.

17. Boundless, "Green Card Processing Times," Boundless Immigration Inc., n.d., https://
www.boundless.com/immigration-resources/average-green-card-wait-times
/#:~:text=In%20most%20cases%2C%20it%20takes,process%20takes%20around
%20three%20years.

18. ABC News, "Faith Leaders to Obama: 'Time Is Now for Immigration Reform',," ABC
News, March 8, 2013, https://abcnews.go.com/ABC_Univision/Politics/obama-talks
-immigration-faith-leaders/story?id=18684791

19. David Ward, "Not So Fast: Evangelicals Differ with Their Leaders on Immigration
Reform," Deseret News, February 22, 2013, https://www.deseret.com/2013/2/22
/20448635/not-so-fast-evangelicals-differ-with-their-leaders-on-immigration-reform.

20. Steven A. Camarota, "Legalization vs. Enforcement: What the American People Think
on Immigration," Center for Immigration Studies, April 2013, https://cis.org/sites
/default/files/poll-legalization-vs-enforcement.pdf.

21. Jeff Coen, "Claims Against Willow Creek's Bill Hybels of 'Sexually Inappropriate' Conduct Are Credible, New Report Says," Chicago Tribune, February 28, 2019, https://
www.chicagotribune.com/2019/02/28/claims-against-willow-creeks-bill-hybels
-of-sexually-inappropriate-conduct-are-credible-new-report-says/. See also Ashley May,
"Willow Creek Church Pastor, Board Resign amid Sexual Misconduct Investigation of
Founder," USA Today, August 9, 2018, https://www.usatoday.com/story
/news/nation-now/2018/08/09/willow-creek-pastor-board-resign-bill-hybels-sex
-scandal/944310002/.

22. For example, here: Evangelical Immigration Table, "300-Plus Pastors, Evangelical
Leaders Urge Protection of DACA Recipients," Evangelical Immigration Table, September 3, 2017, https://evangelicalimmigrationtable.com/300-plus-pastors
-evangelical-leaders-urge-protection-of-daca-recipients/. See also Leonardo Blair, "Willow Creek Church's Lynne Hybels Says Immigration Reform Is Personal," Christian
Post, May 31, 2013, https://www.christianpost.com/news/willow-creek-churchs
-lynne-hybels-says-immigration-reform-is-personal.html.

23. Jonathan Merritt, "Why Evangelicals' Push for Immigration Reform Isn't Working,"
Religion News Service, July 23, 2013, https://religionnews.com/2013/07/23/why
-evangelicals-push-for-immigration-reform-isnt-working/.

24. Edwards, "False Prophets of Open Borders."

25. Griselda Nevarez, "Evangelicals Doing More than Just Praying for Immigration Reform," HuffPost, June 1, 2013, https://web.archive.org/web/20130619163307/http:
/www.huffingtonpost.com/2013/06/01/evangelicals-immigration_n_3371854.html.

See also Erin Kelly, "Evangelical Group to Back Immigration Bill," *USA Today*, August 21, 2013, https://www.usatoday.com/story/news/politics/2013/08/21/evangelicals-immigration-support/2681041/.

26. Betsy Woodruff, "Evangelicals and Immigration," *National Review*, October 24, 2013, https://www.nationalreview.com/2013/10/evangelicals-and-immigration-betsy-woodruff/. *See also* Edwards, "False Prophets of Open Borders."

27. William Hawkins, quoted in Discover the Networks, "National Immigration Forum (NIF)," Discover the Networks, n.d., https://www.discoverthenetworks.org/organizations/national-immigration-forum-nif/.

28. George Soros, "The People's Sovereignty," *Foreign Policy*, October 28, 2009, https://foreignpolicy.com/2009/10/28/the-peoples-sovereignty/.

29. George Soros, "Why I'm Investing $500 Million in Migrants," *Wall Street Journal*, September 20, 2016, https://www.wsj.com/articles/why-im-investing-500-million-in-migrants-1474344001. *See also* Eric Schmitt, "Philanthropist Pledges Help to Immigrants," *New York Times*, October 1, 1996, https://www.nytimes.com/1996/10/01/us/philanthropist-pledges-help-to-immigrants.html.

30. Christian Datoc, "George Soros' 'Open Society Foundations' Named 2016's Least Transparent Think Tank," *Daily Caller*, July 6, 2016, https://dailycaller.com/2016/07/06/george-soros-open-society-foundations-named-2016s-least-transparent-think-tank/.

31. Marjorie Jeffrey, "The Evangelical Immigration Table Exposed as Another Soros Front," Institute for Religion and Democracy, June 5, 2013, https://juicyecumenism.com/2013/06/05/the-evangelical-immigration-table-exposed-as-another-soros-front/. *See also* Julie Roys, "Is Evangelical Immigration Table a Front Group for George Soros?," *Julie Roys* (blog), June 10, 2013, https://web.archive.org/web/20190731193830/https://julieroys.com/is-evangelical-immigration-table-a-front-group-for-george-soros/.

32. Mike Flynn, "Evangelical Group Pushing Immigration Reform Doesn't Legally Exist," Breitbart, June 2, 2013, https://www.breitbart.com/politics/2013/06/02/evangelical-group-pushing-immigration-doesnt-legally-exist/.

33. Matthew Boyle, "National Immigration Forum Funded by Soros and the Left," Breitbart, June 2, 2013, https://www.breitbart.com/politics/2013/06/02/national-immigration-forum-lead-evangelical-jim-wallis-funded-by-george-soros-other-bastions-of-institutional-left/.

34. Tyler O'Neil, "Interview: Eric Metaxas on Biblical Manhood, Christianity in New York City, and Gay Marriage," *Christian Post*, July 11, 2013, https://www.christianpost.com/news/interview-eric-metaxas-on-biblical-manhood-christianity-in-new-york-city-and-gay-marriage-99721/.

35. Ali Noorani, "The Moral Clarity of Resettling Refugees," Bulwark, March 11, 2022, https://www.thebulwark.com/the-moral-clarity-of-resettling-refugees/.

36. Napp Nazworth, "National Immigration Forum Answers Questions About Soros, Chamber of Commerce Funding for Evangelical Immigration Table," *Christian Post*, June 25, 2013, https://www.christianpost.com/news/national-immigration-forum-answers-questions-about-soros-chamber-of-commerce-funding-for-evangelical-immigration-table.html.

37. 2013: Tom Strode, "Moore Prays for Obama, Urges Immigration Steps During White House Session," *Baptist Press*, November 14, 2013, https://www.baptistpress.com /resource-library/news/moore-prays-for-obama-urges-immigration-steps-during -white-house-session/; 2014: Jared A. Favole, "Obama, Evangelical Leaders Discuss Immigration Overhaul," *Wall Street Journal*, April 15, 2014, https://www.wsj.com /articles/BL-WB-44763.

38. Kelly Monroe Kullberg et al., "An Open Letter to the Congress of the United States of America," Evangelicals for Biblical Immigration, June 2013, https://web.archive.org /web/20161023220919/http:/evangelicalsforbiblicalimmigration.com/uncategorized /june-original-open-letter-to-the-congress-of-the-united-states-of-america/.

39. Tim Keller et al., "Top Evangelical Leaders from All 50 States Call on President Trump and Vice President Pence to Support Refugees," *Washington Post*, 2017, https://web .archive.org/web/20170328062753/https:/d3n8a8pro7vhmx.cloudfront.net/worldrlief /pages/18/attachments/original/1486673271/Washington_Post_Evangelical _Leader_Ad_Page_A18_02_08_2017.jpg?1486673271.

40. Nayla Rush, "Low Refugee Admissions So Far in FY 2022: The Biden Administration Is Prioritizing Those Fleeing Poverty, Not War," Center for Immigration Studies, https:// cis.org/Rush/Low-Refugee-Admissions-So-Far-FY-2022.

41. Camila Domonoske, "U.S. Refugee Admissions Pass Trump Administration Cap of 50,000," NPR, July 12, 2017, https://www.npr.org/sections/thetwo -way/2017/07/12/536899605/u-s-refugee-admissions-pass-trump-administration -cap-of-50-000.

42. Suzanne See, "Ways to Welcome the Refugee," *The Gospel Coalition*, Sept. 19, 2015, https://www.thegospelcoalition.org/article/ways-to-welcome-the-refugee/

43. James Simpson, "Is The U.S. Refugee Resettlement System Broken?," *Capital Research*, Issue 8, 2018, https://capitalresearch.org/app/uploads/223145_CRC_Issue8_web.pdf.

44. Evangelical Immigration Table, "About Evangelical Immigration Table," Evangelical Immigration Table, n.d., https://evangelicalimmigrationtable.com/about /#NATIONAL.

45. Baptist Press, "Explainer: ERLC, George Soros and Evangelical Immigration Table," *Baptist Press*, January 9, 2020, https://www.baptistpress.com/resource-library/news /explainer-erlc-george-soros-and-evangelical-immigration-table/.

46. Petaluma Valley Baptist Church, "Our Pastoral Staff," Petaluma Valley Baptist Church, n.d., http://www.petalumabaptist.org/staff.

47. Alan L. Cross, "Evangelical Immigration Table Booth at the SBC, St. Louis, June 13–15," Alan L. Cross, June 10, 2016, https://alancrosswrites.com/evangelical -immigration-table-booth-at-the-sbc-st-louis-june-13-15/.

48. Alan Cross, "Why Pastors Should Lead Their Churches in Disaster Relief," Lifeway Research, August 30, 2016, https://research.lifeway.com/2016/08/30/why -pastors-should-lead-their-churches-in-disaster-relief/. *See also* "Alan Cross" on the ChurchLeaders website, https://churchleaders.com/author/alancross.

49. National Immigration Forum, "Southeast Leaders Urge Legislation for Dreamers," National Immigration Forum, December 14, 2017, https://immigrationforum.org/article /southeast-leaders-urge-legislation-dreamers/.

50. National Immigration Forum, "Consultant: Southeast Regional Mobilizer, Bibles,

Badges and Business," National Immigration Forum, 2014, https://immigrationforum
.org/wp-content/uploads/2014/10/NIF_BBB-Southeast-Regional-Organizer
_11-30-16_FINAL.pdf.

51. DCLeaks, https://web.archive.org/web/20170218135927/http:/soros.dcleaks.com
/view?div=us.

52. Open Society Foundations, "Open Society U.S. Programs Board Meeting," Open Society Foundations, September 3–4, 2013, https://capitalresearch.org/app/uploads
/Open-Society-U.S.-Programs-Board-Meeting-September-3-4-2013.pdf.

53. Open Society Foundations, "Open Society U.S. Programs Board Meeting," Open Society
Foundations, October 1–2, 2015, https://web.archive.org/web/20170219114817/http:
/soros.dcleaks.com/download/?f=/oct%202015%20usp%20board%20book.pdf&t=us.

54. Open Society Foundations, "Open Society U.S. Programs Board Meeting," Open Society Foundations, May 4–6, 2016, https://freebeacon.com/wp-content/uploads/2016
/08/soros-board-book-2016.pdf.

55. Foundation to Promote Open Society, Form 990PF for Fiscal Year Ending December
2020, ProPublica, 2020, https://projects.propublica.org/nonprofits/organizations
/263753801/202113519349100511/full; Foundation to Promote Open Society, Form
990PF for Fiscal Year Ending December 2021, ProPublica, 2021, https://projects
.propublica.org/nonprofits/organizations/263753801/202213209349101601/full.

56. Scott Barkley, "Immigration a Subject Requiring Diligence, Accountability, Say Resolution Authors," *Baptist Press*, August 10, 2023, https://www.baptistpress.com
/resource-library/news/immigration-a-subject-requiring-diligence-accountability-say
-resolution-authors/.

57. Claudia Aoraha, "Staggering Figures Reveal 1.2 Million US-Born Workers Lost Their
Jobs Last Month—Replaced by 688,000 Foreign-Born Staff—as Joe Biden Allows
Migrants to Flood Across the Border," *Daily Mail*, September 4, 2023, https://www
.dailymail.co.uk/news/article-12478977/Staggering-figures-workers-lost-jobs.html.

58. Quinn Owen, Mireya Villarreal, and James Scholz, "'It's Very Challenging': Inside the
Fentanyl Fight at the Border," ABC News, November 7, 2023, https://abcnews.go.com
/Politics/fighting-fentanyl-border-agents-working-thwart-narcotics-smuggling
/stry?id=104689211.

59. Congressional Research Service, "Unaccompanied Alien Children: An Overview,"
Congressional Research Service, September 1, 2021, https://crsreports.congress.gov
/product/pdf/R/R43599.

60. Janna Ataiants et al., "Unaccompanied Children at the United States Border, a Human
Rights Crisis that Can Be Addressed with Policy Change," *Journal of Immigrant and
Minority Health* 20, no. 4 (August 2018): 1000–10, doi: 10.1007/s10903-017-0577-5,
PMID: 28391501, PMCID: PMC5805654.

61. Samuel Smith, "100 Evangelical Leaders Slam Trump's Refugee Ban in Washington
Post Ad," *Christian Post*, February 8, 2017, https://www.christianpost.com/news
/evangelical-leaders-slam-trump-refugee-ban-washington-post-174530/.

62. Ben Zeisloft, "'The Cuban People Will Be Free': Congressman Introduces Resolution to
Support Cuban Protests, Only Republicans Sign On," *Daily Wire*, July 13, 2021, https://
www.dailywire.com/news/the-cuban-people-will-be-free-congressman
-introduces-resolution-to-support-cuban-protests-only-republicans-sign-on.

63. "Beth Moore: God Takes Every Wrong Performed Against Children Personally," *Relevant*, June 18, 2018, https://relevantmagazine.com/current/beth-moore-god-takes -every-wrong-performed-against-children-personally/.

64. Rebecca Paveley, "Clergy in Cuba Are Arrested After Anti-Government Protests," *Church Times*, July 16, 2021, https://www.churchtimes.co.uk/articles/2021/16-july /news/world/clergy-in-cuba-are-arrested-after-anti-government-protests.

65. Belinda Luscombe, "Theologian Russell Moore Has a Message for Christians Who Still Worship Donald Trump," *Time*, January 21, 2021, https://time.com/5932014/donald -trump-christian-supporters/.

66. Russell Moore, "Exclusive: The Letter Russell Moore Will Send Trump About the Refugee Order," *Washington Post*, January 30, 2017, https://www.washingtonpost .com/news/acts-of-faith/wp/2017/01/30/exclusive-the-letter-russell-moore-will-send -trump-about-the-refugee-order/. *See also* Jessica Taylor, "Citing Religious Liberty, Evangelical Leaders Blast Trump's Muslim Ban," NPR, December 9, 2017, https:// www.npr.org/2015/12/09/459086641/citing-religious-liberty-evangelical-leaders -blast-trumps-muslim-ban.

67. Russell Moore (drmoore), "Immigrants, & those fleeing from persecution, are not political ideas," Twitter, October 30, 2018, 11:28 AM, https://twitter.com/drmoore/status /1057293175885365248?s=20.

68. Chiara Fiorillo, "What Is Happening in Cuba? Protests and Unrest Explained," *Newsweek*, July 12, 2021, https://www.newsweek.com/cuba-unrest-protests-havana-covid -food-hunger-poverty-communism-dictatorship-freedoms-tourism-1608679. *See also* *Daily Wire* News, "Critics Blast Biden over Crisis in Cuba: 'They'll Only Allow in People Who Won't Vote Republican,'" *Daily Wire*, July 15, 2021, https://www.dailywire.com /news/critics-blast-biden-over-crisis-in-cuba-theyll-only-allow-in-people-who-wont -vote-republican.

69. Sarah Rumpf-Whitten, "Pro-Palestinian Protests Turn Violent Across Europe," Fox News, November 4, 2023, https://www.foxnews.com/world/pro-palestinian-protests violent-across-europe. *See also* Fox 5 DC Digital Team, "Police Arrest 60 Pro-Palestine Demonstrators After Calls for Ceasefire Erupt in Capitol Rotunda," Fox 5 News, December 19, 2023, https://www.fox5dc.com/news/police-arrest-60-pro -palestine-demonstrators-after-calls-for-ceasefire-erupt-in-capitol-rotunda.

70. J. D. Greear (@jdgreear), quoting Ben Sasse (@BenSasse), "'Family separation is wicked. It is harmful to kids and absolutely should NOT be the default U.S. policy," Twitter, June 18, 2018, 10:00 PM, https://twitter.com/jdgreear/status /1008892254218571778?s=20.

71. "J. D. Greear," *Firing Line with Margaret Hoover*, PBS, aired September 7, 2018, https:// www.pbs.org/wnet/firing-line/video/jd-greear-v5dt98/.

72. Priscilla Alvarez, "Biden Falsely Claims the Obama Administration Didn't Separate Families," CNN, September 12, 2019, https://www.cnn.com/politics/live-news /democratic-debate-september-2019/h_ca819e341152d783479eb2dc6240c08c.

73. J. D. Greear (@jdgreear), "Immigrants known as #Dreamers often have no home other than the US," Twitter, October 11, 2017, 6:00 PM, https://twitter.com/jdgreear/status /918234932450906113?s=20.

74. Committee on Oversight and Accountability, "Border Patrol Chiefs: Biden's Border

Crisis Is 'Overwhelming,'" Committee on Oversight and Accountability, February 7, 2023, https://oversight.house.gov/release/border-patrol-chiefs-bidens-border-crisis-is -overwhelming/.

75. Zeisloft, "'The Cuban People Will Be Free.'"

CHAPTER 3: Hijacking the Pro-life Movement

1. Karen Swallow Prior, "I Prayed and Protested to End Roe. What Comes Next?," *New York Times*, June 24, 2022, https://www.nytimes.com/2022/06/24/opinion/abortion -dobbs-roe-pro-life.html?unlocked_article_code=AAAAAAAAAAAAAAAACEI PuomT1JKd6J17Vw1cRCfTTMQmqxCdw_PIxftm3iWka3DLDmweiOMNAo6B _EGKbKBkfccy2DLeSNhLOqRqXvt_i_dFOAlpSgel5JuYnZBPawMElbWOZEJkl ZTcQeJ_tjbwcmiyLOo4yufk7x_bPGX1DPHehWkmJw9lvZtiJVq1iXYDlaaTFrYk 3oUpzu5hUs4hPUoIZCSJuPnrAx9_KY_GOkmasl9qLrkfDTLDntec6KYCdxFSDD _FRXB_6WU777BMKY9dffa_f1N7Jp2I0fhGAXdoLYypG5Q0W4PS8r1gurXGoh CIo9GkWPYn2uxl9xPEz3UfoQyZ8Q.

2. Karen Swallow Prior (@KSPrior), "Our work now is just starting: we must help and support moms, dads, and babies. Love them all—and in so doing making abortion unimaginable," Twitter, June 24, 2022, 10:30 AM, https://twitter.com/KSPrior/status /1540341632448462848?s=20.

3. Brad Wilcox, *Get Married: Why Americans Must Defy the Elites, Forge Strong Families, and Save Civilization* (New York: Harper Collins, 2024).

4. Adoption Network, "US Adoption Statistics," Adoption Network, n.d., https:// adoptionnetwork.com/adoption-myths-facts/domestic-us-statistics/#:~:text =How%20many%20people%20are%20waiting,one%20and%20two%20million %20couples.

5. Kay S. Hymowitz, "The black Family: 40 Years of Lies," *City Journal*, 2005, https:// www.city-journal.org/article/the-black-family-40-years-of-lies. *See also* Paul E. Pe-terson, "Government Should Subsidize, Not Tax, Marriage," *Education Next* 15, No. 2 (Spring 2015), https://www.educationnext.org/government-subsidize-not-tax -marriage/.

6. Pew Research Center, "The Decline of Marriage and Rise of New Families," Pew Re-search Center, November 18, 2010, https://www.pewresearch.org/social-trends /2010/11/18/ii-overview/#:~:text=Marriage%20rates%20have%20fallen%20among ,share%20had%20dropped%20to%2032%25. See under "Marriage, Family and Race."

7. Richard Fry, "A Record-High Share of 40-Year-Olds in the U.S. Have Never Been Mar-ried," Pew Research Center, June 28, 2023, https://www.pewresearch.org/short -reads/2023/06/28/a-record-high-share-of-40-year-olds-in-the-us-have-never-been -married/.

8. Centers for Disease Control and Prevention, "Births: Final Data for 2018," *National Vital Statistics Reports* 68, no. 13 (November 27, 2019), https://www.cdc.gov/nchs /data/nvsr/nvsr68/nvsr68_13_tables-508.pdf. *See also* Cecilia Lenzen, "Facing Higher Teen Pregnancy and Maternal Mortality Rates, Black Women Will Largely Bear the Brunt of Abortion Limits," *Texas Tribune*, June 30, 2022, https://www.texastribune .org/2022/06/30/texas-abortion-black-women/.

9. Michael D. King, "New Interactive Data Tool Shows Characteristics of Those Who Receive Assistance from Government Programs," United States Census Bureau, May 24, 2022, https://www.census.gov/library/stories/2022/05/who-is-receiving-social-safety-net-benefits.html.

10. Thomas Sowell, "A Painful Anniversary," *The Baltimore Sun*, August 24, 2004, https://www.baltimoresun.com/2004/08/24/a-painful-anniversary-2/.

11. Beth Moore (@BethMooreLPM), "Yes. Step up, church.," Twitter, June 24, 2022, 11:03 AM, https://twitter.com/BethMooreLPM/status/1540349815036547073?s=20.

12. Charlotte Lozier Institute, "Fact Sheet: Pregnancy Help Centers—Serving Women and Saving Lives," Charlotte Lozier Institute, January 18, 2018, https://lozierinstitute.org/fact-sheet-pregnancy-help-centers-serving-women-and-saving-lives/.

13. Charlotte Lozier Institute, "Pro-Life Pregnancy Centers Served 2 Million People with Essential Medical, Education and Support Services in 2019," Charlotte Lozier Institute, October 21, 2020, https://lozierinstitute.org/pro-life-pregnancy-centers-served-2-million-people-with-essential-medical-education-and-support-services-in-2019/.

14. Abigail Abrams and Vera Bergengruen, "Anti-Abortion Pregnancy Centers Are Collecting Troves of Data that Could Be Weaponized Against Women," *Time*, June 22, 2022, https://time.com/6189528/anti-abortion-pregnancy-centers-collect-data-investigation/.

15. Mika Edmondson (@mika_edmondson), "Now that Roe is overturned, I pray that we will provide the access to healthcare, childcare, living wages, education and job opportunities that will support the lives of people in desperate situations," Twitter, June 24, 2022, 10:55 AM, https://twitter.com/mika_edmondson/status/1540347957832286210?s=20.

16. Mika Edmondson (@mika_edmondson), "May the Lord give grace to victims of rape whose pregnancies are daily reminders of the worst violation," Twitter, June 24, 2022, 5:49 PM, https://twitter.com/mika_edmondson/status/1540452109606322176?s=20.

17. Capstone Report, "Reflections on the Revolution in the SBC," Capstone Report, May 25, 2022, https://capstonereport.com/2022/05/25/reflections-on-the-revolution-in-the-sbc/38183/#google_vignette.

18. Russell Moore, "Bonus Episode: A Conversation with Stephen Prothero on Culture Wars Now that 'Roe' Is Gone," *The Russell Moore Show* (podcast), Episode 22, *Christianity Today*, June 24, 2022, https://www.christianitytoday.com/ct/podcasts/russell-moore-show/bonus-episode-stephen-prothero-roe-wade-abortion-culture.html.

19. Russell Moore, "Post-Roe America Needs a Forward-Looking Church," *Christianity Today*, July 14, 2022, https://www.christianitytoday.com/ct/2022/july-web-only/russell-moore-roe-abortion-pro-life-theology-evangelical.html.

20. Russell Moore and Molly Ball, "Evangelicals and America's 'Abortion Wars,'" *Faith Angle* (podcast), July 26, 2022, https://faithangle.podbean.com/e/molly-ball-and-russell-moore-evangelicals-and-america-s-abortion-wars/.

21. Timothy Keller (1950–2023) (@timkellernyc), "THREAD: I recently wrote about how churches should not destroy unity or fellowship over political differences," Twitter, April 29, 2022, https://twitter.com/timkellernyc/status/1520107742110834699?s=20.

22. Steven Begakis, "Tim Keller Is Wrong About Abortion," *Christian Post*, May 11, 2022, https://www.christianpost.com/voices/tim-keller-is-wrong-about-abortion.html.

23. Peter Wehner, "The Moral Universe of Timothy Keller," *The Atlantic*, December 5, 2019, https://www.theatlantic.com/ideas/archive/2019/12/timothy-kellers-moral -universe/603001/.

24. Gregory A. Smith, "Churchgoing Republicans, Once Skeptical of Trump, Now Support Him," Pew Research Center, July 21, 2016, https://www.pewresearch.org/short -reads/2016/07/21/churchgoing-republicans-once-skeptical-of-trump-now-support -him/.

25. Katelyn Beaty, "At a Private Meeting in Illinois, a Group of Evangelicals Tried to Save Their Movement from Trumpism," *The New Yorker*, April 26, 2018, https://www .newyorker.com/news/on-religion/at-a-private-meeting-in-illinois-a-group-of -evangelicals-tried-to-save-their-movement-from-trumpism.

26. Pew Research Center, "Views About Abortion Among Evangelical Protestants," Pew Research Center, n.d., https://www.pewresearch.org/religion/religious-landscape -study/religious-tradition/evangelical-protestant/views-about-abortion/.

27. Daniel Cox and Amelia Thomson-DeVeaux, "Nonreligious Americans Are the New Abortion Voters," FiveThirtyEight, June 29, 2023, https://fivethirtyeight.com/features /nonreligious-americans-are-the-new-abortion-voters/.

28. Elana Schor and Emily Swanson, "Poll: White Evangelicals Distinct on Abortion, LGBT policy," Associated Press, January 2, 2020, https://apnews.com/article/donald-trump-us -news-ap-top-news-elections-immigration-8d3eb99934accc2ad795aca0183290a7.

29. Timothy Keller, "Can Evangelicalism Survive Donald Trump and Roy Moore?," *The New Yorker*, December 19, 2017, https://www.newyorker.com/news/news-desk/can -evangelicalism-survive-donald-trump-and-roy-moore.

30. Premier Christian News, "Tim Keller Says Being a US Evangelical Is 'Harder' Under Trump," Premier Christian News, June 21, 2018, https://premierchristian.news/en /news/article/tim-keller-says-being-a-us-evangelical-is-harder-under-trump.

31. Pew Research Center, "How the Faithful Voted: 2012 Preliminary Analysis," Pew Research Center, November 27, 2012, https://www.pewresearch.org/religion/2012/11 /07/how-the-faithful-voted-2012-preliminary-exit-poll-analysis/.

32. For 2016: Mike Waterhouse, "Borough Breakdown: How NYC Voted for the President (Hint: Clinton Didn't Win Them All)," ABC7 Eyewitness News, November 9, 2016, https://abc7ny.com/election-2016-nyc-results-president/1598306/. For 2020: CNN, "New York," CNN, 2020, https://www.cnn.com/election/2020/results/state/new-york.

33. Elana Schor, "Bipartisan Christian Group Forms Super PAC to Oppose Trump," Associated Press, October 13, 2020, https://apnews.com/article/election-2020 -donald-trump-political-action-committees-christianity-campaigns -942797a20ac8fe9bd9b12edd0adc651a.

34. Michael Wear, "Michael Wear on Political Hopes and Fears," *The Gospel Coalition*, November 17, 2018, https://www.thegospelcoalition.org/video/michael-wear -political-hopes-fears/.

35. Greg Forster, "The Case for Hope from a Former Obama Staffer," *The Gospel Coalition*, March 27, 2017, https://www.thegospelcoalition.org/reviews/reclaiming-hope/.

36. Michael Wear, "This Is How to End Abortion Politics as We've Known It," *Wear We Are* (blog), July 5, 2022, https://wearweare.substack.com/p/this-is-how-to-end-abortion -politics.

37. Katie Jennings, "Abortion by the Numbers," *Forbes*, May 7, 2022, https://www.forbes.com/sites/katiejennings/2022/05/07/abortion-by-the-numbers/?sh=295e91a060a8.

38. Michael Wear, "The Faithful Voters Who Helped Put Biden Over the Top," *New York Times*, November 11, 2020, https://www.nytimes.com/2020/11/11/opinion/biden-evangelical-voters.html.

39. The Trinity Forum, "Evening Conversation with Lecrae and Michael Wear," YouTube video, May 31, 2018, https://www.ttf.org/portfolios/evening-conversation-with-lecrae-and-michael-wear/

40. Chelsea Patterson Sobolik, "Why We Should Celebrate the Dobbs Decision," *The Gospel Coalition*, June 24, 2022, https://www.thegospelcoalition.org/article/celebrate-dobbs/.

41. Karen Swallow Prior (@KSPrior), "Yep. I was for the slow, right way of doing things. That's why I said 50 years. I'm not big on shortcuts," Twitter, May 2, 2022, 11:46 PM, https://twitter.com/KSPrior/status/1521335479341359104?s=20.

42. Karen Swallow Prior (@KSPrior), "I didn't vote for him, so no. That's why I thought it would take 50 more years," Twitter, May 2, 2022, 10:34 PM, https://twitter.com/KSPrior/status/1521317271255359489?s=20.

43. Michelle Boorstein, "Antiabortion Advocate Worked for Years to Overturn Roe, but Worries over Next Steps," *Washington Post*, May 11, 2022, https://www.washingtonpost.com/dc-md-va/2022/05/11/karen-swallow-prior-abortion/.

44. David French (@DavidAFrench), "John Calvin in da house. #NewProfilePic," Twitter, January 27, 2018, 3:47 PM, https://twitter.com/DavidAFrench/status/957354360832479238.

45. David French, "Do Pro-Lifers Who Reject Trump Have 'Blood on Their Hands'?," *The Dispatch*, August 23, 2020, https://thedispatch.com/newsletter/frenchpress/do-pro-lifers-who-reject-trump-have/.

46. Daniel Dench, Mayra Pineda-Torres, and Caitlin Myers, "The Effect of the Dobbs Decision on Fertility," The Institute of Labor Economics, November, 2023, https://docs.iza.org/dp16608.pdf

47. David French, "The Importance of Hope in the Pro-Life Movement," *New York Times*, June 22, 2023, https://www.nytimes.com/2023/06/22/opinion/abortion-law-reality.html.

48. Rachel K. Jones et al., "Long-Term Decline in US Abortions Reverses, Showing Rising Need for Abortion as Supreme Court Is Poised to Overturn Roe v. Wade," Guttmacher Institute, June 15, 2022, https://www.guttmacher.org/article/2022/06/long-term-decline-us-abortions-reverses-showing-rising-need-abortion-supreme-court.

49. Pulse Life Advocates, "True or False: Abortion Rates Drop Under Democratic Presidents?," Pulse Life Advocates, September 25, 2020, https://pulseforlife.org/2020/09/true-or-false/.

50. Graham Vyse, "Democrats Win Total Control of 6 More States. What Will They Do with It?," Governing, November 7, 2018, https://www.governing.com/archive/gov-2018-state-legislative-race-results-trifectas.html.

51. French, "Do Pro-Lifers Who Reject Trump Have 'Blood on Their Hands'?"

52. David French, "Like the President and Hillary, My Views on Marriage Have Evolved,"

National Review, April 27, 2015, https://www.nationalreview.com/2015/04/why-i-changed-my-mind-about-gay-marriage-david-french/.

53. David French, "Pluralism Has Life Left in It Yet," *The Atlantic*, November 18, 2022, https://www.theatlantic.com/newsletters/archive/2022/11/respect-for-marriage-same-sex-religious-freedom/676545/.

54. Dylan Matthews, "Meet David French: The Random Dude Off the Street that Bill Kristol Decided Will Save America from Trump," Vox, May 31, 2016, https://www.vox.com/2016/5/31/11824280/david-french-bill-kristol.

55. Goodstein, "Evangelical Leaders Swing Influence Behind Effort to Combat Global Warming."

56. Hayden Ludwig, "'Creation Care,'" Part 4: "Redefining Pro-Life," Capital Research Center, December 7, 2020, https://capitalresearch.org/article/creation-care-part-4/.

57. Lowe, "Why This Election Isn't Just About Abortion."

58. Sarah Pulliam Bailey, "'I'm Sorry for My Toxicity and Insensitivity': Founder of Evangelical Magazine Steps Aside," *Washington Post*, September 24, 2019, https://www.washingtonpost.com/religion/2019/09/24/im-sorry-my-toxicity-insensitivity-founder-evangelical-magazine-steps-aside/.

59. Beth Moore (@BethMooreLPM), "I'm pro-life, too, Stephanie, but I believe in pro-all-of-life from conception to the grave," Twitter, Dec. 21, 2019, https://twitter.com/BethMooreLPM/status/1208520865660461057

60. Boorstein, "Antiabortion Advocate Worked for Years to Overturn Roe, but Worries over Next Steps."

61. Ian T. Liu, Vinay Prasad, and Jonathan J. Darrow, "Evidence for Community Cloth Face Masking to Limit the Spread of SARS-CoV-2: A Critical Review," *Cato Institute*, November 8, 2021, https://www.cato.org/working-paper/evidence-community-cloth-face-masking-limit-spread-sars-cov-2-critical-review.

62. Karen Swallow Prior, "Being Pro-Life Demands Sacrifice—for a Pandemic, Too," Religion News Service, January 25, 2022, https://religionnews.com/2022/01/25/abortion-covid-masks-vaccines-being-pro-life-demands-sacrifice-in-a-pandemic-too/.

63. National Immigration Forum, "Evangelical Leaders Intensify Calls for Dreamer Solution," National Immigration Forum, January 18, 2018, https://immigrationforum.org/article/evangelical-leaders-intensify-calls-dreamer-solution/.

64. F. Brent Leatherwood, Letter to the Lt. Governor, Speaker, and Every Member of the Legislature of the State of Tennessee, ERLC, https://fox13memphis.com/content/tncms/assets/v3/editorial/0/5b/05b1fc8e-dd96-11ed-9984-9b5f41108387/643e09516fbb9.pdf.pdf.

65. Brett McCracken (@brettmccracken), "We've utterly failed our children when: They can be brutally killed in the womb because enough adults clamor for abortion rights," Twitter, May 24, 2022, 8:06 PM, https://twitter.com/brettmccracken/status/1529252554751635456?s=20.

66. Josh Daws (@JoshDaws), "The right to murder your child is in no way analogous to the right to own a device that is primarily used for self-defense or sport," Twitter, May 25, 2022, 1:33 PM, https://twitter.com/JoshDaws/status/1529516091306811393?s=20.

67. Carl R. Trueman, "The Failure of Evangelical Elites," *First Things*, November 2021, https://www.firstthings.com/article/2021/11/the-failure-of-evangelical-elites.

68. Daniel Dench, Mayra Pineda-Torres, and Caitlin Myers, "The Effects of the Dobbs Decision on Fertility," IZA Institute of Labor Economics, November 2023, https://docs .iza.org/dp16608.pdf.

CHAPTER 4: Christian Media and the Money Men

1. Morgan Lee, "Why the Transgender Conversation Is Changing," *Christianity Today*, April 14, 2021, https://www.christianitytoday.com/ct/podcasts/quick-to-listen /transgender-surgery-sports-bill-legislation-podcast.html.

2. Charlie Dates, "White Churches, It's Time to Go Pro-Life on Guns," *Christianity Today*, June 3, 2022, https://www.christianitytoday.com/ct/2022/june-web-only/uvalde -school-shooting-chicago-go-pro-life-gun-violence.html.

3. Christianity Today, "Immigration," *Christianity Today*, n.d., https://www .christianitytoday.com/ct/topics/i/immigration/.

4. Lilly Endowment Inc., Form 990PF for Fiscal Year Ending Dec. 2016, ProPublica, https://projects.propublica.org/nonprofits/organizati ons/383926408/201943199349105119/IRS990PF.

5. Lilly Endowment, "Lilly Endowment Annual Report 2016," Lilly Endowment, 2016, https://lillyendowment.org/wp-content/uploads/2016/11/complete-report.pdf.

6. Christianity Today International, "Full Filing" for Fiscal Year Ending Dec. 2016, Pro-Publica, https://projects.propublica.org/nonprofits/organizations /520231554/201711299349302376/full.

7. PR Newswire, "Lilly Endowment Awards $750,000 Grant to North Park University," North Park University, February 14, 2017, https://www.northpark.edu/stories/lilly -endowment-awards-750000-grant-north-park-university/.

8. North Park University, "Queers and Allies," North Park University, n.d., https://www .northpark.edu/centers/office-diversity-north-park-chicago/student-organizations /queers-and-allies/.

9. Carl R. Trueman, "The Cancellation of Dr. Nassif," *First Things*, September 1, 2022, https://www.firstthings.com/web-exclusives/2022/09/the-cancellation-of-dr-nassif.

10. Lilly Endowment Inc., Form 990PF for Fiscal Year Ending Dec. 2019, ProPublica, 2019, https://projects.propublica.org/nonprofits/organizations/350868122 /202012829349100221/IRS990PF; for 2021, see https://projects.propublica.org /nonprofits/organizations/350868122/202241329349102664/IRS990PF; for 2022, see https://projects.propublica.org/nonprofits/organizations /350868122/202311359349102611/IRS990PF.

11. Christianity Today, "Christianity Today Gets $1 Million Grant," Oregon Faith Report, December 9, 2022, https://oregonfaithreport.com/2022/12/christianity-today-gets-1 -million-grant/.

12. From https://thrivinginministry.org/. Also of note: Cynthia R. Greenlee, "The Path to Reparations," Thriving in Ministry, July 27, 2021, https://thrivinginministry.org/the -path-to-reparations/; Maria Teresa Gastón, "The Shadows and Fears Cast by US Immi-gration Policy," Thriving in Ministry, September 6, 2022, https://thrivinginministry.org

/fandl_feed_article/the-shadows-and-fears-cast-by-us-immigration-policy/; and Laura Everett, "Working Online from Home Is Fraught for Queer Clergy," Thriving in Ministry, July 26, 2022, https://thrivinginministry.org/working-online-from-home-is-fraught-for -queer-clergy/.

13. "Individual Contributions Data—Christianity Today," Federal Election Commission, https://www.fec.gov/data/receipts/individual-contributions/?data_type=processed &contributor_employer=christianity+today&contributor_employer=christianity +today+international&two_year_transaction_period=2014&two_year_transaction _period=2016&two_year_transaction_period=2018&two_year_transaction _period=2020&two_year_transaction_period=2022. See also "Individual Contribu- tions," https://www.fec.gov/data/receipts/individual-contributions/?contributor _name=meritt+sawyer&two_year_transaction_period=2014&two_year_transaction _period=2016&two_year_transaction_period=2018&two_year_transaction_period =2020&two_year_transaction_period=2022.

14. Sarah Riggs Amico (@SarahRiggsAmico), "Abortion is healthcare. Abortion is health- care. Abortion is healthcare," Twitter, March 4, 2020, 12:42 PM, https://twitter.com /SarahRiggsAmico/status/1235259209756770304?s=20. See also Sarah for Georgia, "On the Issues: Women's Rights," Sarah for Georgia, n.d., https://web.archive.org /web/20220817013648/https://sarahforgeorgia.com/issues/womens-rights/.

15. The Heritage Foundation, "Heritage Explains: The Equality Act," The Heritage Founda- tion, n.d., https://www.heritage.org/gender/heritage-explains/the-equality-act.

16. Albert Mohler, "The Briefing: Wednesday, March 17, 2021," The Briefing (blog), Albert- Mohler.com, March 17, 2021, https://albertmohler.com/2021/03/17/briefing-3-17-21.

17. Simmi Aujla, "Olbermann Suspended After Donations," Politico, November 5, 2010, https://www.politico.com/story/2010/11/olbermann-suspended-after -donations-044734.

18. Dave Levinthal, "Reporters and Editors from the New York Times to the Los Angeles Times Have Been Donating Money in Election 2020, and Democrats Are Getting Most of It," Business Insider, October 30, 2020, https://www.businessinsider.com /journalists-media-news-press-money-trump-biden-contributions-donations-2020-10.

19. Fred Brown, "Political Involvement," Society of Professional Journalists, n.d., https:// www.spj.org/ethics-papers-politics.asp.

20. Elizabeth Warren, "On Senate Floor, Warren Calls for Crackdown on Deceptive and Misleading Practices Used by Many Crisis Pregnancy Centers," August 5, 2022, https://www.warren.senate.gov/newsroom/press-releases/icymi-on-senate-floor -warren-calls-for-crackdown-on-deceptive-and-misleading-practices-used-by-many -crisis-pregnancy-centers#:~:text=It's%20time%20to%20crack%20down,I%20yield.

21. Rod Dreher, "Galli: Elite Evangelicalism's Slide," The American Conservative, October 11, 2021, https://www.theamericanconservative.com/mark-galli-elite-evangelicalism -slide-secularism/.

22. Yonat Shimron, "Christian Reformed Church Brings LGBT Stance into Faith State- ment," Christianity Today, June 15, 2022, https://www.christianitytoday.com/news /2022/june/christian-reformed-church-crc-lgbt-stance-calvin.html. For the interview, see Lee, "Why the Transgender Conversation Is Changing."

23. Kevin J. Jones, "An Arcus News Service? RNS Denies LGBT Money Influences Religion

Coverage," Catholic News Agency, April 1, 2015, https://www.catholicnewsagency.com/news/31788/an-arcus-news-service-rns-denies-lgbt-money-influences-religion-coverage.

24. Yonat Shimron, "Young Evangelicals Are Leaving Church. LGBTQ Bias May Be Driving Them Away," Religion News Service, August 6, 2021, https://religionnews.com/2021/08/06/young-evangelicals-are-leaving-church-resistance-to-lgbtq-equality-is-driving-them-away/.

25. Bob Smietana, "Will Elon Musk Welcome the Babylon Bee Back to Twitter?," *Christianity Today*, November 9, 2022, https://www.christianitytoday.com/news/2022/november/elon-musk-twitter-babylon-bee-christian-satire-suspend.html.

26. Seth Dillon (@SethDillon), "Christianity Today says the Babylon Bee 'has run a number of anti-trans jokes—mocking both particular transgender people like Levine as well as fictional trans people'," Twitter, January 10, 2023, 8:21 PM, https://twitter.com/SethDillon/status/1612982979466248192?s=20.

27. Timothy Dalrymple (@TimDalrymple_), "We don't, but publishing a piece doesn't mean we agree with every detail (this was not the focus of the RNS article) or bit of phrasing," Twitter, January 11, 2023, 8:38 AM, https://twitter.com/TimDalrymple_/status/1613168518471757831?s=20.

28. CRC Staff, "Pierre Omidyar, the Next George Soros," Capital Research Center, August 2, 2022, https://capitalresearch.org/article/pierre-omidyar-the-next-george-soros/.

29. Steve Robinson, "George Soros, Pierre Omidyar Fund Org that Now Controls Most Maine Newspapers," Maine Wire, August 2, 2023, https://www.themainewire.com/2023/08/george-soros-and-pierre-omidyar-fund-org-that-now-controls-major-most-maine-newspapers/. *See also* Open Society Foundations, "Open Society U.S. Programs Board Meeting," Open Society Foundations, September 3–4, 2013, https://capitalresearch.org/app/uploads/Open-Society-U.S.-Programs-Board-Meeting-September-3-4-2013.pdf.

30. Omidyar Network, "Leading Corporations, Foundations and Development Organizations Form 'Better than Cash Alliance' to Accelerate Global Shift to Electronic Payments," Omidyar Network, September 19, 2012, https://omidyar.com/news/leading-corporations-foundations-and-development-organizations-form-better-than-cash-alliance-to-accelerate-global-shift-to-electronic-payments/.

31. Hayden Ludwig, "Omidyar's Political Machine," Part 5: "Funding the Left," Capital Research Center, June 30, 2022, https://capitalresearch.org/article/omidyars-political-machine-part-5/.

32. Hayden Ludwig, "Omidyar's Political Machine," Part 1: "From Tech Billionaire to Mega-Donor," Capital Research Center, June 30, 2022, https://capitalresearch.org/article/omidyars-political-machine-part-1/.

33. Alexander Rubinstein and Max Blumenthal, "How One of America's Premier Data Monarchs Is Funding a Global Information War and Shaping the Media Landscape," *MintPress News*, February 18, 2019, https://www.mintpressnews.com/ebay-founder-pierre-omidyar-is-funding-a-global-media-information-war/255199/.

34. Glenn Greenwald (@ggreenwald), "As I just said, one's funding sources are relevant to one's mission. Liberal billionaires will only fund groups that advance liberal causes (and which define 'disinformation' so as to do so)," Twitter, March 10, 2023, 11:44 AM, https://twitter.com/ggreenwald/status/1634233896433774592.

35. See the Trinity Forum's mention on the Democracy Fund's website: https://democracyfund.org/grant/trinity-forum-inc/; and for donations, see https://projects.propublica.org/nonprofits/organizations/383926408/201943199349105119/IRS990PF (2018), https://projects.propublica.org/nonprofits/organizations/383926408/202003219349106935/IRS990P (2019), https://projects.propublica.org/nonprofits/organizations/383926408/202143569349100609/IRS990PF (2020), and : https://projects.propublica.org/nonprofits/organizations/383926408/202213199349107641/IRS990PF (2021).

36. Michael Wear and Amy E. Black, "Christianity, Pluralism, and Public Life in the United States: Insights from Christian Leaders," The Trinity Forum, n.d., https://www.ttf.org/reports/.

37. Russell D Moore, *Losing Our Religion*, (New York: Penguin), p. 213.

38. David French, "Who Truly Threatens the Church?," *New York Times*, July 9, 2023, https://www.nytimes.com/2023/07/09/opinion/christian-right.html.

39. Kira Mautone, "6th-Grader Speaks Out on Discomfort About Sexually Graphic Book Offered in School Library," Fox News, March 4, 2023, https://www.foxnews.com/media/6th-grader-speaks-discomfort-sexually-graphic-book-offered-school-library.

40. French, "Pluralism Has Life Left in It Yet." See also David French, "Why I Changed My Mind About Law and Marriage, Again," *The Dispatch*, November 20, 2022, https://thedispatch.com/newsletter/frenchpress/why-i-changed-my-mind-about-law-and-marriage-again/; and David French, "An Open Letter to Those Who Think I've Lost My Christian Faith," *The Dispatch*, November 23, 2022, https://thedispatch.com/newsletter/frenchpress/an-open-letter-to-those-who-think-ive-lost-my-christian-faith/.

41. Karen Gilchrist, "The Commercial Surrogacy Industry Is Booming as Demand for Babies Rises," CNBC, March 7, 2023, https://www.cnbc.com/2023/03/07/womb-for-rent-more-women-are-working-in-commercial-surrogacy-industry.html#:~:text=The%20global%20commercial%20surrogacy%20industry,to%20rise%20to%20%24129%20billion.

42. Redeeming Babel, "The After Party Launch Event (with David French, Russell Moore, and Curtis Chang)," YouTube video, March 29, 2023, https://www.youtube.com/watch?v=z8dRBAycfFQ. See also: https://redeemingbabel.org/the-after-party/.

43. Redeeming Babel, "The After Party: Towards Better Christian Politics," Redeeming Babel, n.d., https://web.archive.org/web/20230318143450/https:/redeemingbabel.org/the-after-party/.

44. Alberta, *The Kingdom, the Power, and the Glory*, p. 345.

45. Alison Grubbs, "What Healing Looks Like: Meet the People Working Across Difference to Build Stronger Communities," *New Pluralists: A Sponsored Project of Rockefeller Philanthropy Advisors*, May 2022, https://newpluralists.org/what-healing-looks-like/.

46. Firebelly Design, "Rockefeller Philanthropy Advisors: Introducing Collaborative for Gender and Reproductive Equity," Firebelly Design, n.d., https://www.firebellydesign.com/work/cgre.

47. IKAR, "Supporting Transgender, Non-Binary, and Gender Non-Conforming Community," IKAR, May 4, 2021, https://ikar.org/writings/supporting-transgender-non-binary-and-gender-non-conforming-community/.

48. Tré Goins-Phillips, "BLM Leader Threatens to 'Burn Down the System . . . Literally,'

Calls Jesus a 'Black Radical Revolutionary,'" CBN News, June 25, 2020, https://www2
.cbn.com/news/us/blm-leader-threatens-burn-down-system-literally-calls-jesus-black
-radical-revolutionary.

49. David French, "Why Haley Voters Should Support Biden," *New York Times*, March 10,
2024, https://www.nytimes.com/2024/03/10/opinion/haley-voters-support-biden
.html

50. Principles First, "About the Summit," Principles First, 2024, https://www.principlesfirst
.us/summit/2024/#about.

51. Arizona Pastors Conference, January 29, 2024, https://azpastors.org/.

52. John Stonestreet, "Atheists Are More Political than Evangelicals," *Christian Post*, June
29, 2023, https://www.christianpost.com/voices/atheists-are-more-political-than
-evangelicals.html.

53. George Yancey, "Who's More Political: Progressive or Conservative Christians?," *The
Gospel Coalition*, April 29, 2021, https://www.thegospelcoalition.org/article/political
-progressive-conservative-christians/.

54. Principles First, "About the Summit," Principles First, 2024, https://www.principlesfirst
.us/summit/2024/#about. *See also* Ally Mutnick, "Never Trumpers Rally in D.C., trying
to Find Hope and a Plan Amid Despair," Politico, June 6, 2023, https://www.politico
.com/news/2023/03/06/never-trumpers-rally-dc-00085758.

55. Yonat Shimron, "A Q&A with Evangelical Writer David French on Christian Nationalism," *Washington Post*, February 5, 2021, https://www.washingtonpost.com
/religion/david-french-christian-nationalism/2021/02/05/734865a8-6723-11eb
-8c64-9595888caa15_story.html. *See also* Jon Ward, "Assault on Capitol Was Also an
Attack on Christian Faith, Baptist Leader Russell Moore Says," Yahoo News, January
15, 2021, https://news.yahoo.com/assault-on-capitol-was-also-an-attack-on-christian
-faith-baptist-leader-russell-moore-says-182410188.html.

56. Rockefeller Foundation, Form 990PF for Fiscal Year Ending December 2020, Pro-
Publica, 2020, https://projects.propublica.org/nonprofits/organizations
/131659629/202143079349100824/IRS990PF; Rockefeller Foundation, Form 990PF
for Fiscal Year Ending December 2021, ProPublica, 2021, https://projects.propublica
.org/nonprofits/organizations/131659629/202243159349102059/IRS990PF; Rockefeller Philanthropy Advisors Inc., Form 990PF for Fiscal Year Ending December 2021,
ProPublica, 2021, https://projects.propublica.org/nonprofits/organizations
/133615533/202232859349300818/IRS990ScheduleI.

57. John E. Fetzer Institute Inc., Form 990PF for Fiscal Year Ending June 2021, ProPublica,
2021, https://projects.propublica.org/nonprofits/organizations/386052788
/202240129349100709/IRS990PF. *See also* Bob Boisture, "Not Left or Right, but
Deep: How People of Faith Can Help to Heal America's Divisions," Fetzer Institute,
December 6, 2022, https://fetzer.org/blog/not-left-or-right-deep-how-people-faith
-can-help-heal-americas-divisions.

58. Bill and Melinda Gates Foundation, "Committed Grants: The John E. Fetzer Institute,
Inc.," Bill and Melinda Gates Foundation, 2022, https://www.gatesfoundation.org
/about/committed-grants/2022/11/inv-046857. *See also* Tim Schwab, "Billionaire Bill
Gates Uses Money to Shape the Media," Jacobin, November 27, 2021, https://jacobin
.com/2021/11/bill-gates-foundation-jeffrey-epstein-divorce-journalism/.

59. Sharif Azami, "Faith and Healthy Democracy Report Explores How American Evangelical Christians Might Contribute to Healing Divides," Fetzer Institute, n.d., https://fetzer.org/blog/faith-and-healthy-democracy-report-explores-how-american-evangelical-christians-might. *See also* Paul D. Miller, "An Introduction to 'Faith and Healthy Democracy,'" ERLC, September 26, 2019, https://erlc.com/resource-library/articles/an-introduction-to-faith-and-healthy-democracy/.

60. Os Guinness on the *Fool Proof Theology* podcast hosted by Chase Davis, "85—Os Guinness on Signals of Transcendence and Christians in Revolutionary Times," *Fool Proof Theology*, https://podcasts.apple.com/us/podcast/85-os-guinness-on-signals-of-transcendence/id1529701699?i=1000607092258.

CHAPTER 5: Gracious Dialogue: How the Government Used Pastors to Spread Covid-19 Propaganda

1. Russell Moore, "The Covid-19 Vaccines: A Conversation with Dr. Francis Collins," YouTube video, December 4, 2020, https://www.russellmoore.com/2020/12/11/a-conversation-with-dr-francis-collins-on-vaccine-development-2/.

2. Paul Elias Alexander, "More than 170 Comparative Studies and Articles on Mask Ineffectiveness and Harms," Brownstone Institute, December 20, 2021, https://brownstone.org/articles/studies-and-articles-on-mask-ineffectiveness-and-harms/.

3. Robby Soave, "Masks Make 'Little or No Difference' on COVID-19, Flu Rates: New Study," *Reason*, Feb. 7, 2023, https://reason.com/2023/02/07/masks-covid-dont-work-cochrane-library-review-mandate/. *See also* Emily Joshu, "The Face Mask Effect: Dyslexia and Speech Disorders Among Children Rose 17% During Covid with Nearly One in 10 Kids Now Suffering a Developmental Disability, CDC Report Warns," *Daily Mail*, July 13, 2023, https://www.dailymail.co.uk/health/article-12295645/The-face-mask-effect-Dyslexia-speech-disorders-affect-nearly-one-10-kids-CDC-report-warns.html.

4. Dan Diamond, "Suddenly, Public Health Officials Say Social Justice Matters More than Social Distance," Politico, June 4, 2020, https://www.politico.com/news/magazine/2020/06/04/public-health-protests-301534. *See also* Aaron Greiner et al., "Open Letter Advocating for an Anti-racist Public Health Response to Demonstrations Against Systemic Injustice Occurring During the COVID-19 Pandemic," Google Doc, 2020, https://drive.google.com/file/d/1Jyfn4Wd2i6bRi12ePghMHtX3ys1b7K1A/view.

5. David Zweig, "The CDC's Flawed Case for Wearing Masks in School," *The Atlantic*, December 16, 2021, https://www.theatlantic.com/science/archive/2021/12/mask-guidelines-cdc-walensky/621035/.

6. Moore, "The Covid-19 Vaccines."

7. Belinda Luscombe, "NIH Director Francis Collins Is Fighting This Coronavirus While Preparing for the Next One," *Time*, February 4, 2021, https://time.com/5935658/nih-director-francis-collins-interview/.

8. The Editorial Board, "How Fauci and Collins Shut Down Covid Debate," *Wall Street Journal*, December 21, 2021, https://www.wsj.com/articles/fauci-collins-emails-great-barrington-declaration-covid-pandemic-lockdown-11640129116.

9. Collins on bringing misinformation spreaders to justice: Rachel Roubein, "NIH Director: 'Conspiracies Are Winning Here,'" *Washington Post*, November 19, 2021, https://

www.washingtonpost.com/politics/2021/11/19/nih-director-conspiracies-are-winning-here/. In this video, at the 26:23 mark, Collins insists nature made the virus, though FOIA documents now show he knew the lab leak theory was a very likely possibility: BioLogos, "Science and Faith in Pandemic Times, with Francis Collins," YouTube video, April 6, 2020, https://www.youtube.com/watch?v=EZ3JzHCsPp8&t=2253s. *See also* Jimmy Tobias, "Unredacted NIH Emails Show Efforts to Rule Out Lab Origin of Covid," *The Intercept*, January 19, 2023, https://theintercept.com/2023/01/19/covid-origin-nih-emails/.

10. Deborah Haarsma et al., "Love Your Neighbor, Get the Shot! A Christian Statement on Science for Pandemic Times," BioLogos, https://biologos.org/statement#signatories.

11. Vinay Prasad, "At a Time When the U.S. Needed Covid-19 Dialogue Between Scientists, Francis Collins Moved to Shut It Down," STAT News, https://www.statnews.com/2021/12/23/at-a-time-when-the-u-s-needed-covid-19-dialogue-between-scientists-francis-collins-moved-to-shut-it-down/.

12. Stephen M. Lepore, "'There Needs to Be a Quick and Devastating Take Down': Emails Reveal How Fauci, Head of NIH Colluded to Try to Smear Experts," *Daily Mail*, December 19, 2021, https://www.dailymail.co.uk/news/article-10324873/Emails-reveal-Fauci-head-NIH-colluded-try-smear-experts-called-end-lockdowns.html.

13. Joel Achenbach, "Proposal to Hasten Herd Immunity to the Coronavirus Grabs White House Attention but Appalls Top Scientists," *Washington Post*, October 10, 2020, https://www.washingtonpost.com/health/covid-herd-immunity/2020/10/10/3910251c-0a60-11eb-859b-f9c27abe638d_story.html.

14. Matt Reynolds, "There Is No 'Scientific Divide' over Herd Immunity," *Wired*, July 10, 2020, https://www.wired.co.uk/article/great-barrington-declaration-herd-immunity-scientific-divide.

15. Gregg Gonsalves, "Focused Protection, Herd Immunity, and Other Deadly Delusions," *The Nation*, October 8, 2020, https://www.thenation.com/article/society/covid-jacobin-herd-immunity/. For Gonsalves email to Collins, see https://www.aier.org/wp-content/uploads/2021/12/gonsalvescollins.pdf.

16. Brooks B. Gump, "The Great Barrington Declaration: When Arrogance Leads to Recklessness," *U.S. News and World Report*, November 6, 2020, https://www.usnews.com/news/healthiest-communities/articles/2020-11-06/when-scientists-arrogance-leads-to-recklessness-the-great-barrington-declaration/.

17. Denise Chow, "Why Experts Say We Need to Stop Talking About Herd Immunity," NBC News, November 11, 2020, https://www.nbcnews.com/science/science-news/why-experts-say-we-need-stop-talking-about-herd-immunity-n1247470.

18. Apoorva Mandavilli and Sheryl Gay Stolberg, "A Viral Theory Cited by Health Officials Draws Fire from Scientists," *New York Times*, October 19, 2020, https://www.nytimes.com/2020/10/19/health/coronavirus-great-barrington.html.

19. Grace Ratley, "States Ranked by Age-Adjusted Covid Deaths," The Bioinformatics CRO, December 7, 2022, https://www.bioinformaticscro.com/blog/states-ranked-by-age-adjusted-covid-deaths/.

20. Brandon Showalter, "Doctor Warns of Medical Totalitarianism After License Put Under Review Following Podcast," *Christian Post*, February 3, 2022, https://www.christianpost.com/news/doctor-warns-of-medical-totalitarianism-amid-covid-19-crackdown.html.

21. Greg Wilson, "It Was the Mandates, Not the Fine Print: Fact Checkers Miss Point in Rush to Defend Pfizer," *Daily Wire*, October 15, 2022, https://www.dailywire.com/news/it -was-the-mandates-not-the-fine-print-fact-checkers-miss-point-in-rush-to-defend-pfizer.

22. BBC News, "Covid-19 Disruptions Killed 228,000 Children in South Asia, Says UN Report," BBC News, March 17, 2021, https://www.bbc.com/news/world-asia -56425115.

23. Fox News, "NIH Director Denies Rejecting Lab-Leak Theory," Facebook video, June 2, 2021, https://www.facebook.com/watch/?v=170879315043974.

24. Select Subcommittee on the Coronavirus Pandemic, "The Proximal Origin of a Cover-up: Did the 'Bethesda Boys' Downplay a Lab Leak?," Committee on Oversight and Accountability, July 11, 2023, https://oversight.house.gov/wp-content/uploads /2023/07/Final-Report-7.pdf.

25. BioLogos, "Science and Faith in Pandemic Times, with Francis Collins."

26. Ed Stetzer, "On Christians Spreading Corona Conspiracies: Gullibility Is Not a Spiritual Gift," *Christianity Today*, April 15, 2020, https://web.archive.org/web /20200416092325/https://www.christianitytoday.com/edstetzer/2020/april /christians-and-corona-conspiracies.html.

27. Jonathan Calvert and George Arbuthnott, "What Really Went on Inside the Wuhan Lab Weeks Before Covid Erupted," *Sunday Times*, June 10, 2023, https://archive.is /BoPrc#selection-841.0-852.0.

28. Jerusalem Post Staff, "China Created Covid-19 as a 'Bioweapon,' Wuhan Researcher Claims," *Jerusalem Post*, June 28, 2023, https://www.jpost.com/health-and-wellness /coronavirus/article-748002.

29. Taylor Penley, "Rand Paul Rips Bill Gates' Alleged Tie to Gain-of-Function Research: 'Funding the Biggest Danger to Mankind,'" Fox News, June 18, 2023, https://www .foxnews.com/media/rand-paul-bill-gates-ties-gain-function-research-funding-danger -mankind.

30. Committee on Oversight and Accountability, "Hearing Wrap Up: Suppression of the Lab Leak Hypothesis Was Not Based in Science," Committee on Oversight and Accountability, July 12, 2023, https://oversight.house.gov/release/hearing-wrap-up -suppression-of-the-lab-leak-hypothesis-was-not-based-in-science/.

31. ChurchLeaders.com, "NIH Director Dr. Francis Collins Shares Critical Steps for Back to Church Sunday," YouTube video, September 15, 2021, https://www.youtube.com /watch?v=2JnGZpldjT8.

32. The website is no longer up but can be seen here: https://web.archive.org/web /20200401075609/https://coronavirusandthechurch.com/.

33. https://www.facebook.com/pastorgreear/posts/posting-a-picture-of-myself-getting -the-2nd-vaccine-shot-certainly-solicited-man/291547229003004/

34. https://www.facebook.com/pastorgreear/posts/posting-a-picture-of-myself-getting -the-2nd-vaccine-shot-certainly-solicited-man/291547229003004/

35. Christianity Today, "Where Is God in a Pandemic? A Conversation Between Tim Keller and Francis Collins," Facebook video, May 18, 2020, https://www.facebook .com/watch/live/?ref=watch_permalink&v=557054864999018.

36. Rick Warren, "The Global P.E.A.C.E. Plan." Submitted to the United States Senate

Committee on Appropriations Subcommittee on State, Foreign Operations, and Related Programs, May 6, 2015, https://www.appropriations.senate.gov/imo/media/doc/hearings/050615%20Dr.%20Warren%20Testimony%20-%20SFOPS.pdf

37. HHS Partnership Center, "HHS Partnership Center Special Feature: Dr. Francis Collins + Pastor Rick Warren," YouTube video, November 19, 2020, https://www.youtube.com/watch?v=Lz-WMXld0rk.

38. Pushkala Aripaka, "EU Finds Potential Link Between Heart Inflammation and mRNA Covid shots," Reuters, July 9, 2021, https://www.reuters.com/business/healthcare-pharmaceuticals/eu-regulator-lists-heart-condition-possible-side-effect-mrna-vaccines-2021-07-09/. See also Robert Hart, "Germany, France Restrict Moderna's Covid Vaccine for Under-30s over Rare Heart Risk—Despite Surging Cases," Forbes, April 21, 2022, https://www.forbes.com/sites/roberthart/2021/11/10/germany-france-restrict-modernas-covid-vaccine-for-under-30s-over-rare-heart-risk-despite-surging-cases/?sh=184ee37c2a8a.

39. New Civil Liberties Alliance, "NCLA Challenges Government's Censorship of Support Groups for Victims of Covid Vaccine Injuries," New Civil Liberties Alliance, May 22, 2023, https://nclalegal.org/2023/05/ncla-challenges-governments-censorship-of-support-groups-for-victims-of-covid-vaccine-injuries/.

40. BioLogos, "N. T. Wright and Francis Collins | A Christian Response to Coronavirus," The Language of God (podcast), Episode 51, July 16, 2020, https://podcast.biologos.org/e/nt-wright-francis-collins-a-christian-response-to-coronavirus/. See also John MacArthur, "John MacArthur: The Church's Duty to Remain Open," Decision, September 1, 2020, https://decisionmagazine.com/john-macarthur-the-churchs-duty-to-remain-open/.

41. Emily Brown, "Why Won't Christians Get Vaccinated?" Relevant, September 6, 2021, https://web.archive.org/web/20210907164016/https:/relevantmagazine.com/magazine/why-wont-christians-get-vaccinated/.

42. Meredith Wadman and Jocelyn Kaiser, "NIH Chief Defends Use of Human Fetal Tissue as Opponents Decry It Before Congress," Science, December 13, 2018, https://www.science.org/content/article/nih-chief-defends-use-human-fetal-tissue-opponents-decry-it-congress. See also Justin Lee, "The Cautionary Tale of Francis Collins," First Things, October 29, 2021, https://www.firstthings.com/web-exclusives/2021/10/the-cautionary-tale-of-francis-collins.

43. Stacy Trasancos, "How Aborted Children Are Used in Medical Research in 2020," National Catholic Register, December 15, 2020, https://www.ncregister.com/blog/how-aborted-children-are-used.

44. Sam Dorman, "Doctors Say Pitt Statements Point to Possibility Organs Extracted from Live Fetuses; School Denies Charge," Fox News, August 11, 2021, https://www.foxnews.com/politics/pittsburgh-live-fetus-organs.

45. Nidhi Subbaraman, "Science Misinformation Alarms Francis Collins as He Leaves Top NIH Job," Nature, December 3, 2021, https://www.nature.com/articles/d41586-021-03611-2.

46. Francis Collins, "NIH Stands Against Structural Racism in Biomedical Research," National Institutes of Health, March 1, 2021, https://www.nih.gov/about-nih/who-we-are/nih-director/statements/nih-stands-against-structural-racism-biomedical-research.

See also Subbaraman, "Science Misinformation Alarms Francis Collins as He Leaves Top NIH Job,"

47. Francis S. Collins et al., "Affirming NIH's Commitment to Addressing Structural Racism in the Biomedical Research Enterprise," *Cell* 184, No. 12 (June 10, 2021): 3075–79, https://www.cell.com/cell/fulltext/S0092-8674(21)00631-0?utm_source=EA.

48. Francis Collins, "From the NIH Director: NIH 2021 Pride Month," National Institutes of Health, June 4, 2021, https://www.edi.nih.gov/blog/news/nih-director-nih-2021 -pride-month.

49. National Institutes of Health, "Strategic Plan to Advance Research on the Health and Well-Being of Sexual and Gender Minorities," National Institutes of Health, n.d., https://dpcpsi.nih.gov/sites/default/files/SGMStrategicPlan_2021_2025.pdf.

50. Brandon Showalter, "Testosterone Being Given to 8-y-o girls, Age Lowered from 13: Doctors," *Christian Post*, April 2, 2019, https://www.christianpost.com/news /testosterone-being-given-to-8-y-o-girls-age-lowered-from-13-doctors.html. *See also* https://docs.wixstatic.com/ugd/3f4f51_a929d049f7fb46c7a72c4c86ba43869a.pdf.

51. Ben Zeisloft, "NIH Spends Millions on Study that 'Recruited' Minors to Report Homosexual Activity—Including 'Condomless Anal Sex'—Without Their Parents' Permission," *Daily Wire*, January 29, 2022, https://www.dailywire.com/news /nih-spends-millions-on-study-that-recruited-minors-to-report-homosexual-activity -including-condomless-anal-sex-without-their-parents-pe?%3Futm_source=twitter &utm_medium=social&utm_campaign=dwtwitter.

52. Luscombe, "NIH Director Francis Collins Is Fighting This Coronavirus While Preparing for the Next One."

53. Russell Moore (@drmoore), "I admire greatly the wisdom, expertise, and, most of all, the Christian humility and grace of Francis Collins," Twitter, October 5, 2021, 8:20 AM, https://twitter.com/drmoore/status/1445363320089944064?s=20.

54. David French (@DavidAFrench), "Francis Collins is a national treasure," Twitter, October 5, 2021, 10:47 AM, https://twitter.com/DavidAFrench/status /1445400222780301321?s=20.

55. Michael Gerson, "NIH's Francis Collins, on Covid, Science and Faith," *Washington Post*, October 7, 2021, https://www.washingtonpost.com/opinions/2021/10/07 /francis-collins-nih-covid-science-faith-truth/.

56. Glenn Kessler, "Timeline: How the Wuhan Lab-Leak Theory Suddenly Became Credible," *Washington Post*, May 25, 2021, https://www.washingtonpost.com/politics /2021/05/25/timeline-how-wuhan-lab-leak-theory-suddenly-became-credible/. *See also* Nicholas Wade, "A Covid Origin Conspiracy?," *City Journal*, January 23, 2022, https://www.city-journal.org/article/a-covid-origin-conspiracy.

57. Caroline Downey, "NIH Admits to Funding Gain-of-Function Research in Wuhan, Says EcoHealth Violated Reporting Requirements," *National Review*, October 21, 2021, https://www.nationalreview.com/news/nih-admits-to-funding-gain-of-function -research-in-wuhan-says-ecohealth-violated-reporting-requirements/?utm_source =recirc-desktop&utm_medium=homepage&utm_campaign=hero&utm_content =related&utm_term=first.

58. Timothy Keller (1950–2023) (@timkellernyc), "Thread: Can Christians be leaders in publicly-owned corporations or government agencies that are committed to many non-

Christian values?," Twitter, March 9, 2022, https://twitter.com/timkellernyc/status/1501603866147803137.

59. Subbaraman, "Science Misinformation Alarms Francis Collins as He Leaves Top NIH Job."

60. Mary Louise Kelly, "In the '24th Mile' of a Marathon, Fauci and Collins Reflect on Their Pandemic Year," NPR, March 9, 2021, https://www.npr.org/2021/03/09/975263049/in-the-24th-mile-of-a-marathon-fauci-and-collins-reflect-on-their-pandemic-year.

61. Megan Basham, "Exclusive: In Leaked Audio Former NIH Director/New Biden Science Adviser Laughs Over Threatening Unemployment to Force Vaccines, Blames Trump for Covid Deaths," Daily Wire, March 7, 2022, https://www.dailywire.com/news/exclusive-in-leaked-audio-former-nih-director-new-biden-science-adviser-laughs-over-threatening-unemployment-to-force-vaccines-blames-trump-for-covid-19-deaths.

62. Christianity Today, "How Evangelicals Can Grapple with the Vaccine Using Both Science and Theology: HDI town hall interview with Dr. Francis Collins and Timothy Dalrymple," Christianity Today, June 11, 2021, https://www.christianitytoday.com/better-samaritan/2021/june/how-evangelicals-can-grapple-with-vaccine-using-both-scienc.html.

63. David Shepardson, "Biden Vaccine Mandate Will Test OSHA, U.S. Workplace Regulator," Reuters, September 13, 2021, https://www.reuters.com/legal/government/biden-vaccine-mandate-will-test-us-workplace-regulator-2021-09-13/.

64. Sean Trende, "Vaccine Mandates and Jacobson v. Massachusetts: A Closer Look," American Enterprise Institute, October 12, 2021, https://www.aei.org/articles/vaccine-mandates-and-jacobson-v-massachusetts-a-closer-look/.

65. Nidhi Subbaraman, "How Do Vaccinated People Spread Delta? What the Science Says," Nature, August 12, 2021, https://www.nature.com/articles/d41586-021-02187-1.

66. Basham, "Exclusive: In Leaked Audio Former NIH Director/New Biden Science Adviser Laughs over Threatening Unemployment to Force Vaccines, Blames Trump for Covid Deaths."

67. Peter Wehner, "The Evangelical Church Is Breaking Apart," The Atlantic, October 24, 2021, https://www.theatlantic.com/ideas/archive/2021/10/evangelical-trump-christians-politics/620469/.

68. Megan Best, "The Office of Faith-Based and Community Initiatives: How It Clarified and Developed Government's Partnership with Religious Groups," University of Dallas, November 21, 2013, https://www.georgewbushlibrary.gov/sites/default/files/2021-09/M%20Best%20Paper.pdf. See also Julie Moreau, "New 'Religious Freedom' Division Sows Fears of LGBTQ Discrimination," NBC News, January 20, 2018, https://www.nbcnews.com/feature/nbc-out/new-religious-freedom-division-sows-fears-lgbtq-discrimination-n839256.

69. Rob Crilly, "Only 31 Percent of Americans Trust Fauci's Covid Advice and Just 45 Percent Approve of Biden's Pandemic Response, Another Dire Poll for the Administration Shows," Daily Mail, January 13, 2022, https://www.dailymail.co.uk/news/article-10398941/Only-31-percent-Americans-trust-Faucis-COVID-advice-dire-poll-administration.html.

70. Ryan Saavedra, "It's Official: More Americans Have Died from Coronavirus Under Biden than Trump Despite Biden Pledge to 'Shut Down the Virus,'" *Daily Wire*, December 18, 2021, https://www.dailywire.com/news/its-official-more-americans -have-died-from-coronavirus-under-biden-than-trump-despite-biden-pledge-to-shut -down-the-virus.

71. Jessica Craig, "Charts: How the U.S. Ranks on Covid-19 Deaths Per Capita—And by Case Count," NPR, August 5, 2020, https://www.npr.org/sections/goatsandsoda/2020 /08/05/899365887/charts-how-the-u-s-ranks-on-covid-19-deaths-per-capita-and-by -case-count.

72. Denise Grady and Nicholas St. Fleur, "Fetal Tissue from Abortions for Research Is Traded in a Gray Zone," *New York Times*, July 28, 2015, https://www.nytimes.com /2015/07/28/health/fetal-tissue-from-abortions-for-research-is-traded-in-a-gray -zone.html#:~:text=Companies%20that%20obtain%20the%20tissue,charge%20for %20processing%20and%20shipping.

73. The Center for Medical Progress, "Planned Parenthood Uses Partial-Birth Abortions to Sell Baby Parts," YouTube video, July 14, 2015, https://www.youtube.com/watch?v =jjxwVuozMnU#t=180.

74. Matt Taibbi, "Covid's Origins and the Death of Trust," Racket News, July 20, 2023, https://www.racket.news/p/covids-origins-and-the-death-of-trust?utm_source =substack&publication_id=1042&post_id=135309998&utm_medium=email&utm _content=share&triggerShare=true&isFreemail=true.

75. Redeemer East Side, "In-Person Worship," Redeemer East Side, n.d., https://web .archive.org/web/20210622111120/https:/eastside.redeemer.com/inperson.

76. Mayo Clinic Staff, "Covid-19 in Babies and Children," Mayo Clinic, n.d., https://www .mayoclinic.org/diseases-conditions/coronavirus/in-depth/coronavirus-in-babies -and-children/art-20484405#:~:text=Children%20represent%20about%2018%25 %20of,COVID%2D19%20with%20no%20symptoms.

77. Jared S. Hopkins and Sarah Toy, "Pfizer Study of Covid-19 Vaccine in Pregnant Women Delayed by Slow Enrollment," *Wall Street Journal*, September 22, 2021, https://www .wsj.com/articles/pfizer-study-of-covid-19-vaccine-in-pregnant-women-delayed-by -slow-enrollment-11632310283. *See also* Sharyl Attkisson, "Study: Significant Preterm Births in AstraZeneca Covid-19 Vaccine Study; No Impact on Women's Short-Term Fertility," *Sharyl Attkisson* (blog), October 24, 2021, https://sharylattkisson .com/2021/10/study-significant-preterm-births-in-astrazeneca-covid-19-vaccine -study-no-impact-on-womens-short-term-fertility/.

78. Paige Pauroso, "'Nobody Has Availability': Parents Left Scrambling After Daycare Closes Toddler and Infant Daycare Rooms," WBTV3, October 13, 2021, https://www .wbtv.com/2021/10/13/nobody-has-availability-parents-left-scrambling-after-daycare -closes-toddler-infant-daycare-rooms/.

79. Holly Meyer, "Southern Baptist Convention Mandates Covid-19 Vaccine for Its Missionaries," *Los Angeles Times*, September 17, 2021, https://www.latimes.com /world-nation/story/2021-09-17/southern-baptist-convention-mandates-covid-19 -vaccine-for-its-missionaries.

80. Russell Moore and Walter Kim, "Not the Mark of the Beast: Evangelicals Should Fight Conspiracy Theories and Welcome the Vaccines," *Washington Post*, February 24, 2021,

https://www.washingtonpost.com/religion/2021/02/24/evangelicals-covid-vaccine
-russell-moore-walter-kim/.

81. Redeeming Babel, "Should Pro-lifers Be Pro-vaccine?," YouTube video, March 6, 2021,
https://www.youtube.com/watch?v=rBNptN9D9jU.

82. David French (@DavidAFrench), "When Evangelicals pursue the 'freedom' to make
their neighbors sick, they violate the social compact and undermine their moral standing in politics, law, and culture," Twitter, August 29, 2021, 3:46 PM, https://twitter
.com/DavidAFrench/status/1432067199997460485?s=20.

83. David French, "Did Donald Trump Make the Church Great Again?," *The Dispatch*,
September 19, 2021, https://thedispatch.com/newsletter/frenchpress/did-donald
-trump-make-the-church/.

84. Andy Fell, "Viral Loads Similar Between Vaccinated and Unvaccinated People," University of California, Davis, October 4, 2021, https://www.ucdavis.edu/health
/covid-19/news/viral-loads-similar-between-vaccinated-and-unvaccinated-people. *See
also* Carlos Franco-Paredes, "Transmissibility of SARS-CoV-2 Among Fully Vaccinated
Individuals," *The Lancet Infectious Diseases* (January 2022), https://doi.org/10.1016
/S1473-3099(21)00768-4.

85. Tom Jefferson et al., "Physical Interventions to Interrupt or Reduce the Spread of
Respiratory Viruses," Cochrane Database of Systematic Reviews 2023, Issue 1, Art. No.
CD006207. DOI: 10.1002/14651858.CD006207.pub6.

86. Trinity Bible Chapel (@TBCWR), "There are people like Jennifer in your community,"
Twitter video, January 11, 2022, 12:00 PM, https://twitter.com/TBCWR/status
/1480947649448751106?s=20.

87. Paul D. Miller, "It's Time to Forgive Each Other Our Pandemic Sins," *Christianity Today*, June 1, 2023, https://www.christianitytoday.com/ct/2023/may-web-only/covid
-19-pandemic-amnesty-masks-vaccine-lockdown-church.html.

88. Joel Berry (@JoelWBerry), "I can't help feeling this is like an abusive husband telling his
wife to 'get over it,'" Twitter, June 2, 2023, 7:08 AM, https://twitter.com/JoelWBerry
/status/1664589796390457345.

CHAPTER 6: Critical Race Prophets

1. Truth's Table, "A Podcast by Black Women and for Black Women, Where We Tackle
Politics, Race, Culture, and Gender Issues Through a Christian Lens," Truth's Table,
n.d., https://truthstable.com/.

2. North American Mission Board, "Undivided Session 1: Introduction," YouTube video,
August 20, 2020, https://www.youtube.com/watch?v=dXxJnJb1e80.

3. John A. Broadus, "As to the Colored People," *Standard* (Chicago), 1 Feb. 1883, 1.

4. Margaret Hoover, PBS—*Firing Line*, September 7, 2018, https://www.pbs.org/wnet
/firing-line/video/jd-greear-v5dt98/.

5. Sarah Pulliam Bailey, "Prominent Southern Baptists are dropping 'Southern' name amid
racial unrest," *Washington Post*, September 15, 2020, https://www.washingtonpost.com
/religion/2020/09/15/southern-baptist-name-great-commission-baptist/.

6. The Aspen Institute, "Glossary for Understanding the Dismantling Structural Rac-

ism/Promoting Racial Equity Analysis," The Aspen Institute, n.d., https://www
.aspeninstitute.org/wp-content/uploads/files/content/docs/rcc/RCC-Structural
-Racism-Glossary.pdf.

7. For some of this documentation, see Mike Gonzalez, "Zombie Marxism," The Heritage
Foundation, December 17, 2021, https://www.heritage.org/progressivism/commentary
/zombie-marxism. *See also* Jonathan Butcher and Mike Gonzalez, "Critical Race Theory,
the New Intolerance, and Its Grip on America," The Heritage Foundation, December 7,
2020, https://www.heritage.org/civil-rights/report/critical-race-theory-the-new
-intolerance-and-its-grip-america.

8. Wisevoter, "States that Have Banned Critical Race Theory," Wisevoter, https://
wisevoter.com/state-rankings/states-that-have-banned-critical-race-theory/.

9. Tom Ascol, "Resolution 9 and the Southern Baptist Convention 2019," Founders Ministries, 2019, https://founders.org/articles/resolution-9-and-the-southern-baptist
-convention-2019/.

10. Richard Delgado and Jean Stefancic, "Living History Interview with Richard Delgado
and Jean Stefancic," *Transnational Law and Contemporary Problems* 19, no. 221 (2011),
https://digitalcommons.law.seattleu.edu/cgi/viewcontent.cgi?article=1039&context
=faculty. *See also* Ilana Redstone, "Conflict Theory Doesn't Like You," *Tablet Magazine*,
April 12, 2021, https://www.tabletmag.com/sections/news/articles/conflict-theory
-and-us.

11. Richard Delgado and Jean Stefancic, *Critical Race Theory: An Introduction.* [Third Edi-
tion] (New York: New York University Press, 2017), p. 18.

12. Capstone Report, "Bombshell: Professor Admits Some in SBC Promoting Tools of
Identity Politics," Capstone Report, June 16, 2019, https://capstonereport
.com/2019/06/16/bombshell-professor-admits-some-in-sbc-promoting-tools-of
-identity-politics/32630/.

13. Gerald McDermott, "Is Critical Race Theory Compatible with Christian Faith?," The
Institute on Religion and Democracy, February 11, 2020, https://juicyecumenism.com
/2020/02/11/critical-race-theory/.

14. The Village Church, "How to Understand and Address White Privilege," YouTube
video, January 7, 2017, https://www.youtube.com/watch?v=pzUXZpMQlTQ. *See also*
https://web.archive.org/web/20230406194730/https://www.youtube.com/watch
?v=pzUXZpMQlTQ.

15. Woke Preacher Clips, "Ibram Kendi: Antiracists Fundamentally Reject 'Savior Theology' and Embrace Liberation Theology," YouTube video, March 23, 2021, 2 min. 7 sec.,
https://www.youtube.com/watch?v=azJh4N69Q5k.

16. R. C. Sproul, "The Liberal Agenda," Ligonier, March 1, 2006, https://www.ligonier
.org/learn/articles/liberal-agenda. *See also* John M. Frame, "Liberation Theology," *The
Gospel Coalition*, n.d., https://www.thegospelcoalition.org/essay/liberation
-theology/.

17. Bryan Loritts (@loritts), "Scholars point out how the opposite of racism is not, not being racist, but is to be anti racist (Ibram Kendi)," Instagram, February 28, 2020, https://
www.instagram.com/p/B9HmjGklyQp/. *See also* Bryan Loritts, "Top 10 Books I Read
in 2019," *Dr. Bryan Loritts* (blog), November 25, 2019, https://bryanloritts.com/blog
/top-10-books-i-read-in-2019, and Bryan Loritts, "Top Ten of 2017," tumblr:

bryanloritts, December 20, 2017, https://bryanloritts.tumblr.com/post/168741964420/top-ten-of-2017.

18. CCCU video, "Strategic Transformation: Bryan Loritts," YouTube video, November 4, 2019, https://www.youtube.com/watch?v=lbXGtHNR6kM.

19. Azusa Pacific University, "Allyship and Anti-Racism Resources," Azusa Pacific University, n.d., https://pages.e2ma.net/pages/1767323/23410. *See also* Tom Mackaman, "An Interview with Historian Gordon Wood on the *New York Times*' 1619 Project," World Socialist Web Site, November 28, 2019, https://www.wsws.org/en/articles/2019/11/28/wood-n28.html.

20. Rod Dreher, "On Race, Hillsdale vs. Azusa Pacific," *The American Conservative*, June 18, 2020, https://www.theamericanconservative.com/hillsdale-college-azusa-pacific-black-lives-matter/.

21. Linda A. Livingstone, "Presidential Perspective," Baylor University Office of the President, July 23, 2020, https://president.web.baylor.edu/news/story/2020/presidential-perspective-july-23-2020.

22. Baylor University, "Baylor Diversity and Inclusion Expert Shares 5 Tips to Cultivate Cultural Humility and Antiracism," Baylor University, July 20, 2020, https://news.web.baylor.edu/news/story/2020/baylor-diversity-and-inclusion-expert-shares-5-tips-cultivate-cultural-humility-and.

23. Kenneth Jones and Tema Okun, "White Supremacy Culture," Minnesota Historical Society Department of Inclusion and Community Engagement, n.d., https://www.thc.texas.gov/public/upload/preserve/museums/files/White_Supremacy_Culture.pdf.

24. Laurie Higgins, "Wheaton College's A-Wokening Continues Apace," Illinois Family Institute, March 2, 2022, https://illinoisfamily.org/education/wheaton-college-is-not-your-grandfathers-college/.

25. Wheaton College, "Racial and Cultural Minority Senior Recognition Ceremony," Wheaton College, https://www.wheaton.edu/life-at-wheaton/student-development-offices/vice-president-for-student-development/minority-senior-recognition-ceremony/.

26. Megan Fowler, "Wheaton Pulls Jim Elliot Missionary Plaque to Reword 'Savage' Description," *Christianity Today*, March 19, 2021, https://www.christianitytoday.com/news/2021/march/wheaton-college-missionary-plaque-jim-elliot-waorani.html.

27. Conversations that Matter, "Yes, Grove City College Is Compromised on Social Justice," YouTube video, December 10, 2021, https://www.youtube.com/watch?v=bI3cZV3g4kA&t=1860s.

28. Jemar Tisby, "Is the White Church Inherently Racist?," *New York Times*, August 18, 2020, https://www.nytimes.com/2020/08/18/books/review/white-too-long-robert-p-jones.html.

29. "Save GCC from CRT," Petitions.net, November 10, 2021, https://www.petitions.net/save_gcc_from_crt.

30. "Report and Recommendation of the Special Committee," Grove City College, April 13, 2022, https://www.gcc.edu/Portals/0/Special-Committee-Report-and-Recommendation_0422.pdf.

31. Scott Pendleton, "Seeking Clarity and Unity," Cru, November 6, 2020, https://www.cru.org/content/dam/cru/seeking-clarity-and-unity.pdf.

32. Eliott C. McLaughlin, "Critical Race Theory Is a Lens. Here Are 11 Ways Looking Through It Might Refine Your Understanding of History," CNN, May 27, 2021, https://www.cnn.com/2021/05/27/us/critical-race-theory-lens-history-crt/index.html.

33. George Schroeder, "Seminary Presidents Reaffirm BFM, Declare CRT Incompatible," *Baptist Press*, November 30, 2020, https://www.baptistpress.com/resource-library/news/seminary-presidents-reaffirm-bfm-declare-crt-incompatible/.

34. Matt Smethurst, "On My Shelf: Life and Books with Jarvis Williams," *The Gospel Coalition,* February 28, 2017, https://www.thegospelcoalition.org/article/on-my-shelf-life-and-books-with-jarvis-williams/.

35. Bethlehem College and Seminary, "Ethnic Harmony and the Holy Spirit | PasCon2018," YouTube video, November 11, 2020, https://www.youtube.com/watch?v=Ou0ycm_Bzww.

36. Nell Irvin Painter, "White Identity in America Is Ideology, Not Biology. The History of 'Whiteness' Proves It," NBC News, June 27, 2020, https://www.nbcnews.com/think/opinion/white-identity-america-ideology-not-biology-history-whiteness-proves-it-ncna1232200. For video, see https://otter.ai/u/jEornRtvqfb-AZ2RnPXXbU6_U7U?tab=summary.

37. Coffee and Cream, "13: Seminaries and Racial Reconciliation with Matthew Hall," YouTube video, July 15, 2018, https://www.youtube.com/watch?v=dwI82hKUTgI.

38. Christ Church West Chester, "Race Relations in the Southern Baptist Convention with Dr. Matt Hall," YouTube video, January 17, 2019, https://www.youtube.com/watch?v=zIgJAQFrhrU.

39. ONE SBTS, "ONE Presents: 'Removing the Stain of Racism from the Southern Baptist Convention Panel,'" YouTube video, September 13, 2017, https://www.youtube.com/watch?v=imN8SvGTWz4.

40. For CBS: Peter White, "CBS Ramps Up Off-Screen Diversity Plans; Commits 25% of Script Development Budget to BIPOC Creators and Sets 40% Representation Target in Writers' Rooms," *Deadline*, July 13, 2020, https://deadline.com/2020/07/cbs-diversity-plans-25-script-budget-40-writers-target-1202984315/. For Disney: Lesley Goldberg, "ABC Unveils Ambitious Set of Inclusion Standards," *The Hollywood Reporter*, September 30, 2020, https://www.hollywoodreporter.com/tv/tv-news/abc-unveils-ambitious-set-of-inclusion-standards-exclusive-4069409/. For Fortune 500 companies: Marin Wolf and Kim Bhasin, "Wells Fargo, Delta Join a Nascent Push into Racial Hiring Quotas," Bloomberg, September 1, 2020, https://www.bloomberg.com/news/articles/2020-09-01/can-quotas-fix-diversity-these-major-companies-hope-so?in_source=embedded-checkout-banner. For NASDAQ: Alexander Osipovich and Akane Otani, "Nasdaq Seeks Board-Diversity Rule that Most Listed Firms Don't Meet," *Wall Street Journal*, December 1, 2020, https://www.wsj.com/articles/nasdaq-proposes-board-diversity-rule-for-listed-companies-11606829244.

41. Southeastern Baptist Theological Seminary, "Kingdom Diversity," Southeastern Baptist Theological Seminary, n.d., https://www.sebts.edu/about/kingdom-diversity/.

42. Matt Mullins, "Is Critical Race Theory 'UnChristian [sic],' Part 1: Kingdom Diversity at Southeastern," September 12, 2018, https://web.archive.org/web/20180918002409/http://kingdomdiversity.sebts.edu/index.php/2018/09/12/is-critical-race-theory-unchristian-part-1/.

43. Matt Mullins, "Is Critical Race Theory 'UnChristian [*sic*],' Part 2: Kingdom Diversity at Southeastern," September 14, 2018, https://web.archive.org/web/20180918002318 /http:/kingdomdiversity.sebts.edu/index.php/2018/09/14/is-critical-race-theory -unchristian-part-2/.

44. Matt Mullins, "Is Critical Race Theory 'UnChristian [*sic*],' Part 5: Kingdom Diversity at Southeastern," September 26, 2018, https://web.archive.org/web/20180926182913 /http:/kingdomdiversity.sebts.edu/index.php/2018/09/26/is-critical-race-theory -unchristian-part-5/.

45. Matt Mullins, "Is Critical Race Theory 'UnChristian [*sic*],' Part 6: Kingdom Diversity at Southeastern," October 10, 2018, https://web.archive.org/web/20181113170903 /http:/kingdomdiversity.sebts.edu/index.php/2018/10/10/is-critical-race-theory -unchristian-part-6/.

46. SEBTS Staff, "President Akin Addresses Critical Race Theory at Presidential Q&A," Southeastern Baptist Theological Seminary, May 3, 2021, https://www.sebts.edu /news-and-events/headlines/2021/05/sp21_akin_q_and_a/.

47. Matthew Mullins, "Multiethnic Literatures of the United States," Capstone Report, Spring 2015, https://capstonereport.com/wp-content/uploads/2021/04/Matthew -Mullins-Syllabus.pdf.

48. Thomas Sowell, *Discrimination and Disparities* (New York: Basic Books, an imprint of Hachette Publishing, 2019), p. 183.

49. Sowell, *Discrimination and Disparities*, p. 119.

50. Barcelona School of Economics, "What Is Driving the Racial Marriage Gap in the United States?," Barcelona School of Economics, March 9, 2022, https://focus.bse.eu /what-is-driving-the-racial-marriage-gap-in-the-united-states/#:~:text=In%20 2018%2C%2062%25%20of%20white,gap%20of%2030%20percentage%20points.

51. ERLC, "What Do White Christians Need to Be Mindful of When Speaking Out About Racial Reconciliation?," YouTube video, April 13, 2018, https://www.youtube.com /watch?v=qpo9JR6hucc.

52. *The Gospel Coalition*, "A House Divided Cannot Stand," YouTube video, April 20, 2018, https://www.youtube.com/watch?v=-wmj0i1oH1Q.

53. The Front Porch, "14—JD Greear on Judges 4," YouTube video, July 6, 2019, https:// www.youtube.com/watch?v=plS1NmgkQgk.

54. Voddie T. Baucham, *Fault Lines: The Social Justice Movement and Evangelicalism's Looming Catastrophe* (Washington, DC: Salem Books, an imprint of Regnery Publishing, 2021), p. 92.

55. Adelle M. Banks, "Southern Baptist Church: Racial Prejudice a Factor in Rejection of Black Pastor," Religion News Service, October 30, 2019, https://religionnews.com /2019/10/30/southern-baptist-church-racial-prejudice-a-factor-in-rejection-of-black -pastor/.

56. Ben Terris, "He's Got a 'Downton Abbey'–Inspired Office, but Rep. Aaron Schock Won't Talk About It," *Washington Post*, February 2, 2015, https://www.washingtonpost .com/lifestyle/style/hes-got-a-downton-abbey-inspired-office-but-rep-aaron-schock -wont-talk-about-it/2015/02/02/1d3f1466-ab1f-11e4-abe8-e1ef60ca26de_story.html.

57. Diana Chandler, "Fla. Church Signals Discipline over 'Racial Prejudices,'" *Baptist*

Press, November 1, 2019, https://www.baptistpress.com/resource-library/news/fla
-church-signals-discipline-over-racial-prejudices/.

58. Patrick Riley, "Racism Allegations Rock First Baptist Church Naples After Failed Vote
to Affirm Black Pastor," *Naples Daily News*, November 8, 2019, https://www
.naplesnews.com/story/news/local/2019/11/08/first-baptist-church-naples-vote
-black-pastor-failed-due-racial-prejudice-led-failed-vote-black-past/4169277002/.

59. Matthew Hall (@MatthewJHall), "Sin flourishes in the dark," Twitter, October 31, 2019,
9:16 PM, https://twitter.com/MatthewJHall/status/1190075072960192512?s=20.

60. Bart Barber (@bartbarber), "Celebrating the 81% is the point of considering disci-
plinary action against anyone who disseminated racist sentiments to influence this
process," Twitter, October 31, 2019, 9:04 AM, https://twitter.com/bartbarber/status
/1189890944574857216.

61. Paul Astles et al., Letter to Pastor Marcus Hayes, October 16, 2019, https://acrobat
.adobe.com/link/track?uri=urn%3Aaaid%3Ascds%3AUS%3Ac7c8a426-4926-4e97
-9b27-cab019dc574f&viewer%21megaVerb=group-discover%2FMatthew-Mullins
-Syllabus.pdf.

62. Woke Preacher Clips, "Eric Mason: 'Whiteness Has Caused Blindness of Heart!,'" You-
Tube video, September 23, 2020, https://www.youtube.com/watch?v=O-O6Ufo3GH8.

63. Patrick Riley, "Racism Allegations Rock First Baptist Church Naples After Failed Vote
to Affirm Black Pastor," *Naples Daily News*, November 8, 2019, https://www
.naplesnews.com/story/news/local/2019/11/08/first-baptist-church-naples-vote
-black-pastor-failed-due-racial-prejudice-led-failed-vote-black-past/4169277002/.

64. FBCN Concerned Members, "Concerns Surfacing About Compatibility with Marcus
Hayes," email message to undisclosed recipients, October 24, 2019, https://acrobat
.adobe.com/link/track?uri=urn%3Aaaid%3Ascds%3AUS%3A4dd87981-9696-4b53
-86e2-3157b47ccea5&viewer%21megaVerb=group-discover.

65. Sara Santora, "Actress Dragged for Roe v. Wade Tweet About 'White Supremacist Lawmakers,'" *Newsweek*, May 4, 2022, https://www.newsweek.com/actress-dragged
-roe-v-wade-tweet-about-white-supremacist-lawmakers-1703597.

66. Sarah N. Lynch, "Hate Crimes in US Surged 11.6% in 2021, Fueled by Racial, Ethnic
Bias," Reuters, March 13, 2023, https://www.reuters.com/world/us/hate-crimes-us
-surged-116-2021-2023-03-13/.

67. Lydia Saad, "U.S. Perceptions of White-Black Relations Sink to New Low," Gallup,
September 2, 2020, https://news.gallup.com/poll/318851/perceptions-white-black
-relations-sink-new-low.aspx.

68. Samuel Sey, "White Fragility Is Pro-Racism," Founders Ministries, n.d., https://founders
.org/reviews/white-fragility-is-pro-racism/.

69. Will Hall, "Mitchell: Marxist Concepts Have Footholds at SEBTS, SBTS," *Louisiana
Baptist Message*, March 12, 2020, https://www.baptistmessage.com/mitchell-marxist
-concepts-have-footholds-at-sebts-sbts/.

CHAPTER 7: #MeToo, #ChurchToo, and an Apocalypse

1. Taylor Berglund, "John Crist Cancels 2019 Tour Dates After Reports of Sexting,
Harassment, Manipulation," *Charisma*, November 6, 2019,

https://www.charismanews.com/us/78703-john-crist-cancels-2019-tour-dates
-after-reports-of-sexting-harassment-manipulation.

2. Ed Stetzer and Laurie Nichols, "Ed Stetzer and Laurie Nichols on John Crist, Failure, and Warnings to Heed for Christian Leaders," BCNN1, November 7, 2019, https://web.archive.org/web/20200105173108/https://blackchristiannews.com/2019/11/ed-stetzer-and-laurie-nichols-on-john-crist-failure-and-warnings-to-heed-for-christian-leaders/.

3. John Nekrasov, "Opinion: A Response to John Crist—Why Our Commitment to Truth Demands that We Speak Out Against Abuse in the Church," *Liberty Champion*, November 11, 2019, https://www.liberty.edu/champion/2019/11/opinion-a-response-to-john-crist-why-our-commitment-to-truth-demands-that-we-speak-out-against-abuse-in-the-church/. *See also* Karen Swallow Prior (@KSPrior), "I'm proud of @LibertyU student @john_nekrasov for this excellent essay for @LUChampionNews," Twitter, November 13, 2019, 8:49 PM, https://twitter.com/KSPrior/status/1194794376163184640?s=20&t=MjgCYrdVRv9SWXcf0WUZug.

4. Kate Shellnut, "'Canceled' John Crist Has a New Book, Tour, and Comedy Special," *Christianity Today*, June 20, 2022, https://www.christianitytoday.com/news/2022/june/john-crist-comedy-special-youtube-book-tour-cancel-culture.html.

5. Bekah Eaker, "Responding to the Recent John Crist News," Hope Nation, November 6, 2019, https://hopenation.org/responding-to-the-recent-john-crist-news/.

6. God Is Grey, "When Your Abuser Is a Christian Public Figure | God Is Grey," YouTube video, July 20, 2020, https://www.youtube.com/watch?v=w-Bzze1Ighw.

7. Ashlee Rohnert (@ashleelovelee), "I was a victim of John Crist's predatory sexual, emotional and mental abuse and manipulation," Instagram, July 19, 2020, https://www.instagram.com/p/CC2PPi0J4Ou/?igshid=1jq0laupqpfv8.

8. Task Force Updates, "Resources for Caring for Survivors," Task Force Updates, n.d., https://web.archive.org/web/20220305005911/https://www.sataskforce.net/downloads-1.

9. ERLC, "What Is a Girl Worth?: A Conversation with Rachael Denhollander and Russell Moore on the Church's Abuse Crisis," Vimeo video, October 8, 2019, https://vimeo.com/showcase/6383529/video/365072432.

10. The White House Office of the Press Secretary, "Remarks by the President and Vice President at an Event for the Council on Women and Girls," The White House: President Barack Obama, January 22, 2014, https://obamawhitehouse.archives.gov/the-press-office/2014/01/22/remarks-president-and-vice-president-event-council-women-and-girls.

11. Elizabeth Nolan Brown, "How to Make More Victims of Campus Rape," *Reason*, June 18, 2015, https://reason.com/2015/06/18/how-to-make-more-victims-of-campus-rape/.

12. Scott Clement, "How Did the Post-Kaiser Survey Find 1 in 5 College Women Were Sexually Assaulted?," *Washington Post*, June 16, 2015, https://www.washingtonpost.com/news/grade-point/wp/2015/06/16/how-did-the-post-kaiser-survey-find-1-in-5-college-women-were-sexually-assaulted/.

13. Sofi Sinozich and Lynn Langton, "Rape and Sexual Assault Among College-Age Females, 1995–2013," Bureau of Justice Statistics, December 2014, https://bjs.ojp.gov/library/publications/rape-and-sexual-assault-among-college-age-females-1995-2013.

14. Edward Greer, "The Truth Behind Legal Dominance Feminism's Two Percent False Rape Claim Figure," *Loyola of Los Angeles Law Review* 33, no. 947 (2000), https://digitalcommons.lmu.edu/llr/vol33/iss3/3.

15. Here are the studies for these statistics: For 10 percent: D. Lisak et al., "False Allegations of Sexual Assault: An Analysis of Ten Years of Reported Cases," *Violence Against Women* 16, No. 12 (December 2010): 1318–34, doi: 10.1177/1077801210387747, PMID: 21164210; for 12 percent: Crown Prosecution Service, Great Britain, *A Report on the Joint Inspection into the Investigation and Prosecution of Cases Involving Allegations of Rape*, HM Crown Prosecution Service Inspectorate, HMCPSI/HMIC, 2002, Google Books, https://books.google.com/books/about/A_Report_on_the_Joint_Inspection_Into_th.html?id=zl_qxgEACAAJ; for 25 percent: Benjamin Baughman, *A Study of Rape Investigation Files Involving Female Survivors: A Comparison of Allegations Deemed False and Genuine* (doctoral thesis, University of Huddersfield, 2016), https://eprints.hud.ac.uk/id/eprint/27856/; for 41 percent: E. J. Kanin, "False Rape Allegations," *Archives of Sexual Behavior* 23 (1994): 81–92, https://doi.org/10.1007/BF01541619.

16. Craig Silverman, "Silverman: Examining Tara Reade's Sex Assault Allegations Against Joe Biden," *Colorado Sun*, May 11, 2020, https://coloradosun.com/2020/05/11/joe-biden-tara-reade-sexual-assault-opinion/.

17. Joanne Archambault, "So How Many Rape Reports Are False?," SATI e-News, March 29, 2004, https://web.archive.org/web/20221007041212/https://www.ncdsv.org/images/SoHowManyRapeReportsareFalse.pdf.

18. Henry Otgaar et al., The Return of the Repressed: The Persistent and Problematic Claims of Long-Forgotten Trauma, *Perspectives on Psychological Science*, 14, no. 6 (2019): 1072–95, https://doi.org/10.1177/1745691619862306.

19. Richard J. McNally, *Remembering Trauma* (Cambridge, MA: Harvard University Press), p. 275.

20. Emily Yoffe, "The Bad Science Behind Campus Response to Sexual Assault," *The Atlantic*, September 8, 2017, https://www.theatlantic.com/education/archive/2017/09/the-bad-science-behind-campus-response-to-sexual-assault/539211/.

21. Association of Title IX Administrators, "ATIXA Position Statement," Association of Title IX Administrators, August 16, 2019, https://cdn.atixa.org/website-media/atixa.org/wp-content/uploads/2019/08/20123741/2019-ATIXA-Trauma-Position-Statement-Final-Version.pdf.

22. False Memory Syndrome Foundation, "Frequently Asked Questions," False Memory Syndrome Foundation, n.d., https://www.fmsonline.org/?faq=faq.

23. Elizabeth Nolan Brown, "Bad Science Behind Campus-Rape Guidance Echoes '80s Trauma Myths," *Reason*, September 12, 2017, https://reason.com/2017/09/12/neurobiology-of-trauma/.

24. Janet Halley, "Trading the Megaphone for the Gavel in Title IX Enforcement," *Harvard Law Review* 128, no. 4 (February 2015), https://harvardlawreview.org/forum/vol-128/trading-the-megaphone-for-the-gavel-in-title-ix-enforcement-2/.

25. KC Johnson and Stuart Taylor Jr., *The Campus Rape Frenzy: The Attack on Due Process at America's Universities* (New York: Encounter Books, 2017).

26. Doe v. Purdue, United States Court of Appeals, Seventh Circuit, decided June 28, 2019.

https://law.justia.com/cases/federal/appellate-courts/ca7/17-3565/17-3565-2019-06-28.html

27. Johnson and Taylor, *The Campus Rape Frenzy*, p. 12.

28. Joe Cohn, "Biden Renews Obama's Attack on Campus Due Process," *Wall Street Journal*, June 23, 2022, https://www.wsj.com/articles/biden-renews-obama-attack-campus-due-process-title-ix-sexual-assault-harrasment-civil-rights-11656020306.

29. Emily Yoffe, "The College Rape Overcorrection," *Slate*, December 7, 2014, https://www.slate.com/articles/double_x/doublex/2014/12/college_rape_campus_sexual_assault_is_a_serious_problem_but_the_efforts.html.

30. Guidepost Solutions, *Report of the Independent Investigation: The Southern Baptist Convention Executive Committee's Response to Sexual Abuse Allegations and an Audit of the Procedures and Actions of the Credentials Committee*, Guidepost Solutions, May 15, 2022, https://www.documentcloud.org/documents/22028383-guidepost-investigation-of-the-southern-baptist-convention.

31. David Brooks, "The Dissenters Trying to Save Evangelicalism from Itself," *New York Times*, February 4, 2022, https://www.nytimes.com/2022/02/04/opinion/evangelicalism-division-renewal.html.

32. Emma Green, "Russell Moore and the Fight for the Soul of the Southern Baptist Convention," *The Atlantic*, March 14, 2017, https://www.theatlantic.com/politics/archive/2017/03/russell-moore-southern-baptist-convention/519540/.

33. Jill Waggoner, "2019 National Conference Theme Changes to Confront Sexual Abuse Crisis in the Church," ERLC, April 30, 2019, https://erlc.com/resource-library/press-releases/2019-national-conference-theme-changes-to-confront-sexual-abuse-crisis-in-the-church/.

34. Jack Jenkins, "At Caring Well Conference, SBC Leaders Hear Criticism of Abuse Response," Religion News Service, October 5, 2019, https://religionnews.com/2019/10/05/at-caring-well-conference-sbc-leaders-hear-criticism-of-abuse-response/.

35. Lyell's account: Jennifer Lyell, "My Story of Sexual Abuse and Initial Response in the SBC," lyellstatementonabuse.com, March 8, 2019, https://www.lyellstatementonabuse.com/abuse-disclosure-march-2019.

36. Baptist Press and Biblical Recorder Staff, "New Details of Former SBTS Prof's Resignation Alleged," *Biblical Recorder*, March 8, 2019, https://www.brnow.org/news/New-details-of-former-SBTS-prof-s-resignation-alle/.

37. *Baptist Press* subsequently removed the story from its website and apologized for the fact that, in its judgement, the story "did not accurately communicate the allegations made by Lyell." *See* Baptist Press Staff, "A Statement from Baptist Press," *Baptist Press*, October 15, 2019, https://www.baptistpress.com/resource-library/news/a-statement-from-baptist-press/.

38. This was reported by the author and based on sources on the executive committee, as detailed in Basham, "Southern Baptists' #MeToo Moment."

39. Bob Smietana, "SBC Report Calls 'Never-Trumper' Russell Moore's Agency a 'Significant Distraction' for Southern Baptists," Religion News Service, February 1, 2021, https://religionnews.com/2021/02/01/report-calls-agency-led-by-never-trumper-russell-moore-a-significant-distraction-for-southern-baptists/.

40. Ian Lovett, "Russell Moore, a Top Southern Baptist Convention Official, Resigns," *Wall Street Journal*, May 18, 2021, https://www.wsj.com/articles/russell-moore-a-top-southern-baptist-convention-official-resigns-11621391912.

41. Religion News Service, "Russell Moore to ERLC Trustees: 'They Want Me to Live in Psychological Terror,'" Religion News Service, June 2, 2021, https://religionnews.com/2021/06/02/russell-moore-to-erlc-trustees-they-want-me-to-live-in-psychological-terror/.

42. Religion News Service, "Russell Moore to ERLC Trustees."

43. Russell D. Moore, Letter to J. D. Greear, ERLC, May 31, 2021, https://baptistblog.files.wordpress.com/2021/06/rdm-final-letter.pdf.

44. Phillip Bethancourt, "SBC Whistleblower Report: Southern Baptist Leaders on Sexual Abuse in Their Own Words," Google Doc, June 10, 2021, https://docs.google.com/document/d/1pO2dwKkh7SI5N3V5jDcuSrv_QMHWquOtxxRICjzP0t4/edit.

45. Bob Smietana, "How the 'Apocalyptic' Southern Baptist Report Almost Didn't Happen," *Washington Post*, May 27, 2022, https://www.washingtonpost.com/religion/2022/05/27/how-apocalyptic-southern-baptist-report-almost-didnt-happen/; and Robert Downen, "Southern Baptists to Again Meet Under the Cloud of Abuse Scandals," *Houston Chronicle*, June 12, 2021, https://www.houstonchronicle.com/news/houston-texas/houston/article/Southern-Baptists-to-again-meet-under-the-cloud-16241733.php.

46. Brian Kaylor, "ERLC Trustee Complains About Leaked Letter in Leaked Letter," Word&Way, September 30, 2021, https://wordandway.org/2021/09/30/erlc-trustee-complains-about-leaked-letter-in-leaked-letter/.

47. Jonathan R. Whitehead, "Reference: Letters from Russell Moore; SBC EC and ERLC Resistance to Sexual Abuse Reforms," Letter, September 17, 2021, https://baptistandreflector.org/wp-content/uploads/2021/09/210917-JRW-Letter-to-TF-and-SBC-EC-3.pdf.

48. Rachael Denhollander (@R_Denhollander), "I promised Debbie two years ago that I would never forget," Twitter, June 15, 2021, 2:22 PM, https://twitter.com/r_denhollander/status/1404866872810651648?s=10&t=q-zwIFT8aJNWRKIZph43pQ.

49. Rachael Denhollander (@R_Denhollander), "The importance of waiving privilege is a question I get all the time from institutions in crisis—it's an issue in every case I work on," Twitter, September 20, 2021, 1:48 PM, https://twitter.com/r_denhollander/status/1440010101998432256?s=43&t=q-zwIFT8aJNWRKIZph43pQ.

50. Chantal Da Silva and Kurt Chirbas, "Southern Baptist Leaders Release Once-Secret List of Accused Abusers," NBC News, May 27, 2022, https://www.nbcnews.com/news/us-news/southern-baptist-leaders-release-secret-list-accused-abusers-rcna30807; and Eric Costanzo, "Southern Baptist Convention Has Met a Day of Reckoning. We Must Do Better to Stop Sexual Abuse," *USA Today*, May 29, 2022, https://www.usatoday.com/story/opinion/voices/2022/05/29/southern-baptist-convention-sex-abuse-report/9911082002/.

51. The Lead CNN (@TheLeadCNN), "An explosive investigative report accuses leaders of the Southern Baptist Convention of covering up 20 years of sexual abuse," Twitter, May 23, 2022, 6:49 PM, https://twitter.com/TheLeadCNN/status/1528870886580838403?s=20&t=53npbiicYEuBwyNQ-ZmsaA.

52. Sarah Pulliam Bailey, "Key Takeaways from the Bombshell Sex Abuse Report by

Southern Baptists," *Washington Post*, May 23, 2022, https://www.washingtonpost .com/religion/2022/05/23/sbc-report-sex-abuse-summary/.

53. Ruth Graham and Elizabeth Dias, "Southern Baptist Sex Abuse Report Stuns, from Pulpit to Pews," *New York Times*, May 23, 2022, https://www.nytimes.com/2022/05/23 /us/southern-baptist-sex-abuse-report.html.

54. David French, "The Southern Baptist Horror," *The Atlantic*, May 23, 2022, https:// www.theatlantic.com/ideas/archive/2022/05/southern-baptist-evangelical -allegations-cover-up/629954/.

55. Russell Moore, "This Is the Southern Baptist Apocalypse," *Christianity Today*, May 22, 2022, https://www.christianitytoday.com/ct/2022/may-web-only/southern-baptist -abuse-apocalypse-russell-moore.html.

56. "Abuse of Faith: A 'Chronicle' Investigation," *Houston Chronicle*, 2019, https://www .houstonchronicle.com/news/investigations/abuse-of-faith/.

57. Dylan Sharkey, "Report: 500 Sexual Misconduct Complaints Against Chicago Public School Employees," Illinois Policy, January 6, 2023, https://www.illinoispolicy.org /report-500-sexual -misconduct-complaints-against-chicago-public-school-employees/.

58. Elizabeth L. Jeglic, "Educator Sexual Misconduct Remains Prevalent in Schools," *Psychology Today*, May 17, 2023, https://www.psychologytoday.com/us/blog /protecting-children-from-sexual-abuse/202305/educator-sexual-misconduct -remains-prevalent-in.

59. Terry Gross, "How the Southern Baptist Convention Covered Up Its Widespread Sexual Abuse Scandal," *Fresh Air*, NPR, June 2, 2022, https://www.npr.org/2022/06 /02/1102621352/how-the-southern-baptist-convention-covered-up-its-widespread -sexual-abuse-scand; and Isaac Chotiner, "Decades of Sexual-Abuse Coverups in the Southern Baptist Convention," *The New Yorker*, May 26, 2022, https://www.newyorker .com/news/q-and-a/decades-of-sexual-abuse-coverups-in-the-southern-baptist -convention.

60. Megan Basham (@megbasham), "What the investigation found after looking hard," Twitter, January 28, 2024, 7:33 PM, https://twitter.com/megbasham/status /1751765525225418963

61. Staff Writer, "Guidepost Throws SBC and ARITF Under the Bus in Newest #Churchtoo Lawsuit Filings+ Says It Did NOT Investigate Lyell vs. Sills Claims," Protestia, July 17, 2023, https://protestia.com/2023/07/17/guidepost-throws-sbc-and-artif -under-the-bus-in-newest-churchtoo-lawsuit-filings-says-it-did-not-investigate-lyell -vs-sills-claims/.

62. Isidore The Farmer (@FarmerIsidore), "Is there somewhere that outlines what the abuse specifically was?," Twitter, October 2, 2021, 4:19 PM, https://twitter.com /FarmerIsidore/status/1444396695396265989?s=20.

63. Citygate Films, "Out of Darkness Story Introduction," Vimeo video, May 13, 2022, https://vimeo.com/709689139.

64. Megan Basham, "Southern Baptists' #MeToo Moment," *Daily Wire*, June 14, 2022, https://www.dailywire.com/news/southern-baptists-metoo-moment.

65. Guidepost Solutions, *Report of the Independent Investigation*.

66. Jennifer Lyell, "Update—May 28, 2022," Necessary Statements, May 28, 2022, https://www.lyellstatementonabuse.com/.

67. Robert Downen, "Explosive Report Alleged Sex Abuse by SBC Leader Johnny Hunt. His Accuser Still Waits for Justice," *Houston Chronicle*, June 13, 2022, https://www.houstonchronicle.com/news/investigations/article/sbc-sex-abuse-johnny-hunt-17236965.php.

68. Task Force Updates, "Updated Task Force Challenges and Formal Recommendations," Task Force Updates, June 8, 2022, https://web.archive.org/web/20230315120421/https://www.sataskforce.net/updates/task-force-challenges-and-formal-recommendations-sn54p.

69. Task Force Updates, "Updated Task Force Challenges and Formal Recommendations."

70. Rachael Denhollander (@R_Denhollander), "She's experienced severe trauma," Twitter, July 2, 2022, 9:32 AM, https://twitter.com/R_Denhollander/status/1543226200490926082.

71. Robert Downen, "Texas Supreme Court Rules Against Southern Baptist Leader Accused of Rape, a Win for Survivors," *Houston Chronicle*, April 12, 2022, https://www.houstonchronicle.com/news/houston-texas/houston/article/Texas-Supreme-Court-rules-against-Southern-17076007.php.

72. The Trinity Forum, "Online Conversation—How Much Is a Child Worth? Power, Protection, and Abuse Prevention with Rachael Denhollander," YouTube video, January 22, 2022, https://www.ttf.org/portfolios/online-conversation-with-rachael-denhollander/.

73. Brandon Porter, "Executive Committee Sets Up Hotline for Abuse Claims," *Baptist Press*, May 25, 2022, https://www.baptistpress.com/resource-library/news/executive-committee-sets-up-hotline-for-abuse-claims/.

74. Capstone Report, "Denhollander Has Conflicts of Interest in Relationship with SBC Abuse Hotline," Capstone Report, January 8, 2023, https://capstonereport.com/2023/01/08/denhollander-has-conflicts-of-interest-in-relationship-with-sbc-abuse-hotline/40693/.

75. For a complete and compelling account of the Kavanaugh nomination process, see Carrie Severino and Mollie Hemingway, *Justice on Trial: The Kavanaugh Confirmation and the Future of the Supreme Court* (Washington, DC: Regnery Publishing, 2019).

76. Rachael Denhollander, "I'm a Sexual Assault Survivor. And a Conservative. The Kavanaugh Hearings Were Excruciating," Vox, October 16, 2018, https://www.vox.com/first-person/2018/10/15/17968534/kavanaugh-vote-supreme-court-sexual-assault-christine-blasey-ford.

77. Rachael Denhollander (@R_Denhollander), "These are incredibly important dynamics to understand with abuse," Twitter, July 2, 2022, 9:11 AM, https://twitter.com/R_Denhollander/status/1543220904662106113?ref_src=twsrc%5Etfw%7Ctwcamp%5Etweetembed%7Ctwterm%5E1543220904662106113%7Ctwgr%5Eb38e-874ab0b48877b91154f40767f952ba31dc7d%7Ctwcon%5Es1_&ref_url=https%3A%2F%2Fcapstonereport.com%2F2022%2F07%2F13%2Fsbc-abuse-expert-rachael-denhollander-sided-with-amber-heard%2F38482%2F. *See also* Rasmussen Reports, "More Americans Believe Johnny Depp," Rasmussen Reports, April 26, 2022, https://www.rasmussenreports.com/public_content/lifestyle/entertainment/april_2022/more_americans_believe_johnny_depp.

78. Stephanie Martin, "At PCA General Assembly, Voters Address Gender, Sexuality, and

Sexual Abuse," Church Leaders, June 23, 2023, https://churchleaders.com/news/453673
-presbyterian-church-in-america-general-assembly-gender-sexuality-abuse.html/2.

79. Rachael Denhollander (@R_Denhollander), "Grateful for this step and privileged to be
a part of it," Twitter, July 11, 2022, 7:10 APM, https://twitter.com/R_Denhollander
/status/1546632934760878080?s=20. *See also* Timothy Cockes, "ARITF Releases
Video Interview with Samantha Kilpatrick of Guidepost's 'Faith-Based Solutions,'"
Baptist Press, March 2, 2023, https://www.baptistpress.com/resource-library/news
/aritf-releases-video-interview-with-samantha-kilpatrick-of-guideposts-faith-based
-solutions/; and Chad Burchett, "Southeastern Launches Mandatory Sexual Abuse
Prevention and Response Course," Southeastern Baptist Theological Seminary, July 11,
2022, https://www.sebts.edu/news-and-events/headlines/2022/07/sum22_saprc/.

80. Church Cares, "Becoming a Church that Cares Well for the Abused: About the Training Curriculum," Church Cares, n.d., https://churchcares.com/.

81. Bob Smietana, "Todd Benkert leaves SBC abuse task force over conflict over pastor's
restoration," Religion News Service, February, 17, 2023, https://religionnews
.com/2023/02/17/todd-benkert-leaves-sbc-abuse-task-force-after-conflict-with
-church-that-platformed-johnny-hunt/.

82. Laura Kipnis, *Unwanted Advances: Sexual Paranoia Comes to Campus* (New York: HarperCollins, 2017), Kindle Edition.

83. Ed Kilgore, "The Southern Baptist Church Is Going to Hell in a Handbasket," *New York
Magazine*, June 9, 2021, https://nymag.com/intelligencer/2021/06/southern-baptist
-convention-is-going-to-hell-in-a-handbasket.html. *See also* Yonat Shimron, "The Cost
of Coming Forward: 1 Survivor's Life After #MeToo," Associated Press, November 21,
2019, https://apnews.com/article/religion-baptist-north-carolina-ap-top-news
-greensboro-4b72663ac86d9c0dd195e35e796fbbde.

84. Laura Bullard, "The #ChurchToo Movement Isn't Just About Gender," Jezebel,
June 7, 2018, https://jezebel.com/the-churchtoo-movement-isn-t-just-about-
gender-1826431915. *See also* Sarah Stankorb, "The Southern Baptist Church Ignored Its
Abuse Crisis. She Exposed It," Vice, January 4, 2023, https://www.vice.com/en/article
/qjk9wm/the-southern-baptist-church-ignored-its-abuse-crisis-she-exposed-it.

85. Liam Adams, "Judge Dismisses Claims in High-Profile Suit Against Former SBC
Leader Alleging Victim Intimidation," *The Tennessean*, March 29, 2023, https://www
.tennessean.com/story/news/religion/2023/03/29/paige-patterson-southwestern
-seminary-sbc-abuse/70057334007/.

86. Jayson Larson, "Guidepost Removes Paragraph that Included Out-of-Context Richards
Quote," *Southern Baptist Texan*, June 8, 2022, https://www.texanonline.net/articles
/national/guidepost-removes-paragraph-that-included-out-of-context-richards-quote/.

87. Bob Smietana, "Guidepost Report: Bryan Loritts Mishandled Abuse Allegations at
Former Church but Did Not Cover Them Up," Religion News Service, March 31, 2021,
https://religionnews.com/2021/03/31/report-bryan-loritts-abuse-allegations
-fellowship-summit-church-greear-guidepost-former-church-cover-up/. *See also* Julie
Roys, "Victim and Former Insider Say Bryan Loritts Covered Up Sex Crimes; Dispute
Statements by J. D. Greear and Summit Church," *The Roys Report*, June 9, 2020, https://
julieroys.com/victim-dispute-statements-by-j-d-greear-summit-church/.

88. Julie Roys, "Opinion: Bryan Loritts Is Not 'Qualified for Ministry' and Report Doesn't

Clear Him of Wrongdoing," *The Roys Report*, March 29, 2021, https://julieroys.com/opinion-bryan-loritts-is-not-qualified-for-ministry-report-doesnt-clear-him-of-wrongdoing/.

89. See page B5 of the *Courier-Journal* from Louisville, Kentucky, January 9, 2004, https://www.newspapers.com/newspage/180156990/.

90. WLKY News, "Former Local Teacher Pleads Guilty to Sex Abuse," WLKY News, August 3, 2004, https://www.wlky.com/article/former-local-teacher-pleads-guilty-to-sex-abuse/3714048.

91. Joni Hannigan, "News Analysis: Was SBC #MeToo Resolution on Abuse a Band Aid [*sic*] for Larger Issues?" *The Truth Is in Crisis*, June 26, 2018, https://truthisincrisis.wordpress.com/2018/06/26/news-analysis-was-sbc-metoo-resolution-on-abuse-a-band-aid-for-larger-issues/. *See also* "'Kevin' Ezell's Warning Threatening to Sue Me for Libel After My SBC Story," *The Truth Is in Crisis*, February 3, 2019, https://truthisincrisis.wordpress.com/2019/02/03/a-menacing-message/.

92. Rebecca Keegan and Tatiana Siegel, "How Time's Up Woes Are Overshadowing Its Mission Beyond Hollywood," *The Hollywood Reporter*, September 9, 2021, https://www.hollywoodreporter.com/business/business-news/times-up-initiative-legal-defense-fund-hollywood-scandal-1235008591/.

93. Gene Maddaus, "Time's Up Dissolves Advisory Board that Included Natalie Portman, Jessica Chastain and Reese Witherspoon," *Variety*, September 9, 2021, https://variety.com/2021/film/news/times-up-advisory-board-natalie-portman-jessica-chastain-reese-witherspoon-1235060159/.

94. Jeremy Bauer-Wolf, "Title IX Lawsuits Have Skyrocketed in Recent Years, Analysis Shows," Higher Ed Dive, January 6, 2020, https://www.highereddive.com/news/title-ix-lawsuits-have-skyrocketed-in-recent-years-analysis-shows/569881/.

95. Sarah Brown, "Lawsuits from Students Accused of Sex Assault Cost Many Colleges More than $200,000," *The Chronicle of Higher Education*, August 11, 2017, https://www.chronicle.com/article/lawsuits-from-students-accused-of-sex-assault-cost-many-colleges-more-than-200-000/.

96. Tobin Perry, "2019 Texas Law Seen as a Model to Protect Churches Against Sexual Abuse Predators," Christian Index, October 17, 2022, https://christianindex.org/stories/2019-texas-law-seen-as-a-model-to-protect-churches-against-sexual-abuse-predators,35757.

CHAPTER 8: None Dare Call It Sin: LGBTQ in the Church

1. T. R. Reid, "Anglican Church Leaders Condemn Homosexual Activity," *Washington Post*, August 6, 1998, https://www.washingtonpost.com/archive/politics/1998/08/06/anglican-church-leaders-condemn-homosexual-activity/cf0b18a5-448e-4a87-883a-cdcb1a9fc04e/.

2. Kristjan Archer and Justin McCarthy, "U.S. Catholics Have Backed Same-Sex Marriage Since 2011," Gallup, October 23, 2020, https://news.gallup.com/poll/322805/catholics-backed-sex-marriage-2011.aspx.

3. Ligonier Ministries, "The State of Theology," September 16, 2022, https://www.ligonier.org/posts/2022-state-of-theology

4. Outreach 100, "2019 Largest Participating Churches," Outreach 100, n.d., https://outreach100.com/largest-churches-in-america/2019.

5. Shelia Poole, "North Point Is Named Nation's Second-Largest Church in U.S.," *Atlanta-Journal Constitution*, October 14, 2017, https://www.ajc.com/lifestyles/north-point-named-nation-second-largest-church/f9Y0zcx1D0LqsBqEudPJKO/.

6. Michael Foust, "Andy Stanley's Stance on Homosexuality Questioned," *Baptist Press*, May 2, 2012, https://www.baptistpress.com/resource-library/news/andy-stanleys-stance-on-homosexuality-questioned/.

7. A report here: Ian M. Giatti, "Andy Stanley Says Gay Churchgoers 'Have More Faith than a Lot of You,'" *Christian Post*, January 25, 2024, https://www.christianpost.com/news/andy-stanley-gay-churchgoers-have-more-faith-than-a-lot-of-you.html. The sermon has been removed from the church website: https://northpoint.org/messages/christian/part-5. Several snippets of the sermon are preserved here: Shelby Bowen, "What Did Andy Stanley Actually Say in Sermon Clip on Gay Christians?," *Charisma News*, January 31, 2023, https://www.charismanews.com/culture/91357-what-did-andy-stanley-actually-say-in-sermon-clip-on-gay-christians. Of interest may be J. D. Greear's response to Stanley's sermon here: J. D. Greear, "Downplaying the Sin of Homosexuality Won't Win the Next Generation," *The Gospel Coalition*, February 3, 2024, https://www.thegospelcoalition.org/article/downplay-homosexual-sin-generation/.

8. Foust, "Andy Stanley's Stance on Homosexuality Questioned."

9. Shelby Bowen, "What Did Andy Stanley Actually Say in Sermon Clip on Gay Christians?" *Charisma News*, January 31, 2023, https://www.charismanews.com/culture/91357-what-did-andy-stanley-actually-say-in-sermon-clip-on-gay-christians.

10. "U.S. Foundation Funding for LGBTQ Issues Fell in 2019–20, Study Finds," *Philanthropy News Digest*, July 3, 2022, https://philanthropynewsdigest.org/news/u.s.-foundation-funding-for-lgbtq-issues-fell-in-2019-20-study-finds. *See also* Lyle Matthew Kan, "LGBTQ Philanthropy Since Stonewall: The Top Ten Funders of All Time," Funders for LGBTQ Issues, June 27, 2019, https://lgbtfunders.org/newsposts/lgbtq-philanthropy-since-stonewall-the-top-ten-funders-of-all-time/.

11. Rebecca Voelkel, "A Time to Build Up," National Gay and Lesbian Task Force, 2009, https://www.arcusfoundation.org/wp-content/uploads/2009/01/A-Time-To-Build-Up-Voelkel-2009.pdf.

12. Sarah Johnson, "The Arcus Foundation Focuses on Outreach to Faith Communities," *Inside Philanthropy,* October 13, 2021, https://web.archive.org/web/20151009074449/https://www.insidephilanthropy.com/lgbt/2013/10/21/the-arcus-foundation-focuses-on-outreach-to-faith-communitie.html.

13. Arcus Foundation, "Supporting Safety and Progressive Faith Voices to Secure LGBTQ Social Justice," Arcus Foundation, February 23, 2023, https://www.arcusfoundation.org/supporting-safety-and-progressive-faith-voices-to-secure-lgbtq-social-justice/#main.

14. Here is a breakdown: for 2018: $303,404, https://www.arcusfoundation.org/wp-content/uploads/2019/10/AF-2018-990-PF-Final-for-website.pdf; for 2017: $221,528, https://www.arcusfoundation.org/wp-content/uploads/2018/10/AF-2017-990-PF-Final-for-website.pdf; for 2016: $300,328, https://www.arcusfoundation.org/wp-content/uploads/2017/12/AF-2016-990-PF.pdf; for 2015: $402,158, https://www.arcusfoundation.org/wp-content/uploads/2016/11/AF-2015-990PF-CHAR500.pdf;

for 2014: $379,909: https://www.arcusfoundation.org/wp-content/uploads/2015/10/AF-2014-Form-990PF-signed.pdf; for 2013: $400,000, https://www.arcusfoundation.org/wp-content/uploads/2014/11/AF-2013-Form-990-PF-signed.pdf.

15. Reconciling Ministries Network, "Who We Are—Reconciling Ministries," Reconciling Ministries Network, October 5, 2023, https://rmnetwork.org/who-we-are/.

16. Arcus Foundation, Form 990-PF for Calendar Year 2014, https://www.arcusfoundation.org/wp-content/uploads/2015/10/AF-2014-Form-990PF-signed.pdf.

17. Matthew Vines, "About—Matthew Vines," Matthew Vines, December 17, 2023, https://matthewvines.com/about/.

18. See Arcus Foundation Form 990-PF documents for the following years: 2014: https://www.arcusfoundation.org/wp-content/uploads/2015/10/AF-2014-Form-990PF-signed.pdf; for 2015: https://www.arcusfoundation.org/wp-content/uploads/2016/11/AF-2015-990PF-CHAR500.pdf; for 2016: https://www.arcusfoundation.org/wp-content/uploads/2017/12/AF-2016-990-PF.pdf; for 2017: https://www.arcusfoundation.org/wp-content/uploads/2018/10/AF-2017-990-PF-Final-for-website.pdf; for 2018: https://www.arcusfoundation.org/wp-content/uploads/2019/10/AF-2018-990-PF-Final-for-website.pdf.

19. Arcus Foundation, "LGBT Inclusion Within World's Largest Religions Is a Top Focus of Arcus' Spring 2016 Grants," Arcus Foundation, March 21, 2016, https://www.arcusfoundation.org/lgbt-inclusion-within-worlds-largest-religions-top-focus-arcus-spring-2016-grants/.

20. This language is no longer on the page, but it was used to describe the organization in Vines's bio for this article: Matthew Vines, "10 Reasons God Loves Gay Christians," *Time*, July 11, 2014, https://time.com/2842044/gay-christians/.

21. Matthew Vines, "The Gay Debate: The Bible and Homosexuality," YouTube video, March 10, 2012, https://www.youtube.com/watch?v=ezQjNJUSraY&t=2s.

22. Matthew Vines, *God and the Gay Christian: The Biblical Case in Support of Same-Sex Relationships* (Colorado Springs: Convergent Books, 2015).

23. Scott Hinsche, "Review of Matthew Vines' *God and the Gay Christian*," *Christian Post*, June 5, 2014, https://www.christianpost.com/news/review-of-matthew-vines-god-and-the-gay-christian.html.

24. Greg McDonald et al., *Embracing the Journey: A Christian Parents' Blueprint to Loving Your LGBTQ Child* (New York: Howard Books/Atria, 2020).

25. Mark Wingfield, "Couple Helps Parents of LGBTQ Kids Come Out of the Closet," *Baptist News Global*, July 30, 2020, https://www.baptistnews.com/article/couple-helps-parents-of-lgbtq-kids-come-out-of-the-closet/.

26. Willets's full blurb for the book: "A compelling description of a challenge faced by more and more people in the modern church: how to love God and their gay child without losing their faith or their relationship with either. Each page is filled with striking honesty and first-century courage. An important and helpful resource."—Bill Willits, Executive Director of Ministry Environments, North Point Ministries.

27. Embracing the Journey, "Greg and Lynn's Story," YouTube video, November 17, 2022, https://www.youtube.com/watch?v=KvEwQbhjg0s.

28. Embracing the Journey, "Greg and Lynn's Story."

29. Embracing the Journey, "Greg and Lynn's Story."

30. Greg McDonald et al., *Embracing the Journey: A Christian Parents' Blueprint to Loving Your LGBTQ Child* (New York: Howard Books/Atria, 2020), p. 214.

31. McDonald et al., *Embracing the Journey*, p. 193.

32. McDonald et al., *Embracing the Journey*, p. 198.

33. McDonald et al., *Embracing the Journey*, p. 70.

34. Rosaria Champagne Butterfield, *Five Lies of Our Anti-Christian Age* (Wheaton, IL: Crossway, 2023).

35. Matthew Vines, "The Reformation Project: Training Christians to Eradicate Homophobia from the Church," *HuffPost*, December 16, 2017, https://www.huffpost.com /entry/the-reformation-project-christians-homophobia_b_2790039.

36. The Reformation Project, "About," The Reformation Project, n.d., https://web.archive .org/web/20130404101458/http:/www.reformationproject.org/about. (Link removed).

37. Embracing the Journey, "Your Child's Spiritual Walk," *Embracing the Journey* (newsletter), September 2021, https://www.embracingthejourney.org/september-2021.html.

38. McDonald et al., *Embracing the Journey*, pp. 192, 70. The Q Christian Network returns the favor here: Q Christian Fellowship, "Family Resources," qchristian.org, https:// www.qchristian.org/resources/family.

39. Arcus Foundation, "Spring Grantees Highlight Education, Litigation, and Religious Voices as Ways to Amplify LGBT Advocacy Work," Arcus Foundation, April 6, 2018, https://www.arcusfoundation.org/spring-grantees-highlight-education-litigation -religious-voices-ways-amplify-lgbt-advocacy-work/.

40. Renovus, "Team," Renovus, https://www.renovus.org/team.

41. The video can be found here: Staff Writer, "Exclusive! Andy Stanley's Church Hosts and Promotes Pro-LBGTQ+ Ministry (Part 1)," Protestia, January 26, 2023, https:// protestia.com/2023/01/26/exclusive-andy-stanleys-church-hosts-and-promotes-pro -lbgtq-ministry-part-1/.

42. Embracing the Journey Inc., Form 990PF for Fiscal Year Ending Dec. 2021, ProPublica, 2021, https://projects.propublica.org/nonprofits/organizati ons/474919398/202242039349300914/IRS990.

43. Mark and Jill Savage, "Empty Nest, Marriage, and Loving Your LGBTQ Kids," jillsavage .org, n.d., https://jillsavage.org/welcome-family-life-listeners/.

44. Embracing the Journey, "Thank You," *Embracing the Journey* (newsletter), Holiday Edition 2021, https://www.embracingthejourney.org/holiday-edition-2021.html.

45. "Shauna Habel-Morgan Explains the Moment She Discovered that There . . ." Facebook video, December 8, 2020, https://fb.watch/q2r95rWX50/.

46. Staff Writer, "Radical Pro-LGBTQ+ Activist Is Running SBC Megachurch's Family Ministry," Protestia, February 5, 2023, https://protestia.com/2023/02/05/radical-pro -lgbtq-activist-is-running-sbcs-megachurchs-family-ministry/.

47. Embracing the Journey, "Thank You."

48. Megan Basham (@megbasham), "Here is Saddleback pastor Chris Clark on The Reformation Project's speaker page," Twitter, April 13, 2023, 7:16 PM, https://twitter.com /megbasham/status/1646653705536565248. *See also* https://web.archive.org

/web/20230202172945/https:/reformationproject.org/2021-conference/parents/speakers/. (Link removed).

49. The Dissenter (@disntr), "Saddleback 'pastors,' Andy and Stacie Wood say they 'have no idea' if homosexuals who come to Christ after they get married should get divorced because God hates divorce . . . 'It's a gray area,'" Twitter, February 7, 2023, 1:26 PM, https://twitter.com/disntr/status/1623025474807992363?s=20.

50. Megan Cornwell, "Rick Warren: 'I'm Embarrassed by a Lot of Things Done in the Name of US Evangelicalism,'" *Premier Christianity,* May 2, 2023, https://www.premierchristianity.com/interviews/rick-warren-im-embarrassed-by-a-lot-of-things-done-in-the-name-of-us-evangelicalism/15370.article.

51. Eve Tushnet, "Romoeroticism," *Crisis Magazine,* June 29, 2009, https://crisismagazine.com/opinion/romoeroticism. *See also* Grant Hartley (@TheGrantHartley), "Happy #NationalComingOutDay!," Twitter, October 11, 2019, 3:50 PM, https://twitter.com/TheGrantHartley/status/1182745204706742274?ref_src=twsrc%5Etfw%7Ctwcamp%5Etweetembed%7Ctwterm%5E1182745204706742274%7Ctwgr%5Eda762effe70e0e4e4341777eafa0420ace0f3200%7Ctwcon%5Es1_c10&ref_url=https%3A%2F%2Fevangelicaldarkweb.org%2Fgrant-hartley%2F.

52. Shawn Mathis, "Revoice Gay-Straight Friends Planning a Life Together," *The Aquila Report,* April 2, 2021, https://theaquilareport.com/revoice-gay-straight-friends-planning-a-life-together/

53. Tyler Streckert, "'You Can't Just Tell Us What to Believe,'" *Christianity Today,* October 6, 2017, https://www.christianitytoday.com/ct/2017/october-web-only/you-cant-just-tell-us-what-to-believe.html.

54. Grant Hartley (@TheGrantHartley), "Hey y'all, I have seen some misunderstandings afoot lately, so to clarify," Twitter, February 5, 2022, 7:37 AM, https://twitter.com/TheGrantHartley/status/1489941262761443329.

55. Gregory Coles, "Understanding Celibate Partnerships and Committed Friendships," Center for Faith, Sexuality and Gender, September 28, 2022, https://www.centerforfaith.com/blog/understanding-celibate-partnerships-and-committed-friendships.

56. J. D. Greear, "When Talking with a Transgender Person, Which Pronoun Should You Use?," J. D. Greear Ministries, November 18, 2019, https://jdgreear.com/podcasts/when-talking-with-a-transgender-person-which-pronoun-should-you-use/.

57. Center for Faith, Sexuality and Gender, endorsements webpage, https://www.centerforfaith.com/about/endorsements.

58. Eve Tushnet, "Hope Is the Thing with Feather Boas: Two Small Gay Catholic Thoughts," Patheos, January 30, 2023, https://www.patheos.com/blogs/evetushnet/2023/01/hope-is-the-thing-with-feather-boas-two-small-gay-catholic-thoughts.html.

59. Nate Collins, "What Transgender People Need from Conservative Christians," *Christianity Today,* June 22, 2018, https://www.christianitytoday.com/ct/2018/june-web-only/andrew-walker-transgender-debate-ryan-anderson-harry-sally.html. *See also* "Nate Collins," *The Gospel Coalition,* n.d., https://www.thegospelcoalition.org/profile/nate-collins/.

60. Timothy Keller, "Greg Johnson's Still Time to Care provides a good history & critique of the older ex-gay movement which was a form of the 'prosperity gospel.' It's important that we know its history and, in light of its implosion and ask: now what?," Facebook,

April 26, 2022, https://www.facebook.com/TimKellerNYC/posts
/538381464310230/.

61. Nate Collins (@NateCollins), "The Nashville Statement is 5 years old today. Here's how
to repent from signing it," Twitter, August 29, 2022, 10:27 AM, https://twitter.com
/NateCollins/status/1564258344994578433?s=20.

62. Greg Johnson, *Still Time to Care* (Grand Rapids, MI: Zondervan, 2021), p. 190.

63. Greg Johnson, *On Mission with the LGBTQ+ Community*, p. 4, https://drive.google.com
/file/d/1gu0ZH6igfWes0vypOUnEtnTEMigw9fVu/view?fbclid=IwAR1RfCSB3r1m
_cq5J5FdlRiAvJ8qGUMzi5QFBwJ8eMKncRtbWikIxTQiIUc&pli=1.

64. Wesley Hill, "Revoice and a Vocation of 'Yes'" *First Things*, August 7, 2018, https://
www.firstthings.com/web-exclusives/2018/08/revoice-and-a-vocation-of-yes.

65. Revoice, "Redeeming Queer Culture: An Adventure," YouTube video, February 19,
2019, https://www.youtube.com/watch?v=ijGQEJOHMP8.

66. Mary Jackson and Todd Vician, "Identity Crisis," *World,* October 21, 2022, https://
wng.org/articles/identity-crisis-1666367393.

67. Christianity Today, "Wayfaring: Wesley Hill," *Christianity Today*, n.d., https://www
.christianitytoday.com/ct/opinion/columnists/wayfaring/.

68. Kathryn Post, "Traditional 'Side B' LGBTQ Christians Experience a Renaissance,"
Religion News Service, November 5, 2021, https://religionnews.com/2021/11/05
/traditional-side-b-lgbtq-christians-experience-a-renaissance/.

69. Scott Sauls, "Thoughts on Revoice, Unnecessary Division, and the PCA," scottsauls
.com, http://web.archive.org/web/20230419061433/https://scottsauls.com
/blog/2019/06/21/thoughts-on-revoice-unnecessary-division-and-the-pca/.

70. Chris Bolt, "Revisiting Revoice: The Need for This Discussion," Founders Ministries,
https://founders.org/articles/revisiting-revoice-the-need-for-this-discussion/.

71. *The Gospel Coalition*, "Rachel Gilson," *The Gospel Coalition*, n.d., https://www
.thegospelcoalition.org/profile/rachel-gilson/.

72. Revoice, "Revoice19 Talks: Workshop—Rachel Gilson: Mission and Sexuality," Revoice, n.d., https://watch.revoice.org/revoice19-talks-1/season:5/videos/friday
-workshop-mission-and-sexuality-rachel-gilson.

73. Carson's blurb can be found among the endorsements here: InterVarsity Press, "Single,
Gay, Christian: A Personal Journey of Faith and Sexual Identity," ivpress.com, https://
www.ivpress.com/single-gay-christian.

74. Greg Johnson, "I Used to Hide My Shame. Now I Take Shelter Under the Gospel,"
Christianity Today, May 20, 2019, https://www.christianitytoday.com/ct/2019/may
-web-only/greg-johnson-hide-shame-shelter-gospel-gay-teenager.html.

75. Anugrah Kumar, "PCA Church Explains Why It Allowed Transgender Festival Performance on Its Property," *Christian Post*, March 7, 2020, https://www.christianpost.com
/news/pca-church-explains-why-it-allowed-transgender-festival-performance-on-its
-property.html.

76. Identity in Christ Conference with Tim and Kathy Keller, Living Out, June 21, 2018,
https://www.livingout.org/events/4/identity-in-christ-conference-with-tim-and
-kathy-keller

77. Living Out, "How Biblically Inclusive Is Your Church? The Living Out Church Audit," https://www.livingout.org/resources/articles/65/how-biblically-inclusive-is-your -church-the-living-out-church-audit

78. Bryan Chapell et al., *Report of the Ad Interim Committee on Human Sexuality*, Forty-Seventh General Assembly of the Presbyterian Church in America Ad Interim Committee on Human Sexuality, May 2020, https://pcaga.org/wp-content/uploads/2020/05 /AIC-Report-to-48th-GA-5-28-20-1.pdf.

79. Tim Keller, "What's Happening in the PCA?," *ByFaith*, March 21, 2022, https:// byfaithonline.com/whats-happening-in-the-pca/.

80. Jude 3 and the PCA, "PCA Report on Human Sexuality," https://jude3pca.org/the-pca -report-on-human-sexuality/.

81. Timothy Keller (1950–2023) (@timkellernyc), "Thread: I know some PCA presbyteries are discussing the overtures before us this month," Twitter, January 25, 2022, 7:08 PM, https://twitter.com/timkellernyc/status/1486128754711801858?s=20.

82. Keller, "What's Happening in the PCA?"

83. Timothy Keller, "Greg Johnson's Still Time to Care provides a good history & critique of the older ex-gay movement which was a form of the 'prosperity gospel.' It's important that we know its history and, in light of its implosion and [*sic*] ask: now what?"

84. Becket Cook, "Clarification and Retraction re: Greg Johnson's Book," *Becket Cook* (blog), April 8, 2022, https://web.archive.org/web/20220408183856/https://www .becketcook.com/side-b-retraction.

85. Becket Cook and Brett McCracken, "From Gay to Gospel: The Fascinating Story of Becket Cook," *The Gospel Coalition*, August 23, 2019, https://www.thegospelcoalition .org/article/gay-gospel-becket-cook/.

86. Rosaria Butterfield, "Why I No Longer Use Transgender Pronouns—and Why You Shouldn't, Either," Reformation21, April 3, 2023, https://www.reformation21.org /blog/why-i-no-longer-use-transgender-pronouns-and-why-you-shouldnt-either.

87. Bonnie Kristian, "Rosaria Butterfield Issues Five Battle Cries for the Church Militant," *Christianity Today*, September 22, 2023, https://www.christianitytoday.com/ct/2023 /september-web-only/rosaria-butterfield-five-lies-anti-christian-age.html.

88. D. A. Carson, "But That's Just Your Interpretation!" *Themelios* 44 (2019): 425–32, "https://urldefense.com/v3/__https://www.thegospelcoalition.org/themelios/article /but-thats-just-your-interpretation/.

89. Celeste Gracey and Jeremy Weber, "World Vision: Why We're Hiring Gay Christians in Same-Sex Marriages," *Christianity Today*, March 24, 2014, https://www.christianitytoday .com/ct/2014/march-web-only/world-vision-why-hiring-gay-christians-same-sex -marriage.html.

90. Ruth Graham, "Major Evangelical Adoption Agency Will Now Serve Gay Parents Nationwide," *New York Times*, March 1, 2021, https://www.nytimes.com/2021/03/01 /us/bethany-adoption-agency-lgbtq.html.

91. For each of these schools: Bekah McNeel, "Baylor Grants First Charter to LGBTQ Student Group," *Texas Monthly*, April 27, 2022, https://www.texasmonthly.com /news-politics/baylor-prism-lgbtq-students/; Morgan Lee, "Azusa Pacific Drops

Ban on Same-Sex Student Relationships, Again," *Christianity Today*, March 19, 2019, https://www.christianitytoday.com/news/2019/march/azusa-pacific-university-apu -reversal-gay-relationships.html; Wheaton College, "Refuge," Wheaton College, n.d., https://www.wheaton.edu/life-at-wheaton/student-development-offices/student -wellness/refuge/; Yonat Shimron, "Calvin University Board Votes to Keep Faculty Who Disagree with Stand on Sex," Religion News Service, November 2, 2022, https://religionnews.com/2022/11/02/calvin-university-board-votes-to-keep-faculty -who-disagree-with-stand-on-sex/.

92. Beth Moore, "Why I Removed Some of My Commentary from a Chapter of Praying God's Word," *Living Proof Ministries* (blog), July 6, 2019, https://blog.lproof .org/2019/07/why-i-removed-some-of-my-commentary-from-a-chapter-of-praying -gods-word.html.

93. Beth Moore (@BethMooreLPM), "Nearly makes me cry, David," Twitter, July 5, 2019, 9:49 AM, https://twitter.com/BethMooreLPM/status/1147140392879566848?s=20.

94. Timothy Dalrymple, "Is It Time for Evangelicals to Stop Opposing Gay Marriage?," Patheos, November 26, 2012, https://www.patheos.com/blogs/philosophicalfragments /2012/11/26/is-it-time-for-evangelicals-to-stop-opposing-gay-marriage/.

95. Megan Briggs, "J. D. Greear: Paul's Teaching on Homosexuality Might Surprise You," Church Leaders, February 4, 2019, https://churchleaders.com/pastors/pastor -articles/343307-homosexuality-in-the-bible-jd-greear-apostle-paul.html/2.

96. Kara Bettis Carvalho, "Should I Offer My Pronouns?," *Christianity Today*, August 14, 2023, https://www.christianitytoday.com/ct/2023/september/should-christians -offer-preferred-gender-pronouns.html. *See also* Gregory Coles, "What Pronouns Should Christians Use for Transgender People?," Center for Faith, Sexuality and Gen-der, n.d., https://www.centerforfaith.com/resources/pastoral-papers/11-what -pronouns-should-christians-use-for-transgender-people.

97. Delano Squires, "Squires: 'Pride' Has Infiltrated the Church. Pastors Must Decide Whether They Will Stand for the Cross or Hide in the Closet," Blaze, March 17, 2023, https://www.theblaze.com/fearless/squires-pride-has-infiltrated-the-church-pastors -must-decide-whether-they-will-stand-for-the-cross-or-hide-in-the-closet.

98. Greear, "When Talking with a Transgender Person, Which Pronoun Should You Use?"

99. Nick Eicher, "Culture Friday—J. D. Greear and 'Pronoun Hospitality,'" *World*, Janu-ary 17, 2020, https://wng.org/podcasts/culture-friday-j-d-greear-and-pronoun -hospitality-1617918243.

100. Eliel Cruz, "A Fresh Gay Face Is Shaking Things Up in Evangelical Land," *The Advo-cate*, January 27, 2016, https://www.advocate.com/religion/2016/1/27/fresh-gay-face -shaking-things-evangelical-land#toggle-gdpr.

101. The Reformation Project, "Pastors in Process," The Reformation Project, n.d., https:// reformationproject.org/pastors-in-process-2022/.

102. Kirsten Powers, "My Complicated Feelings About Tim Keller," *Changing the Channel with Kirsten Powers* (newsletter), May 24, 2023, https://kirstenpowers.substack. com/p/my-complicated-feelings-about-tim.

103. Todd Pruitt, "Doctrinal Latitude and the PCA," Reformation21, March 14, 2022, https://www.reformation21.org/blog/doctrinal-latitude-and-the-pca.

Conclusion

1. Sir Thomas Malory, *Le Morte d'Arthur* (London: William Caxton, 1485).

2. Malory, *Le Morte d'Arthur*.

3. John F. MacArthur, *The Vanishing Conscience* (Nashville, TN: Thomas Nelson, 2005)

4. Matthew Loftus, "Is Addiction a Disease? Yes, and Much More," *Christianity Today*, November 23, 2016, https://www.christianitytoday.com/ct/2016/december/is-addiction-disease-yes-and-much-more.html.

5. New America, "Global Cooling?"

6. "Marx vs. Spurgeon—The Philosophical Battle Still Happening Today," Episode 7, *Ideas Have Consequences with Larry Alex Taunton*, Apple Podcasts preview, 2022, https://podcasts.apple.com/us/podcast/marx-vs-spurgeon-the-philosophical-battle-still/id1614308509?i=1000617966228.

7. C. H. Spurgeon, "The Eternal Name," Sermon, Exeter Hall, London, May 27, 1855.

8. Larry Alex Taunton, "Karl Marx and Charles Spurgeon's Epic Struggle for Souls," *The American Spectator*, May 8, 2021, https://spectator.org/karl-marx-charles-spurgeon-socialism-christianity/.

9. Frederick Engels, "Confession," *Works of Frederick Engels 1868*, https://marxists.architexturez.net/archive/marx/works/1868/04/01.htm.

10. Roland Boer, "Keeping the Faith: The Ambivalent Commitments of Friedrich Engels," *Studies in Religion/Sciences Religieuses* 40, no. 1 (March 3, 2011): 63–79, https://doi.org/10.1177/0008429810389019. *See also* Frederick Engels, "On the History of Early Christianity," *Works of Frederick Engels 1894*, https://www.marxists.org/archive/marx/works/1894/early-christianity/#f1.

11. Aaron Earls, "Who Are 'Evangelicals' and Why Knowing That Matters for Your Church," Lifeway Research, July 26, 2021, https://research.lifeway.com/2021/07/26/who-are-evangelicals-and-why-knowing-that-matters-for-your-church/.

Index

Key to frequently used abbreviations:
CRT = critical race theory
ECI = Evangelical Climate Initiative
EEN = Evangelical Environmental Network
EIT = Evangelical Immigration Table
ERLC = Southern Baptist Convention,
    Ethics and Religious Liberty Commission
NAE = National Association of Evangelicals
SBC = Southern Baptist Convention

Abbotoy, Josh, xxvii
abortion, xii, xvi, xx, xxi, xxiii, 51–71
    abortion witnessed in Mozambique,
        51–52
    ACLU abortion campaign, 8
    big-name evangelical leaders
        supporting, 52
    Christian progressives and, 56
    cultural elites and, 71
    Democratic Party and, 60, 61, 62, 71,
        75, 76
    evangelicals as group most opposed
        to, 61
    funding from pro-abortion groups,
        xxii, 20
    Hyde Amendment and, 75
    institutional support for, 66
    Mexico City Policy, 63–64
    monetary motives for, 114–15
    narratives of pro-abortion groups, 53–55
    NIH funding of aborted fetal tissue
        research, 106, 108, 109, 110, 114
    number of lives lost since 1973, 70
    Planned Parenthood and harvesting
        fetal body parts, 114–15
    population reduction and, 20, 28
    purpose of, to kill babies, 69
    rate among Black women, 54, 70
    sanctity of life and, xii, 59
    secular and progressive position on, 53
    as "single issue" voting for Christians, 58
    Wear's compromise position, 63

Women's March (2017) and, xii
    See also pro-life movement
Acts
    17:26, 50
    20, xxii–xxiii
Advocates for Victims of Illegal Alien Crime
    (AVIAC), 33
Against Our Will (Brownmiller), 161
Akin, Danny, 15, 16, 41, 140–42, 145, 148
Alberta, Tim, The Kingdom, the Power, and
    the Glory, xv–xvi
All but Invisible (Collins), 220
Alliance Family Service, 52
Alliance for Citizenship, 44–45
American Baptist Churches USA, 197
American Church (American Protestantism)
    accommodating progressive issues,
        xxvi, xxvii
    accused of protecting white
        supremacy, 84
    adultery, fornication, and, 217
    battling Satan's wolves, 237
    communist infiltration, xvi–xvii,
        xxvii, 128
    co-opted by LGBTQ ideology, 194–231
    co-opted by pro-abortion groups, 20,
        51–71
    co-opted by progressive billionaires
        and left-wing foundations, xxi, xxii,
        72–89
    co-opted to promote government
        climate change policy, xxiv, 5, 7, 10,
        14, 24–30
    co-opted to spread government
        Covid-19 propaganda, xxi, 90–120
    co-opted to support illegal
        immigration, 33–38, 41–42, 50
    co-opting, means of, xxii, xxv, xxviii
    critical race theory, infiltration of,
        121–51
    criticism of, as too right-wing, 83–84
    largest church in the U.S., 198

American Church (American Protestantism)
    (*continued*)
        mankind's need for salvation and, 130
        need for the restraining influence of,
            xxviii
        new Reformation of, 242
        power of the eternal vs. temporal
            preoccupations, xxviii
        progressive buzzwords and, xii, 4–5
        recognizing leaders' political actions
            and rhetoric, xxvii
        Scripture distorted to promote social
            issues, xxiii–xxiv, 8, 26, 30–32, 35,
            94–95, 240
        sexual abuse accusations, #ChurchToo,
            and Title IX policies, xxii, 152–93
American Conservative, The, 132
American Enterprise Institute, 111
American Peace Mobilization, xvii
American Reformer, xxvii
Amico, Sarah Riggs, 75
Amos 3:3, 210
AND Campaign, 63, 68–70
Anderson, Bailey and James, xi–xv, xxix
Andringa, Robert, 11
Annenberg Foundation, 20
Archambault, Joanne, 161
Arcus Foundation, 77, 202, 210, 227–28
    organizations funded by, 77, 203–4,
        210, 211, 212
A Rocha International, 20–21, 23, 24
Aspen Institute, 126–28, 131
Atlantic magazine, 88, 242
    debunking "neurobiology of trauma,"
        165
    editor Wehner, 108
    on evangelicals as voting bloc, xviii
    lionizing Russell Moore, 168
Atlantic Philanthropies, xix
    "A Meeting of Queer Minds" report, xix
Axelrod, David, 110
Azusa Pacific University, 132, 225

Babylon Bee, 78, 119
Baker, Dwight, 95
Ball, Jim, 7–10
Baptist Press, 33, 46
    on EIT-Soros rumors, 41, 42, 45

on First Baptist Church Naples
    controversy, 144
    Lyell-Sills scandal at, 169–70, 177, 179
Barber, Bart, 46, 145, 148, 177, 189–90
Barrett, Amy Coney, 166
Basham, Megan
    on adhering to Scripture, not culture,
        237
    advice for parents, 237
    cancelled interview with Collins, 90, 93
    "How the Federal Government Used
        Evangelical Leaders to Spread
        Covid Propaganda to Churches,"
        90, 94, 102, 108
    on the importance of repentance, 235
    Keller's response to her reporting on
        Collins, 108–9
    lesson on abstaining, 235–36
    on the power of faithful preaching and
        shepherding, 237
    struggle with substance abuse, 232–35
    on telling her story, 236–37
Bassett, W. Todd, 11
Baucham, Voddie, 137, 143
    Fault Lines, 67, 143
    term "ethnic Gnosticism" and, 143
Baylor University, 132, 225
Bean, Lydia, 237–38
Before the Flood (film), 17
Beisner, Cal, 12–15, 19, 22, 27–29
    Cornwall Alliance and, 12–13, 39,
        238–39
Bell, David and Julie, 121–24, 135, 137, 150
Benkert, Todd, 187
Berglund, Taylor, 152, 154–55
Berry, Joel, 119
Bethancourt, Phillip, 172, 173, 174
Bethany Christian Services, 225
Bethlehem College and Seminary, 137
Bhattacharya, Jay, 96, 97–99
Bible Belt, xiii
Bible for Normal People, The (podcast), 196
Biden, Joe, 62, 113
    abortion policy, 60, 61, 63–64, 71
    Covid deaths under administration
        of, 113
    Cuban asylum seekers and, 47–48, 49
    evangelicals for Biden, 61, 62

illegal immigration and, 47, 49
LGBTQ policy and, 61
religious liberty protections and, 61
vaccine mandates and, 110–11
Bill and Melinda Gates Foundation, 82, 126
Biola University, 131, 138
BioLogos, 95–96, 99, 104
"Love Your Neighbor, Get the Shot," 95
Black Lives Matter, xxiii, 86, 92, 140, 150
Blackstone, William, 163, 164
Brannon, Randy, 72–73, 77
Brooks, David, 108
Brown, Patrick, 27
Brownmiller, Susan, *Against Our Will*, 161
Buckley, William F., 41
"Building Momentum for a Roadmap to
    Citizenship" (Noorani), 45
Burk, Denny, 221
Bush, George W., 62, 113
Bush, L. Russ, 17
Butterfield, Rosaria, 209, 224
    Five Lies of Our Anti-Christian Age, 209

Calvary Church, Charlotte, NC, 116
Calvin, John, 228, 241
Calvin University, 225
Campus Crusade for Christ, 134–36, 222
Capital Research Center, 10, 41, 82
Carson, D. A., 222, 225
Carter, Joe, 102, 103
Caudill, Bob and Katy, 145–46, 148
Center for Faith, Sexuality and Gender, 218
Center for Immigration Studies, 36, 41
Center for Reproductive Rights, 20
"champagne ministry," 79–82
Chan, Francis, 219
Chandler, Matt, 131, 219
Chang, Curtis, 85, 86, 88, 117
Charisma magazine, 152
    sexual abuse allegations against John
        Crist, 152–54, 157, 158
Chase, Alexis, 22–23
Chino Cienega Foundation, 20
Christ Central Church, Charlotte, NC,
    121–24, 135
Christian colleges and seminaries, xxix
    Covid-19 and, 95

CRT infiltration of, 128–42, 150–51
DEI departments, 132
EEN and climate change agenda, 16–20
LGBTQ ideology at, 225, 228
pro-abortion Prior as faculty
    member, 54
See also specific schools
Christianity and Liberalism (Gresham), vii
Christianity Today, 6, 73, 83, 219
    as anti-Trump, 73
    articles about homosexuality, 226
    climate change agenda and, 5, 6, 7, 9, 10
    Covid-19 and, 102, 104, 108, 119
    Crist allegations and, 155, 158
    Dalrymple as CEO, 95, 226
    Democratic Party donors at, 75–76
    desire for approval by secular elites,
        76–77
    editor Moore and *Roe v. Wade*, 56
    editor Moore's apocalypse essay 175
    Graham's founding of, 5, 73
    Guinness's criticism of, 89
    on Hayes hiring controversy, 144
    Johnson comes out as gay man in, 222
    Lilly Endowment's funding of, 73–75
    partnership with Arcus Foundation,
        77–78
    progressive views of, xxii, 5, 72–73
    Q&A with Francis Collins, 101–2
    review of *Single, Gay Christian*, 218
    Religious News Service used by, 78
    support for illegal immigration, 73
    support for transgenderism, 78
Christian Post, 38, 60
Christian Reformed Church, 1
Christians for Social Action, 68
Cizik, Richard, 7, 9, 11, 24, 68
Clark, Chris and Elisa, 213, 214
Clergy and Laity United for Economic
    Justice, 34
climate change, xxi, xii, xviii, xx, xxiii, 1–30
    anti-human climate policies, 6, 30
    assumption about human activity
        and, 19, 26
    Beisner and Cornwell Alliance versus
        leftwing ideology, 12–15, 19, 20, 27,
        29, 39, 238–39
    Christian Reformed Church Advent
        devotional and, 1–2

climate change (*continued*)
    co-opting *Christianity Today*, 5, 6, 7,
      9, 10
    creation care movement, 5–12, 16, 18,
      24–30, 68
    distorting Scripture, using "Love your
      neighbor," to promote government
      control, xxiv, 4, 8, 10–11, 14, 19–20,
      26, 30
    downgrading mankind as the
      pinnacle of God's creation, 19
    eco-anxiety and, 26
    evangelicals and, 4, 5–6, 11–12,
      15–23, 237
    funding from left-wing grant makers,
      5, 20
    green policies as harmful, 2–4, 30
    lack of supporting science, 11, 14, 25,
      26, 28
    media manipulation, 29
    myth of scientific consensus on, 27
    narrative of overpopulation, 19
    NOAA and the faith community, xxi
    Ortlund's video and, 24–28
    presented as a moral issue, 6, 16
    risks of questioning the narrative, 27, 29
    skepticism of apocalyptic claims,
      4–5, 25
    targeting fossil fuels, fertilizer, cows,
      3, 17
    targeting young evangelicals, 16–23, 24
    "What Would Jesus Drive?"
      campaign, 8
"Climate Change: Why Christians Should
  Engage" (Ortland, video), 24–28
Clinton, Hillary, 60, 62, 71, 113
Clinton Global Initiative, 9
CNN, xxii, xxiv, 34, 171, 175, 177, 230
Cohn, Joe, 167
Cole, Ben, 143
Coles, Gregory, 218, 227
    Single, Gay Christian, 218, 222
Collins, Francis, 91–115, 119–20
    aborted fetal tissue research at the
      NIH and, 106, 108, 109, 110, 114
    appearances on the Christian media
      circuit, 92–93
    author's cancelled interview with, 90, 93
    background and progressive

      positions, 106–8
    BioLogos founded by, 95
    Christianity Today Q&A, 101–2
    Christian leaders who lauded him,
      107–8
    Covid-19 "conspiracy theories" and, 100
    disparages Trump and evangelicals,
      112–13
    ERLC's webinar with Moore and,
      90–92
    Fauci and, 113
    gain-of-function funding and, 108
    "gracious dialogue" and, 94
    hubris and contempt of, 109
    Keller interview with, 104
    lab leak theory suppressed by, 100,
      101, 108, 271–72n9
    as an LGBTQ "ally," 107, 108
    MacCallum interview on Fox, 100–101
    mandated vaccination and, 110–12
    "pet rock" of, 93
    racial quotas and, 107
    Relevant magazine interview, 106
    role to get Christians to follow
      government mandates, 92–93,
      99–106, 108–10
    transgender research on minors and,
      107, 108, 109
    University of Chicago private forum
      with Moore, leaked audio, 110–14
    Warren's advocacy of, 104–5
    Wright interview with, 105–6
Collins, Nate, 219–20, 224
    All but Invisible, 220
Colossians 3:11, 121
Colson, Chuck, 143
Communist Party USA, xvi–xvii
Community Development Initiatives, 42
Cook, Becket, 224–25
Coppenger, Mark, 130
1 Corinthians
    5:9–10, 210
    5:9–13, 216
    6, 200
    6:9, 197–98
    6:9–10, 209
    6:9–20, 221
    6:18, 235
    9:25–27, 236

13:6, 95
2 Corinthians
2:5–8, 149
5:17–21, 18
10:5, 239
Cornwall Alliance for the Stewardship of
Creation, 12–13, 17, 19, 29, 30, 39, 238
response to ECI public letter, 13–15,
27, 29
Cornwell, Megan, 214–15
Council for Christian Colleges and
Universities, 9, 11, 34, 86
Council on Biblical Manhood and
Womanhood, 221
Covid-19, 90–120
arrogant and elite church leaders,
119–20
church closings, xxix, 91, 92, 99, 118
churches defying closing, 104, 105,
118–19
Collins's role in using Christian
leaders to promote government
policies, xxi, 90–120
"conspiracy theories" and, 95, 96, 100,
101–2, 104
Coronavirus and the Church website,
xxi, 104
deaths under Trump versus Biden, 113
dissent and debate suppressed, 96–98,
101–2
ERLC's webinar with Collins, 90–92
false narratives about, 94
"following Jesus" and, 106
gatherings for Black Lives Matter and, 92
government loss of credibility and, 115
government policies harmful to the
poor and working class, 98, 99
Great Barrington Declaration, 96–97
lab leak theory, 100–103, 108, 115,
271–72n9
leaders using "Love your neighbor"
to justify government policy, xxiv,
94–99, 105, 118
lockdowns and starvation, 98–99
masking and, 91–92, 103–4, 105, 118
media manipulation, 29, 97
non-consensus on approach to, 96–97
risks of questioning the narrative, 29,
97–99

vaccine injuries, 105, 116
vaccine mandates, xv, 103, 110–11, 116
vaccines using fetal cell lines and, 117
violation of First Amendment rights
and, 92
Crist, John, 152–59
abuse allegations, 152–58, 190
critical race theory (CRT), xxiii, xxvi, 121–51
antiracism and, 126, 133–34, 150
antiracist conferences, lessons, 121–24
Aspen Institute and tenets of, 126–28
Campus Crusade for Christ and,
134–36
DEI departments and, 126, 132, 140
diversity mandates at corporations, 138
experience of PCA church members,
Julie and David Bell, 121–24
Greear and, 125–27, 128, 142–43
Grove City College and, 133–34
"How to Understand and Address
White Privilege" (video), 131
Kendi on Christians and, 131–32
Loritts and Christian colleges, 131–32
Marxist roots of, 127–28, 129, 138
as racially divisive, 121–24, 130–31, 150
racial quotas and DEI-based hiring,
142–49
racism defined, 138
removing statues, renaming schools,
125
replacing capitalism with socialism, 139
SBC and, 125–30
at seminaries, 128–42, 150–51
sharing the Gospel as alternative to,
150–51
spiritual jargon of, 125
states blocking in public schools, 128
structural racism defined, 126
unchristian ideas of, 130–31
white privilege, definition, 127, 131
Critical Race Theory (Delgado and Sefancic),
129, 136, 139, 141
Cross, Alan, 42
Cross, Ginna, 51–52, 55, 69
Cuomo, Andrew, 189

Daily Wire, 90
on Barber's investigation of Lyell's
accusations, 177–78

Daily Wire (*continued*)
"How the Federal Government Used
Evangelical Leaders to Spread
Covid Propaganda to Churches"
(Basham), 90, 94, 102, 108
Dalrymple, Timothy, 75, 78, 95, 226
Daniel 6, 109
Davidman, Joy (Mrs. C. S. Lewis), xi
Dawkins, Richard, 80
Daws, Josh, 70
DCLeaks, 44, 46
Delgado, Richard, 129
Critical Race Theory, 129, 136, 139, 141
Democracy Alliance, xix
Democracy Fund, 83, 88
Democratic Party
abortion issue and, 60, 61, 62, 75
big donors, xx
evangelicals as voting bloc and, xviii, 62
faithfulness in the public sphere and,
xxvi
funding for progressive issues, xix
Keller's staffers and, 62
known operatives, xxvii
losses under Obama, 66
progressive issues, xviii
staff of *Christianity Today* and, 75
Denhollander, Rachael, 159, 169–73, 175,
178–80, 183–85
Depp, Johnny, 185
DeSantis, Ron, 97
Devil and Karl Marx, The (Kengor), xvi–xvii
DiAngelo, Robin, 132
White Fragility, 123, 134, 135, 138, 150
DiCaprio, Leonardo, 17
Dillon, Seth, 78
Disciples of Christ, 197
Discrimination and Disparities (Sowell), 141
"Dismantling Structural Racism/Promoting
Racial Equity" (Aspen Institute), 126–28,
131
*Dobbs v. Jackson Women's Health
Organization*, 54, 56, 57, 64, 67, 149
lives saved by, 65–66
Dobson, James, 212
Dougherty, Michael Brendan, 96
Dreher, Rod, 132
Duarte, Amanda, 149–50

Duke, Barrett, 7
Du Mez, Kristin, *Jesus and John Wayne*, xv

Eaker, Bekah, 156
Edmondson, Christine, 83
Edmondson, Mika, 55–56
Eleventh Commandment: Thou shalt not
criticize church leaders, xxvi–xxix
Embracing the Journey (Greg and Lynn
McDonald), 204
Embracing the Journey (organization), 204,
210–12, 215–16, 230
Engels, Friedrich, 240
Environmental Defense Fund, 15
Ephesians
2:1–10, 18
4:15–16, 243
4:22–24, 223
Episcopal Church, xvii, 197
European Union (EU), 3, 4
Evangelical Climate Initiative (ECI), 9–11
cap-and-trade legislation and, 10
eco-fearmongering by, 10
letter: "Climate Change: An
Evangelical Call to Action" and
media push, 10–11, 13
letter rebuttals from Cornwall
Alliance, NAE dissenters, 11–15
Evangelical Environmental Network (EEN),
xviii, 6, 17, 22, 24
Christianity Today, NAE, and, 5, 7
Creation Care and, 7
efforts to turn evangelicals into
environmental activists, 5–12, 15, 22
as the "green Jesus group," 8
hijacking the pro-life movement for
environmental causes, 68
left-wing donors to, 9, 15
recruiting "elite evangelicals," 6
"rent an evangelical" model, 6
targeting Christian colleges and
seminaries, 16–20
targeting SBC, 7
thwarted by Beisner, 13–15, 17, 19,
20, 39
"What Would Jesus Drive?"
campaign, 8
Evangelical Immigration Table (EIT), xviii

Bibles, Badges, and Business program,
42–43, 44, 45
Cuban asylum seekers ignored by, 49
Gang of Eight immigration bill and,
33–40
granting illegals refugee status and, 31
"I Was as Stranger" Bible verses, 35
left-wing funding of, 33–34, 37
linked to World Relief, 41
National Immigration Forum and, 37,
42–43, 45
official launch of, 34, 37
open letter supporting admission of
illegals to the U.S., 40
pushing evangelicals to back federal
legislation, 34, 36
recruitment of Lynne Hybels, 36
SBC targeted by, 41–42, 46
Soros connection, 37, 38, 40, 42–47
victims of illegal alien crime ignored
by, 33
"Welcoming the stranger" tagline, 31,
49, 50
Evangelical Lutheran Church of America, 197
evangelical media
co-opting of, with funding by
progressives, 72–89
co-opting of *Christianity Today*, 72–79
Covid-19 and suppressing dissent,
101–2
Crist allegations and MeToo dogma
in, 152–60
evangelical leaders and, 72
"First Law" applied to, 78–79
French, Moore, Wear, and Chang,
castigating of evangelicals, 83–88
identifying with secular elites, 76–77
journalists donating to political
candidates and, 75–76
lens of biblical doctrine and, 72
LGBTQ agenda and, 211–12
narrative of, what God requires
from Christians participating in
politics, 72
Never Trumpers and, 86, 88
evangelicals, xv–xviii, xxi, xxii, xxiii, xxiv,
xxvi–xxvii
climate change agenda and, 4, 5–6, 8,
15–23, 237

Collins blames for resistance to
vaccine mandates, 112
concern about gender indoctrination, 77
the Eleventh Commandment and,
xxvi–xxix
homosexuality condemned by, 76,
196, 197–98
as less partisan than other groups,
86–87
majority position on immigration, 36
narrative of Republican co-opting
of, xvi
percentage of all U.S. adults, 241–42
percentage of U.S. electorate, xviii, 5
as populists, 87
pro-life position of, 61, 68–70
secular billionaires assault on, xix
stewardship of creation and, 19
Trump voters and, xvi, 48, 57, 60–61,
64–65, 75, 112
well-known Never Trumpers, 58, 65
the Word, unchanging Wisdom of,
and, xv
See also specific issues
Evangelicals for Biblical Immigration, 39
Evangelicals for Social Action (ESA), xxv
Ezekiel 13, xxviii
Ezell, Kevin, 41, 145, 188–89

Farah, Alyssa, xxiv
Farmer-Citizen Movement (Netherlands), 3
Fauci, Anthony, 90, 93, 96–97, 108, 100,
113
Fault Lines (Baucham), 67, 143
Feinstein, Stephen, 128, 129–30
Fenton (public relations firm), 8
Fetzer Foundation, 88
Finding God at Harvard (Kullberg), 39
First Baptist Church Naples, racism charges
and hiring controversy, 143–49
Five Lies of Our Anti-Christian Age
(Butterfield), 209
Floyd, Ronnie, 173–74
Focus on the Family, 34, 212
Ford, Christine Blasey, 184–85
Francis, Pope, 197
Franklin, Benjamin, 163
FreedHearts, 212

French, David, 65, 67, 83–84, 86
    After Party group and, 86
    attacks vaccine and mask resisters,
      117–20
    bizarre arguments on abortion, 66–67
    dubs conservative Christians
      "dominionists," 84
    as a Never Trumper, 65, 67
    on pro-lifer voters for Trump, 65–66, 70
    on same-sex marriage, 67
    self-appointed role of, 88
    as Trinity Forum fellow, 65
    urges getting Covid vaccine, 95
    urges vote for Biden, 86
Fuentes, Nick, 150

Galatians
    1, 240
    2, xxiv, xxvi
    2:11–16, 18
    3:28, 132, 143
    5, xxvi
Gallaty, Robby, 145
Galli, Mark, 76–77
Gates, Bill, 88, 103, 237
Gay Christian Network (GCN), 211
    Evangelical Education Project, 211
    Genesis
      1:27, 224
      1:28, 19
      9, 19
      18, 164
Gerson, Michael, 108
Ghana, green policies and, 3–4
Gilson, Rachel, 222
God and the Gay Christian (Vines), 204, 211
Gospel Coalition, 28, 55, 62, 64, 83, 222, 225
    Cook interview, 224–25
    "Covid conspiracy mongering," 102,
      103
    gun laws as pro-life and, 70
    Keller Center at, 24, 29
    MeToo dogma and, 158
    Wear and, 63, 64
    Williams interview and CRT, 136
    See also Ortlund, Gavin
Grace Community Church, 104, 105
Graham, Billy, xv, 5, 73, 132

Graham, Jack, 144
Greear, J. D., xxvi, 41, 48–49, 132
    Center for Faith, Sexuality and
      Gender and, 219
    Covid-19 and, 104
    CRT ideology and, 126, 127, 128, 149
    DEI-based hiring and, 142–43
    First Baptist Church Naples hiring
      controversy and, 145–47
    LGBTQ ideology and, 227
    media portrayal as antiracist reformer,
      125
    Moore's #ChurchToo letter and, 171–72
    progressive ideology and, 242
    "pronoun hospitality" and, 227
    push to change SBC's name, 125–26
    retiring of SBC presidential gavel, 125
    as SBC president, 146–47, 227
    seeking to bolster his image, 149
    as self-appointed abuse crusader, 188
Greenwald, Glenn, 82–83
Grove City College, 133–34
Grudem, Wayne, 222
Guidepost Solutions, 175, 178, 184
Guinness, Os, 79–80, 88, 89
gun laws, xxiii, 70, 73
Gupta, Sunetra, 96
Gushee, David, 10
Guttmacher Institute, 66

Habel, Doug and Sauna, 212
Hall, Matt, 138, 145, 148
Halley, Janet, 166
Hannigan, Joni, 188–89
Hansen, Collin, 83, 86
Harder, Cherie, 81, 88
Hartley, Grant, 221
Hawkins, William, 37
Hawks, Melissa, 158
Hayes, Marcus, 143–49
Hayhoe, Katharine, 16–17
Heard, Amber, 185
Hebrews, 209
    2:1, 79
    4:12, 243
    10:25, xxix, 91
Henry, Carl F. H., 42
Hescox, Mitch, 22

Hewlett Foundation, 5, 9, 15, 85

Hezekiah, King, xxix

Hill, Wesley, 221, 222, 224

Hitchens, Christopher, 80, 81

homosexuality. *See* LGBTQ movement

Hoover Institution, Stanford University
    Romerstein's papers archived in,
        xvi–xvii

Hope in Times of Fear (Keller), 217

Houston Chronicle, 173, 174, 181–82, 183

"How the Federal Government Used
  Evangelical Leaders to Spread Covid
  Propaganda to Churches" (Basham), 90,
  94, 102, 108

How to Be an Antiracist (Kendi), 131, 134, 135

Hughes, Ben and Sasha, 194–96

Hunt, Johnny, 181–82

Hybels, Bill and Lynne, 36

illegal immigration, xii, xviii, xx, 31–50
    amnesty issue, 34, 37
    cherry-picking Scripture to support,
        xxiv, 31, 32, 35
    church leaders' unequal concerns
        about Trump, 47–49
    co-opting the SBC to support,
        41–42, 46
    Cuban asylum seekers and, 47–48, 49
    death of Maureen Maloney's son and
        illegal alien crime, 31–32, 33, 50
    drug- and sex-trafficking and, 47, 50
    EIT and using "faith voices" to push
        accepting "refugees," 33–40, 46
    evangelical media's support for, 73
    Gang of Eight immigration bill and,
        33–40, 44, 49
    left-wing groups/NGOs that support
        open borders, 33–34, 40–47
    Metaxas and Kullberg open letter
        opposing, 39–40
    not supported by evangelicals, 36, 39
    number of illegal aliens in the U.S.,
        32–33
    replacing American workers, 46–47
    Scripture on national sovereignty, 50
    societal costs of, 47
    Soros funding and, 44–47
    as source of cheap labor, 37

"welcome the stranger" and political
    posturing, 31, 35, 40, 50

Illyn, Peter, 22

Inside Philanthropy, 202–3

Institute on Religion and Democracy, 41–42

Intercept, 82–83

Intergovernmental Panel on Climate
  Change (IPCC), 11, 13, 26, 28

International Mission Board, 143

InterVarsity Christian Fellowship, 34

Ireland, gay lobby and same-sex marriage,
    xix

Isaiah
    1:17, 71
    1:23, 72

James
    1:27, 167
    2:9, 132
    4:7, 236

James, King of England, xv, xviii

Jeremiah 29:11, 66

Jesus and John Wayne (Du Mez), xv

1 John 1:9, 191

John
    1:9, 138
    2:15, 240
    3:16, 18
    8, 159
    10:12–13, 228
    18:36, 131
    171:17, 236

Johnson, Greg, 219–20, 226
    as celibate gay man, 222
    hosts *Transilluminate* exhibition, 222
    Revoice conference and, 220–21
    Still Time to Care, 224

Johnson, KC, 166

Johnson, Lyndon B., 54

Jones, Robert P., 84

Jude, xxiv
    1:3, 12, 18, 232
    1:3–4, 7, 194

Kavanaugh, Brett, 184–85

Keathley, Ken, 16–17

Keller, Tim, 40, 47, 59, 115, 219
    abortion issue and, 59–60, 61

Keller, Tim (*continued*)
    as anti-Trump, 60, 61
    church of, in Democratic district, 62
    church of, Revoice and, 222
    Covid and Francis Collins, 104, 108–9
    Covid arrogance and elitism, 119–20
    death of, 225
    denigrating pro-life evangelicals, 61–62
    disparages pro-life Trump voters, 70
    endorsement of Johnson's book, 224,
        225
    Hope in Times of Fear, 217
        PCA report and LGBTQ ideology,
        222–24
    Powers's memorial article, 230–31
    promotion of Democratic operatives, 62
    on relating the Bible to politics, 59
    Wear's compromise on abortion and, 63
Kendi, Ibram X., 131, 132, 133, 139
    How to Be an Antiracist, 131, 134, 135
Kengor, Paul, *The Devil and Karl Marx*, xvi–xvii
Kilpatrick, Samantha, 185–86
Kim, Walter, 95
    op-ed: "Not the mark of the
        beast: Evangelicals should fight
        conspiracy theories and welcome
        the vaccines," 104
Kingdom, the Power, and the Glory, The
    (Alberta), xv–xvi
King's Chapel, Boston, xv
Kipnis, Laura, 161, 162, 187
    Unwanted Advances, 161
Klusendorf, Scott, 133, 134
Kullberg, Kelly Monroe, 39
    Finding God at Harvard, 39
Kulldorff, Martin, 96
Kwon, Duke, 83

LaMarche, Gara, xix
Land, Richard, 34
Langberg, Diane, 181
La Raza, 37
Leatherwood, Brent, 70
Legates, David, 13
Leno, Jay, 8
Leviticus
    18, 200–201
    19:15, 132

Lewis, C. S., 4, 241
LGBTQ ideology, xii, xiii, xv, xviii, xix, xx,
    xxvi, 194–231
    advice for pastors, 228–31
    Arcus Foundation and, 202–3, 210
    Bible verses as "clobber passages,"
        201, 207
    Biden support for, 61
    Chase's Marriage Militia Project
        and, 23
    Collins, NIH, and, 107, 109
    Embracing the Journey and Northpoint
        megachurch, 204, 210–12
    Episcopal Church and, 197
    Equality Act, 75
    evangelical concerns about gender
        indoctrination, 77
    gay marriage, xxiii, 67, 84, 197, 199,
        207, 209, 210, 214–15, 222, 225
    Greear advises only whispering about,
        227
    Greear and "pronoun hospitality," 227
    Ireland's gay lobby, xix
    LGBTQ-affirming podcasts, 196
    linking to race-based civil rights, 220
    megachurches, Andy Stanley, and
        accommodation of, 198–202
    Newsom's same-sex marriage
        campaign, 8
    North Park University's "Queers and
        Allies" student organization, 74
    organized infiltration of churches,
        225–31
    pastors fear of cancel culture and,
        226–27
    proselytizing sold as compatible with
        Christianity, 195–96, 204–9, 210–12
    Reformation Project, 203–4, 210,
        227–28
    repentance and, 209–10, 224
    Saddleback Church and, 212–16
    Scripture and evangelical rejection of,
        78, 197–98
    Scripture on homosexuality as sinful,
        196–97, 200–201, 204, 205, 206,
        209, 216, 220, 221, 224, 227, 229
    Side A approach, 204, 217, 218, 221
    Side B approach, 217–25, 226
    "spiritual friendships," 218–19

surrogacy trade and, 84
transgenderism or gender dysphoria, xiii, 73, 75, 84, 107, 208, 210, 219, 226, 227, 230
United Methodist Church and, 203
World Vision hiring policy and, 11
youth ministries targeted by, 229–30
Liberty University, 54
Lifeway Christian Resources, survey of evangelicals on homosexuality, 197–98
Lilly Endowment, 73–75
"compelling preaching" initiative, 74
"faithful pastors" project, 74
Thriving in Ministry Initiative, 74–75
Living Out (LGBTQ organization), 222–23
Livingstone, Linda, 132
"5 Tips to Cultivate Cultural Humility and Antiracism," 132
Log Cabin Republicans, 209
Lord of the Rings: The Two Towers (Tolkien), 242
Loreto House, Calcutta, India, 13
Loritts, Bryan, 131, 132, 188
Losing Our Religion (Moore), 84
"Loving God and Neighbor in an Age of Climate Crisis" (Moo), 17–18, 19–22
Lowe, Ben, 21, 23, 68
Lucado, Max, 40, 47, 48
Ludwig, Hayden, 10
Luiten, Erik, 4
Luke
7, 159
14, 231
Luther, Martin, 241, 242
Lyell, Jennifer, 169–70, 172, 177–80, 184

MacArthur, John, 104, 105
MacArthur, John F., 198
The Vanishing Conscience, 235–36
MacArthur Foundation, 5
MacCallum, Martha, 100–101
Machen, J. Gresham, 226, 241
Christianity and Liberalism, vii
Malone College, 7
Maloney, Matthew and Maureen, 31–33
Marisla Foundation, 15
Mark
1:15, 18
10, 231

marriage, xxiii
black couples and well-being, 141–42
definition of, xii
divorce and, xvi
forces that have crushed the American family, 53–54
husbands caring for wives and children, 53
Jesus's teaching in Matthew 19, 74
Obergefell decision and same-sex marriage, xix, 23, 67, 84, 197, 199, 214, 225–26
Scripture and, xxv
Marx, Karl, and Marxism
critical race theory and, 127–28, 129
desire to supplant Christianity, 239
Gaia worship and, 21
MeToo's "power imbalance" and, 159–60
politics of envy and, xxviii
Spurgeon's opposition to, 239–40
using the gospel to transform social structures and, xxv
Mason, Eric, Woke Church, 148
Matthew
5:13–16, 89
6:21, 75
15:9, vii
18, 202
18:15–17, 210
18:15–19, 149
19, 74
24:13–14, 18
28:19–20, 18, 89, 131
Mayorkas, Alejandro, 47
McCain, John, 35
McCracken, Brett, 70
McDermott, Gerald, 131
McDonald, Alonzo, 79
McDonald, Greg and Lynn, 204–9
Embracing the Journey, 204
Embracing the Journey organization, 204, 210–12, 215–16
video for Stanley's Drive Conference, 205–7
McGrath, Alister, 16
Mcintosh, Peggy, 127
McKissic, Dwight, 145

McKitrick, Ross, 13

McLaren, Brian, 11

Merritt, James, 15

Merritt, Jonathan, 15

Metaxas, Eric, 36, 37–39, 50
    Socrates in the City and, 37

#MeToo, #ChurchToo, and Title IX, xxiii,
   152–93
    abuse activists and, 159
    abuse charges and recovered-memory
      craze of the 1980s, 166
    abuse reforms and bureaucratic power
      grabs, 160–62
    American jurisprudence versus Title
      IX approach, 163–67
    "Believe Women" slogan, 167
    Clery Act's definition of sexual
      assault, 161
    Crist scandal and, 152–59, 190
    Denhollander's influence, 170, 178,
      183–86
    Doe v. Purdue and, 166–67
    evangelical media and MeToo dogma,
      152–60
    false accusations and, 160–67, 186,
      189–90
    high profile Church leaders and
      authors "stand with victims"
      position, 155
    Jesus's encounters with women in
      sinful sexual relationships and, 159
    lawsuits for false accusations, 189, 190
    Marxism and "power imbalance,"
      159–60
    media attention for pastors and, 186–87
    misleading and false statistics about
      campus rape, 160, 162, 168
    "neurobiology of trauma" and
      investigations, 164–67, 181, 183, 185
    progressive ideology and, 160, 166
    rate of sexual abuse in the SBC, 175–77
    SBC's Guidepost Report and, 175–82
    SBC's Title IX-style reforms, 182–86
    sexual sin versus sexual abuse, 168
    standards of evidence eliminated,
      162–63
    story of Joseph and, 159
    Title IX and, 160, 162, 163–75,
      187–88, 189

"victim-centered" investigating and,
    164–65
"victim-centered" view of women,
    190–93
worst excesses of MeToo movement in
    the Church, 155, 156, 159

Midwestern Baptist Theological Seminary,
   Center for Public Theology, 129

Milhoan, Kirk, 97

Miller, Paul D., 119

Mitchell, Craig, 150–51

Mohler, Albert, 75, 136, 178, 221

Moo, Jonathan, 26, 29
    A Rocha International and, 20–21
    "Loving God and Neighbor in an Age
      of Climate Crisis," 17–18, 19–22

Moore, Beth, 47, 54, 55, 68–69, 70, 106,
   225–26
    Praying God's Word, 225–26

Moore, Russell, xxii, 34, 35, 36, 40, 48, 60,
   65, 83–84, 86
    After Party group and, 86
    allies and abuse cover-ups, 188
    "apocalypse" essay, 175, 180
    #ChurchToo and, 168
    Covid response and Francis Collins,
      90–92, 104, 108–20
    disparages pro-life Trump voters, 70
    equates amnesty for illegals with pro-
      life movement, 70
    as ERLC head, 168–69
    leaked letters of, 170–73
    Losing Our Religion, 84
    progressive ideology and, 242
    relationships with media, 168, 171, 173
    resignation and accusations against
      SBC, 171–75
    response to overturning of *Roe v.*
      Wade, 56–57
    self-appointed role of, 88

Mullins, Matt, 139, 141
    "Is Critical Race Theory
      'UnChristian,'" series, 139–40

Nashville Statement, 222

Nassar, Larry, 169, 183–84

National Abortion Rights Action League, 20

National Association of Evangelicals (NAE)

climate change agenda and, 4, 5, 7, 9,
11–12
climate report of 2022, 30
co-opting to support government
Covid-19 propaganda, 95
co-opting to support illegal
immigration, 34, 35
leaders targeted by New America, 6
money from a pro-abortion
foundation, xxii
motives of NAE leaders, xxii
"National Day of Prayer for Creation
Care," 68
number of churches and churchgoers, 6
Reagan's "evil empire" speech (1983)
and, 5
National Council of Churches, xvii
National Immigration Forum (NIF)
EIT as project of, 37, 42–43
evangelical groups working with, 34
left-wing groups and aims of, 37
organizing for immigration
legislation, 43
Soros funding for, 44, 45
National Institutes of Health (NIH), 91
Collins as director, 106–9, 114
Covid-19 narratives, 104
DEI grants by, 107
funding for gain-of-function research,
100
funding for sexual and gender
minorities, 107
funding for University of Pittsburgh
fetal scalp research, 106, 108, 110, 114
grants to track homosexuality in teen
boys, 107
masking policies, 92
Stetzer's help in spreading Covid-19
narratives, 104
transgender research on minors, 107,
109
Trump shut-down of fetal cell
research, 107
use of aborted fetal tissue, 106–7,
109, 110
vaccine mandates at, 111–12
See also Collins, Francis
National Religious Partnership for the
Environment, 5

National Review, 41
Natural Resources Defense Council, 15
Netherlands, green policies and, 3
Neuhaus, Richard, 39, 42
New America (Soros-funded think tank),
5–6
Beiser thwarts co-opting
evangelicals, 14
Obama administration alumni and, 6
report on recruiting evangelicals as
climate activists, 14, 16, 22, 23
success with Alexis Chase, 22–23
tactics to co-opt evangelical
institutions, 5–6, 10, 237
Newbell, Trillia, 157
New Evangelicals, The (podcast), 196
Newsom, Gavin, xxiv, 8
New Yorker magazine, Keller on pro-life
evangelicals, 61–62
New York Times, 88, 242
American Peace Mobilization open
letter in, xvii, xviii
Christian support for gay marriage
and, xxiii
columnist David Brooks, 108
columnist David French, 67, 83
Cross op-ed, 42
ECI's full page ad in, 10
on Ghana's oil boom and cocoa
exports, 4
Lewis's "watchful dragons" metaphor
and, 4
lionizing Russell Moore, 168
Moore's accusations against SBC,
173, 174
on SBC's Guidepost Report, 175
"The 1619 Project," 132
Swallow's pro-abortion op-ed, 52–53
Tisby on "white Christians" in, 133
Nichols, Laurie, 155
NOAA (National Oceanic and Atmospheric
Administration), xxi, 26, 28
Noorani, Ali, 38, 42
"Building Momentum for a Roadmap
to Citizenship," 45
North American Mission Board, 41, 142–43,
145, 188
North Park University, 74

North Point Community Church, Atlanta,
198, 199, 201
    LGBTQ advocacy, 202, 203
    McDonalds and Embracing the
        Journey at, 204–5, 210–12, 214
Not Our Faith, 63
Nucatola, Deborah, 114–15
Numbers 32, 242

Obama, Barack, xxii, 17, 34, 62
    on abortion, 66
    administration alumni at New
        America, 6
    Democratic Party losses in Congress
        and governorships under, 66
    DREAM Act and, 35, 49
    faith-based initiatives by, 113
    Gang of Eight immigration bill and,
        35, 38
    illegal immigration and, 40
    reverses ban on aborted fetal tissue
        research, 106–7
    Title IX, sexual abuse reforms, and
        bureaucratic power grabs, 160,
        162–63, 167, 168
Olasky, Marvin, 58, 59, 65
Olbermann, Keith, 76
Omidyar, Pierre, xx, 82–83
    co-opting evangelical churches for
        climate change agenda, 237
    Democracy Fund and, 83, 88
    liberal causes of, 82, 83
    Soros and, 82
    Trinity Forum funding, 83, 87
"On Christians Spreading Corona
    Conspiracies" (Stetzer), 102, 103
One America Movement, 85–86
Open Society Foundations (OSF), xix
    "Building Momentum for a Roadmap
        to Citizenship," 45
    Christian strategy, xix–xx
    efforts to co-opt Southern Baptists,
        44–45
    "faith communities" and "faith
        voices" as priority for, xx
    National Immigration Forum funded,
        37, 44
    "a problem like the Christians" and,
        xix

Soros funding for political access and, 44
    U.S. Programs, xix–xx
Ortlund, Gavin, 24, 26, 29
    "Climate Change: Why Christians
        Should Engage" (video), 24–28
O'Sullivan, John, 78–79
Owen, John, 90

Packer, J. I., 222
Page, Frank, 15
Paris Accords, 3, 28
Paul, Rand, 103
Paul Driessen, 13
Perkins, John, 39
1 Peter 2:11, 235
2 Peter 3:6–7, 1
Pew Research Center, on evangelicals and
    climate alarmism, 4
Phillips, Jack, 226
Piper, John, 137
Planned Parenthood, xxii, 20, 28, 85, 114–15
Politico, on Democracy Alliance, xix
Powers, Kirsten, "My Complicated Feelings
    About Tim Keller," 230–31
Praying God's Word (Moore), 225–26
Preaching Magazine, influential pastors list,
    198, 212
Premier Christianity, Rick Warren interview,
    214–15
Premier Christian News, 61
Presbyterian Church (USA), 197
Presbyterian Church of America (PCA),
    xiv, 220
    impact of CRT on membership of
        Charlotte-area church, 121–25,
        135, 137
    LGBTQ ideology in, 220–24
Prince, David, 174
Principles First, 86, 88
Prior, Karen Swallow, 52–53, 55, 60, 219
    acknowledges Trump voters for Dobbs
        decision, 64–65
    disparages pro-life Trump voters, 70
    equates Covid masking with pro-life
        position, 69
    in evangelical higher education, 54
    hijacking the pro-life movement for
        progressive causes, 69

Revoice and, 222, 225
"stand with victims" position, 155
Prison Fellowship Ministries, 34
pro-life movement, xx, 51–71, 84
adoption alternative to abortion, 53
a baby's inalienable right to life and, 59–60
care for moms and babies and, 55
Cross as Alliance Family Service's executive director, 52
hijacking of, naming progressive causes as pro-life issues, 68–71
lives saved after *Dobbs* decision, 65–66, 67
mission drift and, 69
overturning of *Roe v. Wade*, 52, 54, 55–56
pregnancy centers, 55, 69
right to life and, 52
Trump and, 57, 58, 60, 65, 67
volunteers and costs covered by, 55
See also abortion
Proverbs
24:11–12, 51
29:2, 89
Pruitt, Todd, 231
Psalms
72:13, 167
122:7, 31
Public Religion Research Institute, 84
Purpose Driven Life, The (Warren), 11, 105, 212

racial justice, xii
abortion as ultimate injustice, 70
After Party group and, 86
assumptions of, xiv–xv
critical race theory and, 121–51
"economic equity," xx
generational sins and, xiv
Kwon's advice for Christians, 83
leftist causes and, xiii
PCA church teaching on, xiv, 121–24
progressive influencers and, 83
study group "Be the Bridge," xiii, xiv
"Whiteness 101" reading list, xiii
See also critical race theory
Reagan, Ronald, xvii, 5
Reason magazine, 166
Reclaiming Hope (Wear), 62

Reconciling Ministries Network (RMN), 203
Redeemer Presbyterian Church, New York, 62
vaccination policy, 115–16
Reformation Project, 203–4, 210, 212, 214, 228
annual revenues, 227–28
Arcus funding for, 203–4, 210
Embracing the Journey and, 210–11
speaker lists for conferences, 204
Relevant magazine, 68, 106, 108
Religion News Service (RNS), 52, 77
on hiring controversy at First Baptist Church Naples, 143–44
LGBTQ affirmation in the Church and, 78
publishes Moore's letter to ERLC trustees, 171
Republican Party
American Church and, xvi
climate change agenda and, 6
confusing faith with political positions, xxv–xxvi
EIT campaign to push immigration legislation and, 37, 38–39
EIT pushing pastors to lobby lawmakers for illegals, 34
environmental activists influencing climate legislation through the Church, 22
evangelicals and, xviii
opposition to cap and trade, 7
past presidential candidates, evangelical support for, 62
pro-life evangelicals and, 60
See also Trump, Donald
Revelation 21:1–8, 18
Revoice (LGBTQ organization), 220–25
Rockefeller Brothers Fund, 15
Rockefeller Foundation, 5
Rockefeller Philanthropy Advisors
After Party funding, 83, 85, 87
New Pluralists project, 85
pro-abortion and LGBTQ projects, 85
Rodriguez, Samuel, 35
Rohnert, Ashlee, 158
Roman Catholic Church, 197
Romans
1, 201, 227
1:16, 18

1:26–27, 220
2:11, 143
6, 236
8:22, 19
10:9, 18
10:14, 210
13, 104
13:3–8, 59
13:14, 236
14, 215, 216, 227
16:17, 121
Romerstein, Herbert, xvi–xvii
Romney, Mitt, 62
Roosevelt, Franklin Delano (FDR), xvii

Sadar, Anthony, 27
Saddleback Church, 11, 104
    LGBTQ advocacy at, 203, 212–16
Salvation Army, 11
Samford University, Beeson Divinity School,
    131
Sasse, Ben, 48
Sauls, Scott, 222, 225
Savage, Mark and Jill, 212
Schaeffer, Francis, xxv, 226, 241
Schock, Aaron, 143
Schumer, Chuck, 35
Scott, Jennifer, 118–19
Scripture
    on abortion, 59
    After Party group's misuse of, 85–86
    Book of Jude's "contend for faith"
        and, xxiv
    Christian worldview and rejection of
        apocalyptic climate change, 4–5
    Church's response to sexual abuse
        allegations and, 159
    church teachings and, xv
    consensus not required by, xxiii
    on contending for God's laws in the
        political sphere, 89
    culture replacing in teachings, xv
    evangelical institutions and leaders
        promoting causes unrelated to, xxi
    God's design for sex and marriage
        and, xxv, 53
    on homosexuality, 196–97, 200–201,
        204, 205, 206, 216, 220, 224, 227,
        229

    leaders using "Love your neighbor"
        to justify progressive issues, xxiii–
        xxiv, 8, 26, 30, 31, 32, 94–95
    on leaders appearing to be righteous,
        49
    misused by climate change activists,
        19–20
    misused to justify illegal immigration,
        31, 32, 35, 50
    misused by Marxists, xxv
    on the misuse of power, 71
    on national sovereignty, 50
    presumption of innocence grounded
        in, 164
    private property rights and, xxv
    proclaiming truth and, xxiii
    progressive agenda and distortion of,
        35, 240–41
    on the purpose of government, 59
    sacredness of human life and, xxv
    on sin and repentance, 138
    as source of truth, 243
    the Word, unchanging Wisdom of,
        xv, xxiv
Send Network, 131
Sessions, Jeff, 35
sexual abuse, assault, or harassment. See
    #MeToo, #Church Too, and Title IX
sexuality
    biblical positions on, xii
    "brokenness" applied to, xii
    buzzwords and, xii
    Christian sex ethic as core belief of
        Christianity, 217, 230
    morality and, xv
    Nashville Statement, 222
    Pruitt on biblical clarity about, 231
    Scripture and, xxv
    Southern Baptist Convention and, xxi
    what the Bible teaches about, 228–29
    See also LGBTQ ideology
Sey, Samuel, 149, 150
Sharpton, Al, xxvii
Silliman, Daniel, 76
Sills, David, 169–70, 177, 178, 179
Silverman, Craig, 161
Single, Gay Christian (Coles), 218, 222
Slate, 168
social justice, xvii, xxiii

AND Campaign and Michael Wear, 63
focus on, versus sinful human hearts,
    xxv
using the gospel for transforming
    social structures, xxv
See also critical race theory
Soerens, Matthew, 41
Soros, George, xix, xx, 5, 34
    backing of EIT and, 37, 38, 40, 42–47
    funding for Trinity Forum, 82
    Omidyar as a "core partner," 82
Southeastern Baptist Theological Seminary
    (SEBTS), 185
    climate change agenda and, 16–18, 29
    critical race theory infiltration of, 139–41
    Denhollander and abuse course at,
        185–86
    illegal immigration, EIT, and, 41
    Kingdom Diversity program, 139, 140
    L. Russ Bush Center for Faith and
        Culture, 17
    Moo's lecture on climate and, 17–21
    Mullins's series "Is Critical Race
        Theory 'UnChristian,'" 139–40
    pro-abortion Prior as faculty member, 54
Southern Baptist Convention (SBC)
    abuse allegations and #ChurchToo,
        169–93
    abuse accusations mishandled, 187–88
    abuse allegations and Guidepost
        Report, 168, 175–82, 184, 188–89
    abuse reforms, 159, 174–75, 182–86
    Baptist Press and, 33
    climate change agenda and, 7, 15, 17
    CRT infiltration of, 125–27, 128–30
    the Eleventh Commandment and,
        xxvi–xxix
    emblematic of issues happening
        throughout the Church, xxvii
    Greear and DEI-based hiring, 142–43
    Greear as an abuse crusader, 188
    Greear urges Covid vaccination, 104
    illegal immigration support, 34,
        41–42, 46
    largest Protestant denomination, xx,
        xxvii, 46
    loose structure of, 147, 183
    moving evangelicals to the left and,
        xxviii
    position change on "sexual sins," xxi

progressive billionaires' money and, 89
    sexual abuse rate in churches of, 176
    woke teaching and loss of members, xxvi
Southern Baptist Convention, Ethics and
    Religious Liberty Commission (ERLC),
    xx–xxi, 42
    Covid vaccine pushed by, 104
    DEI-based hiring and, 142
    funding from progressives, xx–xxi,
        88–89
    Leatherwood lobbies for gun control, 70
    Moore and "Abuse Crisis" conference,
        169, 170
    Moore and leftwing ideology, 169
    Moore's resignation and accusations,
        171–75
    Moore's statement supporting
        Obama's Dreamers, 35, 49
    Moore's webinar with Collins on
        Covid-19, 90–92
    racial quotas and, 142
Southern Baptist Convention, International
    Missions Board, 116
Southern Baptist Environment and Climate
    Initiative (SB-ECI), 15
Southern Baptist Theological Seminary
    (SBTS), 130, 136, 139, 221
    CRT infiltration of, 136–38
Southwestern Baptist Theological Seminary,
    150
Sowell, Thomas, 54, 58
    Discrimination and Disparities, 141
    on marriage and well-being, 141–42
Spencer, Richard, 150
Spencer, Roy, 13, 27
Spinrad, Rick, xxi
Sprinkle, Preston, 219, 227
Sproul, R. C., 58, 222
Spurgeon, Charles, 232, 239–40, 241
Sri Lanka, green policies and, 2–3
Stalin, Joseph, xvii
Stanley, Andy, 198–202, 228
    accommodating homosexuality in the
        church and, 199, 200–201, 205–7
    biennial Drive Conference, 200, 201
    influence with pastors, 198
    McDonalds' video at biennial Drive
        Conference, 205
    quoted by the McDonalds, 215–16

Stanley, Andy (*continued*)
    "unhitching" from the Old Testament,
        200
Stanley, Charles, 198
Stearns, Richard, 11
Stefancic, Jean, 129
    Critical Race Theory, 129, 136, 139,
        141
Stetzer, Ed, xxi, xxvi
    Covid policies and Francis Collins,
        103, 108, 115, 119–20
    essay, with Nichols, on Crist abuse
        allegations, 155
    "On Christians Spreading Corona
        Conspiracies," 102, 103, 108
Still Time to Care (Johnson), 224
Stone, Lyman, 176
Strachan, Owen, 129, 130
Stryker, Jon, 202–3

Taibbi, Matt, 115
Taunton, Alex, 80–82, 87
Taunton, Larry, podcast, *Ideas Have
    Consequences*, 239
Taylor, Stuart, 166
1 Thessalonians 5:21, 5
2 Thessalonians
        3:6–14, 53
        3:14, 210
Thomas, Joel, 199
Time magazine, Francis Collins and, 93, 108
Time's Up, 189
1 Timothy
        5, 40
        5:8, 53
2 Timothy
        1:13, 216
        3:4–5, 216
        4, xxvi
Tisby, Jemar, 133
Trende, Sean, 111
Trinity Bible Chapel, Ontario, 118–19
Trinity Forum, 64, 79–82, 87
    After Party group, 85–87
    debate on the existence of God by,
        80–81
    desire for acceptance from secular
        social elites, 81–82
    as elite and explicitly partisan, 87–88

fellows of, in mainstream media,
        83–84, 88
    Guinness's criticism of, 89
    funding sources, 82, 83, 85, 88
    Never Trumpers at, 65
    Wear's report on evangelicals and
        pluralism, 83
Trueman, Carl, 221
Trump, Donald, xvi
    attacks by pro-immigration
        evangelicals, 40
    Collins blames for Covid deaths, 110,
        113
    criticism of border policies by
        evangelical authors and mega-
        pastors, 47, 48, 49
    erects new barriers to state
        interference with religious
        organizations, 113
    evangelical "Never Trumpers," 58, 60,
        65, 86, 88
    evangelicals for, 48, 57, 60–61, 75, 112
    immigration campaign promises, 40
    Mexico City Policy blocking federal
        funds for abortion, 63–64
    moratorium on Muslim refugees, 47
    Not Our Faith super PAC opposing
        re-election of, 63
    overturning *Roe v. Wade* and, 57, 58,
        60, 64
    pro-life evangelicals and, 61, 65, 67,
        70–71
    promises kept by, 61
    shut-down of fetal cell research, 107
Truth's Table podcast, 122
Truth Unites (YouTube channel), 24
Tushnet, Eve, 219

United Church of Christ, 197
United Methodist Church (UMC), 197
    LGBTQ advocacy and, 203
United Nations, xxii
    climate change division (IPCC), 28
    partnership with Planned
        Parenthood, 28–29
University of Chicago
    Collins-Moore private forum, 110–13
    Institute of Politics, 110
University of Pittsburgh, fetal tissue research
    at, 106, 108, 110, 114

Unwanted Advances (Kipnis), 161
USA Today, 175

Vandenberg, Bill, xix–xx
Vanishing Conscience, The (MacArthur), 235–36
VeggieTales (animated series), xxi, 95
View, The (TV show), xxiv
Vines, Matthew, 203–4, 210, 217, 227
    God and the Gay Christian, 204, 211
    Pastors in Process, 228
    YouTube talk (2012), 204
Vischer, Phil, 95
Visconti, Ryan, 198–202
Voskamp, Ann, 40, 47

Walensky, Rochelle, 94
Wallis, Jim, xxvii
Ward, Harry, xvi
Warren, Elizabeth, 76
Warren, Rick, 24, 203
    climate change agenda and, 11
    Embracing the Journey and promoting
        LGBTQ ideology, 212–16
    as a "global influencer," xxii
    The Purpose Driven Life, 11, 105, 212
    support for Francis Collins and Covid
        policies, 104–5, 115, 119–20
    urges using the Christian church to
        promote government programs, 104
    World Economic Forum attendance,
        104
Washington Post, xxii, 72, 88, 242
    Baptist scandals and, 144
    Collins praised in, 108
    discrediting Great Barrington
        Declaration, 97
    Moore's accusations against the SBC
        and, 171, 173
    op-ed: "Not the mark of the
        beast: Evangelicals should fight
        conspiracy theories and welcome
        the vaccines," 104
    open letters in support of illegal
        immigrants, 31, 40, 47
    Prior's disapproval of Trump voters,
        64–65
    on SBC's Guidepost Report, 175
    survey of college campus sexual
        abuse, 160

Wear, Michael, 62–63, 68–70, 86, 88
    advice to the Biden administration on
        abortion, 63–64
    AND Campaign and, 63, 68
    compromise on abortion and, 63
    disapproval of pro-life Trump voters, 64
    elevation of, by leading evangelicals, 64
    Keller and, 63, 64
    Reclaiming Hope, 62
    Trinity Forum report by, 83
Wehner, Pete, 108
Wesleyan Church, 34
Wheaton College
    CRT infiltration of, 132–33
    LGBTQ ideology at, 225
Wheaton College, Billy Graham Center
    Coronavirus and the Church website,
        xxi, 104
    partnering with CDC and NIH, xxi,
        102, 104
    Stetzer as director, 102, 155
    Vox essay, xxvi

White Fragility (DiAngelo), 123, 134, 135,
    138, 150
Whitehead, Jon, 174
white supremacy, xxi, 84, 137, 150
Whitfield, Keith, 130
Willard, Dallas, 80, 81
Williams, Jarvis, 136–38
Willits, Bill, 204–5
Willow Creek Community Church, 36
Woke Church (Mason), 148
Womack, Alisa and Rusty, 181–82
Women's March (2017), xi, xii, xiii
    "pussycat hat," xi, xii
Wood, Andy and Stacie, 214
World Bank, 2, 4
World Economic Forum (WEF), xxii, 17,
    104
World magazine, 58, 59
World Relief, 34, 40–41
World Vision, 11, 225
World War II, xvii
Wright, N. T., 95, 105–6, 108, 119–20

Yancey, Philip, 95

Zuckerberg, Mark, 89

About the Author

MEGAN BASHAM is a culture reporter for the *Daily Wire* and the author of *Beside Every Successful Man: A Woman's Guide to Having It All*. She is a frequent contributor to *Morning Wire*, one of the top ten news podcasts in the United States. She has also written for the *Wall Street Journal*, the *Telegraph*, *First Things*, *National Review*, the *Spectator*, and *WORLD* magazine, where she worked as a film and television editor.